CREDO SERIES

Ecumenical and Interreligious Dialogue

Based on the SL Curriculum Framework Protocol
Option E: Ecumenical and Interreligious Issues

WRITERS
Joseph F. McCann, MEd, PhD, MPhil
Cynthia Cameron, BA, MA

GENERAL EDITOR
Thomas H. Groome, EdD

Professor Theology and Religious Education
Boston College

VERITAS

USA Office: Frisco, Texas

www.veritasreligion.com

The Subcommittee on the Catechism, United States Conference of Catholic Bishops, has found that this catechetical high school text, copyright 2019, is in conformity with the *Catechism of the Catholic Church* and that it fulfills the requirements of Elective Course: E of the *Doctrinal Elements of a Curriculum Framework for the Development of Catechetical Materials for Young People of High School Age.*

CREDO SERIES CONSULTANT: Maura Hyland
PUBLISHER, USA AND THEOLOGICAL EDITOR:
Ed DeStefano
COPY EDITOR: Elaine Campion
DESIGN: Lir Mac Cárthaigh
COPYRIGHT RESEARCH: Emma O'Donoghue;
John Menton

INTERNET RESOURCES
There are internet resources available to support this text. Log on to *www.credoseries.com*

NIHIL OBSTAT
Rev. Msgr. Robert M. Coerver, S.T.L.
Censor Librorum

IMPRIMATUR
† Most Reverend Kevin J. Farrell, D.D.
Bishop of Dallas
May 9, 2016

The *Nihil Obstat* and *Imprimatur* are official declarations that the work contains nothing contrary to Faith and Morals. It is not implied thereby that those granting the Nihil Obstat and Imprimatur agree with the contents, statements or opinions expressed.

See page 324 for copyright acknowledgments

SEND ALL INQUIRIES TO:
Veritas, Customer Service
4848 N Clark Street
Chicago IL 60640
Tel. 866-844-0582
info@veritasreligion.com
www.veritasreligion.com

ISBN 978 1 84730 876 4 (Student Edition)
ISBN 978 1 84730 877 1 (Teacher Resource Edition)
ISBN 978 1 84730 878 8 (E-book: Student Edition)

Printed in the United States of America
1 2 3 4 5 6 7 / 18 19 20 21 22

CONTENTS

This text cites, from the beginning to the end, many resources from the Catholic Church, from non-Catholic Christian faith traditions, and from several other non-Christian religions. All the documents referenced in this text are vital to your understanding the relationship of the Catholic Church with other Christian faith traditions that are not in full communion with the Catholic Church, as well as with non-Christian religions.

First and foremost among these resources are Sacred Scripture and Sacred Tradition—the divinely revealed word of God. We also reference the teaching documents of the pope and bishops. The Church accords these teachings different degrees of authority. Some of these teachings are truths proclaimed to be dogmas/doctrines of the faith. Dogmas are proclaimed by the Magisterium of the Church to be divinely revealed. All the faithful must believe the dogmas of the Church. Among the dogmas of the Church, the mystery of the Holy Trinity is the central mystery of the Christian faith. It is the mystery of God in himself—and is, therefore, the source of all other mysteries.

We also cite documents from other non-Catholic Christian traditions that are not in full communion with the pope and the Catholic Church. The Catholic Church views the texts of other Christian faith traditions as having value, but not always representing actual Divine Revelation.

These non-Catholic Christian faith traditions sometimes propose teachings that are contrary to the teachings of the Catholic Church. Their teachings also contain terms, such as Tradition, sacraments, Eucharist, which they understand and use in ways that are sometimes contrary to the Catholic Church's teachings and use. These other Christian faith communities and religions also accord their texts differing degrees of authority. More significantly, they do not believe in the role of the Magisterium in the divine plan. As a consequence, members of particular faith traditions do not universally accept, understand and use similar terms in the same way.

We introduce the various documents of the Catholic Church, of other non-Catholic Christian traditions, and of non-Christian religions at the opportune points as we go along. This will help you get to know how the Catholic Church views the relative weight and importance of each document.

Important faith words are highlighted in bold type throughout the text and defined in the Faith Glossary. All of these definitions come from either the *United States Catholic Catechism for Adults* or from the *Catechism of the Catholic Church*. These definitions will guide you in understanding correctly both the "commonalities" that other faith traditions share with the Catholic Church and also the "obstacles" that prevent their full communion with the Catholic Church.

CHAPTER 1

The Invitation to Faith

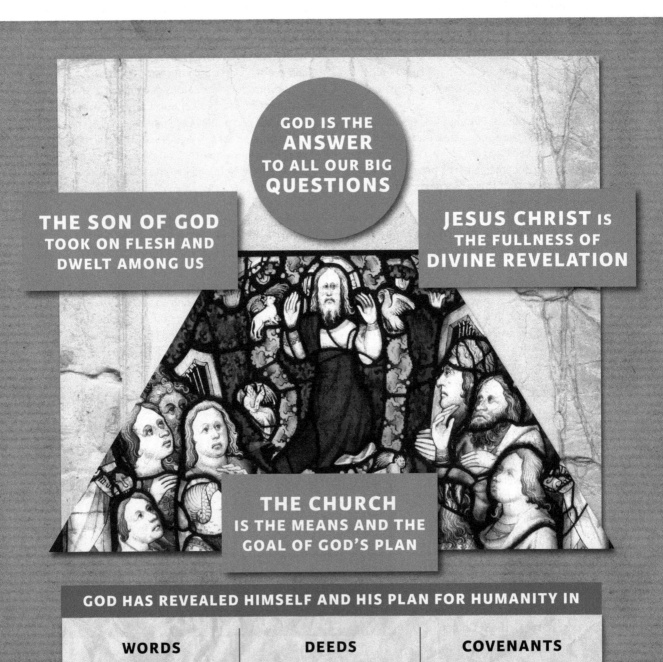

GOD IS THE **ANSWER** TO ALL OUR BIG **QUESTIONS**

THE SON OF GOD TOOK ON FLESH AND DWELT AMONG US

JESUS CHRIST IS THE FULLNESS OF **DIVINE REVELATION**

THE CHURCH IS THE MEANS AND THE GOAL OF GOD'S PLAN

GOD HAS REVEALED HIMSELF AND HIS PLAN FOR HUMANITY IN

| WORDS | DEEDS | COVENANTS |

GOD DID NOT LEAVE US ALONE TO FIGURE OUT THE answers to our deepest questions about life. God has revealed himself and his loving plan to save us "by deeds and words over time and most fully by his sending us his own divine Son, Jesus Christ" (*United States Catholic Catechism for Adults*, Glossary, "Revelation," 526). This chapter explores the human search for God and the unique role of the Catholic Church in the divine plan for humanity.

SOURCES OF DIVINE REVELATION:

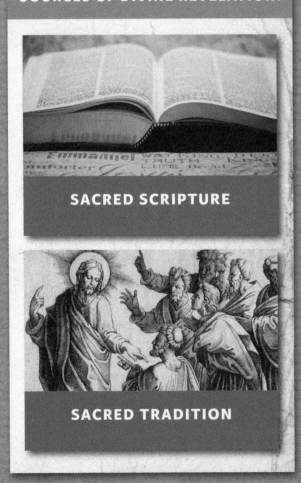

SACRED SCRIPTURE

SACRED TRADITION

Faith Focus: These teachings of the Catholic Church are the primary focus of the doctrinal content presented in this chapter:

- ⊙ "Creation is the foundation of 'all God's saving plans' [*General Catechetical Directory*, no. 51], the 'beginning of the history of salvation' that culminates in Christ" (*Catechism of the Catholic Church*, no. 280).
- ⊙ Through the gift of intelligence, human beings have the ability to discover the Creator at work through his creation.
- ⊙ God revealed himself to Abraham and Moses and formed his Chosen People, the People of Israel.
- ⊙ Jesus Christ, the Incarnate Word of God, is the fullness of Revelation.
- ⊙ Jesus revealed the Trinity, the central mystery of faith.
- ⊙ God desires that all people live in communion with him.
- ⊙ The Church, divinely instituted by Christ and prefigured in the People of Israel, is the new People of God.
- ⊙ Jesus entrusted the proclamation of the Gospel to the Apostles.
- ⊙ Divine Revelation ended with the death of the last Apostle.

Discipleship Formation: As a result of studying this chapter and discovering the meaning of the faith of the Catholic Church for your life, you should be better able to:

- ⊙ understand the foundation of the Catholic Church's commitment to ecumenical and interreligious dialogue;
- ⊙ trace Divine Revelation through the history of salvation;
- ⊙ describe the connection between Divine Revelation and the Catholic Church;
- ⊙ share your faith in Jesus Christ, the Eternal Word of God and the fullness of Revelation.

Scripture References: These scripture references are quoted or referred to in this chapter:
OLD TESTAMENT: Genesis 3:15, 9:16, 15:5, 17:1–22; **Exodus** 3:14; **Deuteronomy** 5:1–22; **Psalms** 90:1–2, 104:1–35, 117:22, 147:1–11; **Proverbs** 8:22–31; **Isaiah** 7:14, 44:24; **Jeremiah** 33:19–2
NEW TESTAMENT: Matthew 1:22–23, 6:25–34, 13:51–52, 16:13–20, 18:20, 21:42, 28:18–20; **Luke** 1:26–38, 3:21–22; **John** 1:1–5 and 14, 8:48–58, 10:22–30, 14:1–13 and 17, 17:1–26; **Acts of the Apostles** 2:1–47, 4:11, 17:16–33; **Romans** 6:4, 12:5; **1 Corinthians** 3:1–23, 12:12–20 and 27; **2 Corinthians** 5:19; **Ephesians** 1:9 and 23, 2:18 and 21–22, 4:12; **Colossians** 1:18; **1 Timothy** 6:16; **Hebrews** 1:1–2; **1 Peter** 2:7; **2 Peter** 1:4; **1 John** 4:9–16; **Revelation** 14:4

Faith Glossary: Familiarize yourself with or recall the meaning of these key terms. Definitions are found in the Glossary: **Church, covenant, Deposit of Faith, divine providence, Divine Revelation, ecclesial communities, ecumenism, evangelization, Exodus, interreligious dialogue, Magisterium, natural revelation, original holiness, original justice, Original Sin, religion, Sacred Scripture, Sacred Tradition, salvation, Trinity**

Faith Words: Divine Revelation; evangelization
Learn by Heart: Matthew 28:18–20
Learn by Example: Thomas Merton

Why do human beings have so many questions?

Have you ever spent much time with a two-year-old? If you have, you probably noticed that "Why?" is among the most common words they speak. Two-year-olds are discoverers and questioners. As time goes on, a child also begins to ask, "Who?" "What?" "When?" "Where?" and "How?" The truth is that we remain two-year-olds at heart. We never seem to grow out of questioning. We have an insatiable desire and need to know and to learn.

OPENING REFLECTION

⊙ What are some things about life that you really want to know?

⊙ What are some of the great truths of life that you can learn from reflection on your own experience? On Sacred Scripture? On the teachings of the Catholic Church?

⊙ Take a moment and write these down in the form of questions. Refer back to your list as you work your way through this chapter.

RESTLESS HEARTS: OUR NEED TO ASK AND TO KNOW

Human beings tend to ask some pretty basic questions about life and about our human nature: "*Why* is there so much suffering?" "*Who* am I?" "*What* is the meaning of my life?" "*Where* is my life headed?" "*When* will we get there?" "*How* can I lead a good life?"—and the list goes on. Asking these and similar questions and searching for satisfying answers never ceases.

The problems that weigh heavily on people's hearts are the same today as in past ages. What is humanity? What is the meaning and

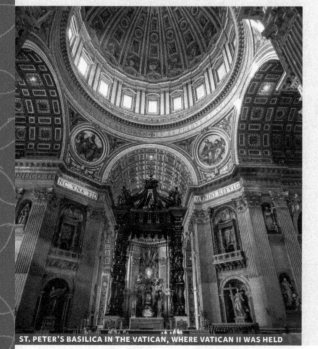

ST. PETER'S BASILICA IN THE VATICAN, WHERE VATICAN II WAS HELD

Key Resource: Documents of Vatican II

In the section "Restless Hearts: Our Need to Ask and to Know" we reference one of the sixteen documents of the Second Vatican Council, which is also called Vatican II. Vatican II met from 1962 to 1965 and is the twenty-first Ecumenical Council of the Church in her two-millennium history. An Ecumenical Council is "a gathering of the world's bishops, exercising their collegial authority over the universal Church in union with the pope" (*United States Catholic Catechism for Adults* [USCCA], 511). An Ecumenical Council issues some of the Church's most authoritative teaching documents. We will be quoting from Vatican II documents extensively throughout this course of study.

purpose of life? What is upright behavior, and what is sinful? Where does suffering originate, and what end does it serve? How can genuine happiness be found? What happens at death? What is judgment? What reward follows death? And finally, what is the ultimate mystery, beyond human explanation, which embraces our entire existence, from which we take our origin and toward which we tend?

—Vatican II, *Declaration on the Relation of the Church to Non-Christian Religions (Nostra Aetate)*, no. 1

St. Augustine of Hippo (354–430) was a great questioner and searcher for the meaning of human life. He captured the heart of his own questioning and searching and that of every restless heart in these often repeated words from his autobiography, which is called the *Confessions:* "You have made us for yourself, O Lord, and our heart is restless until it rests in you."

We know that it took an unbelieving and searching Augustine many years before he would utter those words. His life was running into one dead end after another. So he searched and asked questions. He studied the writings of and debated both Christian and pagan philosophers and theologians. He listened to the admonitions of his mother, St. Monica. He prayed and reflected on the Scriptures. Finally, he could say, "My heart is listening, Lord; open the ears of my heart. . . . Let me run toward this voice and seize hold of you. . . . Do not hide your face from me."

ST. MONICA | ST. AUGUSTINE CHURCH, LEBANON, KY

Key Resources: *Catechism of the Catholic Church* and *United States Catholic Catechism for Adults*

Throughout this text we reference the *Catechism of the Catholic Church* (CCC) and the *United States Catholic Catechism for Adults* (USCCA) as resources. A catechism is a book produced by the Church that gives an authoritative explanation of the Catholic faith.

CATECHISM OF THE CATHOLIC CHURCH

The CCC was produced in 1992, and its final Latin edition issued in 1997. The CCC was written to offer the local churches of the world an authoritative resource for teaching the faith, and for developing their own national catechisms (CCC, nos. 1–25). For example, our bishops produced the *United States Catholic Catechism for Adults*.

The *Catechism of the Catholic Church* incorporated Vatican II's teachings and reflected its general approach of wanting to reach out to, and dialogue with, the world. Although the Glossary in the English translation of the *Catechism* is not part of the text's official teachings, its definitions offer helpful descriptions of the points they cover.

UNITED STATES CATHOLIC CATECHISM FOR ADULTS

The USCCA is a catechism based on the CCC drawn up by the United States Conference of Catholic Bishops (USCCB) for use in the United States. The USSCB approved the USCCA in 2004. Because the USCCB, as a national bishops' conference, does not participate directly in the teaching office of the pope, or with the pope and all world bishops together, its authority is only as delegated by the pope. The USCCB, therefore, submitted the USCCA to the Vatican for approval. The USCCA was subsequently approved by the Vatican in 2006, and published.

HEADS OF PAGAN DEITIES (1ST CENTURY BC) AT MOUNT NEMRUT, TURKEY

This awareness and recognition results in a way of life that is imbued with a deep religious sense.
—*Declaration on the Relation of the Church to Non-Christian Religions*, no. 2

GOD—THE ANSWER TO OUR BIGGEST QUESTIONS

God has created every person with the abilities both to come to know him and to choose to live in communion with him, with other people and with all creation. God makes himself known in many ways. "In the creation of the world and of man, God gave the first and universal witness to his almighty love and his wisdom, the first proclamation of the 'plan of his loving goodness,' which finds its goal in the new creation in Christ" (CCC, no. 315).

The Creator in his goodness did not leave us only with the ability to come to an "awareness" of his existence. God freely chose to reveal what we could never come to know about him, about ourselves and about the divine plan of goodness, of creation and of **salvation**.

Jesus, the Incarnate Word, is the divine light sent into the world to dispel the darkness in human minds and hearts. (Check out John 1:1–5.) Jesus Christ, the Incarnate Son of God, fulfills the deepest desires of the human heart. He is the answer to life's deepest questions. He is the Good News of salvation to both believers and non-believers, to Jews and Gentiles. Jesus Christ, who is truly God and truly man, is the truth we seek, the way to God that we struggle to know, and the life we all desire. (Check out John 14:1–13.)

LET'S PROBE DEEPER: A SCRIPTURE ACTIVITY

- ⊙ Recall for a moment St. Peter's marketplace addresses to the Jewish pilgrims on Pentecost and St. Paul's addresses to the Epicurean and Stoic philosophers in Athens. Read and reflect on Acts of the Apostles 2:14–36 and 17:16–33.
- ⊙ What do these addresses reveal about:
  - the human person coming to know, love and serve God?
  - the role of religion in the human search for God?
  - the role of Jesus Christ in that search?
- ⊙ Share reflections as a class.

THE PLACE OF RELIGION IN THE HUMAN QUEST FOR MEANING

At the heart of the human story, or history, we discover that "People look to their different religions for an answer to the unsolved riddles of human existence" (*Declaration on the Relation of the Church to Non-Christian Religions,* no. 1).

Where do we come from? Where are we going? From the most ancient times, **religions** have expressed the wide range of answers to these and other questions which are "decisive for the meaning and orientation of our life and actions" (CCC, no. 282). In the religions of the world, people come face to face with the mystery of the origin and purpose of life, God.

Throughout history, to the present day, there is found among different peoples a certain awareness of a hidden power, which lies behind the course of nature and the events of human life. At times, there is present even a recognition of a supreme being, or still more of a Father.

Evangelization

This is the ministry and mission of proclaiming and witnessing Christ and his Gospel with the intention of deepening the faith of believers and inviting others to be baptized and initiated into the Church.

—USCCA, Glossary, 512

Divine Revelation

God's communication of himself and his loving plan to save us. This is a gift of self-communication, which is realized by deeds and words over time and most fully by his sending us his own divine Son, Jesus Christ.

—USCCA, Glossary, "Revelation," 526

JESUS PREACHING ON THE SEA OF GALILEE | 19TH-CENTURY ENGRAVING

THE GREAT COMMISSION

Since apostolic times the Church has taught: "It pleased God, in his goodness and wisdom, to reveal himself and to make known the mystery of his will, which was that people can draw near to the Father, through Christ, the Word made flesh, in the holy Spirit, and thus become sharers in the divine nature" (Vatican II, *Dogmatic Constitution on Divine Revelation* [*Dei Verbum*], no. 2).

"In Christ God was reconciling the world to himself" (2 Corinthians 5:19). In his **Church** is found the fullness of the means for this reconciliation, for salvation. The risen Christ commissioned the Apostles and his Church to proclaim the Good News of salvation, to pass on his teachings and to "make disciples of all nations" (Matthew 28:19–20). Fulfilling this commission to proclaim the Gospel, or **evangelization**, is the primary work of the Church.

In this text we explore the human person's deepest questions, trace **Divine Revelation** through the history of salvation as God's response to those questions, and examine the Catholic Church's role in passing on that Revelation in our own times.

We build our treatment of Revelation on the teachings in four documents promulgated, or officially issued, by the Pope and by the Second Vatican Council, namely, *Dogmatic Constitution on the Church* (*Lumen Gentium*); *Dogmatic Constitution on Divine Revelation* (*Dei Verbum*); *Decree on Ecumenism* (*Unitatis Redintegratio*), and *Declaration on the Relation of the Church to Non-Christian Religions* (*Nostra Aetate*).

Dogmatic Constitution on the Church: This document teaches on the nature and mission of the Church in the divine plan for humanity. The Church is "a sign and instrument . . . of communion with God and of the unity of the entire human race" (no. 1). The Church, the new People of God, is catholic, or universal. "And to it belong, or are related in different ways: the catholic faithful, others who believe in Christ, and finally all of humankind, called by God's grace to salvation" (no. 13).

Dogmatic Constitution on Divine Revelation: God did not leave humanity on its own to come to know him. "It pleased God, in his goodness and wisdom, to reveal himself and to make known the mystery of his will (see Ephesians 1:9), which was that people can draw near to the Father, through Christ, the Word made flesh, in the holy Spirit, and thus become sharers in the divine nature (see Ephesians 2:18; 2 Peter 1:4)" (no. 1). Divine Revelation is passed on in **Sacred Scripture** and **Sacred Tradition**.

Decree on Ecumenism: At the Last Supper Jesus prayed to his Father that the community of his disciples would always be one as he and the Father are one. (Check out John 17:1–26.) The Acts of the Apostles and the New Testament letters attest to the reality that the Church, the one Body of Christ (see 1 Corinthians 12:12–13), experienced divisions from her beginning (see 1 Corinthians 3:1–23), divisions that she must always strive to avoid and heal when they occur. Dialogue and consultation between the Catholic Church and non-Catholic **ecclesial communities** that "leads toward full and perfect unity, in accordance with what God in his kindness wills" (no. 8) is the work of **ecumenism**.

Declaration on the Relation of the Church to Non-Christian Religions: In this document the Church teaches: "The Catholic Church rejects nothing of what is true and holy in these [non-Christian] religions. . . . The church, therefore, urges its sons and daughters to enter with prudence and charity into discussion and collaboration with members of other religions" (no. 2). Dialogue and collaboration with non-Christian religions is the work of **interreligious dialogue**.

READ, REFLECT AND SHARE
- Matthew 28:19–20 has been called "The Great Commission." Reread and reflect on that Gospel passage.
- Share any connections you see between that passage and the Church's works of ecumenism and interreligious dialogue.

OVER TO YOU
- What opportunities do you have to share your faith with family and friends?
- How are you participating in the Great Commission by such sharing?

The Catholic Church rejects nothing of what is true and holy in non-Christian religions

Emmanuel—"God is with us"

Someone to watch over us

George Gershwin (1898–1937) is a well-known name in early twentieth-century music. George and Ira Gershwin were children of Russian Jewish immigrants who emigrated to Brooklyn, New York. The Gershwin brothers blazed a trail for records, musical shows and movies; their work set the idiom for American popular music. One of their earliest songs was: "Someone to Watch Over Me"; it included these lyrics:

> There's a somebody I'm longin' to see
> I hope that he turns out to be
> Someone to watch over me

BUST OF GEORGE GERSHWIN IN KIELCE, POLAND

OPENING REFLECTION

⊙ Have you ever felt the need and desire for somebody "to see" and "to watch over" you?
⊙ To what or to whom did you turn? Were you satisfied? Are you still searching?
⊙ Can you recall what Jesus had to say about that desire?

DIVINE PROVIDENCE

The universal human need and desire for God to "watch over" us is one of the "unsolved riddles of human existence" named in the *Declaration on the Relation of the Church to Non-Christian Religions*. God did not leave humanity to solve this riddle on its own.

In the very beginning, in the work of creation, God revealed himself to be a Triune God. Creation originates with the Father and is brought into being through the Word (Jesus Christ) by the power of the Holy Spirit.

The *Catechism* teaches that the first human beings had undisturbed communion with the Triune God through their state of **original justice** and **original holiness** (CCC, nos. 375 and 376). They "preferred themselves" to God and they disobeyed and turned away from God— known as the Fall. They lost the state of original holiness and justice, and a new situation arose (CCC, nos. 385–387). They lost their original communion with God and harmony with creation. They entered the state of **Original Sin**. As a consequence, human nature was weakened. "Adam and Eve transmitted to their descendants human nature wounded by their own first sin and hence deprived of original holiness and justice" [CCC, no. 417] (CCC, nos. 396–400, 416-418).

After the Fall and before God made himself known to us through Divine Revelation, humanity could come to know some of the truths *about* God. The human person would be able to know these truths through the use of the God-given gift of intellect and the power of reasoning.

At his own appointed time, God sent Jesus, in flesh and blood, so that we could see and understand the truth of his Revelation

These truths include that God exists and that God has certain attributes, such as goodness and beauty, and that God is all-loving, all-knowing and all-powerful (CCC, no. 286) Thus, humanity had to *search* for God, while not being able to restore a relationship of "intimate friendship" with him. This truth shapes all the subject matter discussed by this book.

Knowing these things does not answer all of our questions. We need God to "watch over" us by revealing himself to us, redeeming us from our state of Original Sin and our personal sins, and restoring us to holiness of life, in which we live in an intimate relationship of friendship with God. That is how we find out *who* God is and *what* the relationship is that God created us to have with him.

GOD MAKES HIMSELF AND HIS PLAN KNOWN

God made all this possible through his plan of salvation. God revealed this plan gradually and over time—first to the ancient Israelites and, finally and most clearly, in Jesus Christ. Through the history of the Israelites, God revealed himself to be among them, watching over and caring for them. At his own appointed time, God sent Jesus, in flesh and blood, so that we could see and understand the truth of his Revelation.

The Son of God took on flesh and dwelt among us. Reflecting on this Revelation and referring to the writings of the prophet Isaiah (7:14), Matthew the Evangelist wrote:

All this took place to fulfill what had been
spoken by the Lord through the prophet:
"Look, the virgin shall conceive and bear a son,
    and they shall name him Emmanuel,"
which means "God is with us."

—Matthew 1:22–23

God has revealed himself to be the true and only solution to this riddle of human existence.

(Check out Matthew 6:25–34.) The Church uses the term **divine providence** to name "God's loving care and concern for all he has made; he continues to watch over creation, sustaining its existence and presiding over its development and destiny" (USCCA, Glossary, 510).

OVER TO YOU

- Read Matthew 6:25–34.
- What do these very words of God say to your heart—today?

SMALL ANSWERS TO BIG QUESTIONS

Sometimes we can work out answers for ourselves. We can call this "science" or "history" or "philosophy" or "politics" or "economics" and so on. We reflect on our own human experiences to find reason and order and system in the universe and in our lives.

We probe our surroundings—the weather, mountains and valleys, seas and rivers, awesome places and special times on our planet Earth, all of which can put us in touch with the Creator. We reach into the depths of our being, drill below our thoughts and feelings and consciousness and identity to seek and discover the foundations of existence. We work at trying to make sense of the world, to get on, survive and prosper.

We speculate about, speak to and try to listen for the "Power" that we identify or recognize above, behind or beneath everything that we experience. Since the dawn of history, humankind has sought to find what kind of "powers" might exist and whether or not they "watch over" us. Our natural reasoning, however, does not yield answers to other questions so easily. In this text we will be learning about the Catholic Church and her relation to the great world faith traditions that have transpired from this search across the centuries.

OVER TO YOU

- Pause, read and reflect on Psalm 90:1–2 and Psalm 147:1–11.
- What do these very words of God say to your heart—today? How do they reflect your faith and trust in God?

God comes to meet us

By natural reason man can know God with certainty, on the basis of his works. But there is another order of knowledge, which man cannot possibly arrive at by his own powers: the order of divine Revelation. Through an utterly free decision, God has revealed himself and given himself to man. This he does by revealing the mystery, his plan of loving goodness, formed from all eternity in Christ, for the benefit of all men. God has fully revealed this plan by sending us his beloved Son, our Lord Jesus Christ, and the Holy Spirit.

—CCC, no. 50

IT IS I, BE NOT AFRAID | A.N. MIRONOV

THE GIFTS OF REVELATION

"God has revealed himself to man by gradually communicating his own mystery in deeds and in words" (CCC, no. 69). The Catholic Church speaks of **natural revelation** and **Divine Revelation**. Natural revelation is the "evidence God gives of himself in created realities" (*Dogmatic Constitution on Divine Revelation*, no. 2).

Natural revelation: All creation manifests the existence, goodness and beauty of its Creator. The Creator has blessed the human person with the gifts of reason and free will. Through the use of the gift of reason, the human person can come to know of God's existence with certainty. Through the use of the gift of free will, the human person can choose to honor the Creator, who has clearly revealed that his goodness, power and love brought us into being. God the Creator is the origin and destiny of all that he created, of both visible and invisible created realities. "When he listens to the message of creation and to the voice of conscience, man can arrive at certainty about the existence of God, the cause and the end of everything" (CCC, no. 46).

Human reason also enables us to come to know the natural moral law that God has "written and engraved in the soul of each and every man" (CCC, no. 1954; quoting Pope Leo XIII). "The moral law presupposes the rational order, established among creatures for their good and to serve their final end, by the power, wisdom, and goodness of the Creator" (CCC, no. 1951).

The gift of free will enables us to choose to live our life according to the demands of the *natural* moral law. "Man participates in the wisdom and goodness of the Creator who gives him mastery over his acts and the ability to govern himself with a view to the true and the good. The natural law expresses the original moral sense which enables man to discern by reason the good and the evil, the truth and the lie" (CCC, no. 1954).

Though human reason is, strictly speaking, truly capable by its own natural power and light of attaining to a true and certain knowledge of the one personal God, who watches over and controls the world by his providence, and of the natural law written in our hearts by the Creator; yet there are many obstacles which prevent reason from the effective and fruitful use of this inborn faculty. For the truths that concern the relations between God and man wholly transcend the visible order of things, and, if they are translated into human action and influence it, they call for self-surrender and abnegation. The human mind, in its turn,

All creation manifests the existence, goodness and beauty of its Creator

GOD REVEALS HIMSELF TO MOSES | 19TH-CENTURY ENGRAVING

is hampered in the attaining of such truths, not only by the impact of the senses and the imagination, but also by disordered appetites which are the consequences of original sin. So it happens that men in such matters easily persuade themselves that what they would not like to be true is false or at least doubtful.

—CCC, no. 37, quoting Pius XII, *Humani Generis*, no. 561

Divine Revelation: Divine Revelation is a different order of knowing than knowing by the use of our natural faculties.

God, who "dwells in unapproachable light", wants to communicate his own divine life to the men he freely created, in order to adopt them as his sons in his only-begotten Son (see 1 Timothy 6:16). By revealing himself God wishes to make them capable of responding to him, and of knowing him and of loving him far beyond their own natural capacity.

—CCC, no. 52

Divine Revelation goes beyond natural revelation, or the manifestation of the Creator in his works of creation. The *Catechism* elaborates on this truth of our faith:

Thus the revelation of creation is inseparable from the revelation and forging of the covenant of the one God with his People. Creation is revealed as the first step towards this covenant, the first and universal witness to God's all-powerful love (see Genesis 15:5; Jeremiah 33:19–26).

—CCC, no. 288

Divine Revelation is God's free and direct *communication* of himself and his divine plan for humanity. This gift of Divine Revelation came about gradually over time. God first revealed himself to Abraham and the descendants of Abraham, the Israelites, also known as Hebrews and Jews. Divine Revelation was fully realized by God "sending us his own divine Son, Jesus Christ" (USCCA, Glossary, "Revelation," 526). Divine Revelation is passed on in the one "divine well-spring" of Revelation, namely, **Sacred Scripture** and **Sacred Tradition**.

THINK, PAIR AND SHARE

⊙ How can the distinction between natural revelation and Divine Revelation facilitate an open dialogue between Catholics and non-Christians?

⊙ Share reflections as a class.

Key resources: Roman Missal and Compendium of the Catechism of the Catholic Church

In the sections "The Old Testament" and "The New Testament" we introduce two more key resources, namely, the *Roman Missal* and the *Compendium of the Catechism of the Catholic Church*.

Roman Missal: The *Roman Missal* is the book containing the prayers and rites that the Roman Catholic Church uses for celebrating the Mass. The *Roman Missal* was first published in 1570. It has been updated, or revised, several times to make adjustments to the wording of prayers and to the rites. The current *Roman Missal* was published in Latin in 2008 and in English in 2011. This "new" *Roman Missal* is also periodically updated to include feasts of newly canonized saints and other feasts (such as "Mary, Mother of the Church," added in 2018).

Compendium of the Catechism of the Catholic Church: The *Compendium of the Catechism of the Catholic Church* is a shorter, digested version of the CCC, which was issued in English in 2006. It is not intended to replace the Catechism. The Compendium uses a question-and-answer, or dialogic, format. "This dialogic format also lends itself to brevity in the text, by reducing it to what is essential. This may help the reader to grasp the contents and possibly memorize them as well" (Compendium, "Introduction," p. xvi, no. 4).

THE ONE DIVINE WELL-SPRING OF REVELATION

Sacred Scripture and Sacred Tradition flow from the same "divine well-spring." Both Scripture and Tradition "are bound closely together, and communicate one with the other. Flowing from the same divine well-spring, both of them merge, in a sense, and move towards the same goal" (*Dogmatic Constitution on Divine Revelation*, no. 9). Both Scripture and Tradition "make up a single sacred deposit of the Word of God, in which, as in a mirror, the pilgrim Church contemplates God, the source of all her riches" (CCC, no. 97).

God is the author of Sacred Scripture. "Sacred scripture is the utterance of God put down as it is in writing under the inspiration of the holy Spirit. And tradition transmits in its entirety the word of God which has been entrusted to the apostles by Christ the Lord and the holy Spirit. . . . Hence, both scripture and tradition must be accepted and honored with equal devotion and reverence" (*Dogmatic Constitution on Divine Revelation*, no. 9).

SACRED SCRIPTURE

The Scriptures, both the Old Testament and the New Testament, speak to us in a human way. They teach faithfully and without error all that God inspired the human authors to communicate about salvation.

THE OLD TESTAMENT

God "manifested himself to our first parents from the very beginning. After the fall, he buoyed them up with the hope of salvation, by promising redemption (see Genesis 3:15); and he has never ceased to take care of the human race, in order to give eternal life to all those who seek salvation by persevering in doing good" (*Dogmatic Constitution on Divine Revelation*, no. 3).

Abraham and the beginnings of a people of faith: In response to humanity's turning away from God, God made a promise with our first parents (see Genesis 3:15). The Church believes this promise to be the first announcement of the Good News of salvation in Jesus Christ, not only for the Chosen People but for all humanity. God responded to humanity's continuing rejection of him and of the divine plan of goodness by entering a **covenant** with Noah and all creation (see Genesis 9:16). God has never revoked this promise.

Then, at God's appointed time, he revealed himself to and entered a covenant with Abraham and his descendants. (Check out Genesis 17:1–22.) In and through Abraham's descendants, God formed the People of Israel, God's Chosen People. "Israel" was the name given to Jacob, the grandson of Abraham. The descendants of the twelve sons of Jacob would become the Twelve Tribes of Israel, and they would guide the Chosen People.

This covenant with Abraham marked the birth of a people of faith that began with the Israelites and achieved universal significance and scope in the new People of God. During the celebration of the Eucharist, the Church professes this apostolic belief. She declares Abraham to be "our father in faith" (*The Roman Missal*, Eucharistic Prayer I).

Moses and the formation of the People of God: God chose Moses to reveal the divine name, "I AM WHO I AM" (Exodus 3:14), and to liberate the Israelites from slavery in Egypt. During that **Exodus** journey, God revealed himself to be present with his Chosen People to guide them to the new land that he promised them. At Sinai he gave them the Decalogue, a code of worship and morality for living the covenant. (Check out Deuteronomy 5:1–22.)

During the Exodus journey, God revealed himself to be present with his Chosen People to guide them to the new land that he promised them

The Decalogue, or Ten Commandments, is rooted in the heart of every person. It reveals the responsibilities for living in right relationship with God, others and all creation. The Ten Commandments point the way to live a life committed to justice and peace rooted in love (charity) of God and neighbor.

Over time the Israelite people gathered together a record of God's Revelations to them. The Church eventually assembled these accounts into the writings that make up the Old Testament. Throughout the forty-six books of the Old Testament we hear God's promise through his prophets to send a messiah and savior. *(We will explore God's Revelation to the Jewish people in more detail in chapter 7, "Judaism and the Jewish People.")*

THE NEW TESTAMENT

At God's appointed time the Triune God fully revealed himself and the divine plan of goodness. "The full and definitive stage of God's revelation is accomplished in his Word made flesh, Jesus Christ, the mediator and fullness of Revelation. . . . In the sending of the Son and the gift of the

MOSES LEADS THE EXODUS | 13TH-CENTURY ILLUMINATED MANUSCRIPT

Spirit, Revelation is now fully complete, although the faith of the Church must gradually grasp its full significance over the course of centuries" (*Compendium of the Catechism of the Catholic Church*, no. 9). The Church has gathered the inspired written account of this final Revelation in the twenty-seven books of the New Testament.

The Person of Jesus Christ, his life and teachings and the Paschal Mystery of his Passion and Death, Resurrection and Ascension are the center of the New Testament. For this reason "the four Gospels occupy a central place because Jesus Christ is their center" (CCC, no. 139). The New Testament does not replace the Old Testament. "The Old Testament prepares for the New and the New Testament fulfills the Old; the two shed light on each other; both are true Word of God" (CCC, no. 140)

SACRED TRADITION

Jesus is the fullness of God's Revelation. This Revelation, which Jesus entrusted to his Apostles, ended with the death of the last Apostle. Our understanding of Divine Revelation continues through the **Magisterium** of the Church, which Jesus instituted on the foundation of the Apostles.

The Church, over time and under the guidance of the Holy Spirit, has reflected on God's Revelation in the Scriptures. She continues to deepen her understanding of God's great truths for our lives and for our salvation. It is the mission of the Church to teach and witness authentically to Divine Revelation over time and to share this Revelation with "all nations" (Matthew 28:19).

The Magisterium of the Catholic Church, that is, the "teaching office of the pope, and bishops in communion with him, guided by the Holy Spirit" (USCCA, Glossary, 519), is entrusted with teaching *authentically* and *authoritatively* the whole **Deposit of Faith**. This Deposit of Faith is the "heritage of faith contained in Sacred Scripture and Tradition, handed on in the Church from the time of the Apostles, from which the Magisterium draws all that it proposes for belief as divinely revealed" (USCCA, Glossary, 509).

The Magisterium preserves and hands on that Deposit of Faith faithfully, as ever old and

JESUS SURROUNDED BY SYMBOLS OF THE FOUR EVANGELISTS | 13TH-CENTURY IVORY CASKET

The four Gospels occupy a central place because Jesus Christ is their center.

CCC, NO. 139

ever new. (Check out Matthew 13:51–52.) The Magisterium leads the Church toward a deeper understanding and living of the Gospel. "It is clear, therefore, that, in the supremely wise arrangement of God, sacred tradition, sacred scripture and the magisterium of the church are so connected and associated that one of them cannot stand without the others. [For example, the Church's dogma on the Immaculate Conception, which was defined as a dogma of the Church in 1854, is rooted in the earliest beliefs of the Church and devotion of the Church to Mary.] Working together, each in its own way under the action of the one holy Spirit, they all contribute effectively to the salvation of souls" (*Dogmatic Constitution on Divine Revelation,* no. 10). *(We will explore Revelation and the Catholic Church in more detail in the next section of this chapter.)*

REFLECT AND SHARE

- ⊙ What insights did you receive about Divine Revelation?
- ⊙ What is the wisest and best attitude we can take toward God's Revelation for our lives? Give reasons for your response.
- ⊙ How might a Christian share those insights with non-Christians? Why is it important to do so?

OVER TO YOU

- ⊙ Reflect: Divine Revelation is God's self-communication about who he is and his loving plan of creation and salvation. That amounts, of course, to a revelation about yourself—about God's relationship with you and your God-given destiny.
- ⊙ Why is reading and reflecting on Scripture so vital to your identity as a disciple of Jesus Christ?
- ⊙ Might you give reading and praying the Scriptures a greater role in your daily schedule? How will you go about doing so?

THE IMMACULATE CONCEPTION | JOHANN LUCAS KRACKER

The Immaculate Conception was defined as a dogma of the Church in 1854

The Church, the new People of God

PENTECOST | CHURCH OF ST. VITUS, RAVENSBURG, GERMANY

The Mission of the Holy Spirit

When the work which the Father gave the Son to do on earth (see John 17:4) was completed, the holy Spirit was sent on the day of Pentecost to sanctify the church continually and so that believers might have access to the Father through Christ in the one Spirit (see Ephesians 2:18).

—*Dogmatic Constitution on the Church,*
no. 4

THE COMING OF THE HOLY SPIRIT

The old city is thronged with visitors. The narrow streets are packed with traffic, pedestrians, carts, donkeys, horses. It is mid-morning; everyone is out and about, buying breakfast at stalls, greeting old friends, talking and laughing, and making the acquaintance of total strangers.

This is Jerusalem on the Feast of Weeks, or Pentecost. Jewish pilgrims from many nations have converged on Jerusalem in multitudes to thank God for the new harvest. Suddenly, from one of the houses, a small band of people, men and women, spill out into the street, shouting and hallooing in joy.

Questions ripple through the crowd in countless languages: "Who are they?" "Why are they so filled with joy?" "What has happened to them?" The answers are shouted out in a babble of foreign words and phrases. Then one of the men, who seems to be the leader, addresses everyone. His name is Peter. He and his companions are followers of Jesus of Nazareth.

Something amazing happens: without translation, the people in that vast crowd, who are from many nations with different languages, hear Peter's words, each in their own language. As they listen they are "cut to the heart" and they ask Peter and the other apostles: "Brothers, what should we do?"

Peter [says] to them, "Repent, and be baptized every one of you in the name of Jesus Christ so that your sins may be forgiven; and you will receive the gift of the Holy Spirit. For the promise is for you, for your children, and for all who are far away, everyone whom the Lord our God calls to him."

—Acts of the Apostles 2:37–39

Peter, "filled with the Holy Spirit," proclaimed to the crowd that the divine plan of salvation that God had promised was fulfilled in Jesus Christ

On that Pentecost in the marketplace in Jerusalem, the Holy Spirit came upon the Apostles and the other disciples, just as Jesus, the Incarnate Son of God and the Second Person of the Trinity, had promised would happen (check out John 14:15–31), and they began fulfilling the mission their Risen Lord had given them. About three thousand people welcomed Peter's message and were baptized on that day.

OPENING REFLECTION

- You can read the full account of the coming of the Holy Spirit on that Pentecost day in Jerusalem in Acts of the Apostles 2:1–47.
- Place yourself in the minds and hearts of the Apostles and other disciples on that day.
  - Imagine your enthusiasm as you approach the crowd of "devout Jews from every nation under heaven living in Jerusalem" (Acts of the Apostles 2:5).
  - Imagine your response when about three thousand pilgrims come forward to be baptized and join you in following Jesus.
- Filled with the gift of the Holy Spirit, what do you take from this New Testament passage for your own life now as a disciple of Jesus Christ?

JESUS CHRIST, THE CENTER OF THE DIVINE PLAN OF CREATION AND SALVATION

Peter, "filled with the Holy Spirit" (Acts of the Apostles 2:4), proclaimed to the crowd that the divine plan of salvation that God had promised and that they were longing for was fulfilled in Jesus Christ. Jesus fulfilled both the Law and the Prophets. Jesus was the Son of God and the Christ, or "Anointed One" of God, whom God had foretold through the prophets of Israel. Peter said to the people, "Therefore let the entire house of

ST. PETER PREACHING | EARLY 20TH-CENTURY ILLUSTRATION

Israel know with certainty that God has made him both Lord and Messiah, this Jesus whom you crucified" (Acts of the Apostles 2:36).

Jesus Christ, the Lord and Messiah, is the Eternal Word made man (see John 1:1, 14). The Gospels clearly attest to this fact. Recall the account of the Annunciation in Luke 1:26–38 (Luke the Evangelist is also the author of the Acts of the Apostles). Also recall the accounts of the baptism of Jesus by John the Baptist in Luke 3:21–22; of Peter the Apostle's confession of faith in Jesus as Lord at Caesarea Philippi in Matthew 16:13–20; and of Jesus' own revelation of his divine Sonship in John 8:48–58 and John 10:22–30.

READ, REFLECT AND SHARE

- Work in small groups.
- Each group member selects and reads one or several of these gospel passages: Luke 1:26–38; Luke 3:21–22; Matthew 16:13–20; John 8:48–58; John 10:22–30.
- Share what you think each passage reveals about the identity of Jesus.

The Church: The Means and the Goal of God's Plan

THE LAMB ON MOUNT ZION AND THE REDEEMED | YORK MINSTER, ENGLAND

Through the Church all of us can now participate in the very inner life of God, being sustained in living as disciples of Jesus by God's grace and the presence to us of the Holy Spirit. Bonded together in Christ by Baptism, as members of the Church we continue the saving and life-giving work of the Triune God in the world by the power of the Holy Spirit. "The Church is both the means and the goal of God's plan: prefigured in creation, prepared for in the Old Covenant, founded by the words and actions of Jesus Christ, fulfilled by his redeeming cross and his Resurrection, the Church has been manifested as the mystery of salvation by the outpouring of the Holy Spirit. She will be perfected in the glory of heaven as the assembly of all the redeemed of the earth (see Revelation 14:4)" (CCC, no. 778).

THE CHURCH, THE NEW PEOPLE OF GOD, FOR ALL NATIONS

God the Father planned the Church from the beginning of time. "[God] . . . willed to make men holy and save them, not as individuals without any bond or link between them, but rather to make them into a people who might acknowledge him and serve him in holiness" (CCC, no. 781). God has given the Church a unique role and responsibility in the divine plan. The Church, prefigured in the People of Israel and divinely instituted by Jesus Christ, the Incarnate Son of God and Second Person of the Trinity, is the new People of God. The Church is a gift to all nations, to all humanity.

THE CHURCH'S FOUNDATION

Jesus Christ is the Head of his Church, the Body of Christ, and the baptized are its members (see Romans 12:5; 1 Corinthians 12:12, 14–20, 27; Ephesians 1:23, 4:12; Colossians 1:18). "The Church is one with Christ" (CCC, no. 795). In Christ "the whole structure is joined together and grows into a holy temple in the Lord; in whom you also are built together spiritually into a dwelling-place for God" (Ephesians 2:21–22).

Often, . . . the church is called God's *building* (see 1 Corinthians 3:9). The Lord compared himself to the stone which the builders rejected, but which was made into the cornerstone (see Matthew 21:42; Acts of the Apostles 4:11; 1 Peter 2:7; Psalm 117:22). On this foundation the church is built by the apostles (see 1 Corinthians 3:11) and from this it receives stability and cohesion.
    —*Dogmatic Constitution on the Church*, no. 6

The apostolic Church acknowledged the Apostles to be the first leaders of the Church. Luke's account of the Gospel attests to this when it teaches that members of the Church, from her earliest days, "devoted themselves to the apostles' teaching. . . ." (Acts of the Apostles 2:42).

THINK, PAIR AND SHARE

⦿ Pause and read Paul's descriptions of the Body of Christ in 1 Corinthians 12:12–20, 27; Ephesians 1:23, 4:12; Colossians 1:18.

⦿ Discuss with a partner why every member is vital to the life and functioning of the Body of Christ.

⦿ Share what you have learned from this text for your own vocation as a member of the Body of Christ in the world.

THE CHURCH'S WORK OF EVANGELIZATION

St. Peter, St. Paul and the other Apostles continued the work of the Church begun in Jerusalem. "The Church exists by the will of God the Father and his plan to gather all people under the Lordship of his Son" (USCCA, 115). They proclaimed the Gospel to Jews and Gentiles, believers and pagans, making disciples in *all nations*. They baptized, as Jesus taught, in the name of God the Holy Trinity—"in the name of the Father and of the Son and of the Holy Spirit" (Matthew 28:19). The Church grew in numbers as the Apostles and their companions taught the baptized to obey everything that Jesus had commanded.

For more than two millennia the Church has been working to fulfill this responsibility, the Great Commission. The same Spirit, the Paraclete, whom Jesus promised and whom he and his Father sent upon the Apostles at Pentecost, "bestows upon [the Church] varied hierarchic and charismatic gifts" (*Dogmatic Constitution on the Church*, no. 4; quoted in CCC, no. 768), and with the Father and the Son guides, sustains and sanctifies the Church today.

This ministry and mission, the work of evangelization, is the primary work of the Church. Today the pope (the successor of St. Peter and bishop of Rome) and the bishops of the world (the successors of the other Apostles) in communion with the pope, carry forward this work with Jesus Christ "to the end of the age" (Matthew 28:20b).

REFLECT AND SHARE

⊙ Where do you see the Church at work among believers? Among non-believers? Describe that work.

⊙ How does that work build on and flow from the ministry and mission of the Apostles?

JOURNAL EXERCISE

⊙ Reflect on and describe ways you can join in the Church's work of evangelization.

OVER TO YOU

⊙ Take a moment and pray the Apostles' Creed, the faith of the Church that has been handed down from apostolic times.

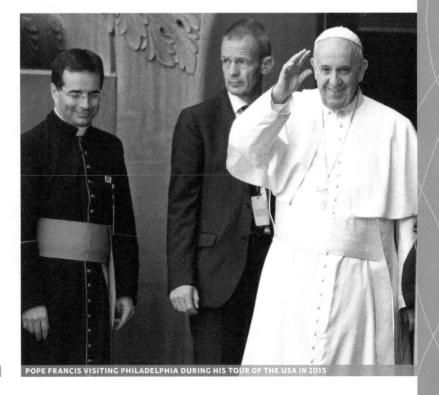

The pope and the bishops of the world carry forward the work of evangelization

POPE FRANCIS VISITING PHILADELPHIA DURING HIS TOUR OF THE USA IN 2015

Jesus Christ, the love of God made flesh

MANIFESTATIONS OF TRUE LOVE

The musical *Fiddler on the Roof* depicts Jewish life in a village in Tsarist Russia in the year 1905. Tevye the milkman and his wife Golde have five daughters, and one by one the daughters choose their husbands out of love rather than by the traditions of their family. Tevye finds this hard to understand; but each time he reluctantly agrees to the marriage. His love for his daughters always wins out.

This experience drives Tevye to ask Golde: "Do you love me?" Golde, somewhat confused, replies: "Do I love you? For twenty-five years I've washed your clothes, Cooked your meals, Cleaned your house, Given you children, Milked the cow. After twenty-five years, why talk about love right now?"

OPENING REFLECTION

⊙ What are signs of someone's true love for another person?

⊙ What are the signs of God's love in your life right now?

⊙ What signs of God's love did Jesus reveal?

JESUS CHRIST, GOD "WHO IS LOVE" INCARNATE

The unfolding story of God's Revelation is well summarized in the New Testament Letter to the Hebrews: "Long ago God spoke to our ancestors in many and various ways . . . but in these last days he has spoken to us by a Son" (Hebrews 1:1–2).

The whole life of Jesus Christ, the Incarnate Son of God, constantly revealed that God is a God of unconditional love. John, the Apostle and Beloved Disciple, many years after Jesus' Death, Resurrection and Ascension, wrote to the whole Church:

God's love was revealed among us in this way: God sent his only Son into the world so that

The Meaning and Purpose of Life

"By love, God has revealed himself and given himself to man. He has thus provided the definitive, superabundant answer to the questions that man asks himself about the meaning and purpose of his life" (CCC, no. 68).

At Jesus' baptism in the Jordan River, "the Holy Spirit descended upon him in bodily form like a dove" (Luke 3:22)

THE BAPTISM OF JESUS | LORENZO GHIBERTI

we might live through him. In this is love, not that we loved God but that he loved us and sent his Son to be the atoning sacrifice for our sins. Beloved, since God loved us so much, we also ought to love one another. No one has ever seen God; if we love one another, God lives in us, and his love is perfected in us.

By this we know that we abide in him and he in us, because he has given us of his Spirit. And we have seen and do testify that the Father has sent his Son as the Savior of the world. God abides in those who confess that Jesus is the Son of God, and they abide in God. So we have known and believe the love that God has for us.

God is love, and those who abide in love abide in God, and God abides in them.

—1 John 4:9–16

THE CENTRAL MYSTERY OF OUR FAITH

Jesus, the Incarnate Son of God, revealed, as we have seen, that God is a Triune God—Father, Son and Holy Spirit—whose inner divine life and work among humanity is an expression of divine love. The Holy Trinity, the central mystery of our faith, is divine love. "The mystery of the Most Holy Trinity is the central mystery of the Christian faith and of Christian life. God alone can make it known to us by revealing himself as Father, Son and Holy Spirit" (CCC, no. 261).

You will recall that at the beginning of Jesus' ministry, at his baptism in the Jordan River, "the Holy Spirit descended upon him in bodily form like a dove. And a voice came from heaven, 'You are my Son, the Beloved; with you I am well pleased' " (Luke 3:22).

God has revealed his love for humanity most fully in the Paschal Mystery of Jesus' Passion, Death and Resurrection. The work of Jesus, the Incarnate Son of God, is the work of divine love; it is the work of the Holy Trinity. We have no greater testimony to the Holy Trinity's love for humanity than God the Father sending the Son to become one of us, and the Son freely sacrificing his life for our salvation, and the Father and the Son sending the Holy Trinity to make us partakers once again in the very life of God.

"By the grace of Baptism 'in the name of the Father and of the Son and of the Holy Spirit,' we are called to share in the life of the Blessed Trinity, here on earth in the obscurity of faith, and after death in eternal light" (CCC, no. 265). Because of Jesus' Paschal Mystery, those who are united with him through Baptism can also rise with him and "walk in newness of life" (Romans 6:4).

The Cross reminds us that God is in solidarity with all who suffer

THE CRUCIFIXION | CHAPELLE NOTRE-DAME-DES-FONTAINES, FRANCE

All these works of Jesus were the work of the Triune God among us. Jesus made it clear: "The Father and I are one" (John 10:30) and "whoever has seen me has seen the Father" (John 14:9). Likewise, Jesus promised to send "the Spirit of truth . . . [who] abides with you" and who "will be in you" (John 14:17).

All the baptized have the responsibility to proclaim the Gospel of God's loving and merciful solidarity with people. All the baptized are to give witness in both words and deeds to the Trinity's love for all people. Joined to Christ, made adopted children of the Father and temples of the Holy Spirit through Baptism, all the baptized are to fulfill the Great Commission according to their state of life in the Church by being living images of God who is love.

REFLECT AND PRAY

- ⊙ Take a moment to become aware of God's presence with you.
- ⊙ Pray the Glory Prayer.

GOD OF COMPASSION AND MERCY

The Cross reminds us that God is in solidarity with all who suffer. Jesus' whole life and public ministry was one of deep compassion and mercy for all. He fed the hungry, healed the sick and drove out evil wherever he encountered it. He welcomed all to his table and rejected unjust social structures, both religious and civil. Jesus offered healing and hope to all, with special favor and care for those most in need. In his parable of the judgment of nations, Jesus demands that we do the same.

THINK, PAIR AND SHARE

- ⊙ Reflect: Jesus said, "Whoever has seen me has seen the Father" (John 14:9).
- ⊙ Discuss: What can Christians do so that others, believers and non-believers, can come to know God through Jesus?

JOURNAL EXERCISE

- ⊙ Take a look at a typical day in your life right now.
- ⊙ How can you give witness to the faith you profess with the Church in the Apostles' Creed?
- ⊙ Write your decisions in your journal. Return to this journal entry and add to it during this course of study.

JUDGE AND ACT

REVIEW AND SHARE WHAT YOU HAVE LEARNED

Look back over this chapter and reflect on what you have learned about Divine Revelation and the story of God reaching out to humanity to reveal his plan of salvation. Share what you have learned about the:

- ⊙ place of religion in the human quest for the meaning of life;
- ⊙ role of evangelization in the mission of the Church;
- ⊙ relationship between natural revelation and Divine Revelation;
- ⊙ connection uniting Sacred Scripture and Sacred Tradition;
- ⊙ pre-eminent role of Jesus Christ in the divine plan for humanity;
- ⊙ role of the Church in the divine plan for humanity;
- ⊙ central mystery of the Christian faith.

OVER TO YOU

- ⊙ What have you learned about God from your reflection on creation?
- ⊙ What have you come to know about God from your study of Sacred Scripture and Sacred Tradition that you cannot come to know from creation?
- ⊙ What have you come to know about your Catholic identity from your study of Scripture and the teachings of the Catholic Church?
- ⊙ What have you come to know about God's love for all people from the lives of Christians, both living and deceased?

LEARN BY EXAMPLE

Thomas Merton (1915–68), priest and "man of dialogue"

You may already have encountered Thomas Merton in Son of God and Son of Mary, *the second book of the* Credo *series.*

Thomas Merton came to know the love of God for all people and the desire of all people to live in communion with God. Merton was born in France in 1915; his mother was born in the United States of America and his father in New Zealand. During his youth Merton could have been described as a *seeker*. In 1939, while a student at Columbia University in New York City, he was baptized into the Roman Catholic Church and received the Eucharist.

In 1941 Merton became a professed member of the Trappists, or the Order of Cistercians of the Strict Observance, and he was ordained a priest in 1949. As a Trappist he was a prolific author, worked for social justice and committed himself to dialogue with non-

Christian Asian religions. He died in Bangkok while participating in an East–West monastic dialogue.

Pope Francis, in his address to the Congress of the United States of America on

September 24, 2015, chose to hold up Merton as one of four exemplary Americans who have worked for the common good of humanity. The pope said:

"A century ago, at the beginning of the Great War, which Pope Benedict XV termed a 'pointless slaughter,' another notable American was born: the Cistercian monk Thomas Merton. He remains a source of spiritual inspiration and a guide for many people. In his autobiography he wrote: 'I came into the world. Free by nature, in the image of God, I was nevertheless the prisoner of my own violence and my own selfishness, in the image of the world into which I was born. That world was the picture of Hell, full of men like myself, loving God, and yet hating him; born to love him, living instead in fear of hopeless self-contradictory hungers.' Merton was above all a man of prayer, a thinker who challenged the certitudes of his time and opened new horizons for souls and for the Church. He was also a man of dialogue, a promoter of peace between peoples and religions."

The pope concluded his remarks by saying that Merton exemplifies "the fruit of a faith which becomes dialogue and sows peace in the contemplative style."

TALK IT OVER

- ⊙ Why is open and honest dialogue essential to sharing the faith of the Catholic Church with others—both believers and non-believers?
- ⊙ Why is prayer central to that dialogue?

SHARE FAITH WITH FAMILY AND FRIENDS

- ⊙ Make a list of the groups, societies and associations that your family either contributes to financially or actively participates in.
- ⊙ How many of these organizations are religious? How do you feel about your own and your family's involvement in Church?
- ⊙ What is the difference between contributing financially and participating through active involvement?
- ⊙ Perhaps you could discuss these questions with members of your family.

JUDGE AND DECIDE

- ⊙ What is the most important truth that you have learned from this chapter for your own life of faith?
- ⊙ How might it help you understand your connection to people, no matter what their religion?

LEARN BY HEART

Jesus said, "All authority in heaven and on earth has been given to me. Go therefore and make disciples of all nations, baptizing them in the name of the Father and of the Son and of the Holy Spirit, and teaching them to obey everything that I have commanded you. And remember, I am with you always, to the end of the age."

MATTHEW 28:18–20

PRAYER REFLECTION

All gather and become aware of the presence of Christ, who said, "For where two or three are gathered in my name, I am there among them" (Matthew 18:20).

LEADER

The Church has been gifted with an awesome privilege and responsibility.
God has called us to give witness to the Revelation of the divine plan of creation and salvation.
On Good Friday each year, at the Liturgy of Friday of the Passion of the Lord, we pray for the Church, that she may persevere in fulfilling the mission God has given her. (*Pause*)

Let us pray, dearly beloved, for the holy Church of God,
that our God and Lord be pleased to give her peace,
to guard her and to unite her throughout the whole world,
and grant that, leading our life in tranquility and quiet,
we may glorify God the Father almighty.

All pray in silence, asking for the wisdom and strength to glorify God in both words and deeds.

LEADER

Almighty ever-living God,
who in Christ revealed your glory to all the nations,
watch over the works of your mercy,
that your Church, spread throughout all the world,
may persevere with steadfast faith in confessing your name.
Through Christ our Lord.

RESPONSE

Amen.
—*The Roman Missal,* Friday of the Passion of the Lord (Good Friday), "The Solemn Intercessions, I. For Holy Church"

Pray the Sign of the Cross together.

EL SALVADOR DEL MUNDO MONUMENT, SAN SALVADOR, EL SALVADOR

CHAPTER 2

The Church: The One Body of Christ

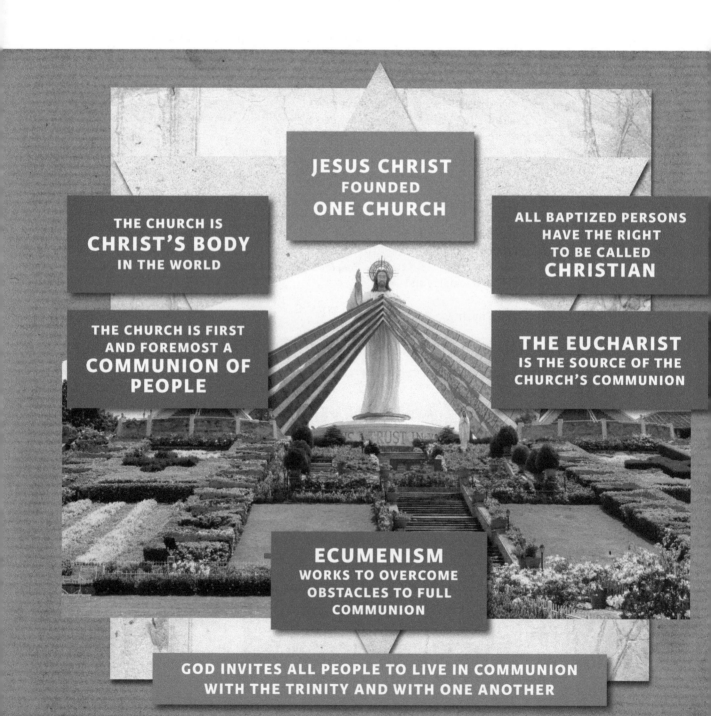

JESUS CHRIST FOUNDED ONE CHURCH

THE CHURCH IS CHRIST'S BODY IN THE WORLD

ALL BAPTIZED PERSONS HAVE THE RIGHT TO BE CALLED CHRISTIAN

THE CHURCH IS FIRST AND FOREMOST A COMMUNION OF PEOPLE

THE EUCHARIST IS THE SOURCE OF THE CHURCH'S COMMUNION

ECUMENISM WORKS TO OVERCOME OBSTACLES TO FULL COMMUNION

GOD INVITES ALL PEOPLE TO LIVE IN COMMUNION WITH THE TRINITY AND WITH ONE ANOTHER

JESUS CHRIST FOUNDED ONE CHURCH. HIS CHURCH IS a mystery of communion uniting all the baptized with the Trinity and with one another. His Church is also an instrument of salvation. St. Paul taught about the oneness, or unity, of the Church. All the baptized are to be united and function as the parts of a body, all working together to make up Christ's body in the world. Since apostolic times this unity has been challenged and divisions have arisen within the Church. The Church continues to strive to overcome the divisions that separate Christians.

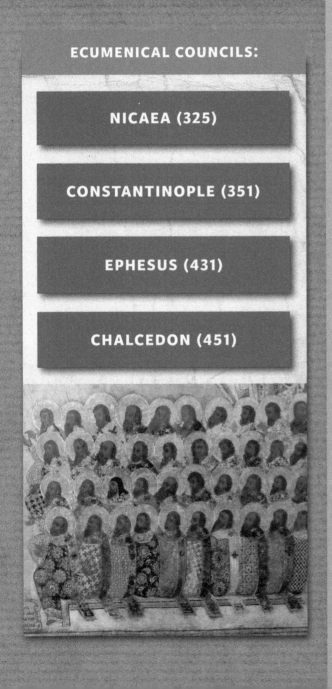

ECUMENICAL COUNCILS:

NICAEA (325)

CONSTANTINOPLE (351)

EPHESUS (431)

CHALCEDON (451)

Faith Focus: These teachings of the Catholic Church are the primary focus of the doctrinal content presented in this chapter:

- Jesus Christ instituted one Church.
- All baptized persons are members of the Church and have the right to be called Christian.
- From the beginning there have been rifts and serious dissensions that resulted in breaks from the full communion of the Church.
- Members of the Orthodox Church and its member churches are in imperfect union with the Catholic Church.
- Protestant denominations, or ecclesial communities, are in imperfect communion with the Catholic Church.
- The fullness of the Church founded by Jesus Christ is found "in the present world . . . in the Catholic Church" (*Dogmatic Constitution on the Church* [*Lumen Gentium*], no. 8).
- Receiving Holy Communion deepens one's communion with the Trinity and the Church.
- Ecumenism is the efforts of the Church to restore unity and full communion within the one Church of Christ.

Discipleship Formation: As a result of studying this chapter and discovering the meaning of the faith of the Catholic Church for your life, you should be better able to:

- describe why the Church is "one";
- understand and articulate why the Church is a mystery of communion;
- explain the significance of the Church as an image of the Triune God;
- name the early divisions that occurred in the first centuries of the Church;
- deepen your commitment to regular participation in the Eucharist;
- work to restore unity within the Church.

Scripture References: These scripture references are quoted or referred to in this chapter:
OLD TESTAMENT: 2 Maccabees 12:46
NEW TESTAMENT: Luke 1:28, 30 and 41; **John** 4:1–42, 17:20–24, 19:25b–27; **Acts of the Apostles** 15:1–35; **Romans** 10:9; **1 Corinthians** 1:10–14, 10:16–17, 11:1–33, 12:1–31, 13:1–13, 15:3–5; **Ephesians** 4:3–5; **Colossians** 3:19; **1 Thessalonians** 3:12–13; **1 Timothy** 3:9; **1 Peter** 2:9–10

Faith Glossary: Familiarize yourself with or recall the meaning of these key terms. Definitions are found in the Glossary: **Church, Communion of Saints, Creed, dogma, Ecumenical Council, ecumenism, hypostatic union, Marks of the Church, Purgatory, Resurrection, sanctifying grace, schism, tradition, Trinity**

Faith Words: Church; Communion of Saints; Ecumenical Council
Learn by Heart: 1 Corinthians 12:13, 27
Learn by Example: The Paulist Fathers

Why do Christians strive to be one?

CELEBRATING *DIA DE LOS MUERTOS*

Miguel invited his friend Sean to celebrate *Dia de Los Muertos* ("Day of the Dead") with his family on November 1. Sean was a bit confused; he wondered how anyone could "celebrate" a day for the dead. He was even more surprised when Miguel explained that the members of his family were all meeting in the cemetery. Since Sean had a day off from school for All Saints Day, he went along. He noticed that many of Miguel's relatives were wearing costumes depicting skeletons (*calacas*) and others had skull-like masks (*calaveros*), and all were in a celebratory mood. There was music and games, good food and drink.

As Miguel sat eating his *enchilada* beside his grandparents' grave with Sean, he explained that many of the dishes were his grandparents' favorites. He told Sean that he believed their spirits would be enjoying the fun, saying with a smile, "Oh, we're sure that my grandparents are in heaven with God, so why be sad for them."

OPENING REFLECTION

- The custom of *Dia de Los Muertos* is rooted in the Catholic teaching on praying for those who may have died in God's friendship, but are in need of purification before entering heaven. "This teaching is also based on the practice of prayer for the dead, already mentioned in Sacred Scripture: 'Therefore [Judas Maccabeus] made atonement for the dead, so that they might be delivered from their sin' (2 Maccabees 12:46). From the beginning the Church has honored the memory of the dead and offered prayers in suffrage for them, above all the Eucharistic sacrifice, so that, thus purified, they may attain the beatific vision of God. The Church also commends almsgiving, indulgences, and works of penance undertaken on behalf of the dead" (*Catechism of the Catholic Church* [CCC], no. 1032).
- Think about your own attitude toward death.
- Who among your relatives or friends have died?
- Do you remember and celebrate their lives? Do you pray for them? When and how do you do so?

THE EMPTY TOMB | FRA ANGELICO

Hope of resurrection in Christ

In Preface I for the Dead, the celebrant prays, in part:

In him [Christ] the hope of blessed resurrection has
    dawned, . . .
Indeed for your faithful, Lord,
life is changed not ended,
and, when this earthly dwelling turns to dust,
an eternal dwelling is made ready for them in heaven.
    —*The Roman Missal*

ALL SAINTS (DETAIL) | LIEVEN VAN LATHEM

Church

The name given the "convocation" or "assembly" of the People God has called together from "the ends of the earth." In Christian usage, the word "Church" has three inseparable meanings: the People that God gathers in the whole world; the particular or local church (diocese); and the liturgical (above all Eucharistic) assembly. The Church draws her life from the Word and the Body of Christ, and so herself becomes Christ's Body. In the Creed, the sole Church of Christ is professed to be one, holy, catholic, and apostolic.

—CCC, Glossary

Communion of Saints

This refers to members of the Church through all time—those now in the Church and those members who have already gone before us and are either in Purgatory or heaven.

—*United States Catholic Catechism for Adults* (USCCA), Glossary, 507

THE CHURCH: A COMMUNION OF SAINTS

On November 1 the Church celebrates All Saints Day, which is a holy day of obligation. We celebrate all the saints in heaven; those named saints by the Catholic Church and those not officially canonized. We celebrate the hope that the **Resurrection** of Jesus Christ gives us. On November 2, All Souls Day, or "The Commemoration of all the Faithful Departed," we remember and pray for all the faithful departed in **Purgatory**.

The celebration *Dia de Los Muertos* is a Mexican cultural expression, or **tradition**, of the **Church**. It celebrates the Church as the **Communion of Saints**.

The term "saint" is often used in the New Testament letters. For example, St. Paul often describes the members of the Body of Christ, the Church, as saints. In the First Letter to the Church in Thessalonica we read:

And may the Lord make you increase and abound in love for one another and for all, just as we abound in love for you. And may he so strengthen your hearts in holiness that you may be blameless before our God and Father at the coming of our Lord Jesus with all his saints.

—1 Thessalonians 3:12–13

A good question to ask is why do Catholics hold to such deep communion with all the baptized, both living *and* dead. Catholics treat all the faithful departed, those in heaven and those in Purgatory, as members of the Church who now live in a new way, in life everlasting. We remember and celebrate that the bond of our Baptism is never broken, not even by death. We are baptized into the life, Death *and* Resurrection of Jesus Christ. The life of a person whose body has died "is changed not ended" (*The Roman Missal*, Preface I for the Dead).

THINK, PAIR AND SHARE

⊙ Why do Catholics have a tradition of asking the saints to intercede with God on our behalf?

⊙ Why do Catholics pray *for* the faithful departed, as we do on All Souls Day?

THE LAST SUPPER | EL GRECO

One Lord, One Faith, One Baptism

> The Church is one: she acknowledges one Lord, confesses one faith, is born of one Baptism, forms only one Body, is given life by the one Spirit, for the sake of one hope (see Ephesians 4:3–5), at whose fulfillment all divisions will be overcome.
>
> —CCC, no. 866

THE CHURCH IS ONE

In the Nicene Creed we profess "I believe in one, holy, catholic, and apostolic Church." *One, holy, catholic* and *apostolic* are the four **Marks of the Church** founded by Jesus Christ. "These four characteristics, inseparably linked with each other, indicate essential features of the Church and her mission" (CCC, no. 811).

The Church is one because of "her *source*," the Holy Trinity; "her *founder*," Jesus Christ, the Word made flesh; and "her *soul*," the Holy Spirit (see CCC, no. 813). God the Father has gathered his Church in the name of Jesus Christ. Jesus Christ instituted the Church to be and to live as one People in communion with him and the Father and the Spirit.

Recall these words from the priestly prayer of Jesus at the Last Supper. He prays for his disciples *and* for those who will come to believe in him "through their word"; in other words, Jesus prays for the Church:

> "I ask not only on behalf of these, but also on behalf of those who will believe in me through their word, that they may all be one. As you, Father, are in me and I am in you, may they also be in us, so that the world may believe that you have sent me. The glory that you have given me I have given them, so that they may be one, as we are one, I in them and you in me, that they may become completely one, so that the world may know that you have sent me and have loved them even as you have loved me. Father, I desire that those also, whom you have given me, may be with me where I am, to see my glory, which you have given me because you loved me before the foundation of the world.
>
> —John 17:20–24

DISPUTES, RIFTS AND DIVISION IN THE APOSTOLIC CHURCH

Recall for a moment Paul's teaching on the Church as the Body of Christ, which we explored briefly in chapter 1.

The very first Christian communities worked at

preserving unity within the one Body of Christ. For example, Paul had received word that the members of the Church at Corinth were dividing into camps. The Apostle responded by writing a letter in which he addressed several issues that were causing disunity within the community. (Check out 1 Corinthians 11:1–33.)

Before his inspiring exhortation on the Church as the Body of Christ, Paul first chided the church community at Corinth: "Now I appeal to you, brothers and sisters, by the name of our Lord Jesus Christ, that all of you should be in agreement and that there should be no divisions among you, but that you be united in the same mind and the same purpose" (1 Corinthians 1:10). Paul made this appeal because some were claiming to belong to Paul, others to Apollos, others to Cephas (Peter). After pointing out the foolishness of such claims, he asked rhetorically, "Has Christ been divided?" (Check out 1 Corinthians 1:10–14.)

Paul then moved on to deepen their understanding of the mystery of their oneness in Christ and with one another. He reminded them that it is the Holy Spirit who gifts each of the baptized for the good of the whole Church. Each member should use their gifts to unify and not divide the Church. (Check out 1 Corinthians 12:1–31.)

Paul concluded this teaching with his well-known hymn on the gift of love. The members of the Church are bound in love for Christ and one another. Love is at the center of the Body of Christ, the Church, just as it is at the center of the life of God the Trinity. (Check out 1 Corinthians 13:1–13.) "Above all, clothe yourselves with love, which binds everything together in perfect harmony" (Colossians 3:19; see also Vatican II, *Dogmatic Constitution on the Church* [*Lumen Gentium*], no. 14).

REFLECT AND SHARE

⊙ Imagine you are at Corinth as Paul's letter is being read aloud.
⊙ Reflect: What stands out for you as you listen? What questions might you have?
⊙ Share reflections as a class.

LET'S PROBE DEEPER: A SCRIPTURE ACTIVITY

⊙ Read Acts of the Apostles 15:1–35.
⊙ Reflect:
  – What was the controversy that was causing a rift between the Apostles Peter and Paul, and between Jews and Gentile Christians?
  – What did the elders gathering in council do to resolve the issue?
  – What does their approach reveal about their understanding of the nature of the Church?
⊙ Discuss responses as a class.

Acts 15:1–35 reveals how a rift between the Apostles Peter and Paul and between Jews and Gentile Christians was resolved

SAINTS PAUL AND PETER | ALTAR OF ST. CATHERINE, SCHWABACH, GERMANY

The Church: a mystery of communion

OPENING REFLECTION

- What do you understand to be the meaning of the term "mystery"?
- Is there a difference between a *mystery* of science, a *mystery* novel, and a *mystery* of faith?

THE MYSTERY OF THE HOLY TRINITY

In common speech "mystery" usually means something that we cannot yet explain or do not know and try to solve. When St. Paul writes of "the mystery of the faith" (1 Timothy 3:9), the Apostle is referring to deep truths that are of God and that give us insight into the very meaning of life. The mystery of the Holy **Trinity** is the central mystery of the Christian faith and life.

Your great-grandparents and grandparents may have used the *Baltimore Catechism* to learn about this central mystery of faith. The *Baltimore Catechism* used a question-and-answer format to teach these truths. Here are answers to some of the questions about the Trinity that your older relatives would have learned and, more than likely, memorized:

- "There is but one God."
- "In God there are three Divine Persons, really distinct, and equal in all things—the Father, the Son, and the Holy Ghost."
- "The Blessed Trinity is one God in three Divine Persons."
- "'First,' 'second,' and 'third' with regard to the persons of the Trinity do not mean that one person was before the other or that one is greater than the other; for all the persons of the Trinity are eternal and equal in every respect."

Key Resource: *Baltimore Catechism*

In the section "The Mystery of the Holy Trinity" we reference the *Baltimore Catechism*. The *Baltimore Catechism* was a catechism written for the Catholics in the United States by the bishops of the Church in the United States following the Third Synod of Baltimore in 1885. The *Baltimore Catechism* contained 421 questions and answers. It was superseded by the *Catechism of the Catholic Church* and the *United States Catholic Catechism for Adults*. (*New Catholic Encyclopedia*, Vol. 3, 2nd Edition, "Catechisms," 239–246)

THE TRINITY | TADDEO CRIVELLI

The Church as Communion

The concept of *communion* lies *"at the heart of the Church's self understanding"* (John Paul II, *Address to the Bishops of the United States of America* [1987]), insofar as it is the Mystery of the personal union of each human being with the divine Trinity and with the rest of mankind, initiated with the faith. . . . It is essential to the Christian understanding of *communion* that it be recognized above all as a gift from God, as a fruit of God's initiative carried out in the paschal mystery. The new relationship between man and God, that has been established in Christ and is communicated through the sacraments, also extends to a new relationship among human beings.
— Congregation for the Doctrine of the Faith, *Letter to the Bishops of the Catholic Church on Some Aspects of the Church Understood as Communion* (1992), no. 3

ORTHODOX BOGOYAVLENSKAYA CHURCH IN OREL, RUSSIA

⊙ "The three Divine Persons are one and the same God, having one and the same Divine Nature."
—*Baltimore Catechism* No. 3, "Lesson Third: On the Unity and Trinity of God"

The *United States Catholic Catechism for Adults* summarizes the **dogma**, or doctrine, of the Trinity. This summary includes three truths of faith that you have learned in your *Credo* texts. These truths of faith are:

First, the Trinity is One. We do not speak of three gods but of one God. Each of the Persons is fully God. They are a unity of Persons in one divine nature.

Second, the Divine Persons are distinct from each other. Father, Son, and Spirit are not three appearances or modes of God, but three identifiable persons, each fully God in a way distinct from the others.

Third, the Divine Persons are in relation to each other. The distinction of each is understood only in reference to the others. The Father cannot be the Father without the Son, nor can the Son be the Son without the Father. The Holy Spirit is related to the Father and the Son who both send him forth.

All Christians are baptized in the name of the Father and of the Son and of the Holy Spirit. The Trinity illumines all the other mysteries of faith.
—USCCA, 52–53

REFLECT AND SHARE

⊙ Imagine yourself as a catechist in your parish Confirmation program. Your session focuses on the mystery of the Holy Trinity.
⊙ Pause and, drawing upon what you have already learned about the Most Blessed Trinity, reflect:
  – How would you explain the meaning of the Catholic Church's teaching on the Holy Trinity?
  – How would you help the young people come to apply the meaning of that mystery of faith to their lives?
⊙ Share reflections as a class.

THE CHURCH: AN IMAGE OF TRINITARIAN COMMUNION

The Church has come to understand and teach that the Holy Trinity is an *inseparable* communion of three distinct Divine Persons. The Church has also come to understand and teach that this mystery of faith is not only about God. It

Key Resource: Congregation for the Doctrine of the Faith

In the section "The New People of God—One People with a Common Goal" we introduce the Congregation for the Doctrine of the Faith (CDF) as a resource. We cite its 1992 *Letter to the Bishops of the Catholic Church on Some Aspects of the Church Understood as Communion* (1992). The CDF is the Church office that examines what people are saying about the faith worldwide, especially teachings proposed by her theologians. The CDF participates in the pope's teaching authority. When necessary, the CDF issues letters explaining why certain ideas do or do not faithfully express Catholic doctrine. Pope Benedict XVI, the former Cardinal Joseph Ratzinger, was head of the CDF from 1981 until his election as pope in 2005.

CARDINAL JOSEPH RATZINGER BECAME POPE BENEDICT XVI

is also the mystery that reveals the dignity and destiny of every human person and of the human community as a whole.

The life of the individual Christian *and* the life of the whole Church is ordered to a *communion* of life "with the divine Trinity and with the rest of mankind." Through Baptism a person receives the gift of **sanctifying grace** to participate in and partake of the life of God "established in Christ and . . . communicated through the sacraments."

By the grace of Baptism "in the name of the Father and of the Son and of the Holy Spirit," we are called to share in the life of the Blessed Trinity, here on earth in the obscurity of faith, and after death in eternal light (see Paul VI, *Credo of the People of God: Solemn Profession of Faith,* §9).
—CCC, no. 265

This new relationship with God in Christ "also extends to a new relationship among human beings." The Holy Trinity calls the whole Church to be in communion together and to be co-responsible for the good of the whole of creation. All the baptized are to be a sacramental people who actively participate in worshiping the Trinity *together* and in making visible the Holy Trinity's saving work in the world. The universal Church is to be "a people made one by the unity of the Father, the Son and the Holy Spirit" (St. Cyprian [d. 258], Bishop of Carthage in modern-day Tunisia, quoted in *Dogmatic Constitution on the Church,* no. 4).

OVER TO YOU

⊙ Identify practical ways in which you could give witness to God's invitation to all people to live in communion with the Trinity.

THE NEW PEOPLE OF GOD—ONE PEOPLE WITH A COMMON GOAL

The word "church" comes from the Latin *ecclesia* and the Greek *ek-kalein,* meaning "to call out of." The First Letter of Peter reveals that the Apostles came to understand that God had called and chosen the community of Jesus' disciples, the Church, to be God's own people: "You are a chosen race, a royal priesthood, a holy nation, God's own people. . . . Once you were not a people, but now you are God's people" (1 Peter 2:9–10). This image, as we saw, is deeply grounded in the Old Testament Scriptures.

The Second Vatican Council (1962–65) passed on this Apostolic Tradition. The title of chapter 2 of the Council's *Dogmatic Constitution on the Church* is "The People of God." It teaches that the

Church is the messianic people that has Christ as its head and that fulfills the covenant God made with his Chosen People, the Israelites.

The Church instituted by Christ is first and foremost foremost a *communion of people*. She is "the sign and the instrument of the communion of God and men" (CCC, no. 780). This communion, which God has chosen to be the visible sacrament of his saving work in Christ, is, however, wounded. It is divided in the world today, and includes other Christian churches and ecclesial communities not in full communion with the Catholic Church. "Nevertheless, many elements of sanctification and of truth are found outside its visible confines. Since these are gifts belonging to the church of Christ, they are forces impelling towards catholic unity" (*Dogmatic Constitution on the Church*, no. 8). The one Church Christ founded subsists, or is found in its fullness, in the Catholic Church.

"The Christian faithful are therefore not permitted to imagine that the Church of Christ is nothing more than a collection—divided, yet in some way one—of Churches and ecclesial communities; nor are they free to hold that today the Church of Christ nowhere really exists, and must be considered only as a goal which all Churches and ecclesial communities must strive to reach" (Congregation for the Doctrine of the Faith, *The Mystery of the Church*, no. 1). In fact, "the elements of this already-given Church exist, joined together in their fullness in the Catholic Church and, without this fullness, in the other communities" (St. John Paul II, *Ut Unum Sint*, no. 14). "Therefore, these separated Churches and communities as such, though we believe they suffer from defects, have by no means been deprived of significance and importance in the mystery of salvation. For the spirit of Christ has not refrained from using them as means of salvation which derive their efficacy from the very fullness of grace and truth entrusted to the Catholic Church" (Vatican II, *Decree on Ecumenism*, no. 3).

—Congregation for the Doctrine of the Faith, *Declaration on the Unicity and Salvific Universality of Jesus Christ and the Church (Dominus Iesus)*, no. 17

God's saving work among and through his pilgrim people is not finished; there is a journey ahead as well as behind. We must continue to work together for the values of God's reign of life, love and truth so that we may arrive at eternal light.

REFLECT AND SHARE

- ⊙ What insights does the biblical image of the Church as a people whom God has gathered together give you into the nature and mission of the Church?
- ⊙ Share reflections as a class.

WHAT ABOUT YOU PERSONALLY?

- ⊙ Reflect on these words from the *Dogmatic Constitution on the Church*, no. 10: "All the disciples of Christ . . . should everywhere on earth bear witness to Christ and give an answer to everyone who asks a reason for their hope of eternal life."
- ⊙ How can *your* words and actions give an answer to anyone who would ask about the source of *your* hope of eternal life?

EUCHARIST: SOURCE OF THE CHURCH'S COMMUNION

The Eucharist makes the Church. The first association many Catholics have with the word "communion" is when they receive Holy Communion during the celebration of the Eucharist. St. Paul wrote, "The bread that we break, is it not a sharing in the body of Christ? Because there is one bread, we who are many are one body, for we all partake of the one bread" (1 Corinthians 10:16–17). The Eucharist is the source of the Church's communion.

"Really sharing in the body of the Lord in the breaking of the eucharistic bread, we are taken up into communion with him and with one another. 'Because the bread is one, we, though many, are one body, all of us who partake of the one bread' (1 Corinthians 10:17)." (See also *Dogmatic Constitution on the Church*, no. 7.)
—*Letter to the Bishops of the Catholic Church on Some Aspects of the Church Understood as Communion*, no. 5

Receiving the Body and Blood of Christ in Holy Communion augments our communion with Christ, his Father and the Holy Spirit; it unites and strengthens our relationship with all the faithful; it separates us from sin; it commits us to the poor and to seek full communion with the baptized who have separated themselves from the Catholic Church.

JOURNAL EXERCISE

- ⊙ Reflect on your participation in the Eucharist.
  - Do you see regular participation in the Eucharist as vital to your life as a member of the Church?
  - Do you see your receiving of Holy Communion as bonding you more closely with Christ and with the Church?
  - Do your reflections increase your commitment to receive Holy Communion more regularly?
- ⊙ Summarize your reflections in your journal.

The bread that we break, is it not a sharing in the body of Christ?

1 CORINTHIANS 10:16

Divisions and disunity in the Church

Christianity in the United States of America Today

Christianity in the United States of America is diverse. In addition to the Roman Catholic

WORSHIPERS AT NEW ISRAEL BAPTIST CHURCH, NEW ORLEANS

Church, the Eastern Catholic Churches and the Orthodox Churches, there are numerous Protestant denominations that are divided among themselves over doctrine and practices. These Christian denominations, or ecclesial communities, include, according to the Pew Research Center, Baptists, Methodists, Pentecostals, Lutherans, Presbyterians, Restorationists, Episcopalians/Anglicans, Holiness, Congregationalists, Adventists, Anabaptists, Reformed, Pietist and nondenominational groups.

OPENING REFLECTION

- ⊙ Which of the Protestant denominations, or ecclesial communities, named above are you aware of?
- ⊙ Do you have family, friends or neighbors who are members of any of those denominations or ecclesial communities? What do you know about the teachings and practices of their faith?

CREEDS AND COUNCILS

In the first section of this chapter we learned that the Church professes one faith received from the Apostles. Two of the ways in which the Church authentically passes on that apostolic faith is through her Creeds and councils. We will now review each of these, which you have already studied in detail in *The Body of Christ: The Church* text in the *Credo* series.

Creeds: St. Ambrose (c. 340–397), the fourth-century Bishop of Milan, Italy, described the Creed as "the spiritual seal, our heart's meditation and an ever-present guardian; it is, unquestionably, the treasure of our soul" (*Explanation of the Creeds*, 17). The Creeds of the Church are also called Symbols of Faith. "A symbol of faith is a summary of the principal truths of the faith and therefore serves as the first and fundamental point of reference for catechesis" (CCC, no. 188).

The Creeds are rooted in the celebration of the Sacrament of Baptism. As remains the case today, those seeking Baptism in the early Church were asked to state or profess the faith of the Church prior to their actual Baptism. The Letter to the Romans and the First Letter to the Corinthians provide us with examples of creedal formulae or statements of faith in the Apostolic Church. (Check out Romans 10:9 and 1 Corinthians 15:3–5.)

THE CREED (DETAIL) | 16TH-CENTURY BRUSSELS TAPESTRY

Many Creeds arose in the Church throughout her history. They are brief, normative statements or professions of Christian faith. The Apostles' Creed and the Niceno-Constantinopolitan Creed (or Nicene Creed) are the most familiar and most widely used today. The Church professes the Apostles' Creed or the Niceno-Constantinopolitan Creed at Mass during the Liturgy of the Word. At Baptism, the Creed is professed in question-and-answer format.

The Apostles' Creed, while not written by the Apostles, is so-called because "it is rightly considered to be a faithful summary of the apostles' faith. It is the ancient baptismal symbol of the Church of Rome. Its great authority arises from this fact: it is 'the Creed of the Roman Church, the See of Peter, the first of the apostles, to which he brought the common faith (see St. Ambrose, *Explanation of the Creeds*, 7)' " (CCC, no. 194).

The Niceno-Constantinopolitan (Nicene) Creed formulated the teachings of the First Council of Nicaea in AD 325 and the First Council of Constantinople in AD 381. Both of these early councils formulated the faith of the Church as a response to serious dissension and disputes that were dividing the communion of the Church.

Councils: Following the example of the Council at Jerusalem, local Christian churches held councils to decide local issues. At the beginning of the fourth century, however, a universal controversy was raging around whether Jesus could be said to be fully divine. This controversy was rooted in a dispute over the relationship of the Three Persons of the Trinity.

The controversy became so intense that it was threatening the peace of the Roman Empire. This prompted the Emperor Constantine to call a meeting of the whole Church, or an Ecumenical Council.

THE EARLY ECUMENICAL COUNCILS

The first Ecumenical Council met at Nicaea in 325. Since then, there have been twenty more gatherings of the world's bishops exercising their collegial authority over the universal Church in union with the pope. We will now take a brief look at the first four Ecumenical Councils of the Church and their impact on the communion of the Church.

The First Council of Nicaea (AD 325)
The First Council of Nicaea passed on the apostolic faith in the Trinity and condemned the Arian heresy. Arianism denied that the Son of God was of one substance and one nature with God the Father. As a consequence, Arianism falsely taught that Jesus, the Incarnate Son of God, was not truly and fully divine.

The First Council of Constantinople (AD 381)
The First Council of Constantinople reaffirmed the teachings of the First Council of Nicaea and rejected Arianism. This council taught that Jesus was "of the same substance" as God, or of the same nature as God. In other words, Jesus was fully God. Jesus, the Incarnate Son of God, was truly divine and truly human. The First Council of Constantinople also addressed the relationship of the Father and Son with the Holy

Spirit. The words the council used to describe the relationship created another theological and doctrinal controversy that intensified the controversy between the Church in the East and the Church in the West. As we will discuss in chapter 4, it was one of the major doctrinal issues that contributed to the Great Schism in 1054—a schism that continues to this day.

OVER TO YOU

- These teachings of the First Council of Nicaea and the First Council of Constantinople are stated, as we have seen, in the Niceno-Constantinopolitan (or Nicene) Creed.
- Take a moment and recall these words of the *Catechism of the Catholic Church*, "To say the Credo with faith is to enter into communion with God, Father, Son, and Holy Spirit, and also with the whole Church which transmits the faith to us and in whose midst we believe" (CCC, no. 197).
- Pause, reflect and pray the Nicene Creed.

The Council of Ephesus (AD 431)

After the Councils of Nicaea I and Constantinople I, a new challenge to the full humanity and divinity of Jesus arose. This challenge was led by Nestorius (c. 381–451), the Patriarch of Constantinople, the center of the Church in the East. Nestorius claimed that Jesus was really *two persons*, having *two natures* that were totally separate. He and his followers claimed that Jesus was a human person

only joined to the Divine Person of the Son of God. The council taught that Jesus is one Divine Person in whom the divine nature and a human nature are united. This dogma of the Church is called the hypostatic union. Jesus, the Incarnate Son of God, is inseparably true God and true man.

As a consequence of their false understanding of the Apostolic Tradition of the Church, Nestorius and his followers reasoned that Mary was only the mother of the human person Jesus and not the Mother of God. They believed that Mary could be called *Cristotokos*, the Mother of Christ, but not *Theotokos*, the Mother of God. The third Ecumenical Council held at Ephesus condemned Nestorius and taught that "Mary truly became the Mother of God by the human conception of the Son of God in her womb" (CCC, no. 466).

This dispute led to some churches, such as the Assyrian Church, breaking away from full communion with the pope and the Catholic Church. Modern dialogue with those who have not accepted the authority and office of the pope has made progress in healing this schism. "Those baptized are fully in the communion of the Catholic Church on this earth who are joined with Christ in its visible structure by the bonds of the profession of faith, the sacraments, and ecclesiastical governance" (*Code of Canon Law*, canon 205). The visible union between bishops as well as all other members of the Church is found in the office of the Roman Pontiff by virtue of his

Key Resource: Code of Canon Law

In the section "The Council of Ephesus (AD 431)" we introduce the Catholic Church's *Code of Canon Law* as a resource. The Church's canon law governs her life, discipline, and the practice of the sacraments. The Code was last revamped in 1983 to incorporate the teachings of Vatican II.

COUNCIL OF EPHESUS | NOTRE-DAME DE FOURVIÈRES, LYON, FRANCE

FAITH WORD

Ecumenical Council

A gathering of all the bishops of the world, in the exercise of their collegial authority over the universal Church. An ecumenical council is usually called by the successor of St. Peter, the Pope, or at least confirmed or accepted by him.

—CCC, Glossary, "Council, Ecumenical"

being the Vicar of Christ. Later some of these churches accepted the authority of the pope and returned to full communion with the Catholic Church.

OVER TO YOU

⊙ Read Luke 1:28, 30, 41 and John 19:25b–27.
⊙ Pray the Hail Mary slowly, pausing and reflecting after you pray the words "Holy Mary, Mother of God."
  – Can you imagine Christians refusing to give the title Mother of God to Mary? Why might they do so?
  – What does it mean for Christian faith to pray to Mary, Mother of God?

The Council of Chalcedon (AD 451)

The controversies over the Church's doctrine of the hypostatic union and the divisions that resulted from those disputes did not cease. Eutyches (c. 380–c. 456), an Orthodox monastic priest from Constantinople who took part in the Council of Ephesus, went to the other extreme from Nestorius. Eutyches argued that there was only one nature in Christ, a human nature. The humanity of Jesus was totally absorbed into his divinity. Eutyches' heresy is called Monophysitism, a Greek term meaning "one nature."

The fourth Ecumenical Council, the Council of Chalcedon in 451, reiterated and summarized the teaching of the previous councils, declaring that Jesus was fully divine, fully human, and

yet one Divine Person. The council taught: "We unanimously teach and confess one and the same Son, our Lord Jesus Christ: the same perfect in divinity and perfect in humanity, the same truly God and truly man . . . consubstantial with the Father as to his divinity and consubstantial with us as to his humanity. . . . The distinction between the two natures was never abolished by their union" (quoted in CCC, no. 467).

Those who believed the Monophysite heresy also broke away from full communion with the Church and formed what are called Oriental Orthodox Churches. Modern dialogue with the Oriental Orthodox Churches has made progress in healing this schism. (*We will explore the Orthodox and other churches in the East in more detail in chapter 4.*)

REFLECT, PAIR AND SHARE

⊙ Where in the Creeds do we find the summary statements of the doctrine of the Church on the Trinity?
⊙ Where in the Creeds do we find the summary statements of the doctrine of the Church that Jesus is one Person who is truly and fully divine and truly and fully human?
⊙ Share what those doctrines reveal about your relationship with God.

OVER TO YOU

⊙ How do Ecumenical Councils preserve and deepen the communion of the Church?

The call to unity

WEEK OF PRAYER FOR CHRISTIAN UNITY

Each year in January Christians around the globe unite to celebrate the Week of Prayer for Christian Unity. Two Episcopalian priests, Reverend Paul Wattson and Reverend Spenser, first proposed the Week of Prayer in 1908. Today this week of prayer is celebrated in the United States of America and other countries in the northern hemisphere during the week when the Church also celebrates the Feast of the Conversion of Saint Paul the Apostle (January 25). Christians in countries in the southern hemisphere gather around Pentecost. During this week of prayer Christians acknowledge their shared identity as brothers and sisters related to one another by Baptism.

OPENING REFLECTION

- ⊙ When have you gathered for prayer with other Christians? Why did you gather?
- ⊙ Are you aware of when your diocese celebrates the Week of Prayer for Christian Unity? If not, make it a point to research the day, time and prayer. Would you consider participating in the celebration?
- ⊙ Take a moment and pray: "Lord, may we become one as you and the Father and the Holy Spirit are one"; or use a prayer of your own.

ECUMENISM

The term "ecclesial communities" expresses the apostolic faith that the Church is a "mystery of

Brothers and Sisters by Baptism

"The Church knows that she is joined in many ways to the baptized who are honored by the name of Christian, but who do not however profess the Catholic faith in its entirety or have not preserved unity or communion under the successor of Peter" (Vatican II, Dogmatic Constitution on the Church, no. 15). Among the non-Catholic Churches and Christian communities, there are indeed to be found many elements of the Church of Christ, which allow us, amid joy and hope, to acknowledge the existence of a certain communion, albeit imperfect.

—Congregation for the Doctrine of the Faith, Letter to the Bishops of the Catholic Church on Some Aspects of the Church Understood as Communion, no. 17

ECUMENICAL CHAPEL IN WARSAW CHOPIN AIRPORT, POLAND

The *Decree on Ecumenism* (*Unitatis Redintegratio*) of the Second Vatican Council, the twenty-first Ecumenical Council of the Church, promoted those efforts. The decree described the division within the communion of the Church as a scandal for which all sides are to share the blame. The decree also made clear that all Christians now share the responsibility to work for the unity that Jesus Christ intended. The decree opens:

> The restoration of unity among all Christians is one of the principal concerns of the Second Vatican Council. Christ the Lord founded one church and one church only. However, many christian communities present themselves to people as the true inheritance of Jesus Christ; all indeed profess to be followers of the Lord but they differ in outlook and go their different ways, as if Christ himself were divided. Certainly, such division openly contradicts the will of Christ, scandalizes the world, and damages the sacred cause of preaching the Gospel to every creature.
>
> —*Decree on Ecumenism*, no. 1

communion," a concept we have learned about in the "Hear the Story" section of this chapter. We have also seen that from apostolic times the Church has experienced divisions and rifts in the unity of that communion. In response to Jesus' desire which he expressed in his prayer to the Father, the Church has always made efforts to heal those divisions and restore unity within the communion of the Church, the Body of Christ. **Ecumenism** is the term the Church uses to name the efforts aimed at fostering unity between the Catholic Church and other Christian churches and ecclesial communities.

Key Resource: Apostolic Exhortations

APOSTOLIC EXHORTATION

In the "Reflect and Share" activity that follows the section "Full and Imperfect Communion," we introduce Pope Francis' apostolic exhortation *The Joy of the Gospel* (*Evangelii Gaudium*) as a resource.

Most commonly, an apostolic exhortation is a teaching document from the pope on a specific issue of the time. The pope commonly issues an apostolic exhortation after a meeting of bishops called a synod. A synod typically discusses a topic of current concern to the life and mission of the Church; for example, the Synods on the Family (2014 and 2015); the Synod on Young people, the Faith and Vocational Discernment (2018). At a synod the bishops develop a series of recommendations to address the topic. The pope takes the recommendations into account when he writes the apostolic exhortation to teach the faithful about the topic. The pope may also issue an apostolic exhortation on other occasions. For example, on March 19, 2018 Pope Francis issued the apostolic exhortation *Gaudete et Exsultate* (Rejoice and Be Glad). The theme of *Gaudete et Exsultate* is the call to holiness in today's world.

FULL AND IMPERFECT COMMUNION

What does it mean for other Christian churches and ecclesial communities to be in *full communion* with the Catholic Church? Baptized people are in full communion with the Catholic Church when they are joined with Christ in the visible structure of the Church through the profession of faith, the reception of the sacraments, and show respect and obedience toward those in authority in the Church.

The *Catechism of the Catholic Church* teaches: "But the unity of the pilgrim Church is also assured by visible bonds of communion:

- profession of one faith received from the Apostles;
- common celebration of divine worship, especially of the sacraments;
- apostolic succession through the sacrament of Holy Orders, maintaining the fraternal concord of God's family" (CCC, no. 815)

What does it mean for other Christian churches or ecclesial communities to be in *imperfect communion* with the Catholic Church? The *Decree on Ecumenism* states that "in Catholic doctrine there exists an order or 'hierarchy' of truths, since they vary in their relation to the foundation of the christian faith" (*Decree on Ecumenism* [*Unitatis Redintegratio*], no. 11). The communion is imperfect because of differences in doctrine, discipline, and/or ecclesiastical structure that are obstacles to full communion. The ecumenical movement works to foster unity between the Catholic Church and other Christian churches and ecclesial communities through dialogue and striving to overcome obstacles to full communion.

First, there are the divisions with the Churches in the East. Christian churches, such as the Orthodox Churches, are those with a validly ordained priesthood and validly celebrated Eucharist. Ecclesial communities are those Christian denominations that do not have a validly ordained priesthood, and the Eucharist they celebrate is not fully recognized by the Catholic Church (*We will explore the imperfect communion of the Catholic Church with the Orthodox Churches in more detail in chapter 4.*)

Second, there are the divisions that occurred in the West stemming from the Protestant

Pope Francis met with Russian Orthodox Patriarch Kirill in Cuba in February 2016, the first such meeting between patriarch and pope since the Great Schism of 1054

POPE FRANCIS AND RUSSIAN ORTHODOX PATRIARCH KIRILL IN CUBA IN FEBRUARY 2016

Reformation. In chapters 5 and 6 we explore in more detail the imperfect communion of the Catholic Church with these ecclesial communities—the common ties that we share and the differences that separate us. (*We will continue our discussion of the ecumenical efforts among Christians in the next chapter.*)

REFLECT AND SHARE

- Pope Francis in his apostolic exhortation *The Joy of the Gospel* (*Evangelii Gaudium*) wrote: "We must never forget that we are pilgrims journeying alongside one another. This means that we must have sincere trust in our fellow pilgrims" (*The Joy of the Gospel*, no. 244). "If we concentrate on the convictions we share, and if we keep in mind the principle of the hierarchy of truths, we will be able to progress decidedly towards common expressions of proclamation, service and witness" (*The Joy of the Gospel*, no. 246).

- What wisdom do you see in Pope Francis' guidance that we "concentrate on the convictions we share" while we acknowledge our differences in giving witness to Christ?

- How do you see your parish and school following the Pope's wisdom?

WHAT ABOUT YOU PERSONALLY?

- Do any of your words or actions contribute to disunity among Christians?

- How might you contribute to the unity among Christians?

We must never forget that we are pilgrims journeying alongside one another

PILGRIMS ATTENDING WORLD YOUTH DAY, KRAKÓW, POLAND IN 2016

REVIEW AND SHARE WHAT YOU HAVE LEARNED

Review what you have learned in this chapter about the Church's teaching that the Church is the Body of Christ, bonded in deep communion and moving through history as a new "People of God" *in* Jesus Christ. Share the teachings of the Catholic Church that you have learned on these statements:

⊙ The Church, the Body of Christ, is one.

⊙ The life of the individual Christian and the life of the whole Church is ordered to a communion of life "with the divine Trinity and with the rest of mankind."

⊙ The Church is "the sign and the instrument of the communion of God and men" (CCC, no. 780).

⊙ The Eucharist is the source of the Church's communion.

⊙ The one Church founded by Jesus Christ is found in its fullness in the present world in the Catholic Church.

⊙ The Creeds and Ecumenical Councils of the Church pass on authentically the one faith received from the Apostles.

⊙ Ecumenism is the effort of the Church to foster unity among all Christians.

TALK IT OVER

⊙ What has learning that the Church is a mystery of communion added to your understanding of the Church?

LEARN BY EXAMPLE

The Paulist Fathers, giving the Word of God a voice

Father Isaac Hecker (1819–88) founded the Missionary Society of St. Paul the Apostle, or the Paulist Fathers, on July 7, 1858 to evangelize both believers and non-believers. Hecker and three other Redemptorist missioners shared a common concern for Protestants, who often came to hear them preach. Their impact on Protestants is evidenced by the fact that the majority of the early Paulist Fathers were Protestants who converted to Catholicism.

From their beginning the Paulists have used a variety of methods to fulfill their mission. They carried out their early ministry primarily by preaching and the use of the printing press. For example, in April 1865 Hecker founded the monthly magazine *The Catholic World*. In the early 1900s Paulists began serving on college campuses as chaplains. In the 1940s and 1950s they established Catholic Information Centers. The Centers in various cities around

FATHER ISAAC HECKER C. 1887

the country welcomed "seekers from other faiths or no faith at all to an understanding of the teachings and way of life of the Catholic

Church." Today the Paulist Fathers continue to proclaim the Gospel using a variety of web-based and other contemporary social media "to give voice to the words of Christ—the Word Himself—to a new generation of Americans."

Evangelization has been the primary mission of the Paulists from their founding. The Paulist Office for Ecumenical and Interfaith Relations "serves as a concrete expression of the Paulist Community's commitment to work for unity among the followers of Christ (Ecumenism) and to build bridges of understanding, respect, and collaboration with members of other world religions (Interfaith Relations)."

The Paulist Fathers' mission statement on their website includes these summary statements relating to their work:

⊙ We give the Word of God a voice in pulpits and print, on radio and television, on the Web and the wide screen.

⊙ We search out those who have no church home, and welcome home those who have been away.

⊙ We share the passion of St. Paul for unity in faith and solidarity in mission among all the baptized in the body of Christ.

⊙ We build bridges of respect and collaboration with people of other world religions.

⊙ We welcome people of diverse racial and cultural backgrounds in our parish, city center and campus worshipping communities.

⊙ The Gospel we preach calls for all the children of God to be treated with dignity and justice.

OVER TO YOU

⊙ Reflect on these words from the mission statement of the Paulist Fathers: "The one Spirit of Christ, poured into all hearts, urges us to work with our brothers and sisters for union in faith, life, worship and mission towards the unity God wills for the one church of Christ."

⊙ How can you support and take part in that work, right now?

SHARE FAITH WITH FAMILY AND FRIENDS

⊙ Recall those of your relatives, neighbors and good friends who are Christian but not Catholic.

⊙ Do you respect and treat them as sisters and brothers in Christ?

⊙ Identify ways you can bring an "ecumenical spirit" to your personal relationship with them.

JUDGE AND DECIDE

⊙ Do you see signs of disrespect among Catholics and other Christians in your community? Would you name those signs acts of prejudice?

⊙ How do the efforts of the Paulist Fathers and the ecumenical work of the Catholic Church strive to break down prejudice?

⊙ What can you do to take part in those efforts?

LEARN BY HEART

In the one Spirit we were all baptized into one body—Jews or Greeks, slaves or free—and we were all made to drink of one Spirit. . . . Now you are the body of Christ and individually members of it.

1 CORINTHIANS 12:13, 27

Introduction

LEADER

Sprinkles water over the students, saying:
This water, from different sources, is a symbol of
our unity, which is real, though still incomplete.

Invitation to Prayer

LEADER

Almighty God, breathe into us the wind of unity
that recognizes our diversity.

ALL

Breathe into us tolerance that welcomes and
makes us community.

LEADER

Breathe into us fire that unites what is torn apart
and heals what is ill.

ALL

Breathe into us grace that overcomes hatred and
frees us from violence.

LEADER

Breathe into us life that faces down and defeats
death.

ALL

Blessed be the God of mercy, who is Father, Son
and Holy Spirit, and makes all things new. Amen!

DIVINE MERCY SHRINE, EL SALVADOR CITY, PHILIPPINES

Prayer of Contrition

LEADER

In humility, as children of God and sisters and
brothers in Christ, we receive God's mercy and
respond to God's call to make new all relationships.

READER

Merciful Lord, your Spirit hovered over the
waters where diversity sprouted and flourished.
We confess our difficulty to live with legitimate
differences. Forgive us those attitudes of mind,
words and actions that do violence to unity in
diversity.

ALL

O Lord, have mercy upon us.

READER

Merciful Christ, grace and joy of the multitude,
listener and teacher, you give birth to new visions
of hope and heal the wounds of mind and body.
We confess that we have failed to listen to voices
different from our own, failed to say words that
bring healing and hope, and we have perpetuated
exclusive attitudes to those who cry out for
solidarity and fellowship.

ALL

O Lord, have mercy upon us.

READER

Merciful Lord, you are the source of all creation,
the Eternal and life-giving Word.

We confess that we do not listen to your creation that groans and cries out for liberation and renewal.
Help us to walk together and to hear your voice in all living things that suffer and yearn for healing and care.

ALL
O Lord, have mercy upon us.

LEADER
O God, fountain of mercy and grace, pour over us your pardon. May your love transform us into a source of living waters to restore the strength of your people. We make our prayer through Christ our Lord.

ALL
Amen.

Gospel Proclamation

Proclamation or dramatization of the Gospel of John 4:1–42.
All reflect on the Gospel.

Affirmation of Faith

The Nicene-Constantinopolitan Creed, the Apostles' Creed or another affirmation of faith may be used, for example, the renewal of baptismal promises.

Intercessory Prayer

LEADER
God of eternal compassion,
as individuals and as community,
we ask for light, so we may become more welcoming and understanding toward others and reduce the suffering in our world.

ALL
Hear us, God of love! Hear this our cry!

LEADER
God of eternal compassion,
teach your children that charity, hospitality and unity are expressions of your revelation and will for humanity.

ALL
Hear us, God of love! Hear this our cry!

LEADER
God of eternal compassion,
we beseech you, grant us peace;
teach us and guide us to be builders of a tolerant and non-violent world.

ALL
Hear us, God of love! Hear this our cry!

LEADER
God of eternal compassion,
who spoke to us through creation,
then through the prophets and then through your Son Jesus Christ,
grant us wisdom to listen to your voice that calls us to unity in our diversity.

ALL
Hear us, God of love! Hear this our cry!

All who wish to do so may add other prayers.
All pray the Lord's Prayer together.

> **May Jesus Christ the living water be behind us to protect us, before us to guide us, by our side to accompany us, within us to console us, above us to bless us.**

Benediction

LEADER

May the Lord God
bless us and protect us,
fill our heart with tenderness and our soul with
joy,
our ears with music and our nostrils with
perfume,
our tongue with song giving face to hope.

May Jesus Christ the living water be
behind us to protect us,
before us to guide us,
by our side to accompany us,
within us to console us,
above us to bless us.

May the life-giving Spirit
breathe into us that our thoughts may be holy,
act in us so that our work is holy,
draw our heart so that we love what is holy,
strengthen us that we will defend what is holy.

May he make his home in our heart,
water its dryness, and melt its coldness,
kindle in our innermost soul the fire of his love
and bestow upon us a true faith, and firm hope,
and a sincere and perfect love.

ALL

Amen.

Sharing Peace and Sending Forth

LEADER

May God, who teaches us to welcome each other
and calls us to practice hospitality, grant us peace
and serenity as we move forward on the path of
Christian unity.
As we go in the peace of Christ let us share with
each other the sign of peace.

—International Prayer for Christian Unity 2015,
prepared by The Pontifical Council for Promoting
Christian Unity and The Commission on Faith and
Order of the World Council of Churches

JESUS AND THE SAMARITAN WOMAN | GEORG RAPHAEL DONNER

Ecumenical and Interreligious Dialogue

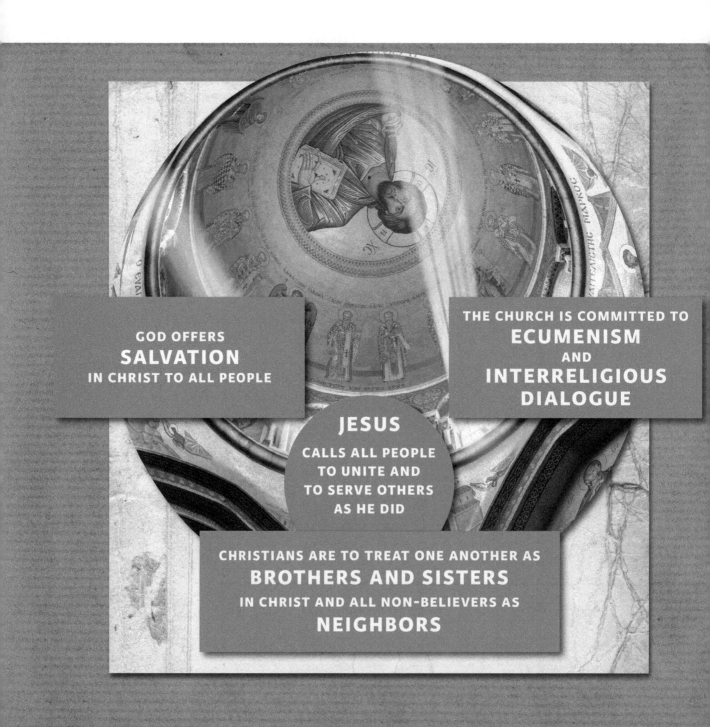

GOD OFFERS
SALVATION
IN CHRIST TO ALL PEOPLE

THE CHURCH IS COMMITTED TO
ECUMENISM
AND
**INTERRELIGIOUS
DIALOGUE**

JESUS
CALLS ALL PEOPLE
TO UNITE AND
TO SERVE OTHERS
AS HE DID

CHRISTIANS ARE TO TREAT ONE ANOTHER AS
BROTHERS AND SISTERS
IN CHRIST AND ALL NON-BELIEVERS AS
NEIGHBORS

CHAPTER 3 EXAMINES THE PRINCIPLES, HISTORY and goals of the Catholic Church's ecumenical dialogue with other Christian churches and ecclesial communities and also her interreligious dialogues with non-Christian religions. We explore the impetus that Vatican II gave to this work. We also look at the ecumenical and interreligious mission of the Church at both global and national levels, including the efforts of the recent popes. In the remaining chapters of this text we examine this work in more detail.

"THE CHURCH IS THE PLACE WHERE HUMANITY MUST REDISCOVER ITS UNITY AND SALVATION."
—CATECHISM OF THE CATHOLIC CHURCH, NO. 845

Faith Focus: These teachings of the Catholic Church are the primary focus of the doctrinal content presented in this chapter:

- ☉ Christ calls all his disciples to unity.
- ☉ Commitment to ecumenism responds to the prayer of the Lord Jesus that "they may all be one" (John 17:21).
- ☉ All Christians are to work as the one Body of Christ to serve all people in need.
- ☉ Salvation is a gift of grace available through faith in Jesus Christ.
- ☉ The Catholic Church is the ordinary means of salvation willed by God.
- ☉ God can lead to salvation those who through no fault of their own are ignorant of the Gospel and seek him with a sincere heart.
- ☉ The Church has the obligation and sacred right to evangelize all people.

Discipleship Formation: As a result of studying this chapter and discovering the meaning of the faith of the Catholic Church for your life, you should be better able to:

- ☉ renew your faith in Christ and his Church;
- ☉ foster the unity of the Church by joining with Catholic and non-Catholic Christian friends to serve people in need;
- ☉ pray regularly for the unity of the Church;
- ☉ respect non-believers and support their efforts to do God's will as they have come to know it;
- ☉ work against injustice rooted in religious bigotry and support efforts that foster the religious liberty of all people.

Scripture References: These scripture references are quoted or referred to in this chapter:
NEW TESTAMENT: Matthew 5:13–16; **Luke** 2:19 and 51, 10:25–37; **John** 8:31a–32, 14:1–14, 17:20–23; **Romans** 8:32, **1 Timothy** 3:15; **Jude** 3

Faith Glossary: Familiarize yourself with or recall the meaning of these key terms. Definitions are found in the Glossary: **Apostolic Succession, Beatific Vision, ecumenism, hierarchy of truths, interreligious dialogue, New Evangelization, Orthodox Churches, parable, proselytism**

Faith Words: ecumenism; hierarchy of truths
Learn by Heart: John 8:31a–32
Learn by Example: Pilgrimages of Trust on Earth

Why is dialogue among Christians vital?

PREJUDICE AND DISCRIMINATION AMONG CHRISTIANS

Katie's family moved from New Jersey to Texas during the summer after Katie had completed elementary school. She was looking forward to beginning high school in her new surroundings and making lots of new friends. A short time after she had started in high school Katie came home and asked, "Dad, are Catholics Christians?"

Her dad replied, "Of course we're Christians? Catholics are Christians just as your friend Sabrina who is Baptist is a Christian, and Emily who is Lutheran is a Christian. Why are you asking?"

"Well, after history class one of my classmates told me, 'Catholics are not real Christians.' "

At dinner that evening Katie and her family talked about how Christians of different denominations and backgrounds can be prejudiced against and even hostile toward one another.

OPENING REFLECTION

- ⊙ Do you consider all non-Catholic Christians to be "real" Christians? Why or why not?
- ⊙ When have you experienced firsthand or learned about prejudice or bullying or discrimination among Christians?
- ⊙ Can you recall from your study of history times when the differences that separated Christians resulted in violence? Resulted in acts of injustice?

CHRISTIAN DIFFERENCES TURNED INTO VIOLENCE AND INJUSTICE

Down the centuries some Christians have used differences between their faith beliefs to justify wars and other acts of violence and injustice, which have scarred the face of Christianity.

Conflicts in Europe: Historians point out that Europe enjoyed only thirty years of peace in the period following the Protestant Reformation. Between 1562 and 1598 there were numerous civil wars and outbreaks of violence that were clearly motivated by religious differences. For example, Protestantism was declared illegal in France. By 1609 the Holy Roman Empire had fragmented into two hostile alliances—the Protestant Union and the Catholic League. The Thirty Years War (1618–48) was the greatest of these wars on the European continent.

Conflicts in the United States of America: Violence and injustice also scarred the face of Christianity in the United States of America from its early days. One historian writes:

A deep anti-Catholic sentiment, inherited from Great Britain, existed in colonial America. Some colonies had laws restricting or banning Catholicism. The settling of the colony of

Maryland by English Catholics was perhaps the only exception. . . . Protestants resented Catholicism on theological grounds, often making fun of and belittling Catholic religious rites and customs. The common Christian link between Protestantism and Catholicism meant little. . . .

As American Catholicism spread during the 19th century, anti-Catholic violence saw churches burned, Catholics massacred, property destroyed, and the growth of anti-foreigner and anti-Catholic organizations like the "Know Nothings." Beyond violence, Catholics routinely became victims of discrimination in employment and housing.

—Elliot Eastman, *Life in the USA*, "Discrimination Against Catholics"

As Catholics grew in numbers and Catholics and Protestants lived and worked side by side, this discrimination gradually eroded and gave way to inclusivity. In 1960 John F. Kennedy, a Catholic, was elected the 35th President; and in 2008 Joe Biden was elected the first Catholic Vice-President. By 2015 thirty-one percent of Congress, including the Speaker of the House of Representatives and the House Minority Leader, and six justices of the Supreme Court were Catholic, and the pope addressed a joint session of the Congress.

REFLECT AND SHARE

⦿ What factors do you think contributed toward Catholics and other Christians living together peaceably and justly?

THE GOOD SAMARITAN

The **parable** of the good Samaritan is found only in Luke's account of the Gospel. Jesus told this parable to conclude his response to an expert in Jewish law who had asked him, "Teacher, what must I do to inherit eternal life?" To which Jesus replied with the question, "What is written in the law?"

The lawyer rightly answered Jesus' question by quoting the Torah, "You shall love the Lord your God with all your heart, and with all your soul, and with all your strength, and with all your mind; and your neighbor as yourself." Jesus responded, "You have given the right answer; do this, and you will live." Jesus then told the parable of the good Samaritan to open up the meaning of these two Great Commandments of the Torah.

One of the key messages of Luke's Gospel is that God offers salvation in Christ to all people. Jewish laws in Jesus' time discriminated against Samaritans. You will recall that Samaritans had intermarried with non-Jews. In response, Jewish law stipulated that Samaritans could not be "real" or "true" Jews. Jewish laws were written to exclude Samaritans from participation in Jewish life. Yet in his parable Jesus holds up the Samaritan who stopped to care for the wounded traveler—and not the priest or Levite who did not stop—as an example of a Jew who lives and practices the Torah and the Law of God.

Clearly, for Jesus, one's "neighbor" is not just the person or group of people with whom we agree or who meet our standards. Those who follow the Law of God treat everyone as their neighbor. Jesus says to all Christians, as he said to the Jewish lawyer, "Go and do likewise."

THE GOOD SAMARITAN (DETAIL) | HEINRICH ALDEGREVER

Pope Francis House

THE POPE FRANCIS HOUSE, ST. LOUIS, MISSOURI

"In imitation of our Master, we Christians are called to confront the poverty of our brothers and sisters, to touch it, to make it our own and to take practical steps to alleviate it. . . . In the poor and outcast we see Christ's face; by loving and, helping the poor, we love and serve Christ." (Pope Francis)

In 2015 Christians united and worked together on building the Pope Francis House, a Habitat For Humanity effort, in St. Louis, Missouri. The Pope Francis House, a two-story home, is located behind Cardinal Glennon and St. Louis University Hospitals.

LET'S PROBE DEEPER: A SCRIPTURE ACTIVITY

⊙ Read the parable of the good Samaritan in Luke 10:25–37.
⊙ Apply the lesson of the parable to the relationship between Christians today.
⊙ What can the parable teach Christians?
⊙ Share reflections as a class.

A MESSAGE FOR CHRISTIANS TODAY

There is a message in the parable of the Good Samaritan for Christians today. Christians are to treat one another as *brothers and sisters* in Christ and all non-believers as *neighbors*. Serving others—all others—gives witness to our shared faith in Jesus Christ. The building of Pope Francis House in St. Louis, Missouri, is but one example.

Jesus is always calling us to unite and to serve others as he did. Jesus commands us to be open, friendly, helpful, kind and responsive to all, especially to those in need. This includes serving not only those with whom we identify, but also the stranger, the outsider, the marginalized. Any time we are tempted to divide people into "us" and "them," and to walk by "those others," we are failing to live up to Jesus' call and challenge.

Jesus calls all his disciples to be united as one so that people will believe in him and his Gospel (see John 17:21). Jesus and his Gospel demand that we engage our Christian sisters and brothers in a spirit of neighborliness. The work of **ecumenism** is a response to that call.

READ, REFLECT AND SHARE

⊙ Reread John 17:20–23.
⊙ Reflect:
  – How can the efforts of Christians from different traditions working together to serve people in need contribute to fulfilling Jesus' prayer to his Father?
  – Why or how would Christians being "one" help people come to believe in Jesus Christ?
⊙ Share reflections as a class.

WHAT ABOUT YOU PERSONALLY?

⊙ Are there opportunities for you to join with non-Catholic youth in serving people in need? Have you taken advantage of those opportunities?
⊙ What was the impact of those efforts on your coming to know young people of non-Catholic traditions?

The ecumenical movement

POPE FRANCIS MEETS THE ECUMENICAL PATRIARCH OF CONSTANTINOPLE

On June 8, 2014 Pope Francis, as his predecessors had done, met with the Ecumenical Patriarch of Constantinople, Bartholomew I, at the Vatican. The Ecumenical Patriarch of Constantinople is the first among equals of the Churches that make up the **Orthodox Churches**, or the Churches in the East not in full communion with the Catholic Church. As part of their meeting, Pope Francis and Ecumenical Patriarch Bartholomew joined in an interfaith summit of Jews, Christians and Muslims.

On November 29 and 30 of that same year Pope Francis reciprocated by visiting Ecumenical Patriarch Bartholomew in Constantinople. Together the Pope and Patriarch took part in festivities surrounding the Feast Day of the Apostle Andrew. Tradition teaches that Andrew, the younger brother of St. Peter, first preached the Gospel in what today is Turkey and Western Russia.

OPENING REFLECTION

- ◉ What have you learned about the effects of open and honest dialogue with people with whom you disagree?
- ◉ Why is dialogue essential to restoring full communion between the Catholic Church and the Orthodox Churches and ecclesial communities that are currently separated from the Catholic Church?

THE BEGINNINGS OF THE CONTEMPORARY ECUMENICAL MOVEMENT

The twentieth century saw an increased effort at reconciling and restoring the unity of Christians. For many church historians, the World Missionary Conference held at Edinburgh, Scotland, in 1910 is the historical marker for the beginning of these efforts on an international scale.

FAITH WORD

Ecumenism

The efforts among all Christians to bring about the fulfillment of Christ's will for the unity of his followers.

—*United States Catholic Catechism for Adults (USCCA), Glossary, 511*

POPE FRANCIS MEETING ECUMENICAL PATRIARCH BARTHOLOMEW IN 2014

In 1920 Ecumenical Patriarch Germanus V of Constantinople made another significant contribution to this movement among the Orthodox Churches. He promulgated an encyclical that proposed a "fellowship of Churches." The Patriarch's efforts were opposed by many who believed that the encyclical intentionally overlooked the tradition and foundation of the Orthodox Churches.

In 1948 the World Council of Churches (WCC) held its first meeting. The WCC promotes unity among Protestant and many Eastern and Western Orthodox Churches. The WCC describes itself as:

a community of churches on the way to visible unity in one faith and one eucharistic fellowship, expressed in worship and in common life in Christ. It seeks to advance towards this unity, as Jesus prayed for his followers, "so that the world may believe" (John 17:21).

The WCC "has no legislative authority over members. It exists to facilitate common action by the churches, to promote cooperation in study, to stimulate the growth of ecumenical and missionary consciousness in all the churches" (*New Catholic Encyclopedia*, Vol. 14, 2nd edition, 841). While the Roman Catholic Church is not a member of the World Council of Churches, a joint working group of the WCC and the Roman Catholic Church has been meeting annually since the close of the Second Vatican Council in 1965.

VATICAN COUNCIL II (1962–65)—A FRESH IMPETUS FOR ECUMENISM

St. John XXIII invited Protestant "observers" to the Second Vatican Council. The Council's *Decree on Ecumenism (Unitatis Redintegratio)* was a watershed in marking Catholic participation in the ecumenical movement. The *Decree on Ecumenism* opens, "The restoration of unity among all Christians is one of the principal concerns of the Second Vatican Council" (no. 1).

THE POPES' COMMITMENT TO ECUMENISM

St. John Paul II: In his 1995 encyclical, *On Commitment to Ecumenism (Ut Unum Sint)*, St. John Paul II reaffirmed the commitment of the Church to ecumenism. The Pope opened his encyclical:

Ut unum sint! The call for Christian unity made by the Second Vatican Ecumenical Council with such impassioned commitment is finding an ever greater echo in the hearts of believers, . . .

Christ calls all his disciples to unity. My earnest desire is to renew this call today, to propose it once more with determination, repeating what I said at the Roman Coliseum on Good Friday 1994, at the end of the meditation on the *Via Crucis* prepared by my Venerable Brother Bartholomew, the Ecumenical Patriarch of Constantinople. There I stated that believers in Christ, united in following in the footsteps of the martyrs, cannot remain divided. If

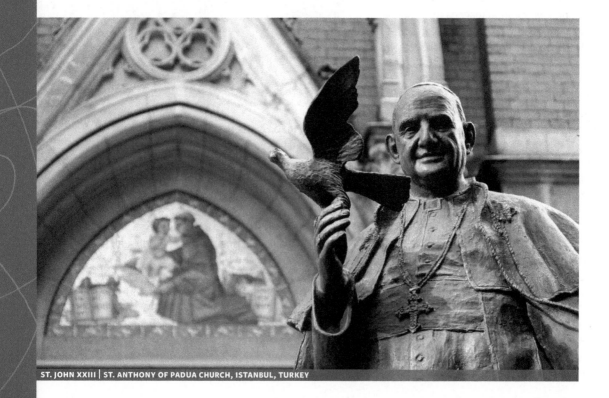

ST. JOHN XXIII | ST. ANTHONY OF PADUA CHURCH, ISTANBUL, TURKEY

Key Resource: Encyclical Letters

In the section "The Popes' Commitment to Ecumenism" we introduce an encyclical letter. An encyclical letter is a teaching letter written by the pope on his own authority to all the bishops to guide them in fulfilling their teaching ministry. In an encyclical letter a pope teaches on a matter that he considers to be important at that point in time. An encyclical letter "leads to better understanding of Revelation in matters of faith and morals" (CCC, no. 892).

The teaching of an encyclical letter is not proposed as a dogma/doctrine, or a divinely revealed truth. The faithful, however, "are to adhere [to it] with religious assent" (CCC, no. 892; quoting *Lumen Gentium*, no. 25) of the mind and the will "which, though distinct from the assent of faith, is nonetheless an extension of it" (CCC, no. 892)

ENCYCLICAL LETTERS OF ST. JOHN PAUL II

they wish truly and effectively to oppose the world's tendency to reduce to powerlessness the Mystery of Redemption, they must *profess together the same truth about the Cross*. The Cross! An anti-Christian outlook seeks to minimize the Cross, to empty it of its meaning, and to deny that in it man has the source of his new life. It claims that the Cross is unable to provide either vision or hope. Man, it says, is nothing but an earthly being, who must live as if God did not exist.

—*On Commitment to Ecumenism*, no. 1

Pope Benedict XVI: On April 20, 2005, in an address to the cardinals on the day after his election to the papacy, Pope Benedict XVI reaffirmed his commitment to work for Christian unity. Speaking of himself in the third person he stated:

Peter's current Successor takes on as his primary task the duty to work tirelessly to rebuild the full and visible unity of all Christ's followers. This is his ambition, his impelling duty. He is aware that good intentions do not suffice for this. Concrete gestures that enter hearts and stir consciences are essential, inspiring in everyone that inner conversion that is the prerequisite for all ecumenical progress.

Among other efforts, Pope Benedict XVI in November 2006 traveled to Istanbul, Turkey, to meet with Patriarch Bartholomew of Constantinople. Together the Pope and the Patriarch renewed their commitment to work toward full communion of the Churches. In that same month and year Pope Benedict XVI met with Rowan Williams, the Anglican Archbishop of Canterbury. They signed a Common Declaration specifying the faith shared by the Catholic Church and the Anglican Communion and acknowledged the service common among Catholics and Anglicans. In March 2007 Pope Benedict XVI sent a message to the gathering of the Lutheran World Federation and encouraged both Catholics and Lutherans to remain committed to their ecumenical efforts.

Pope Francis: Pope Francis has often asserted his and the Church's commitment to ecumenism. For example, in his November 24, 2013 apostolic exhortation, *The Joy of the Gospel (Evangelii Gaudium)*, Pope Francis wrote:

Commitment to ecumenism responds to the prayer of the Lord Jesus that "they may all be

"...we must have sincere trust in our fellow pilgrims, putting aside all suspicion or mistrust"

POPE FRANCIS

one" (John 17:21). The credibility of the Christian message would be much greater if Christians could overcome their divisions and the Church could realize "the fullness of catholicity proper to her in those of her children who, though joined to her by baptism, are yet separated from full communion with her" (*Decree on Ecumenism*, no. 4). We must never forget that we are pilgrims journeying alongside one another. This means that we must have sincere trust in our fellow pilgrims, putting aside all suspicion or mistrust, and turn our gaze to what we are all seeking: the radiant peace of God's face.

—*The Joy of the Gospel*, no. 244

For Pope Francis, as it was for his predecessors, the ecumenical movement "is not just about being better informed about others,

but rather about reaping what the Spirit has sown in them, which is also meant to be a gift for us. . . . Through an exchange of gifts, the Spirit can lead us ever more fully into truth and goodness" (*The Joy of the Gospel*, no. 246).

BRAINSTORM AND SHARE
- ◉ Work in small groups.
- ◉ Brainstorm a list of concrete ways in which Christian young people today can contribute to building unity within the Church.
- ◉ Share lists as a class.

OVER TO YOU
- ◉ Make one personal decision about ecumenism for your own life–faith–life journey.
- ◉ Reflect on how you can integrate that decision into your daily life.

Seeking truth through dialogue

THE SEARCH FOR TRUTH

Searching for the truth is a central theme that runs through works of literature and opera. The protagonists in these works discover early on that they do not know the full truth about something and they launch a quest to find it. This is true in our daily lives too. Often, just when we think we have learned the truth about something or someone, we learn that the *whole truth* is deeper, more complicated and more profound than we had imagined.

OPENING REFLECTION

◉ How do you go about seeking and learning the truth—about the meaning of life, about God, about the role of religion and faith, and other important life questions?

◉ How does this search enrich your understanding and living of the Catholic faith?

JESUS CHRIST—TRUTH INCARNATE

The search for the truth is a universal quest. Seeking the truth about life, about God and about one's self is a central and fundamental aspect of our human condition. You will recall that Jesus saw and replied to this need in his disciples. (Take a moment and read John 14:1–14.)

FAITH WORD

Hierarchy of Truths

The order (hierarchy) of the truths in Catholic doctrine, insofar as they vary in their relation to the central mystery and foundation of Christian faith, the mystery of the Holy Trinity.
—*Catechism of the Catholic Church* (CCC), Glossary

To know Jesus is to know the truth about God, about one's self and about the purpose and destiny of human life. Jesus Christ is the fullest and clearest Revelation of the truth that every human seeks and needs to know. Later on in his account of the Gospel, John once again connects Jesus and "truth." Speaking to his disciples, Jesus says: "If you continue in my word, you are truly my disciples; and you will know the truth, and the truth will make you free" (John 8:31a–32).

READ, REFLECT AND SHARE

◉ Reflect on the two passages from John's Gospel.

◉ Why is Jesus' revelation that he is "the way," the "truth" and "the life" important for living as a faithful disciple of Jesus?

◉ Why does knowing Jesus and living the truth he reveals set one free?

THE HOLY TRINITY | 15TH-CENTURY MANUSCRIPT

FRANCISCAN FRIARS AND PILGRIMS AT THE CHURCH OF THE HOLY SEPULCHRE, JERUSALEM

Pope Francis reminds us that our search for the truth, as a pilgrim people, has not reached the end

THE CHURCH: A PILGRIM PEOPLE IN SEARCH OF THE TRUTH

From the time of the Apostles, as the writings in the New Testament reveal, the Church has been a *pilgrim people* on her way toward comprehending the fullness of divine truth. This image is a particularly helpful guide for ecumenical dialogue. The Second Vatican Council taught:

The tradition that comes from the apostles makes progress in the church, with the help of the holy Spirit. There is a growth in insight into the realities and words that are being passed on. This comes about through the contemplation and study of believers who ponder these things in their hearts (see Luke 2:19 and 51). It comes from the intimate sense of spiritual realities which they experience. And it comes from the preaching of those who, on succeeding to the office of bishop, have received the sure charism of truth. Thus, as the centuries go by, the church is always advancing towards the plentitude of divine truth, until eventually the words of God are fulfilled in it.

—*Dogmatic Constitution on Divine Revelation (Dei Verbum)*, no. 8

This pilgrim journey has oftentimes led to essential differences in doctrines and practices that have divided the unity of the Church. Reflecting on these differences and on the participation of the Catholic Church in the ecumenical efforts among Christians, Pope Francis teaches: "If we concentrate on the convictions we share, and if we keep in mind the principle of the hierarchy of truths [bold type added], we will be able to progress decidedly towards common expressions of proclamation, service and witness" (*The Joy of the Gospel*, no. 246).

The Pope reminds us that our search for the truth, as a pilgrim people, has not reached the end. Ecumenical dialogue helps us see and understand our Catholic faith with fresh and wondering eyes. It gives us access to the accumulated wisdom and goodness of other Christian communities. It helps us journey together to come to know, love and serve God revealed in Jesus Christ, the Second Person of the Trinity and the Incarnate Son of God, who is "the way, and the truth, and the life" (John 14:6). Ecumenical dialogue helps us live together as good neighbors—respecting, supporting and loving one another on our common pilgrim journey to our final discovery of Eternal Truth—the Beatific Vision.

THINK, PAIR AND SHARE

- In what ways does the image of the Church as a pilgrim people resonate with your own search to come to know Jesus and all that he has revealed?
- Share with a partner how the Church guides you in coming to know Jesus.
- Suggest an image for the Church that points to her search for a deeper understanding of Jesus and all that he has revealed.

CHURCH OF THE HOLY SEPULCHRE, JERUSALEM

The Catholic Church and Ecumenical Dialogue

Since the promulgation of the *Decree on Ecumenism* on November 21, 1964, the Catholic Church, both worldwide and in the United States of America, has engaged in a number of ecumenical dialogues. Many of these dialogues have led to closer ties between the Catholic Church and other churches and ecclesial communions. For example, on a global level:

- In 1965 the Catholic Church and Eastern Orthodox Churches officially removed the mutual excommunications that each had imposed on the other in 1054. Since this time, Catholic and Orthodox dialogue has worked toward resolving issues such as the primacy of the pope and the mutual recognition of each church's sacraments. There are still barriers to full communion between the two churches, but real progress is being made. We will examine these commonalities and obstacles in chapter 4.

- The Faith and Order Commission is a working group of the World Council of Churches (WCC). The Vatican participates in this group, which seeks to build consensus around a variety of theological issues. The Faith and Order Commission has released a number of very important consensus documents, including "Baptism, Eucharist, and Ministry." The Commission also provides a forum for joint ecumenical projects, such as the Week of Prayer for Christian Unity.

- The Lutheran–Catholic dialogue has been particularly fruitful. Several major declarations have been released in which theologians demonstrate that there is significant theological agreement on a number of issues, despite different emphases. The most important of these declarations is the *Joint Declaration on the Doctrine of Justification* (1999). We will look more closely at this Joint Declaration in chapter 5.

- Methodists signed the Catholic–Lutheran Joint Declaration in 2011. In 2012 Catholics and Methodists, in connection with their theological dialogue on the Eucharist, issued a joint statement on the connection between the Eucharist and the relationship of believers to creation and environmental stewardship. We will look at this Joint Declaration more closely in chapter 6.

ECUMENICAL DIALOGUES IN THE UNITED STATES OF AMERICA

The Committee on Ecumenical and Interreligious Affairs of the United States Conference of Catholic Bishops (USCCB) has the mandate to give guidance in ecumenical and interreligious affairs in the United States of America. According to the USCCB website, the committee's responsibilities include:

⊙ fostering spiritual ecumenism according to the principles laid down in the *Decree on Ecumenism* (see especially no. 8) about public and private prayer for the unity of Christians;

⊙ promoting friendliness, cooperation and charity between Catholics and their brothers who are not in full communion;

⊙ initiating and guiding full dialogue with them, bearing in mind the adaptation to be made to the types of participants according to nos. 9 and 11 of the *Decree on Ecumenism*;

⊙ promoting in common with our brothers not in full communion joint witness to the Christian faith as well as cooperation in such areas as, for example, education, morality, social and cultural matters, learning and the arts (see *Decree on Ecumenism*, no. 12, also the *Decree on the Missionary Activity of the Church* [*Ad Gentes*], no. 15).

IN SUMMARY: THE PRINCIPLES OF ECUMENICAL DIALOGUE

"Concern for restoring unity involves the whole church, faithful and clergy alike" (*Decree on Ecumenism*, no. 5). Mutual respect and neighborliness shown in ecumenical dialogue allow Christians to dialogue about both their commonalities and the obstacles to full communion, and to remain as loving, neighborly and hospitable partners in dialogue. The Catholic Church teaches that ecumenical activities require:

⊙ a visible continuity with the ancient Church, namely, "the passing on of the office of bishop from the Apostles to bishops, and from them to other bishops down each generation, by means of ordination" (USCCA, Glossary, "Apostolic Succession").

⊙ a permanent *renewal* of the Church in greater fidelity to her vocation; such renewal is the

> The Church is the pillar and bulwark of the truth. She hands on from generation to generation the Apostles' confession of faith

12TH-CENTURY PILLAR CAPITAL, SAINT-NECTAIRE, AUVERGNE, FRANCE

driving-force of the movement toward unity (see *Decree on Ecumenism*, no. 6);

- *conversion of heart* as the faithful "try to live holier lives according to the Gospel" (*Decree on Ecumenism*, no. 7§3); for it is the unfaithfulness of the members to Christ's gift which causes divisions;

- *prayer in common*, because "change of heart and holiness of life, along with public and private prayer for the unity of Christians, should be regarded as the soul of the whole ecumenical movement, and merits the name 'spiritual ecumenism' " (*Decree on Ecumenism*, no. 8§1);

- *fraternal knowledge of each other* (see *Decree on Ecumenism*, no. 9);

- *ecumenical formation* of the faithful and especially of priests (see *Decree on Ecumenism*, no. 10);

- *dialogue* among theologians, and meetings among Christians of the different churches and communities (see *Decree on Ecumenism*, nos. 4, 9, and 11);

- *collaboration* among Christians in various areas of service to mankind (see *Decree on Ecumenism*, no. 12). ["Human service" is the idiomatic phrase.]

—CCC, no. 821

THINK, PAIR AND SHARE
- What do these principles tell you about the commitment of the Catholic Church to ecumenism?
- Which of these principles can Christian young people integrate into their life right now? What difference would that make?

ECUMENICAL DIALOGUE AND FULL COMMUNION

The Catholic Church possesses the fullness of the means of salvation willed by God as the ordinary way of saving all people. "To reunite all his children, scattered and led astray by sin, the Father willed to call the whole of humanity together into his Son's Church. The Church is the place where humanity must rediscover its unity and salvation" (CCC, no. 845).

The Church is the pillar and bulwark of the truth. She hands on from generation to generation the Apostles' confession of faith.

Apostolic Succession represents a visible continuity with the ancient Church

(Check out 1 Timothy 3:15 and Jude 3.) In the words of St. Irenaeus, the Church's message "is true and solid, in which one and the same way of salvation appears throughout the whole world" (*Against Heresies* 1, 10).

There are many doctrinal disagreements and practices, however, that have arisen among Christians and that are dividing the Church. These need to be resolved in order for there to be full unity within the Church in passing on "the Apostles' confession of faith." The Catholic Church, in her ecumenical dialogues with other Christian churches and ecclesial communities, strives to promote this unity. There is greater hope of restoring the full communion of the Catholic Church with other Christian churches and ecclesial communities where there is:

⊙ *a visible* continuity with the ancient Church (**Apostolic Succession**);

⊙ *a shared understanding* of interpreting revealed truth (Scripture read through the lens of Tradition); for example, such a starting point exists with the Orthodox Churches;

⊙ practice of the sacraments as fundamental encounters with Christ and effective mediations of God's grace.

Given these three areas where common beliefs and practices are found, it is not surprising that ecumenical dialogue between the Catholic Church and the Eastern Orthodox Churches, between Catholics and Lutherans, and between Catholics and Anglicans (Episcopalians) has been the most ongoing and fruitful.

Greater obstacles, however, continue to arise in doctrine and in practice, for example, with churches and ecclesial communities who permit women and non-celibate homosexuals to serve as ordained ministers. No matter how far apart the Christian churches may seem, the bond of Baptism and our common faith in Jesus binds us and calls us to the ongoing search for unity through dialogue. We will explore these dialogues in more detail in the next three chapters.

WHAT ABOUT YOU PERSONALLY?

⊙ How does your study and practice of the Catholic faith prepare you to dialogue and share your faith with other Christian youth?

⊙ How can you commit to finding agreement and acknowledging disagreement in matters of faith with others, and doing so with love, respect and openness?

Interreligious dialogue

AGREEING TO DISAGREE

Mahatma Gandhi (1869–1948), a Hindu, successfully led India's struggle for independence from British rule by a campaign of non-violent civil disobedience. Gandhi's efforts included not only campaigns against a wide range of social injustices but also efforts to build religious and ethnic amity, or *mitrata*. *Mitrata* is a Hindu word meaning "a state of friendship and cordiality."

Gandhi named the guiding principle of his efforts *satyagraha*. *Satyagraha* comes from two Sanskrit words meaning "truth" and "love." Gandhi committed himself to champion the truth, as he knew it, with love and a spirit of respect and cordiality. *Satyagraha* demands affirming and maintaining one's own understanding of the truth with an openness that builds trust rooted in friendship and cordiality.

OPENING REFLECTION

⊙ Have you had an open and honest conversation with someone even though you disagreed strongly with them? What was that experience like?

⊙ How might *satyagraha* provide inspiration for ecumenical dialogue between the Catholic Church and other Christians? For interreligious dialogue with non-Christians?

⊙ How can such dialogue help us to learn about and learn from others even when we do not reach an agreement?

Augustin Cardinal Bea (1881–1968), Jesuit priest and scholar

One German Lutheran observer at Vatican II said of Cardinal Bea that, after Pope John XXIII, Bea "will live on in the memory of many as the most impressive figure" at the Council. Cardinal Bea is perhaps best remembered for the fact that he was the first President of the Secretariat (now the Pontifical Council) for Promoting Christian Unity, from its foundation in 1960 until his death, aged eighty-seven, in 1968.

AUGUSTIN CARDINAL BEA IN 1963

It was Bea who first suggested that non-Catholic observers should be invited to the Second Vatican Council; in the end, 60 observers attended. One of the leading American Protestant participants, Robert McAfee Brown, said that Bea's spirit "endeared him to the Protestant world." Given his position, Bea was the principal architect of the *Decree on Ecumenism*. . . . It was he who was charged with drawing up the declaration on the Jews, which eventually evolved into the Decree *Nostra aetate* on the relationship between Catholicism and non-Christian religions as a whole.

—Oliver P. Rafferty, SJ, "Agustin Bea: Scholar, Teacher, Cardinal"

INTERRELIGIOUS DIALOGUE

In chapter 1 we learned that the Second Vatican Council addressed the work of interreligious dialogue in its *Declaration on the Relation of the Church to Non-Christian Religions*, or *Nostra Aetate*. *Nostra Aetate* approached the relationship of the Catholic Church and the other non-Christian religions of the world with a spirit of openness and respect for the truth and goodness that is found in these religions.

Interreligious dialogue is a dimension of the Church's work of the New Evangelization. It is the "proclamation of Christ and his Gospel (Greek: *evangelion*) by word and the testimony of life, in fulfillment of Christ's command" (CCC, Glossary, "Evangelization"). Dialogue with non-Christian religions is not a contemporary form of proselytism with a new face. In the negative sense, proselytism implies attempting to gain converts even by recourse to means that compromise the freedom and dignity of the human person.

Unlike ecumenical dialogue, interreligious dialogue is not meant to lead to unity among the world's religions. Its immediate purpose is to increase knowledge and understanding and to build deeper relationships of friendship, mutual trust and respect. There are many forms of interreligious dialogue. These include the dialogue of:

⊙ daily life in religiously pluralistic societies and communities;
⊙ shared service to the needy;
⊙ theologians and scholars;
⊙ shared spiritual experiences.

In 2014 the Committee on Ecumenical and Interreligious Affairs of the United States Conference of Catholic Bishops (USCCB) summarized the twenty years of dialogues between the Catholic Church and Muslims. The bishops wrote: "Perhaps most importantly, our work together has forged true bonds of friendship that are supported by mutual esteem and ever-growing trust that enables us to speak candidly with one another in an atmosphere of respect. Through dialogue we have been able to work through and overcome much of our mutual ignorance, habitual distrust, and debilitating fear . . . we are convinced that the encounter and dialogue with persons different than ourselves offers the best opportunity for fraternal growth, enrichment, witness, and ultimately peace."

The Pontifical Council for Promoting Christian Unity (PCPCU) continues to be the Church's primary authority for conducting ecumenical dialogue with other Christians. The PCPCU "exercises a double role. First of all, it is entrusted

Interreligious dialogue aims to increase understanding and to build friendship, mutual trust and respect

Pope Paul VI established the Secretariat for Non-Christians in 1964. It was renamed the Pontifical Council for Interreligious Dialogue in 1988

STATUE OF POPE PAUL VI ON MOUNT TABOR, ISRAEL

with the promotion, within the Catholic Church, of an authentic ecumenical spirit . . . At the same time, the Pontifical Council is active in all areas that can contribute to promoting Christian unity by strengthening relationships with other Churches and Ecclesial Communities. It organizes and oversees dialogue and collaboration with other Churches and World Communions" (The Pontifical Council for Promoting Christian Unity, Vatican Website).

LET'S PROBE DEEPER

- Read and reflect on these words from the *Declaration on the Relation of the Church to Non-Christian Religions*: "The Catholic Church rejects nothing of what is true and holy in these [other] religions. It has a high regard for the manner of life and conduct, the precepts and the doctrines which, although differing in many ways from its own teaching, nevertheless often reflect a ray of that truth which enlightens all men and women" (*Nostra Aetate*, no. 2).
- How does this teaching of the Catholic Church help form your attitude and behavior toward non-Christian religions? Give specific examples.
- Share reflections as a class.

THE CATHOLIC CHURCH'S WORK OF INTERRELIGIOUS DIALOGUE

The commitment of the Catholic Church to interreligious dialogue is carried out on a global level through the work of the Pontifical Council for Interreligious Dialogue. The Catholic Church

in the United States of America participates in these dialogues, as we have seen, through the work of the Bishops' Committee on Ecumenical and Interreligious Affairs.

Pontifical Council for Interreligious Dialogue: On Pentecost Sunday, 1964, Pope Paul VI established the Secretariat for Non-Christians. In 1988 it was renamed the Pontifical Council for Interreligious Dialogue (PCID). The PCID, however, does not have responsibility for Christian–Jewish relations. These dialogues come under the Pontifical Commission for Religious Relations with the Jews, which is housed in the Pontifical Council for Promoting Christian Unity. According to the Pontifical Council for Interreligious Dialogue web page, this council has the responsibilities to:

- promote respect, mutual understanding and collaboration between Catholics and the followers of other religious traditions;
- encourage the study of religions;
- promote the formation of persons dedicated to dialogue.

CHRISTIAN AND MUSLIM ICONOGRAPHY AT THE HAGIA SOPHIA, ISTANBUL, TURKEY

Committee on Ecumenical and Interreligious Affairs: Interreligious dialogue takes place most often at a national rather than a global level. In the United States of America the Committee on Ecumenical and Interreligious Affairs of the United States Conference of Catholic Bishops, in addition to its work for Christian unity, is actively involved in dialogue and other forms of cooperation with non-Christian religions, especially in working together in service to those in need.

The bishops' committee sponsors joint projects with a variety of Jewish, Muslim and Buddhist communities. Particularly important since 2001 has been the bishops' involvement in Catholic–Muslim cooperation and dialogue—a dialogue aimed at reducing anti-Muslim bias and at improving the relationships between these two communities.

All efforts at interreligious dialogue require participants to show mutual respect and to work honestly and openly to understand differences in culture, as well as commonalities and differences in belief. To achieve such goals requires

participants to be trained in accurate knowledge of one another's religions. The Tantur Ecumenical Institute, a project of the University of Notre Dame that is located in Jerusalem, is one example of this ongoing effort. The aims of the Institute, as presented on its website, are:

⊙ We assist the search for Christian unity and interchurch harmony among the diverse Christian communions.
⊙ We seek a broader and deeper understanding of each other's faith and traditions, ethics and social witness, liturgies and pieties.
⊙ We explore the relationships between Christians and peoples of other world faiths, especially Jews and Muslims.
⊙ We participate in the search for world peace and justice, through theological study and through exploring human rights and conflict resolution in different religious and social contexts.

In addressing the June 2013 meeting of the Tantur Ecumenical Institute Ecumenical Advisory Board, Bishop Denis Madden asked, "What are we called to do as a Church to cultivate and prepare for this new springtime?" He continued:

Earlier this year Bishop Brian Farrell, Secretary of the Pontifical Council for Promoting Christian Unity, reasserted that ecumenical formation is a key aspect of the search for full unity among Christians when he said: *"Formation is a kind of condition sine qua non for ecumenical awareness effectively to take hold."* Bishop Farrell went on to insist the ecumenical formation must be programmed and adapted to the variety of vocations, charisms, and ministries in the Church. Ecumenical formation is not just an exercise in pragmatic thinking to network individuals and institutions at the service of unity, but a profound requirement of the doctrine of our Church.

—From USCCB website

REFLECT, ANALYZE AND SHARE

- ◉ Have you witnessed or experienced cooperative efforts between Christians and non-Christians in your community? What differences did those efforts make to your community?
- ◉ Do you think prejudice and lack of trust divides Christians and non-Christians in your community? Share examples of and reasons for that prejudice and lack of trust.

WHAT ABOUT YOU PERSONALLY?

- ◉ How does your Catholic faith guide you in working to overcome such prejudice and distrust?

PROCLAIM AND DIALOGUE

The Catholic Church has a long tradition of believing that all people of good will who follow the truth, as best they know it, can be saved in ways known by God himself. The Church at the Second Vatican Council taught:

Salvation Outside the Church

Those who, through no fault of their own, do not know the Gospel of Christ or his church, but who nevertheless seek God with a sincere heart, and, moved by grace, try in their actions to do his will as they know it through the dictates of their conscience—these too may achieve eternal salvation.
—*Dogmatic Constitution on the Church* [*Lumen Gentium*], no. 16

CICERO, WHOM THE CHURCH REGARDS AS A "VIRTUOUS PAGAN"

For since Christ died for everyone (see Romans 8:32), and since all are in fact called to one and the same destiny, which is divine, we must hold that the holy Spirit offers to all the possibility of being made partners, in a way known to God, in the paschal mystery.

—*Pastoral Constitution on the Church in the Modern World* (*Gaudium et Spes*), no. 22

The risen Christ commissioned the Apostles, their successors and the whole Church to proclaim the Gospel to all peoples. The Catholic Church strives to fulfill this commission, in part, through open, honest and respectful ecumenical and interreligious dialogue. The Catholic Church commits herself fully to these dialogues because in her is the fullness of the means of salvation willed by God as the ordinary way of saving all people.

The Catholic Church proclaims faithfully the Good News, or Gospel, of salvation: "All salvation comes from Christ the Head through the Church which is his Body" (CCC, no. 846). This salvation and participation in the life of God, now and eternally, is a gift of grace from the one Triune God, which he makes available through faith in Jesus Christ.

ANALYZE, COMPARE AND SHARE

- Describe the differences between ecumenical and interreligious dialogue. How are they similar to and different from each other?
- Is there one purpose that unites both efforts?
- Share responses as a class.

JOURNAL EXERCISE

- Take a close look at a typical day and week in your life.
- Identify opportunities you might have to take part in the Church's works of ecumenism and interreligious dialogue.
- Describe how you could take advantage of those opportunities.

The holy Spirit offers to all the possibility of being made partners in the paschal mystery

AGNUS DEI (LAMB OF GOD) | JORLUNDE CHURCH, DENMARK

JUDGE AND ACT

REVIEW AND SHARE WHAT YOU HAVE LEARNED

Review what you have learned in this chapter about the Church's teaching on ecumenism and interreligious dialogue. Share the teachings of the Catholic Church that you have learned in this chapter on these statements:

⊙ Differences among Christians have caused divisions within and wounded the unity of the Church.

⊙ The Catholic Church's commitment to ecumenism responds to the prayer of the Lord Jesus that "they may all be one" (John 17:21).

⊙ Vatican Council II gave a fresh impetus to ecumenism.

⊙ The Catholic Church participates in ecumenical dialogues at both global and national levels.

⊙ "Concern for restoring unity involves the whole church, faithful and clergy alike" (*Decree on Ecumenism*, no. 5).

⊙ Dialogue with non-Christians, or interreligious dialogue, is part of the Church's mission to evangelize all people.

⊙ The Catholic Church rejects nothing of what is true and holy in non-Christian religions.

⊙ The immediate purpose of the Catholic Church's participation in interreligious dialogue is to increase knowledge and understanding and to build deeper relationships of friendship, trust and respect in a mutual search for truth.

⊙ The Catholic Church participates in the work of interreligious dialogue at both global and national levels.

OVER TO YOU

⊙ Reflect: The search for truth is a universal quest. To know Jesus is to know the truth about God, about one's own self, and about how Jesus is always calling the members of his Church to unity.

⊙ Is the way you live your faith in Christ an invitation to non-Catholic Christians and non-Christians to know Christ as the way and the truth and the life?

FACING RELIGIOUS DISCRIMINATION HEAD-ON

Today the United States is considered the most religiously diverse nation in the world. In addition to Christians and Jews, Muslims, Buddhists, Hindus, Sikhs, Mormons, Bahá'ís and others have taken their place in and are making significant contributions to our society. Yet, the efforts of non-Christians and non-Jews are often met with bigotry and prejudice, distrust and fear, and sometimes violent hostility. In turn, Muslims and others treat Christians and Jews with similar violence.

Religious-based bias and discrimination is particularly insidious and can often be subtle. We would like to think that since the Holocaust we have learned how to avoid such bigotry. But egregious hatred and violence continues to scar our country and the world. As Catholics, we must do all we can to fight this religious hatred and strive to establish peace and respect among people of all religious traditions. This is an urgent matter of gospel justice rooted in love.

TALK IT OVER

⊙ How can ecumenical and interreligious dialogue build bridges of trust among people? Establish peace among people of good will?

Pilgrimages of Trust on Earth

The *Credo* series text *The Promised One: Servant and Savior* introduced the story of Frère Roger and the Taizé community. You will recall that Taizé is an ecumenical community of Catholics and Protestants in Taizé, France. Taizé exists "to be a sign of reconciliation between divided Christians and between separated peoples."

Young adults between the ages of seventeen and thirty gather in Taizé throughout the year. These meetings usually last from Sunday to Sunday. The schedule of a typical day includes morning, midday and evening prayer, workshops and meals.

Participants in the meetings return to their dioceses, parishes or other communities to undertake a "Pilgrimage of Trust on Earth." During these pilgrimages, hospitality breaks down many barriers and prejudices.

One participant described these gatherings: "The pilgrimage of trust is first of all a meeting; with the Risen Christ and with others. Thanks to the times of prayer together, we make ourselves available for God. Through sharing and hospitality, everyone agrees to overcome barriers and differences in order to welcome and enrich one another" (Taizé web page).

Following one such pilgrimage meeting, another young person wrote: "The pilgrimage is an event for those who make it, those who dare to leave their homes and risk failure, but also for those who receive guests and discover that they receive much more. Thousands of young pilgrims have joined thousands of people who have agreed to open their homes to strangers. They shared more, much more than their possessions; they shared their lives, their beliefs, their hopes" (Taizé web page).

A pilgrimage of trust is but one example of young people from various Christian and other religious traditions building bridges of trust. Such bridge building is the keystone for successful ecumenical and interreligious dialogues.

TALK IT OVER

- Have you ever participated in a meeting between Catholic and non-Catholic youth? Did that meeting build bridges of trust and understanding among participants?

SHARE FAITH WITH FAMILY AND FRIENDS

- Non-Christian holidays, such as Hanukkah, Eid Al-Fitr and Diwali, can increase our awareness and understanding of people from the many religious traditions that make up our nation.

- Make a commitment to learn about some of the religious holidays of non-Christian religions. If possible, talk to people of other faiths about their religious holidays. Share what you learn with family and friends.

JUDGE AND DECIDE

- Take a moment and analyze the religious profile of your group of friends.

- How can you actively involve yourself in the process of learning about non-Catholic Christian traditions and non-Christian religious traditions? You might begin by dialoguing with friends who are not Catholic.

- Identify one way you can practice the virtues of respect and neighborliness toward people who belong to religious traditions other than your own.

LEARN BY HEART

"If you continue in my word, you are truly my disciples; and you will know the truth, and the truth will make you free."

JOHN 8:31A–32

All gather quietly and take up a position appropriate and conducive to prayer. After a moment of silence all pray the Sign of the Cross together.

Invitation to Prayer

LEADER

The Taizé community is committed to fostering Christian unity. Shared meditative prayer by its members is among the community's best known characteristics. In that spirit we gather today to honor God in song and in silence. We open our prayer in song.

All join in singing an appropriate song.

Gospel Proclamation

READER

A reading from the holy Gospel according to Matthew.

ALL

Glory to you, O Lord.

READER

Proclaim Matthew 5:13–16.

The Gospel of the Lord.

ALL

Praise to you, Lord Jesus Christ.

Song Response

All join in singing an appropriate song.

Reflection and Decision

All silently reflect on the reading and apply it to their life.

Intercessory Prayer

LEADER

God, our Creator,
you are the origin and source of life for all
 peoples.
You desire that all humanity live in friendship and
 harmony with you and with one another,
as you Father and Son and Holy Spirit live in
 perfect harmony and love.
Send forth your Holy Spirit
to kindle in all hearts the fire of your love,
that we may strive with the grace of your Spirit
to mend what divides your family.
We ask this in the name of your Son, Jesus Christ,
 in whose image we have been created,
who lives and reigns with you in the unity of the
 Holy Spirit,
one God, forever and ever.

RESPONSE

Amen.

Concluding Song

All join in singing an appropriate song.

CHAPTER 4

The Orthodox and Catholic Churches in the East

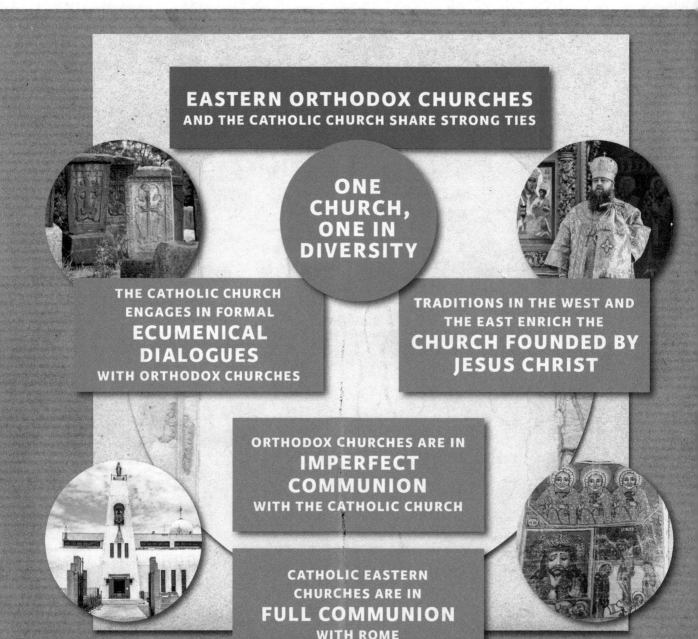

EASTERN ORTHODOX CHURCHES
AND THE CATHOLIC CHURCH SHARE STRONG TIES

**ONE
CHURCH,
ONE IN
DIVERSITY**

THE CATHOLIC CHURCH
ENGAGES IN FORMAL
**ECUMENICAL
DIALOGUES**
WITH ORTHODOX CHURCHES

TRADITIONS IN THE WEST AND
THE EAST ENRICH THE
**CHURCH FOUNDED BY
JESUS CHRIST**

ORTHODOX CHURCHES ARE IN
**IMPERFECT
COMMUNION**
WITH THE CATHOLIC CHURCH

CATHOLIC EASTERN
CHURCHES ARE IN
FULL COMMUNION
WITH ROME

THE CHURCH AT VATICAN II REAFFIRMED THE original unity of the one Church founded by Jesus Christ. In chapter 2 we learned that this unity was becoming fractured in her earliest days. In this chapter we examine the Eastern Orthodox Churches; their separation, or schism, from the pope and the churches in full communion with him. We also explore the ties that unite and the differences that are obstacles to the full communion of the Catholic Church and the Eastern Orthodox Churches. Finally, we examine the Eastern Catholic Churches, who remain in communion with the pope.

SCHISMS IN THE CHURCH
SCHISM OF 451
SCHISM OF 1054

Faith Focus: These teachings of the Catholic Church are the primary focus of the doctrinal content presented in this chapter:

- The Apostles established the Church throughout the world.
- The Bishop of Rome, the pope, the successor of St. Peter, "is the perpetual and visible source and foundation of the unity both of the bishops and of the whole company of the faithful" (Vatican II, *Dogmatic Constitution on the Church*, no. 23).
- The Catholic Church and the Eastern Orthodox Churches were one until the Schism of 1054.
- Many cultural, political and economic factors, as well as theological, contributed to the Schism of 1054.
- The Catholic Church includes the Roman, or Latin, Rite in the West and twenty-two Catholic Churches of a diversity of rites in the East.
- Traditions in both the Church in the West and the Churches in the East contribute to and enrich the faith and life of the Church.

Discipleship Formation: As a result of studying this chapter and discovering the meaning of the faith of the Catholic Church for your life, you should be better able to:

- integrate true and authentic dialogue concerning faith into your relationships with others;
- appreciate the oneness of the Church, which is expressed in a diversity of authentic traditions;
- understand the reasons for the schisms separating the Catholic Church from the Eastern Orthodox Churches and the Oriental Orthodox Churches;
- be aware of the Orthodox Churches in your community;
- value the diversity that Eastern Catholic Churches contribute to the Catholic Church.

Scripture References: These scripture references are quoted or referred to in this chapter:
NEW TESTAMENT: Matthew 16:18–19; **John** 16:13–15, 17:20–24; **Acts of the Apostles** 9:32, 10:1—11:18, 11:27—14:28, 15:36—18:23, 18:24—21:14, 27:1—28:31; **1 Corinthians** 12:4–6, 12–31; **Ephesians** 4:15-16

Faith Glossary: Familiarize yourself with or recall the meaning of these key terms. Definitions are found in the Glossary: **Apostolic Succession; Apostolic Tradition, celibacy, collegiality, diaspora, dogma, Eastern Churches, Ecumenical Council,** *Filioque,* **icon, Immaculate Conception, indissolubility of marriage, infallibility, Monophysitism, Orthodox Churches, perpetual virginity of Mary, rites, schism, synod,** *Theotokos*

Faith Words: Orthodox Churches; Eastern Churches
Learn by Heart: 1 Corinthians 12:4–6
Learn by Example: Blessed Paul VI and Patriarch Athenagoras I of Constantinople

How has the Church preached the Gospel to the world from her beginning?

RUDYARD KIPLING

Oh, East is East and West is West, and never the
  twain shall meet,
Till Earth and Sky stand presently at God's great
  Judgment Seat;
But there is neither East nor West, Border, nor
  Breed, nor Birth,
When two strong men stand face to face, tho'
  they come from the ends of the earth!

"The Ballad of East and West" addresses
a universal human experience: honest and
open personal interaction can contribute to the
healing of wounds and divisions. Reflection on
"The Ballad of East and West" offers some insight
into the importance of face-to-face encounter
and dialogue between the Western Church and
the Eastern Orthodox Churches.

OPENING REFLECTION

⊙ What insight does Kipling's opening/closing
  verse give you into what can happen when
  people from very different cultures "stand face
  to face"?

⊙ Have you ever met someone from a different
  culture and been struck by both the
  similarities and differences between you?
  Recall your experiences.

EAST AND WEST: ONE WORLD, ONE GOSPEL
Jesus lived and died in Palestine, a province of
the Roman Empire in what is today the Middle
East. The Acts of the Apostles attests that the
evangelizing efforts of the Apostles took place
throughout Asia Minor (modern-day Turkey) and
Eastern Europe. The one Church founded by Jesus
Christ spread from Jerusalem, the center of the
Jewish world, to Rome, the center of the Roman
Empire. (Check out the map, "The Church Born in
Jerusalem Spreads Out into the World.")

THE BALLAD OF EAST AND WEST
The English novelist and poet Rudyard Kipling
(1865–1936) was born in Bombay, India. In 1871 he
went to England for his education. He returned
to India, where his parents were living, in 1882, at
the age of sixteen. In 1889 he returned to England
and published "The Ballad of East and West."
  In the ballad an English officer and an
Afghan who stole a horse from the officer's son
encounter each other and, through dialogue,
become friends. Kipling's ballad uses the imagery
of the relationship between the officer and the
horse-thief to describe the relationship between
eastern and western civilizations. The ballad
begins and ends with the same verse:

The Apostle Peter: St. Luke in his Acts of the Apostles writes that Peter "went here and there" (Acts of the Apostles 9:32) with the other Apostles as they preached Christ and his Gospel not only in Jerusalem but also in the **diaspora**. (Check out Acts of the Apostles 10:1—11:18.) Church tradition teaches that Peter traveled to and resided in Rome, a tradition found in St. Ignatius of Antioch's *Letter to the Romans*. St. Ignatius, who was martyred in Rome about AD 110, was born a pagan in Syria, converted to Christianity and became Bishop of Antioch, an ancient Greek–Roman city in modern-day Turkey.

According to several traditions of the Church, the Apostle Peter was martyred in Rome, where he was buried. St. Clement, who was the Bishop of Rome from AD 92 to 96, passes on that tradition in his *Letter to the Corinthians*. Clement attests: "To these men [Peter and Paul] who lived such holy lives there was joined a great multitude of the elect who by reason of rivalry were victims of many outrages and tortures and who became outstanding examples among us" (*Letter to the Corinthians*, 6:1).

The Apostle Paul: St. Paul's evangelizing efforts took him primarily to the eastern part of the Roman Empire, namely to Syria, Asia Minor (modern-day Turkey) and Greece. (Check out Acts of the Apostles 11:27—14:28; 15:36—18:23; and 18:24—21:14.) This Apostle to the Gentiles established churches in Galatia, an area in modern Turkey; at Thessalonia, a city in modern Greece; at Colossae, a city in the southwest corner of modern Turkey; at Corinth, a commercial port-city in ancient Greece connecting the East and the West; at Ephesus, a seaport city in ancient Greece which is part of modern Turkey; and other places throughout the region.

Acts of the Apostles 27:1—28:31 describes St. Paul's journey to Rome. Church tradition asserts that he and St. Peter founded the Church and were martyred in that city. These ancient verses praise St. Peter and St. Paul as the "Fathers of great Rome":

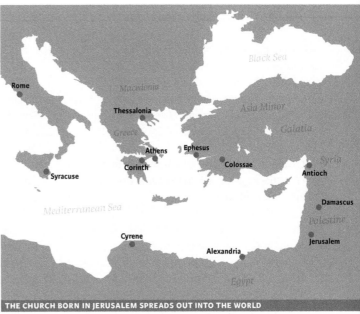

THE CHURCH BORN IN JERUSALEM SPREADS OUT INTO THE WORLD

Peter and Paul, the Fathers of great Rome,
Now sitting in the Senate of the skies,
One by the cross, the other by the sword,
Sent to their thrones on high, to Life's eternal
   prize.

The other Apostles: Other Apostles also preached outside of Palestine. As we learned in chapter 3, St. Andrew the Apostle brought the Gospel to and established the Church in modern-day Turkey and in Eastern Russia. Tradition also teaches that St. John the Apostle lived the last days of his life, died and is buried in Ephesus. An ancient tradition of the Church, passed on by St. Ambrose (c. 340–397) and St. Jerome (c.340–420), attests that Thomas the Apostle brought the Gospel to and established the Church in India, where he was martyred. The evangelization efforts of the other Apostles are not known.

THE PRIMACY OF THE BISHOP OF ROME

The New Testament attests to the primacy and the governing and teaching authority of St. Peter among the Apostles. St. Clement, who died around AD 80, affirmed and claimed for himself the primacy and authority granted to St. Peter by becoming the Bishop of Rome. Clement wrote to the Church at Corinth: "If anyone disobeys the things which have been said by Him [Christ] through us, let them know that they will involve themselves in transgressions and in no small danger."

St. Irenaeus, in the late second century AD, wrote: "The blessed apostles [Peter and Paul], having founded and built up the church [of Rome] . . . handed over the office of the episcopate to Linus" (*Against Heresies* 3:3:3). Linus was the immediate successor of St. Peter as the Bishop of Rome.

St. Damasus I, who was the Bishop of Rome from AD 366 to 384, claimed the same primacy and authority. He wrote:

Likewise it is decreed: . . . [W]e have considered that it ought to be announced that . . . the holy Roman Church has been placed at the forefront not by the conciliar decisions of other churches, but has received the primacy by the evangelic voice of our Lord and Savior, who says: "You are Peter, and upon this rock I will build my Church, and the gates of hell will not prevail against it; and I will give to you the keys of the kingdom of heaven, and whatever you shall have bound on earth will be bound in heaven, and whatever you shall have loosed on earth shall be loosed in heaven" (Matthew 16:18–19). The first see [today], therefore, is that of Peter the apostle,

that of the Roman Church, which has neither stain nor blemish nor anything like it.
—*Decree of Damasus* 3

The Catholic Church today affirms and passes on this same **Apostolic Tradition**: "The Roman Pontiff, as the successor of Peter, is the perpetual and visible source and foundation of the unity both of the bishops and of the whole company of the faithful" (Vatican Council II, *Dogmatic Constitution on the Church* [*Lumen Gentium*], no. 23).

REFLECT AND SHARE

⊙ There is much coverage of the pope in the media today. Share what you have read or heard about the pope and his activities in recent times. How does he demonstrate his leadership of the Church by his words and/or actions?

⊙ Share any reports that you have seen, read or heard about the pope working with other bishops. Give specific examples.

OVER TO YOU

⊙ How does the pope lead, inspire or motivate you to live your faith in Jesus Christ?

THE VATICAN COAT OF ARMS INCORPORATES THE KEYS OF ST. PETER

The schism of the East from the West

Pope Francis on the Nature of True Dialogue

At a meeting in Brazil, Pope Francis said: "When leaders in various fields ask me for advice, my response is always the same: dialogue, dialogue, dialogue. It is the only way for individuals, families, and societies to grow, the only way for the life of peoples to progress, along with the culture of encounter, a culture in which all have something good to give and all can receive something good in return." . . . Dialogue does not mean denying objective truth, but rather respecting the

POPE FRANCIS IN BRAZIL, 2013

dignity of the other person "in a way that everyone can see in the other not an enemy, not a rival, but a brother or sister to be welcomed and embraced."

—Vatican Radio, October 31, 2015

OPENING REFLECTION

- What common ground do you see between Pope Francis' words on dialogue and Kipling's message in the opening and closing verse of "The Ballad of East and West"?
- Have you ever experienced a time when you and a family member or friend had a serious disagreement?
  - Did you work at resolving the disagreement?
  - What was the result of your efforts, or lack of efforts?
- What guidance do you take from Pope Francis' words on dialogue for your relationships with other Christians with whom you disagree?

THE CHURCH IN THE EAST AND THE WEST

In AD 313 Emperor Constantine issued the Edict of Milan. This edict gave Christians the legal right to gather and worship publicly. In AD 326 Constantine founded a second capital of the Roman Empire and moved his primary seat of government from Rome to Byzantium. He renamed Byzantium "Constantinopolis."

In AD 380 Emperor Theodosius I declared Christianity the official religion of the whole Roman Empire. The Roman Empire, in the West and in the East, was now united both politically and religiously.

Upon the death of Theodosius I in AD 395, the Roman Empire permanently split and came under the administration of two emperors—Honorius in the West, and Arcadius in the East. When Rome fell to the Visigoths two years later, the governing power of the whole Roman Empire shifted to Constantinople. These divisions affected the governance of the Church and remain today.

RECALL AND REFLECT

- Recall and reflect on what you have already learned in the first section of this chapter about the primacy and authority of the pope, the Bishop of Rome.

DISPUTES AND DIVERSITY LEAD TO SCHISM

The Schism of 451: Disagreements and disputes within the Church grew in scope and intensity from the mid-fourth century. Following the Council of Chalcedon (AD 451), those who supported the false teachings of what has become known as **Monophysitism** merged. The Monophysite heresy, as you learned in chapter 2 of this text, argued that there was only one nature in Christ: a divine nature. The humanity of Christ was totally absorbed into his divinity. Because of misunderstandings about the Person of Jesus Christ, following the Council of Chalcedon, several churches broke away from the Catholic Church and formed today's Oriental Orthodox Churches.

The Oriental Orthodox Churches never officially adopted the Monophysite heresy, even though they have been accused of such. Sadly, they are often referred to as Monophysites. The **Schism** of 451, or the Chalcedonian Schism, continues today.

The Schism of 1054: The two parts of the Roman Empire continued gradually to grow politically further and further apart. Constantine IX, the Byzantine emperor from 1042 to 1055, tried to reunite the empire to defend it from the Norman invasions. This reunion, in great part, depended upon the agreement of the Bishop of Rome, St. Leo IX, and the Patriarch of Constantinople, Michael Cerularius. Negotiations between the legates of the Pope and the Patriarch failed.

After the death of St. Leo IX on April 19, 1054, Cardinal Humbert, one of the Pope's legates, stood before the altar in the Cathedral in Constantinople and delivered a declaration excommunicating Cerularius and his clergy. Cerularius, in response, convoked a synod which excommunicated the legates who had represented Leo IX. Emperor Constantine's attempts to mend fences failed. The Schism of 1054 divided the Churches in the East from the Churches in the West. The former Churches are named the Eastern Orthodox Churches.

Many factors, including cultural, political and economic, as well as doctrinal, contributed

THE ORTHODOX CHURCH OF THE INTERCESSION ON THE NERL, RUSSIA

FAITH WORD

Orthodox Churches

The term "Orthodox Churches" refers to those Churches belonging to the two Orthodox families, namely the Eastern Orthodox Churches and the Oriental Orthodox Churches. The Eastern Orthodox Churches include those of the Byzantine tradition who are linked in some way to the Patriarchate of Constantinople. The Oriental Orthodox Churches are those who did not accept the Council of Chalcedon (AD 451) and now make up a communion of six churches. The Orthodox Churches "are separated from the Catholic Church (schism), yet are in an imperfect but deep communion with the Catholic Church by reason of our common Baptism, the profession of the Creed, and the possession of true sacraments by reason of apostolic succession of their priesthood" (*Catechism of the Catholic Church* [CCC], Glossary).

to the Schism of 1054. First, different forms of church governance had emerged. Second, disputed theological issues, such as the *Filioque* controversy, remained unresolved. (*In the "Embrace the Vision" section of this chapter we will explore the meaning and significance of the term "Filioque" and the controversy surrounding it in more detail*.) Third, cultural, spiritual and political factors contributed to different understandings and practices of the faith. For example, there wasn't one common language, which could have contributed to creating a shared unity and identity. Greek was the predominant language in the East, whereas Latin was the language in the West. Both languages gave rise to different explanations and understandings of church doctrine.

REFLECT, ANALYZE AND SHARE

⊙ Reflect on the events leading up to the Schism of 1054.
⊙ Discuss with a partner: What do these events and their consequences say about the potential dangers of politics and religion becoming overly interconnected?
⊙ Share reflections as a class.

EASTERN ORTHODOX CHURCHES

The term "Eastern Orthodox Churches" refers to all the **Orthodox Churches** of the Byzantine tradition. This family of Orthodox Churches tend to be organized by national identity: for example, the Orthodox Church of Greece, Orthodox Church of Poland, Orthodox Church of Russia and so on. There are fifteen independent Eastern Orthodox Churches in full communion with one another and with the Ecumenical Patriarchate of Constantinople.

In the United States the largest Orthodox Church is the Greek Orthodox Archdiocese of America, which has about 1,500,000 members in 540 parishes served by 800 priests. Among the smaller Orthodox Churches in the U.S. are the Antiochian Archdiocese based in the Middle East, the Orthodox Church of America (OCA), and other groups linked to Orthodox Churches in Serbia, Ukraine, Romania, Bulgaria, and so on. The Orthodox Church in America was founded in 1794 as a mission by Russian Orthodox to

Alaska. It was granted its independence by the Russian Orthodox Patriarch in 1970. The OCA has more than 85,000 members and more than 700 parishes, monasteries and other ecclesial institutions in fourteen archdioceses and dioceses in the United States of America and Canada.

Each Orthodox Church is independent from the other Orthodox Churches in its governance, or administration. A patriarch, metropolitan or archbishop presides over each Orthodox Church. The relationship between patriarchs and other

The OCA has more than 85,000 members in the United States of America and Canada

AN ORTHODOX CHURCH BUILDING IN ALASKA

church leaders is synodal and collegial. They meet as a **synod** and consult with priests and laity. The collective wisdom of the synod guides the decision-making process. No one patriarch, metropolitan or archbishop has authority over any other regarding doctrinal or moral teaching and administrative or other practices. This Orthodox understanding and practice of collegiality, as we will explore in the next section of this chapter, differs from the teaching and practice of **collegiality** in the Catholic Church.

LET'S PROBE DEEPER

⊙ The Synod on the Family, or the Fourteenth Ordinary General Assembly of the Synod of Bishops, met at the Vatican from October 4 to October 25, 2015.
⊙ Work in small groups. Research this synod, and then discuss:
  – Who participated in the synod?
  – What was the theme of the synod?
  – What was the Pope's role in relation to the synod?

OVER TO YOU

⊙ Are you familiar with an Orthodox Church in your area? If not, research the location of the Orthodox Church nearest to where you live.
⊙ Find out about when the members of this Church celebrate their liturgy, the holy days they observe, and about the activities that are provided for the young people.
⊙ Record the information you find and add to it as you learn more about the beliefs and practices of the Orthodox Churches in the next section of this chapter.

In the next section of this chapter we will explore, in more detail, (1) the bonds that unite the Catholic Church and the Orthodox Churches, (2) the issues that continue to be obstacles to the full communion of the Catholic Church and the Orthodox Churches, and (3) the efforts to reunite the Catholic Church and the Orthodox Churches.

Strong ties and differences

PORTALS INTO THE REALM OF THE HOLY

Icons are portals into the realm of the holy. They are a vital element of Eastern Orthodox prayer and devotional life and are rich in symbolic meaning. "Icons are more than sacred pictures. Everything about them is theological. For example, they are always flat, flat so that we who inhabit the physical world will understand that the world of the spirit where Christ, His Mother, the angels, the saints, and the departed dwell, is a world of mystery which cannot be penetrated by our five senses" (Fr. Michael Azkoul).

OPENING REFLECTION

- Reflect prayerfully on the images of the icons on this page.
- What strikes you? Does reflecting on them help you enter into deeper communion with God?

STRONG TIES BETWEEN ORTHODOX CHURCHES AND THE CATHOLIC CHURCH

In the Second Vatican Council's *Decree on Ecumenism* (*Unitatis Redintegratio*), the Catholic Church acknowledges her strong ties with the Orthodox Churches. We will now explore some of the key elements that continue to bond the Catholic Church and the Orthodox Churches. One key expression of the dialogue between the two since Vatican II has been joint statements. These statements may or may not be considered official teaching statements by one or more signatories. But even when they do not represent official teaching, they can be useful expressions of the state of discussion.

Core doctrines and beliefs: Catholic and Orthodox Churches "confess the same basic Christian faith, as expressed in the Christian canon of Scripture and in the Churches'

PART OF AN ICONOSTASIS IN AN ORTHODOX CHURCH

traditional creeds" (United States Conference of Catholic Bishops, "Steps Towards a Reunited Church: A Sketch of an Orthodox–Catholic Vision for the Future," The North American Orthodox–Catholic Theological Consultation, October 2, 2010, no. 6b). Again, although a theological consultation does not represent authoritative Catholic teaching, it can offer a useful portrait of shared elements of beliefs.

Both Churches profess faith in the Triune God; in the full divinity and humanity of Jesus Christ, the Incarnate Son of God; in the mission of the Holy Spirit; and in the unique role of the Blessed Virgin Mary in the divine plan. The Catholic Church and the Orthodox Churches accept the same canon of Scripture and also share many moral teachings on issues related to war, justice, sexual morality and the value of all human life.

The Church: In 1989 the Catholic Church and the Orthodox Churches agreed: "The Church is the mystery of God-given unity among human beings, who are bound together by their faith in the risen Lord and by the transforming gift of the Holy Spirit into the divine and human fellowship (*koinonia*) we call the Body of Christ (1 Corinthians 12:13)." One enters the Church through Baptism and the profession of faith. The mystery of the Church is most fully realized and celebrated in the Eucharist. The Church strives toward the fullness of the Kingdom of God when, at God's appointed time, Christ will come again in glory.

Apostolic Succession: Both the Catholic Church and the Orthodox Churches subscribe to the doctrine of Apostolic Succession, that is, the "passing on of the office of bishop from the Apostles to bishops, and from them to other bishops down each generation, by means of ordination" (*United States Catholic Catechism for Adults* [USCCA], Glossary, "Apostolic Succession"). The Catholic Church and Orthodox

ST. BASIL THE GREAT | ENGRAVING C. 18TH CENTURY

Churches recognize and teach that "the Church of God exists where there is a community gathered together in the Eucharist, presided over, directly or through his presbyters, by a bishop legitimately ordained into the apostolic succession, teaching the faith received from the apostles, in communion with other bishops and their Churches" (Joint International Dialogue, *Ravenna Statement* [2007], no. 18). The heading on the Vatican website above the Ravenna Statement indicates that the Statement is not to be taken as a document of official Catholic teaching. The Statement, however, offers a helpful listing of elements of shared beliefs.

The ministerial priesthood: The Catholic Church and the Orthodox Churches hold that the valid ordination by a bishop sets some baptized men apart for a permanent sacramental ministry and leadership within the Church.

Liturgical and sacramental life: The Catholic Church and the Orthodox Churches celebrate the same Seven Sacraments. Both profess that the life of the Church is centered in the liturgy, especially the Eucharist, and that participation in the Seven Sacraments both forms and nourishes the faithful. The Catholic Church and the Orthodox Churches also recognize and celebrate in their liturgy the life of many of the same saints, especially those from the early centuries of the Church; for example, Saints Basil, Clement, Athanasius, Gregory, John Chrysostom, and Cyril and Methodius.

There are, however, differences in the liturgical rites in each tradition. For example, in the Latin Rite (the rite of the Church in the West), the Sacrament of Baptism is ordinarily received in infancy; the Eucharist is first received around the age of seven; and Confirmation is most often celebrated at a later time after the first reception of the Eucharist. The Orthodox Churches follow the ancient tradition of celebrating Baptism, Confirmation and Eucharist (in that order) at the same time, even for infants. The Roman Catholic Church follows that same ancient tradition when initiating non-baptized children of catechetical age, youth and adults into the Church. This diversity enriches the Church and

The Council of Ephesus in AD 431 formally taught that Mary is *Theotokos*, or the "Bearer of God"

ORTHODOX ICON OF THEOTOKOS

points to her true catholic nature: "The Church is catholic, capable of integrating into her unity, while purifying them, all the authentic riches of cultures" (CCC, no. 1202).

Mary/Theotokos: The Catholic and the Orthodox Churches "venerate Mary, the Mother of God, as the foremost among those transformed by the grace of Christ's redemption" ("Steps Towards a Reunited Church: A Sketch of an Orthodox–Catholic Vision for the Future," no. 4). The Council of Ephesus in AD 431 formally taught that Mary is *Theotokos*, or the "Bearer of God." The Blessed Virgin Mary truly conceived by the power of the Holy Spirit and gave birth to the Person of Jesus Christ, in whom the divine nature and a human nature were united. Both Churches confess the perpetual virginity of Mary—Mary was a virgin during the conception and birth of Jesus, and she remained a virgin for the rest of her life.

REFLECT AND SHARE

- ⊙ Has your exploration of the similarities between the Catholic Church and the Orthodox Churches deepened your own appreciation of your Catholic faith?
- ⊙ Share with a partner the aspects of your faith that you treasure.

OBSTACLES TO FULL COMMUNION

Substantial differences in beliefs and practices remain as obstacles to full reunion, or full communion, between the Catholic Church and the Orthodox Churches.

The authority of the pope: The chief obstacle to restoring the full communion of the Catholic Church and the Orthodox Churches is the issue of the authority of the pope, the Bishop of Rome. St. John Paul II, in his 1995 encyclical *On Commitment to Ecumenism* (*Ut Unum Sint*), acknowledged that "the Catholic Church's conviction that in the ministry of the Bishop of Rome she has preserved, in fidelity to the Apostolic Tradition and the faith of the Fathers, the visible sign and guarantor of unity, constitutes a difficulty for most other Christians, whose memory is marked by certain painful recollections" (no. 88).

Orthodox Churches, as so Protestants, claim that the Catholic teaching on the authority of the pope is at odds with Scripture and Apostolic Tradition. While Orthodox Churches honor the primacy of the Bishop of Rome, they reject the teaching of the Catholic Church on the pope's primacy of jurisdiction over the universal Church. That teaching of the Catholic Church is: "The bishop of the Roman Church, in whom continues the office given by the Lord uniquely to Peter, the first of the Apostles, and to be transmitted to his successors, is the head of the college of bishops, the Vicar of Christ, and the pastor of the universal Church on earth" (*Code of Canon Law*, canon 331).

All three Divine Persons of the Holy Trinity share the one and same divine nature

Orthodox Churches, as we have seen, use a synodal and collegial form of teaching and governance. The Orthodox understanding and exercise of collegiality differs from the Catholic Church's teaching and practice of collegiality: "This college of bishops together with, but never without, the Pope has supreme and full authority over the universal Church" (CCC, Glossary, "Collegiality").

The Orthodox Churches, consistent with their practice of collegiality, also reject the teaching of the Catholic Church on papal infallibility. The dogma on infallibility teaches, in part: "[The Roman Pontiff's] definitions are rightly said to be irreformable by their very nature and not by reason of the consent of the church, in as much as they were made with the assistance of the holy Spirit promised to him in blessed Peter; and as a consequence they are not in need of the approval of others, and do not admit of appeal to any other tribunal" (Vatican II, *Dogmatic Constitution on the Church*, no. 25).

The *Filioque* controversy: In the Niceno-Constantinopolitan (Nicene) Creed the Catholic Church professes: "I believe in the Holy Spirit, the Lord, the giver of life, / who proceeds *from the Father and the Son*, [italics added] / who with the Father and the Son is adored and glorified, / who has spoken through the prophets" (English translation of *The Roman Missal*, copyright 2010).

The clause "who proceeds from the Father and the Son" is used to teach the eternal origin and divinity of the Holy Spirit and the consubstantial unity of all three Divine Persons of the Holy Trinity—that is, all three Divine Persons share the one and same divine nature. (The word *filioque* refers to the phrase "and the Son,"—"and (*que*) the son (*filio*)." The eastern tradition does not include the use of the *Filioque* in the Nicene Creed, that is, the Holy Spirit proceeds from the Father "and the Son." The eastern tradition professes that the Holy Spirit "*comes from* the Father *through* the Son" to express the same mystery of faith. The Orthodox Churches base their dispute on the fact that the *Filioque* was not included in the original Niceno-Constantinopolitan Creed, but was added later by the Church in the West.

The challenge of Catholic–Orthodox consultations is to come to an agreement *on the words* to be used to express this central mystery and dogma of the Christian faith, which both traditions confess.

Ecumenical Councils: The Orthodox Churches only recognize the teaching authority of the first seven Ecumenical Councils, namely, the First Council of Nicaea (325), the First Council of Constantinople (381), the Council of Ephesus (431), the Council of Chalcedon (451), the Second Council of Constantinople (553), the Third Council of Constantinople (680–681), and the Second Council of Nicaea (787). They base their rejection of the authority of the later councils, which are recognized as ecumenical by the Catholic Church, on the claim that the later councils were not truly ecumenical, or "pan-Orthodox," in their representation.

Mary: The Catholic Church and the Orthodox Churches differ in their teachings on Mary being free from all sin. The Catholic Church, in the dogma of the Immaculate Conception, teaches "from the first moment of her conception, Mary—by the singular grace of God and by virtue of the merits of Jesus Christ—was preserved immune from original sin" (CCC, Glossary, "Immaculate Conception"). The Catholic Church teaches that Mary was free from Original Sin and its effects throughout her life. Because of their different understanding of Original Sin, the teachings of the Orthodox Churches on Mary's freedom from sin differ from the teaching of the Catholic Church.

Marriage: The Catholic Church and the Orthodox Churches teach that a baptized man and a baptized woman who are married sacramentally are living signs of the union of Christ and his Church. Both the Orthodox Churches and the Catholic Church affirm the sanctity of marriage and see it as a lifelong commitment. Their teachings on divorce and remarriage, however, are contrary to each other.

The Catholic Church affirms the indissolubility of marriage and prohibits divorced spouses who have entered a valid sacramental marriage from remarrying without first having their marriage annulled. An annulment is a declaration by the Church that a marriage lacked one or more of the essential conditions for a true sacramental marriage.

The Orthodox Church, while opposed to divorce, does permit remarriage without a declaration of nullity: "Out of pastoral consideration and in order better to serve the spiritual needs of the faithful, the Orthodox Church tolerates remarriage of divorced persons under certain specific circumstances as it permits the remarriage of widows and widowers under certain specific circumstances" (Joint Committee of Orthodox and Catholic Bishops—a non-authoritative consultation of the two Churches in the United States that began in 1981). Remarriage is an exception to the rule, as it were; and its celebration, unlike one's first marriage, has a penitential character.

Both the Orthodox Churches and the Catholic Church see marriage as a lifelong commitment

THE BRIDE AND GROOM ARE CROWNED AS PART OF THE ORTHODOX WEDDING CEREMONY

Holy Orders: The Orthodox Church allows a man who marries before ordination to be ordained to the priesthood and to live a non-celibate life within his marriage. The priest's marriage and family life are seen to serve as a model for the community. If an unmarried man is ordained to the priesthood, however, he may not marry and must remain celibate after his ordination to the priesthood.

The discipline of the Roman Catholic Church requires her members who seek ordination to the priesthood to live a celibate life as an essential condition for ordination. Mandatory celibacy is also required in some Eastern Catholic Churches. There is one exception to this discipline of the Roman Catholic Church. The Roman Catholic Church does permit married clergy from some other Christian communities who desire full communion with the Catholic Church to be ordained and serve as priests. As of 2017, there were 120 married priests in the United States. The Catholic Church does permit a married man to be ordained a deacon. A married deacon, however, cannot be ordained to the priesthood while his wife is still living.

REFLECT AND SHARE

⊙ Given their common ties and their differences, how might the Catholic Church and Orthodox Churches work together to proclaim the Gospel?

⊙ Share ideas as a class.

CATHOLIC—ORTHODOX DIALOGUES AND CONSULTATIONS

Since the Second Vatican Council, the Catholic Church has been engaged in formal ecumenical dialogues both at national levels and worldwide.

Eastern Orthodox Churches: The North American Orthodox–Catholic Theological Consultation has been meeting on a regular basis for almost forty-five years. At these consultations representatives from both the Orthodox Churches and the Catholic Church have dialogued on a wide variety of issues, including: The Holy Eucharist (1969), Respect for Life (1974), The Church (1974), Baptism, Eucharist and Ministry (1984), Faith, Sacraments, and the Unity of the Church (1988), Search for Full Communion (1994), The Filioque: A Church Dividing Issue? (2003), and Steps Towards

AN ORTHODOX BISHOP AT THE HIGH MONASTERY OF ST. PETER, MOSCOW

a Reunited Church: A Sketch of an Orthodox–Catholic Vision for the Future (2010). Again, although these statements are not official Catholic teaching documents, they do offer the fruits of mutual pursuit of shared understanding, which itself helps foster Christian unity.

Similarly, on a more global level the Pontifical Council for Promoting Christian Unity has been meeting with the Orthodox Churches. In 1979 the Joint Commission for Theological Dialogue between the Roman Catholic Church and the Orthodox Church was established. The issues the Joint Commission discussed include: The Mystery of the Church and the Eucharist in the Light of the Mystery of the Holy Trinity (1980); Faith, Sacraments and the Unity of the Church (1984); the Role of the Bishop of Rome in the Communion of the Church (2009, 2010); Primacy and Synodality in the Church (2014). Again, while commissions do not offer official teaching, their shared statements help build mutual understanding.

In 1965 Pope Paul VI and the Ecumenical Patriarch of Constantinople, Athenagoras I, formally rescinded the mutual excommunications that each Church had imposed on the other in 1054. This signified a new beginning and a commitment to new dialogue and collaboration, and, hopefully, the beginning of a return to unity. (See "Learn by Example" in the Judge and Act section of this chapter.) And in 2016 Pope Francis and Patriarch Kirill, the Russian Orthodox Patriarch, met in Cuba. This was the first meeting of a pope and a Russian Orthodox patriarch since the Schism of 1054. While there is still a long way to go, many important steps have been taken.

Oriental Orthodox Churches: The Oriental Orthodox Communion today includes six churches that are in full communion with one another. These churches are: the Armenian

THE ETHIOPIAN ORTHODOX CHURCH OF ST. GEORGE, CARVED FROM THE ROCK WHERE IT STANDS

Apostolic Church, the Coptic Orthodox Church of Alexandria, the Ethiopian Orthodox Tewahedo Church, the Eritrean Orthodox Tewahedo Church, the Indian Orthodox Church, and the Syriac Orthodox Church of Antioch (or simply, Syrian Orthodox Church).

The international dialogue between the Catholic Church and the Oriental Orthodox Churches began in 2004. These dialogues are built on the work of Blessed Paul VI and St. John Paul II. In October 1971 the Syrian Orthodox Patriarch Ignatius Jacoub III and Pope Paul VI, at the end of the Patriarch's visit in October 1971, issued a joint statement. It reads in part:

> Pope Paul VI and Patriarch Mar Ignatius Jacoub III are in agreement that there is no difference in the faith they profess concerning the mystery of the Word of God made flesh and become really man, even if over the centuries difficulties have arisen out of different theological expressions by which this faith was expressed.

In commenting on this statement the United States Conference of Catholic Bishops wrote in 1980:

The Oriental Orthodox Churches are those who did not accept the Council of Chalcedon (AD 451)

THE COUNCIL OF CHALCEDON | VASILY SURIKOV

This agreement provides us with a solid basis for the hope that in "speaking the truth in love" (Ephesian 4:15a) this dialogue will make a contribution to our further growth together "into him who is the head, into Christ, from whom this whole body, joined and knit together by every joint with which it is supplied, when each part is working properly, makes bodily growth and builds itself in love" (Ephesians 4:15b–16).
—"Purpose, Scope, and Method of the Dialogue Between the Oriental Orthodox and Roman Catholic Churches," Introduction, USCCB website

In 1984 St. John Paul II and the Patriarch of the Syrian Orthodox Church declared:

[W]e find today no real basis for the sad divisions and schisms that subsequently arose between us concerning the doctrine of Incarnation. In words and life we confess the true doctrine concerning Christ our Lord, notwithstanding the differences in interpretation of such a doctrine which arose at the time of the Council of Chalcedon.
—From Common Declaration of St. John Paul II and His Holiness Mar Ignatius Zakka I, June 23, 1984

The international dialogue between the Catholic Church and the Oriental Orthodox Churches has been in progress since 2004. The first meeting was held in Cairo, Egypt on January 27–30, 2004. Since their inception, fourteen meetings have been held from 2004 through 2017. This dialogue has issued agreed statements on the nature of the Church and the ways the Churches expressed full communion in the period before the schism following the Council of Chalcedon in 451. The Catholic Church in the United States, under the guidance of the Secretariat for Ecumenical and Interreligious Affairs of the USCCB, has also been in consultation with the Oriental Orthodox Churches since 1977.

ECUMENISM WITHIN THE ORTHODOX CHURCHES

St. John Paul II and His Holiness Mar Ignatius Zakka II issued a joint statement on June 23, 1984. In addition to this joint authoritative statement, there is ongoing ecumenical dialogue between the Oriental Orthodox and the Eastern Orthodox Churches. The goal of this latter dialogue addresses the division within the Orthodox family of Churches. These latter dialogues, which arose unofficially in 1964, officially began in 1985. Their purpose is to recognize that "both families have always loyally maintained the authentic Orthodox Christological faith, and the unbroken continuity of the apostolic tradition, though they may have used Christological terms in different ways" and also to recognize that "political, sociological, cultural, linguistic and even psychological factors in creating tension have also played a role in the division" (From *The Dialogue Between the Eastern Orthodox and Oriental Orthodox Churches*, Christine Chaillot, editor, Volos Academy Publications, copyright 2017).

REFLECT AND SHARE

- ◉ How are the efforts at reunion of the Churches a response to the priestly prayer of Jesus in John 17:20–24?
- ◉ What is the role of the Holy Spirit in these dialogues? Check out John 16:13–15.
- ◉ Share reflections as a class.

JOURNAL EXERCISE

- ◉ How can you more consciously call upon the Holy Spirit to help you reconcile your differences with others?
- ◉ What can you do in your school, parish and local community to foster opportunities for Catholic and Orthodox Christians to come together to learn about and from each other?

How are the efforts at reunion of the Churches a response to the priestly prayer of Jesus in John 17:20–24?

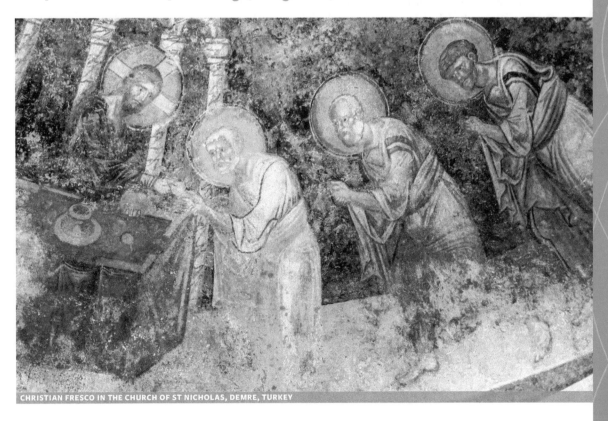

CHRISTIAN FRESCO IN THE CHURCH OF ST NICHOLAS, DEMRE, TURKEY

Diversity expressing the unity of the Church

A MULTI-CULTURAL PARISH

Diversity is a key characteristic of St. Joseph's Catholic Community. Parishioners come from a wide diversity of cultural backgrounds and include Nigerian, Vietnamese, Korean, Chinese, Mexican and Ecuadorian people. The display of international foods at the annual St. Joseph's Table celebration is an image of the unity and shared bond that has been created through a lived faith in service to others.

OPENING REFLECTION

⊙ Do you belong to any communities where there are different cultural traditions and expressions? What have you learned from this diversity?

⊙ How can diversity enrich a community?

⊙ How can you cherish and respect every member of your own school and parish communities?

EASTERN CATHOLIC CHURCHES

We tend to speak of the Catholic Church and the Roman Catholic Church as if the designations are synonymous—in reality, they are not. The Catholic Church includes the Roman, or Latin, **rite** in the West and twenty-two Catholic Churches of a diversity of rites in the East. All these Churches are equal in dignity and are "part of the divinely revealed, undivided heritage" of the one, holy, catholic and apostolic Church.

The Catholic Church values highly the institutions of the eastern churches, their liturgical rites, ecclesiastical traditions and their ordering of the christian life. For in those churches, which are distinguished by their venerable antiquity, there is clearly evident the tradition which has come from the apostles through the Fathers and which is part of the divinely revealed, undivided heritage of the universal church.

—Vatican II, *Decree on the Catholic Eastern Churches (Orientalium Ecclesiarum)*, no. 1

While the Orthodox Churches and the Roman Church are not yet fully unified, all the Catholic

MEDIEVAL ARMENIAN CHRISTIAN KHACHKARS (CROSS STONES)

FAITH WORD

Eastern Churches

Churches of the East in union with Rome (the Western Church), but not of [the] Roman rite, with their own liturgical, theological and administrative traditions, such as those of the Byzantine, Alexandrian or Coptic, Syriac, Armenian, Maronite, and Chaldean rites. The variety of particular churches with distinctive traditions witnesses to the catholicity of the one Church of Christ, which takes root in distinct cultures.

—CCC, Glossary

One Church, One in Diversity

The holy Catholic Church, which is the Mystical Body of Christ, is made up of the faithful who are organically united in the holy Spirit by the same faith, the same sacraments and the same government, and who, coming together in various hierarchically linked different groups, thus form particular churches or rites.
—*Decree on the Catholic Eastern Churches*, no. 2

MARONITE CHURCH OF THE ANNUNCIATION, NAZARETH

Eastern Churches are in full communion with Rome, the Western Church, and with one another. All profess the same faith and all submit to the authority of the pope, the Bishop of Rome, whom they acknowledge to be the successor of St. Peter, the Vicar of Christ, the Pastor of the universal Church on earth and the visible foundation of the Church founded by Christ. The rites used by the Eastern Catholic Churches, however, differ from the Roman rite used in the Western, or Latin, Church.

AUTHENTIC DIVERSITY WITHIN THE CHURCH

The presence of the Eastern Catholic Churches lends a wonderful variety of customs and practices to the family that is the Catholic Church. It is a rich banquet, marked by unity in the midst of diversity. "These individual churches, both eastern and western, while they differ somewhat among themselves in what is called "rite," namely in liturgy, in ecclesiastical discipline and in spiritual tradition, are none the less all . . . of equal rank, so that none of them is superior to the others because of its rite" (*Decree on the Catholic Eastern Churches*, no. 3). For example, in many Eastern Catholic Churches, married men can be ordained priests, but they cannot be bishops or monks.

The Eastern Catholic Churches attest to the truth that the one Church founded by Jesus Christ is both diverse and unified. In other words, it is catholic: "From the beginning, this one Church has been marked by a great diversity which comes from both the variety of God's gifts and the diversity of those who receive them. Within the unity of the People of God, a multiplicity of peoples and cultures is gathered together" (CCC, no. 814).

LET'S PROBE DEEPER: A SCRIPTURE ACTIVITY

- Recall St. Paul's teaching in 1 Corinthians 12:12–31 on the Church as the one Body of Christ.
- How does St. Paul's image of the Body of Christ apply to the relationship between the Western and Eastern Catholic Churches?
- Share reflections as a class.

OVER TO YOU

- What insights into the nature of the Catholic Church have you learned from hearing about the Eastern Catholic Churches?

REVIEW AND SHARE WHAT YOU HAVE LEARNED

Review what you have learned in this chapter about the Eastern Catholic Churches and the Orthodox Churches. Share the teachings of the Catholic Church that you have learned in this chapter on these statements:

- ⊙ The Bishop of Rome, the pope, is the visible source and foundation of the unity of the Church.
- ⊙ Disputes within the Church led to schisms between the Church in the West and the Church in the East.
- ⊙ There are strong ties between the Catholic Church and the Orthodox Churches.
- ⊙ Traditions in both the Catholic Church in the West and the Catholic Church in the East contribute to and enrich the authentic unity of the Church.
- ⊙ The Catholic Church is in dialogue with the Orthodox Churches.

OVER TO YOU

- ⊙ What does the relationship between the Catholic Church in the West (the Roman Catholic Church) and the Catholic Churches in the East teach us about authentic diversity within the Church?
- ⊙ What has learning about the connection between the Orthodox Churches and Eastern Catholic Churches contributed to your understanding of the Church?

LEARN BY EXAMPLE

Blessed Pope Paul VI and Patriarch Athenagoras I of Constantinople

Blessed Paul VI was the first pope since the ninth century to visit the East and the first pope in centuries to meet with an Orthodox patriarch. As the Second Vatican Council was drawing to a close, Paul VI reached out to the Orthodox Churches. Fortunately, the Pope had a receptive partner, Athenagoras I (1886–1972), the Ecumenical Patriarch of Constantinople.

In 1964 Paul VI and Athenagoras I met in Jerusalem, a place that both of them had deliberately chosen. This historic meeting prompted the Catholic–Orthodox Joint Declaration of 1965. This declaration publicly rescinded the mutual excommunications that had marked the Schism of 1054. This meeting between the East and the West also signified the beginning of a Catholic–Orthodox dialogue. The express purpose of the new dialogues would be to explore ways the two Churches could work toward reunion. The declaration stated, in part:

PATRIARCH ATHENAGORAS I AND POPE PAUL VI, NAZARETH

Pope Paul VI and Patriarch Athenagoras I with his synod realize that this gesture of justice and mutual pardon is not sufficient to end both old and more recent differences between the Roman Catholic Church and the Orthodox Church.

Through the action of the Holy Spirit those differences will be overcome through cleansing of hearts, through regret for historical wrongs, and through an efficacious determination to arrive at a common understanding and expression of the faith of the Apostles and its demands....

They hope . . . that the whole Christian world, especially the entire Roman Catholic Church and the Orthodox Church will appreciate this gesture as . . . an invitation to follow out in a spirit of trust, esteem and mutual charity the dialogue which, with God's help, will lead to living together again, for the greater good of souls and the coming of the kingdom of God, in that full communion of faith, fraternal accord and sacramental life which existed among them during the first thousand years of the life of the Church.

Blessed Paul VI, St. John Paul II, Benedict XVI and Francis have all met and dialogued with patriarchs. These meetings demonstrate that, no matter how high the roadblocks, the path to peace lies through dialogue, respect and face-to-face encounters.

The popes and the patriarchs give clear witness that mutual respect needs to be at the heart of the relationship between the Catholic and Orthodox Churches. The mutual respect for the culture, dignity and practices of one another's traditions is vital to the healing of the schism that separates the Churches.

TALK IT OVER

- What have the encounters between Blessed Paul VI and Ecumenical Patriarch Athenagoras I taught you about the connection between respect and reconciliation?
- Share clear, concrete examples of situations in the world today where Christians need to demonstrate respect for one another and work at reconciling their differences in the manner modeled by Paul VI and Athenagoras I and their successors.

SHARE FAITH WITH FAMILY AND FRIENDS

- Is there an Orthodox or an Eastern Catholic church in your parish/diocese that you could arrange to visit?
- Contact its youth minister to see whether you can tour the church. Perhaps a member of its youth group could be your guide.
- Invite family members and/or friends to join you.

JUDGE AND DECIDE

- What is one way you can help embrace and promote diversity within the Church— through your participation in parish, school or local community activities?
- Commit to following up on this, and invite others to join you.

OVER TO YOU

- Research a prayer practice that comes from the Orthodox or Eastern Catholic tradition.
- How might that tradition enrich your practice of the Catholic faith?
- Perhaps choose an icon to display in your home or bedroom.

LEARN BY HEART

Now there are varieties of gifts, but the same Spirit; and there are varieties of services, but the same Lord; and there are varieties of activities, but it is the same God who activates all of them in everyone.

I CORINTHIANS 12:4–6

PRAYER REFLECTION

All stand and pray the Sign of the Cross together.
Conclude by praying together:
Glory to you, our God, glory be to you!

LEADER
Heavenly Ruler, Comforter, the Spirit of Truth,
present in all places and filling all things,
Treasury of Goodness and Giver of Life:
come and abide in us.
Cleanse us from every stain of sin
and save our souls, O gracious God.

ALL
Holy God! Holy mighty! Holy immortal! Have
mercy on us.
Holy God! Holy mighty! Holy immortal! Have
mercy on us.
Holy God! Holy mighty! Holy immortal! Have
mercy on us.

Glory to the Father and the Son and the Holy
Spirit,
both now and forever and to the ages of ages.
Amen.

LEADER
All Holy Trinity, have mercy on us.
Lord, forgive our sins
and pardon our transgressions.
Holy One, visit and heal our infirmities, for the
glory of your name.

Lord, have mercy.
Lord, have mercy.
Lord, have mercy.

Glory to the Father and the Son and the Holy
Spirit,
both now and forever and to the ages of ages.
Amen.

ALL
All pray the Our Father together, ending with:
For yours is the kingdom and the power
and the glory of the Father and the Son and the
Holy Spirit,
both now and forever and to the ages of ages.
Amen.

Lord, have mercy.
Lord, have mercy.
Lord, have mercy.

All focus on the icon (opposite) and pray silently.

LEADER
Let us all pray together this final hymn of praise:

ALL
Glory to God, who has shown us the Light!
Glory to God in the highest, and on earth, peace,
good will toward all!
We praise you! We bless you! We worship you!
We glorify you and give thanks to you for your
great glory!
O loving God, heavenly ruler, God the almighty!
O Lord, the Only-begotten Son, Jesus Christ, and
the Holy Spirit!

O Lord God, Lamb of God, Son of the Father,
who take away the sins of the world, have mercy
on us!
You, who take away the sins of the world, receive
our prayer!
You, who sit on the right hand of God the Father,
have mercy on us!
For you alone are holy, and you alone are Lord.
You alone, O Lord Jesus Christ, are most high in
the glory of God the Father,
in unity with the Holy Spirit, one God, forever
and ever.
Amen.

LEADER

Let your mercy be upon us, loving God,
even as we have set our hope on you.
Blessed are you, O God; teach us your statutes.
Blessed are you, O Master; make us to
understand your commandments.
Blessed are you, O Holy One; enlighten us with
your precepts.

Your mercy endures forever, O God!
To you belongs worship, to you belongs praise, to
you belongs glory:
to the Father and to the Son and to the Holy
Spirit,
now and forever and to the ages of ages.

ALL

Amen.

CHAPTER 5

The Lutheran, Anglican (Episcopalian) and Reformed Christian Communities

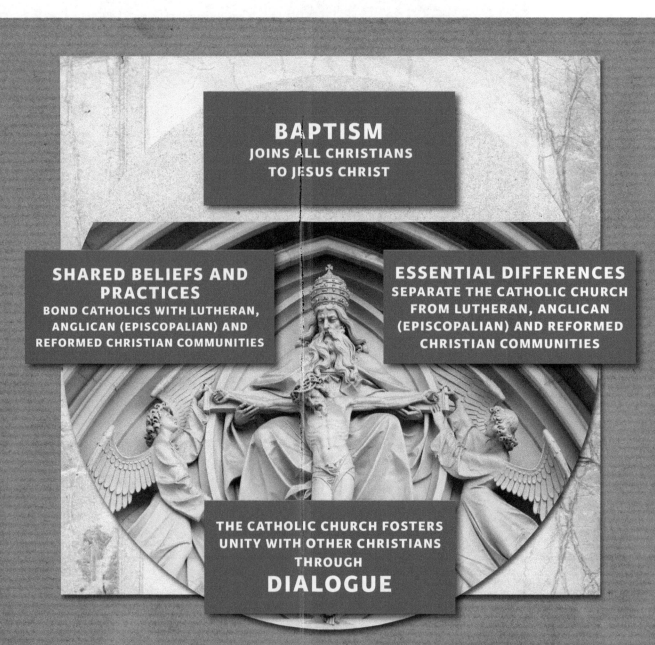

BAPTISM
JOINS ALL CHRISTIANS
TO JESUS CHRIST

SHARED BELIEFS AND PRACTICES
BOND CATHOLICS WITH LUTHERAN, ANGLICAN (EPISCOPALIAN) AND REFORMED CHRISTIAN COMMUNITIES

ESSENTIAL DIFFERENCES
SEPARATE THE CATHOLIC CHURCH FROM LUTHERAN, ANGLICAN (EPISCOPALIAN) AND REFORMED CHRISTIAN COMMUNITIES

THE CATHOLIC CHURCH FOSTERS UNITY WITH OTHER CHRISTIANS THROUGH
DIALOGUE

ALL CHRISTIANS, CATHOLIC AND NON-CATHOLIC, HAVE been joined to Christ and incorporated into his Church at Baptism. The Second Vatican Council teaches: "The church has many reasons for knowing that it is joined to the baptized who are honored by the name of Christian, but do not profess the faith in its entirety or have not preserved unity of communion under the successor of Peter" (*Dogmatic Constitution on the Church*, no. 15). The Catholic Church is committed to dialogue aimed at fostering unity with these ecclesial communities. In this chapter we explore the relationship of the Catholic Church with Lutheran, Anglican (Episcopalian), and Reformed Christian communities.

"COMMITMENT TO ECUMENISM RESPONDS TO THE PRAYER OF THE LORD JESUS THAT 'THEY MAY ALL BE ONE' "
—POPE FRANCIS

Faith Focus: These teachings of the Catholic Church are the primary focus of the doctrinal content presented in this chapter:

- ⊙ Baptism is the foundation of the mystery of the communion uniting all Christians.
- ⊙ The Catholic Church is committed to and engaged in open and honest ecumenical dialogue with non-Catholic Christian denominations, or ecclesial communities.
- ⊙ The Catholic Church shares common ties in doctrine and practices with other Christian traditions.
- ⊙ There are differences in doctrine and practices that are obstacles to full communion between other Christian denominations and the Catholic Church.

Discipleship Formation: As a result of studying this chapter and discovering the meaning of the faith of the Catholic Church for your life, you should be better able to:

- ⊙ describe the origins of the Lutheran, Anglican (Episcopalian), and Presbyterian and other Reformed Christian communities;
- ⊙ name the key doctrines and practices that unite Lutherans, Anglicans (Episcopalians), and Presbyterian and other Reformed Christian communities with the Catholic Church;
- ⊙ name the key differences that are obstacles to the full communion of Lutherans, Anglicans (Episcopalians), and Presbyterian and other Reformed Christian communities with the Catholic Church;
- ⊙ engage in dialogue about the Catholic faith with non-Catholic Christian family members and friends.

Scripture References: These scripture references are quoted or referred to in this chapter:
OLD TESTAMENT: Psalm 126:1–6; **Zechariah** 8:20–23
NEW TESTAMENT: Matthew 22:37–39, 25:34b, 28:16–20; **Mark** 1:15; **John** 17:11, 20–24; **Acts of the Apostles** 2:42; **Romans** 3:21–26, 8:15–30; **Ephesians** 1:4–5 and 9–11, 2:20, 4:5; **Philippians** 2:12; **1 Thessalonians** 5:1–11; **2 Timothy** 1:9–14; **James** 2:14–26; **Revelation** 21:14

Faith Glossary: Familiarize yourself with or recall the meaning of these key terms. Definitions are found in the Glossary: **Anglican Communion, annulment, Apostolic Succession, Calvinism, Catholic Reformation (Counter-Reformation), economy of salvation, Divine Revelation, ecclesial communities, ecumenism, grace, heresy, indulgences, justification, Magisterium, merit, predestination, Protestant Reformation, Real Presence, sacramental economy, sacraments, Sacred Scripture, Sacred Tradition, salvation,** *sola fide, sola gratia, sola scriptura,* **transubstantiation**

Faith Words: justification; predestination
Learn by Heart: Romans 3:23–24
Learn by Example: Dietrich Bonhoeffer

What unites and what separates Christians?

Many Branches of the Christian Family Tree

The Pew research forum in 2015 provided this profile of the religious landscape in the United States of America: Evangelical Protestants (25.4 percent); Unaffiliated (22.8 percent); Catholics (20.8 percent); Mainline Protestant (14.7 percent); Non-Christian faiths (5.9 percent). Mainline Protestants include, among others, these ecclesial communities: the United Methodist Church, the American Baptist Churches USA, the Evangelical Lutheran Church in America (ELCA), the Presbyterian Church USA, and the Episcopal Church.

OPENING REFLECTION

⊙ Create a profile of Christianity in your local community.

⊙ Do you know personally or are you aware of Anglican, Baptist, Episcopalian, Lutheran, Methodist or Presbyterian Christians?

⊙ Have you ever shared your faith with other Christians who are not Catholic? What have you shared and with whom? Did your sharing increase your mutual understanding of each other's tradition?

ECCLESIAL COMMUNITIES

It is helpful to make an important distinction at this point. The Lutheran, Anglican (Episcopalian), and Reformed Christian communities identify as "churches" in their formal titles. We will learn in this chapter why the Catholic Church does not consider these and other Protestant denominations to be churches as the Catholic

Church understands and defines "church." The Catholic Church identifies these Protestant denominations as ecclesial communities—a term introduced by Vatican II.

The Catholic Church teaches that the term "Church" designates only those *Christian faith traditions who maintain apostolic succession*, or a direct historical connection with the original Apostles. The term "ecclesial community" is used to designate all Christian denominations who do not maintain Apostolic Succession. That is the reason for the change in terminology from the last chapter, where we discussed the Orthodox Churches. In ecumenical discussion, the Catholic Church's agents, such as pontifical councils, commissions, and organized dialogues, use the designation "church' for Protestant ecclesial communities who use the term "church" in their formal title.

THE CATHOLIC CHURCH AND ECUMENISM

The Christian landscape in the United States of America is one of diversity and division. Such diversity and division calls for open and honest dialogue. This dialogue among Christians aimed at fostering unity between Christ's followers, as we have seen, is the work of **ecumenism**.

Pope Francis, as you will recall from your study of ecumenism in chapter 3, summarized the Catholic Church's commitment to ecumenism in his first apostolic exhortation, *The Joy of the Gospel* (*Evangelii Gaudium*):

Commitment to ecumenism responds to the prayer of the Lord Jesus that "they may all be one" (John 17:21). . . . We must never forget that we are pilgrims journeying alongside one another. This means that we must have sincere trust in our fellow pilgrims, putting aside all suspicion or mistrust, and turn our gaze to what we are all seeking: the radiant peace of God's face."

—*The Joy of the Gospel*, no. 244

You will also recall that there are many interrelated dimensions to the ecumenical activity of the Catholic Church. These include:

(1) a visible continuity with the ancient Church (Apostolic Succession); (2) the Spirit-guided renewal of the Catholic Church in fidelity to her vocation; (3) a conversion of heart of all the faithful; (4) prayer in common when appropriate; (5) understanding of and respect for one other; (6) proper and adequate formation of clergy and laity in the beliefs and practices of one another; (7) honest and open dialogue among the representatives of different churches and communities; and (8) collaboration in works of service to others.

THINK, PAIR AND SHARE

⊙ Share with a partner your awareness of the ecumenical efforts of the Catholic Church in your diocese.

"ONE LORD, ONE FAITH, ONE BAPTISM" (EPHESIANS 4:5)

The Sacrament of Baptism is the foundation upon which life in the one Church of Jesus Christ is built. The Catholic Church teaches: "Baptism constitutes the foundation of communion among all Christians, including those who are not yet in full communion with the Catholic Church" (*Catechism of the Catholic Church* [CCC], no. 1271).

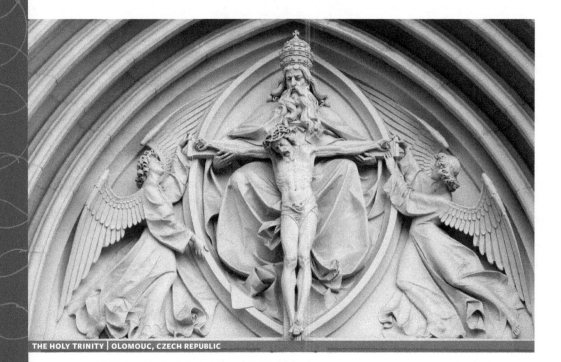

THE HOLY TRINITY | OLOMOUC, CZECH REPUBLIC

This Sacrament of Christian Initiation joins all Christians to Jesus Christ and incorporates them into the one Body of Christ, the Church.

The Catholic Church recognizes as valid all celebrations of Baptism that include these three elements: (1) the immersion of the candidate three times into water or the pouring of water three times over the candidate's head; (2) the use of a Trinitarian formula: "N., I baptize you in the name of the Father, and of the Son, and of the Holy Spirit"; and (3) the person baptizing has the intention to baptize according to the mind of the Church.

The ritual for the celebration of Baptism in the Eastern liturgies, while essentially the same as the liturgies of the Church in the West, differs slightly: "In the Eastern liturgies the catechumen turns toward the East and the priest says: 'The servant of God, N., is baptized in the name of the Father, and of the Son, and of the Holy Spirit.' At the invocation of each person of the Most Holy Trinity, the priest immerses the candidate in the water and raises him up again" (CCC, no. 1240).

The Catholic Church does not re-baptize a validly baptized non-Catholic who seeks full communion with the Catholic Church. She acknowledges all the baptized, including those in imperfect communion with the Catholic Church, to be members of Christ's Body. All the baptized have the right to be called Christian. All are brothers and sisters to the members of the Catholic Church.

TALK IT OVER
- How would you respond to someone who claims that to be a Christian, one must be a Catholic?
- How would you respond to someone who claims that Catholics are not really Christian?

OTHER COMMON TIES
There are a number of other shared beliefs and practices, in addition to the Sacrament of Baptism, bonding the Catholic Church and Anglicans (Episcopalians), Lutherans, Presbyterians and other non-Catholic Christians. These include:
- Confession of the faith of the Church, summarized in the Nicene Creed and Apostles' Creed.
- Belief in the Trinity.
- Beliefs about Jesus Christ derived from **Sacred Scripture** and **Sacred Tradition**. The Catholic Church teaches that "at the heart of [our faith] we find, in essence, a Person, the Person of Jesus of Nazareth, the only Son from the

Father" (CCC, no. 426). It is important to point out that although these ecclesial communities do not have the same understanding of Tradition as the Catholic Church, they increasingly believe in Tradition. (*New Catholic Encyclopedia*, Vol. 14, 2nd edition, 133 and 138.)

◉ Moral commitments rooted in the Decalogue, the Beatitudes and the Great Commandments. These include:
  – compassion for people in need, seeking justice rooted in charity (love) for people, and working for the common good of society;
  – promotion of the sacredness of human life; albeit, as we will see, with differing understandings of what is considered a human life that merits legal protection;
  – working for peace and reconciliation in a non-violent manner.

◉ Liturgical practices; for example:
  – the celebration of Sunday as the Lord's Day, the day of the Lord's Resurrection;
  – the use of a common cycle of scripture readings for worship celebrations.

REFLECT AND DISCUSS
◉ Where do you see Catholics working alongside other Christians? What are they doing? How are they giving witness to their shared faith?
◉ Have you worked alongside other Christians? What were you working for?

◉ How do you think those efforts contributed to fulfilling the prayer and desire of Jesus that "they may all be one" (John 17:21)?
◉ How might this work contribute to the good of the Church? Of the human family?

DIFFERENCES—OBSTACLES TO FULL COMMUNION
While the Catholic Church and other Christian traditions share, to one degree or another, many common ties, there are also many essential differences that separate the Catholic Church from these ecclesial communities. The teachings and practices of the Catholic Church that are not accepted by other Christian traditions include:

◉ The hierarchical structure of the visible Church on earth, of which the ordained ministry of bishops and priests is essential.
◉ The divinely given authority of the pope, the Vicar of Christ and successor of St. Peter the Apostle, and of the Magisterium.
◉ Sacred Scripture *and* Sacred Tradition flow from the "same divine well-spring." Together they form one Divine Revelation. They "come together in some fashion to form one thing, and move toward the same goal [see Vatican II, *Dei Verbum*, no. 9]. Each of them makes present and fruitful in the Church the mystery of Christ, who promised to remain with his own 'always, to the close of the age' [see Matthew 28:20]" (CCC, no. 80).

Sacred Scripture *and* Sacred Tradition flow from the "same divine well-spring"

- A **sacramental economy**, or **economy of salvation**, that includes the Seven **Sacraments**.
- Bishops are in the direct line of succession to the Apostles (**Apostolic Succession**) and have the authority to ordain other baptized men as bishops and priests and deacons.
- Marriage is ordained by God to be between *one man* and *one woman*. This is the foundation of the Catholic Church's teaching on marriage. Some ecclesial communities reject this teaching, which the Catholic Church teaches as divinely revealed, and permit same-sex marriages.
- A valid sacramental marriage is indissoluble. A civil divorce does not end a valid sacramental marriage.
- Abortion, the direct killing of an unborn person in the womb of a mother, is a moral evil and sin and is never justified.

The greatest hope for restoring full communion exists when there is (1) a visible continuity with the ancient Church (Apostolic Succession); (2) a shared understanding on interpreting revealed truth (Sacred Scripture read through the lens of Sacred Tradition) as already exists with the Orthodox Churches; and (3) the practice of the Seven Sacraments.

HOW WOULD YOU RESPOND?

- A non-Catholic Christian friend says, "The Catholic Church is just wrong about so many things. There is no evidence in the Bible to support so much of what the Catholic Church teaches."
- How can you affirm the teachings of the Catholic Church and respond respectfully *and* honestly to your friend's statement?
- Role-play examples.

In the next three sections of this chapter we will explore the relationship between the Catholic Church and the Lutheran, Anglican (Episcopalian), and Reformed Christian communities. As we do so, it is important to keep in mind that within and among each of these ecclesial communities there is a diversity of doctrinal, sacramental and liturgical, and moral teachings.

The Lutheran tradition

LUTHER PLACE MEMORIAL CHURCH, WASHINGTON DC

The Lutheran World Federation

The Lutheran World Federation is a "global communion of churches in the Lutheran tradition." It includes 72 million members in 145 member churches in 98 countries. The Evangelical Lutheran Church in America (ELCA), the largest Lutheran ecclesial community in the United States, is one of those members. The Lutheran Missouri Synod and the Wisconsin Evangelical Lutheran Synod, the next two largest Lutheran ecclesial communities in the United States, are not members.

OPENING REFLECTION

- ◉ What are the Lutheran congregations in your community?
- ◉ Do you have any Lutheran friends? Do you share your faith in Jesus Christ with them?
- ◉ How might that faith-sharing deepen a friendship? Deepen understanding of and respect for each other?

THE DESIRE FOR REFORMATION

The desire to reform itself was a hallmark of the fifteenth/sixteenth-century Church in the West. Some of the reformers, such as the Dutch writer Desiderius Erasmus (c. 1466–1536), remained loyal to the Church and sought to reform it from within. Other reformers, such as the English theologian John Wycliffe (1330–84), the French theologian and pastor John Calvin (1509-64), and the German Augustinian priest Martin Luther (1483–1546), and their followers chose to separate themselves from the Catholic Church.

Martin Luther and the Protestant Reformation: The roots of the Lutheran faith tradition are founded in Martin Luther's calling the Catholic Church to reform itself. Luther was a Catholic priest and a member of the Order of Saint Augustine, or Augustinians. He directed his reforms at the clergy and at certain teachings and practices of the Church, such as **indulgences**, which he claimed were abuses of authority and not found in Scripture and the apostolic Church. Luther nailed his Ninety-five Theses to the door of the cathedral church in Wittenberg, Germany on October 31, 1517 to promote his reform efforts. This event eventually became identified as the launching of the **Protestant Reformation**.

Luther's preaching and writings continued to set him at odds with the Church. In 1521 Pope Leo X declared Luther's erroneous teachings to be **heresy** and invited him to repent. When Luther refused, Leo excommunicated him. Kings and princes averse to the pope and church authority supported Luther and his efforts. This support

MICHELANGELO'S *LAST JUDGMENT* IS A COUNTER-REFORMATION MASTERPIECE

Justification

The term used to refer to the action of God by which we are freed from our sins and sanctified and renewed by the grace of God.
—*United States Catholic Catechism for Adults* (USCCA), 517

contributed to solidifying the division of the Church.

The Catholic Reformation, or Counter-Reformation: The Catholic Church responded to the Reformers with her own internal reformation. These efforts have been named the **Catholic Reformation**, or the **Counter-Reformation**. The Council of Trent (1545–63) was the center of the Catholic Reformation. The council reasserted the Church's doctrinal teachings that Luther had denied and it also decreed the reformation of practices, in areas such as the education of clergy, which Luther rightly identified as harmful to the Church.

REFLECT AND SHARE
- According to St. Augustine of Hippo, the Church is *semper reformanda* (always in need of reform, or always reforming).
- What wisdom is found in this teaching of St. Augustine?
- How do you see the Catholic Church today following that wisdom?

LUTHERAN CORE BELIEFS: SCRIPTURE, GRACE AND FAITH
Luther's teachings remain at the heart of Lutheranism today. They are summarized in *The Book of Concord: The Confessions of the Lutheran Church*, in which we read: "As Christians, the Lutheran faith is centered on the person and work of Jesus Christ. We believe that God is three in one, or triune. We believe that the Son of God became a human being to suffer and die for the sins of the world so that all who believe in Him will not perish but through His substitution for us on the cross we are given forgiveness and eternal life."

The three expressions *sola scriptura*, *sola gratia* and *sola fide* capture Luther's teachings on Scripture, grace and faith in the divine plan of **salvation**, and **justification** and the Christian's pursuit of holiness of life. While the Catholic Church agrees with Lutherans on many aspects of their understanding of Scripture, grace and faith, there are also many differences in understandings and teachings between the two traditions. The ongoing Catholic–Lutheran dialogue seeks to affirm those commonalities and to reconcile those differences.

Sola scriptura **(Only Scripture):** Lutherans, as Catholics do, believe in the centrality of Sacred Scripture to the Christian life. Luther's belief in the power of Sacred Scripture to transform lives urged him to translate the New Testament into German from the Latin Vulgate in 1522. He undertook this monumental task so as to give every Christian the opportunity to read the

Gospel. The term *sola scriptura*, in some sense, points to Luther's reverence for both Scripture and the power of Scripture.

Luther himself rarely used the term *sola scriptura*. The term, which means Scripture alone or only Scripture, can be interpreted to mean that Scripture alone is the authoritative source for the beliefs and practices of the Christian faith. Such an interpretation of Luther could lead one to draw the conclusion that Luther rejected the authority of Sacred Tradition. Indeed, this was and is the way many Protestants and some Lutherans understood and continue to understand Luther's teaching on the interpretation of Scripture.

The evidence, however, shows: "According to Luther, Holy Scripture does not oppose all tradition but only so-called human traditions" (Lutheran-Roman Catholic Commission on Unity, *From Conflict to Communion: Lutheran-Catholic Common Commemoration of the Reformation in 2017*, no. 200). Holy Scripture is the primary principle (*primum principium*) "on which all theological statements must directly or indirectly be grounded" (*From Conflict to Communion*, no. 196).

The Catholic Church at the Council of Trent responded to this doctrinal issue. The council taught that the teaching authority of the Church, the Magisterium, guides the authentic interpretation of Scripture. This truth is reaffirmed by the *Catechism of the Catholic Church*.

Sola gratia (Only grace): Luther experienced a deep sense of personal sinfulness. This spiritual experience moved him to assert that forgiveness and salvation are pure gifts of God. Only the grace of God through the redeeming work of Jesus Christ can save a person. The expression *sola gratia* summarizes this teaching of Luther.

Catholics and Lutherans confess: "By grace alone, in faith in Christ's saving work and not because of any merit on our part, we are accepted by God and receive the Holy Spirit, who renews our hearts while equipping and calling us to good works" (Catholic–Lutheran *Joint Declaration on the Doctrine of Justification*, no. 15).

Sola fide (Only faith): The Catholic Church teaches that faith and grace and good works are interconnected in the divine plan of salvation

MARTIN LUTHER AND THE PROTESTANT REFORMERS | BERLIN CATHEDRAL, GERMANY

and the pursuit of holiness of life. Luther taught that God saves through one's faith and trust in Jesus Christ *alone.* No good works a person performs can merit salvation and justification. This teaching is captured in the expression *sola fide.* While Luther did acknowledge that good works performed in cooperation with the grace of the Holy Spirit are essential to the Christian life, his belief that God saves through faith alone diminished the role of good works in the life of a Christian.

SCRIPTURE ACTIVITY

- Read and reflect on Romans 3:21–26 and James 2:14–26.
- Discuss: What do these New Testament passages reveal about grace and justification, faith and good works?

LET'S PROBE DEEPER: THE CATHOLIC DOCTRINE OF JUSTIFICATION

Here is a summary of the Catholic Church's teaching on merit and justification:

- Justification, or righteousness, is a free gift of God's love. It is the merciful and free act of God which takes away our sins. It is brought about by the grace of the Holy Spirit which has been merited or earned for us by the Passion of Christ and given to us in Baptism. This grace of the Holy Spirit makes us sharers in the life of the Holy Trinity. It is called habitual or sanctifying grace because it sanctifies us or restores us to a state of holiness.
- Merit usually refers to the right to compensation for what we have done. We cannot merit or earn this grace of justification and salvation on our own.
- God gives us the possibility of *acquiring merit* through our union with the love of Christ, who alone is the source of our merit before God.
- Moved by the grace of the Holy Spirit and joined to Christ, we can merit for ourselves and for others the graces needed for our sanctification (holiness of life) and for eternal life.
- All Christians must be governed by holiness, not by sin; holiness alone will lead to eternal life.

   —Based on *Compendium of the Catechism of the Catholic Church,* nos. 422–423, 425–428

TALK IT OVER

- Compare the observations you made on Romans 3:21–26 and James 2:14–26 with the

THE HOLY SPIRIT | CHURCH OF THE NATIVITY, JONAVA, LITHUANIA

Holy Communion is offered on a regular basis in a Lutheran church but it may not be offered every Sunday

LUTHERAN CHURCH IN RIDGEWAY, NORTH DAKOTA

summary of the Catholic doctrine in the "Let's Probe Deeper" above.

◉ Have you learned anything new or understood anything more clearly about the Catholic doctrine on grace and justification from the summary? Explain.

OVER TO YOU

◉ How are you responding to the Trinity's invitation to live in communion with God and the Church on earth and in heaven? What else might you do?

SEEKING FULL COMMUNION: COMMON TIES AND DIFFERENCES

Catholics and Lutherans celebrate their common ties and acknowledge their differences. Here are several key examples:

◉ **Worship**: The reading of Scripture and the preaching of the Gospel is the heart of Lutheran liturgy, which is also sometimes called the Divine Service. Holy Communion is offered on a regular basis but it may not be offered every Sunday. The Catholic celebration of Mass always includes both the proclamation of the Word of God *and* the celebration of the Eucharist.

◉ **Sacraments**: Catholics and Lutherans teach that Christ gave his Church sacraments. Lutheran teaching on the sacraments differs from Catholic teaching in respect of the number, the nature and the role of sacraments in the divine plan of salvation. For example:
 – The Catholic Church teaches that there are seven sacraments. Lutherans teach that Christ only gave his Church Baptism and Holy Communion (the Lord's Supper or Eucharist).
 – Lutherans and Catholics profess a belief in the Eucharist, or Lord's Supper, as indispensable for the life and building up of the Church. Catholics and Lutherans believe in the presence of Christ in the Eucharist. Lutherans, as Luther did, reject the doctrine of **transubstantiation**. On this issue the Roman Catholic–Lutheran dialogue has reached this agreed understanding: "Lutherans and Catholics can together affirm . . . 'In the Sacrament of the Lord's Supper Jesus Christ, true God and true man, is present wholly and entirely, in his Body and Blood, under the signs of bread and wine' (*The Eucharist: Final Report of the Joint Roman Catholic-Lutheran Commission*, 1978, no. 16). This

common statement affirms all the essential elements of faith in the eucharistic presence of Jesus Christ without adopting the conceptual terminology of transubstantiation" (*From Conflict to Communion*, no. 154). Lutheran traditions, such as the Evangelical Lutheran Church in America (ELCA), Lutheran Missouri Synod (LMS) and the Wisconsin Evangelical Lutheran Synod (WEL) in the United States, differ among themselves in their understanding and explanation of this key belief of Lutherans and Catholics.

– Holy Orders: Lutherans lack a sacrament of Holy Orders. Lutheran bishops are not in a direct line of succession from the Apostles; and Lutheran bishops do not sacramentally or validly ordain their bishops and ministers. Consequently, Lutherans do not have a valid celebration of the Eucharist. The Evangelical Lutheran Church in America (ELCA) also ordains women, a practice contrary to the doctrine of the Catholic Church.

⊙ **The sanctity of every human life**: Lutherans and the Catholic Church both teach that human life begins at the moment of conception. The ELCA, contrary to the teaching of the Catholic Church, allows direct abortion, however, as the last resort when the life of the mother is threatened, or when abnormalities in the development of the fetus pose a fatal threat to a newborn, or the pregnancy is the result of rape or incest.

⊙ **Marriage**: Catholics and Lutherans teach that divorce is contrary to God's original design and intention for marriage. Lutherans, however, permit divorce under certain circumstances, for example, in cases of adultery or where one spouse deserts the other. Lutherans also permit divorced persons to remarry in the Church. The Catholic Church, as you will recall, teaches that every valid sacramental marriage is indissoluble. Catholics in a valid sacramental marriage may remarry only after they have received a declaration of **annulment** of their marriage.

Lutheran teachings on same-sex marriage are diverse. The ELCA sanctions same-sex marriages. Other Lutherans prohibit same-sex marriages, as does the Catholic Church.

- What new insights into what unites and separates Catholics and Lutherans did the study of this section of the chapter give you?
- Share those insights as a class or with a partner.

THE LUTHERAN–ROMAN CATHOLIC DIALOGUE

The Catholic Church continues to be in ecumenical dialogue with Lutherans, both worldwide and in the United States. Representatives of the Roman Catholic Church in the United States and of the Evangelical Lutheran Church in America meet twice a year.

In 2010 the Lutheran–Catholic Dialogue issued the joint statement, "The Hope of Eternal Life." The Preface of this statement reiterates the importance of these dialogues: "We affirm as Lutherans and Catholics in the dialogue process a commitment to the goal of full communion, even as we recognize that further agreements are necessary before full, sacramental communion can be restored."

In October 2016, as we have already seen, the Lutheran–Roman Catholic Commission on Unity met in Sweden. The meeting took place at the beginning of a yearlong series of events leading up to the 500th anniversary of the Reformation and the 50th anniversary of dialogue between Lutherans and Catholics. At the conclusion of the meeting, the Lutheran–Roman Catholic Commission on Unity issued a joint declaration, *From Conflict to Communion: Lutheran-Catholic Common Commemoration of the Reformation in 2017*. The declaration concludes: "The ecumenical journey enables Lutherans and Catholics to appreciate together Martin Luther's insight into and spiritual experience of the gospel of the righteousness of God, which is also God's mercy" (no. 244). . . . "The beginnings of the Reformation will be rightly remembered when Lutherans and Catholics hear together the gospel of Jesus Christ and allow themselves to be called anew into community with the Lord" (no. 245).

It is important to remember once again that, while national dialogues are not authoritative statements of Catholic teaching, they do offer examples of the current state of ongoing discussions between Catholics and Lutherans.

TALK IT OVER
- Why is ecumenical dialogue vital to the Body of Christ, the Church?

WHAT ABOUT YOU PERSONALLY?
- How might you contribute to the Catholic–Lutheran search for unity?

How might you contribute to the Catholic–Lutheran search for unity?

The Anglican (Episcopalian) Communion

C.S. LEWIS—A FAITH-INSPIRED WRITER

C.S. Lewis (1898–1963) was an Irish novelist, poet and Christian apologist who was a faithful member of the Church of England. Lewis had this to say about his faith in Christ: "I believe in Christianity as I believe that the sun has risen: not only because I see it, but because by it I see everything else."

OPENING REFLECTION

⊙ Are you familiar with Lewis's series of fantasy novels *The Chronicles of Narnia*, the most famous of which is *The Lion, the Witch and the Wardrobe*? What truths about the Christian faith did you discover Lewis sharing through these novels?

⊙ What other novels or films have you read or seen that share the Christian faith?

The Anglican Communion

The word "Anglican" comes from the thirteenth-century Latin term *ecclesia anglicana,* which means "English Church." The members of the Anglican Communion are descendants from the Church of England. Some Anglicans identify themselves as Episcopalian. Episcopalians are in seventeen nations, including the United States of America. The Episcopal Church in the United States is a member of the Anglican Communion.

The Anglican Communion, or Anglican Episcopal ecclesial community, is a worldwide communion of independently governed members. There are 44 national and regional Anglican ecclesial communities, comprising 85 million people in over 165 countries. The Anglican Communion describes itself as a "fellowship, within the one holy catholic and apostolic church, . . . in communion with the see of Canterbury." It does not set teachings and practices for its members. Members of the Anglican Communion can differ one from the other in their teachings and practices, for example, in the practice of marrying same-sex couples.

THE ARCHBISHOP OF CANTERBURY, JUSTIN WELBY

MEDAL OF POPE CLEMENT VII

Pope Clement VII refused Henry VIII's request for an annulment and asserted the Church's teaching on the indissolubility of marriage

ORIGINS OF THE CHURCH OF ENGLAND

Missioners brought the Gospel to Britain, a province of the Roman Empire, no later than the third century. The writings of Tertullian (c. 155–c. 220) and other early Christian writers and the martyrdom of St. Alban around 304 attest to this fact. The beliefs, liturgy and hierarchical structure of the early Church in Britain were part of Western Christianity and under the authority of the pope. The established Christian community in seventh-century England was in communion with Rome. Missionaries had been sent to England by Pope Gregory the Great. Further, the name "Church of England" after the sixteenth century refers to a schismatic ecclesial community, which separated itself from the pope and the Catholic Church.

In the early stages of the Protestant Reformation King Henry VIII (1491–1547) found himself at odds with the authority of the pope. Henry, whom the pope had named "Defender of the Faith" because of his defense of the Church against the Lutheran reformers, requested that Pope Clement VII annul his four-year marriage to Catherine of Aragon. Catherine was unable to bear him a son as his heir to the throne.

The pope refused Henry's request and asserted the Church's teaching on the indissolubility of marriage. Henry eventually responded by declaring himself to be the Supreme Head of the Church of England, and the Archbishop of Canterbury to be its primary bishop. That separation remains today. The Church of England is the established religion of England, but Anglican churches elsewhere do not have any official status, even in the other countries of the British Commonwealth. The ruling monarch, the King or Queen of England, and the Archbishop of Canterbury remain the primary leaders of the Church of England, but have only symbolic significance for other Anglicans.

REFLECT AND DISCUSS

⊙ King Henry VIII challenged the allegiance of St. Thomas More, who was a high official in Henry's government, to the pope. More chose to remain faithful to the pope and the Catholic teaching on the indissolubility of marriage. More would neither publicly nor privately approve of Henry's divorce and remarriage. More's response has been immortalized in his words to the crowds who came to witness his execution, "I die the king's faithful servant, but God's first."

⊙ What can we learn from St. Thomas More when other Christians challenge our practice of the Catholic faith?

THE EPISCOPAL TRADITION

There are Episcopal ecclesial communities and parishes in the United States of America, such as the Episcopal Church in the United States of America, and in sixteen other nations. The

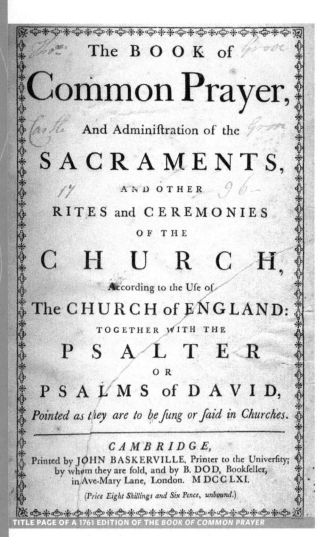

The BOOK of

Common Prayer,

And Adminiſtration of the

SACRAMENTS,

AND OTHER

RITES and CEREMONIES

OF THE

CHURCH,

According to the Uſe of

The CHURCH of ENGLAND:

TOGETHER WITH THE

PSALTER

OR

PSALMS of DAVID,

Pointed as they are to be ſung or ſaid in Churches.

CAMBRIDGE,

Printed by JOHN BASKERVILLE, Printer to the Univerſity;
by whom they are ſold, and by B. DOD, Bookſeller,
in Ave-Mary Lane, London. M DCC LXI.

(*Price Eight Shillings and Six Pence, unbound.*)

Episcopalians and other Anglicans around the world. The *Book of Common Prayer* contains an "Outline of the Faith," or catechism. This catechism is a brief summary and not a complete statement of Episcopal beliefs and practices.

REFLECT AND SHARE

⊙ Are there Anglican and Episcopal congregations in your community? Perhaps you know someone who identifies themselves as either Anglican or Episcopalian.

⊙ Share what you know about the beliefs and practices of these congregations.

ROMAN CATHOLIC–EPISCOPAL CONSULTATION

The Roman Catholic–Episcopal ecumenical dialogue or consultation in the United States is part of the worldwide consultation of the Catholic Church with the Anglican Communion. These consultations have taken place since 1965, the year that the Second Vatican Council closed. Over the years the consultations have produced joint statements on the Eucharist as sacrifice, authority in the Church, the purpose of the Church, Mary, grace and hope in Christ, the ordination of women, and a diversity of ethical/moral issues.

The "Mary: Grace and Hope in Christ" section of the 2004 Joint Statement of the Anglican–Roman Catholic International Commission (ARCIC) asserts the common tradition of both Anglicans and Catholics on the Blessed Virgin Mary "as the pattern of grace and hope . . . and as a figure of the Church . . . who is one with us in that vast community of love and prayer we call the communion of saints" (Preface by the Co-Chairmen, Joint Statement).

In particular, the Joint Statement finds much common ground regarding the Catholic doctrine of the Immaculate Conception of Mary and the Assumption of Mary, although most Anglicans do not believe that these teachings must be held as articles of faith.

Our Agreed Statement concerning the Blessed Virgin Mary as pattern of grace and hope is a powerful reflection of our efforts to seek out what we hold in common and celebrates

Episcopal Church in the United States is a descendant of the Church of England. It is the only Province of the Anglican Communion in the country, although there are some smaller groups of Anglicans who look to bishops from the Provinces of the Southern Hemisphere for pastoral support. The Episcopal Church in the United States of America became independent of the Church of England after the American Revolution, when its clergy and other leaders refused allegiance to the British monarch. Today, it is the largest member of the Anglican Communion in the United States of America.

The *Book of Common Prayer: And Administration of the Sacraments and Other Rites and Ceremonies of the Church*, which was first published in the sixteenth century, is the foundational written source of unity for important aspects of our common heritage. Mary, the mother of our Lord Jesus Christ, stands before us as an exemplar of faithful obedience, and her "Be it to me according to your word" is the grace-filled response each of us is called to make to God, both personally and communally, as the Church, the body of Christ. It is as figure of the Church, her arms uplifted in prayer and praise, her hands open in receptivity and availability to the outpouring of the Holy Spirit, that we are one with Mary as she magnifies the Lord. "Surely," Mary declares in her song recorded in the Gospel of Luke, "from this day all generations will call me blessed."

—Preface, *Mary: Grace and Hope*: The Seattle Statement, Feast of the Presentation, February 2, 2004

Again, it is important to remember that even though consultations and dialogues do not constitute official Catholic teaching, they offer signs of progress toward bringing about full communion with the Catholic Church.

SEEKING FULL COMMUNION: COMMON TIES AND DIFFERENCES

The Catholic Church and the Anglican (Episcopalian) Communion share many doctrines and practices. There are also serious differences that remain obstacles to the full communion of Episcopalians and other Anglicans with the Catholic Church. Here are examples of key commonalities and differences that are part of the ongoing consultations of the Catholic Church and the Episcopal Church in the United States:

⊙ **The Church**: In their Creeds, Catholics and Episcopalians profess the Church to be "one, holy, catholic and apostolic." The members of the Anglican (Episcopalian) Communion assert that their origin is in the apostolic Church. The understanding of "apostolic"

of the Anglican Communion differs from the teaching of the Catholic Church. "The Church is apostolic because she is founded on the apostles, in three ways: she was and remains built on 'the foundation of the Apostles' [see Ephesians 2:20 and Revelations 21:14], the witnesses chosen and sent on mission by Christ himself [see Matthew 28:16-20]; with the help of the Spirit dwelling in her, the Church keeps and hands on the teaching [see Acts of the Apostles 2:42], the 'good deposit,' the salutary words she has heard from the apostles (see 2 Timothy 1:13-14); she continues to be taught, sanctified, and guided by the apostles until Christ's return, through their successors in pastoral office: the college of bishops, 'assisted by priests, in union with the successor of Peter, the Church's supreme pastor' [see *Decree on the Church's Missionary Activity*, no. 5] " (CCC, no. 857). The Catholic Church teaches that the bishops of the Anglican Communions are not in direct historical line with the Apostles.

⊙ **Authority of the pope**: The Episcopal Church in America and the other members of the Anglican Communion reject the teaching that the pope "has been granted by God supreme, full, immediate, and universal power in the care of souls" (Vatican II, *Decree on the*

'THE ROCK OF THE EVER-STANDING ROMAN CATHOLIC CHURCH' | HENRY SCHILE

Pastoral Office of Bishops in the Church [*Christus Dominus*], no. 2).

⊙ **Worship and Creed**: Common worship, as contained in the *Book of Common Prayer*, is the unifying element of the Anglican (Episcopalian) Communion. "Although it subscribes to the historic Creeds (the Nicene Creed and the Apostles' Creed), . . . the Episcopal Church grants great latitude in interpretation of doctrine. It tends to stress less the confession of particular beliefs than the use of the *Book of Common Prayer* in public worship."

The structure and rites of Sunday worship celebrated at an Episcopal parish are very similar to the rites of the celebration of Mass. There are shared prayers, a confession of sins, proclamation of the Word of God, a homily, profession of the Creed, and a shared Eucharist. Contrary to Catholic discipline, all baptized persons are invited to receive Holy Communion.

⊙ **Sacraments**: Episcopalians and the other members of the Anglican Communion teach that only the Sacraments of Baptism and the Holy Eucharist have been given to the Church by Jesus Christ. While they celebrate other "sacramental" rites for Confirmation, Marriage, Ordination, Reconciliation of a

Penitent, Ministration to the Sick and at Time of Death, Episcopalians do not see these rites *as equal* to Baptism and Holy Eucharist.

   – **Eucharist**: Episcopalians teach that Jesus Christ is present in the Eucharist; but their understanding and teaching on the meaning of the mystery of Christ's presence differs from that of the Catholic Church. Episcopalians and other Anglicans have not reached a consensus regarding the dogmas of the Catholic Church on transubstantiation and the Real Presence of Christ in the Eucharist. While some Anglicans accept these teachings, many others explain this mystery of faith differently. They believe that the eucharistic bread and wine are an outward and visible *sign* of an inward and spiritual grace.

   – **Holy Orders**: The Catholic Church and the Anglican (Episcopalian) Communion are served by baptized men who have been "ordained." The Catholic Church does not recognize the "ordination" of the bishops and priests and deacons of the Anglican Communion to be valid. This is so, as we have seen, because bishops of the Anglican Communion do not share in Apostolic

RAPHAEL'S FRESCO *THE DISPUTATION OF THE HOLY SACRAMENT* IN THE VATICAN DEPICTS A DEBATE ON THE REAL PRESENCE

Succession. Also, if an Anglican priest converts to Catholicism, he is ordained by a bishop of the Catholic Church.

Some members of the Anglican Communion also ordain women as bishops, priests and deacons. Not all Episcopalian and other member churches of the Anglican Communion implement this practice. The Catholic Church teaches that ordination is reserved to baptized men.

– **Marriage**: The Anglican (Episcopalian) Communion recognizes that a sacramental marriage truly entered may die and the sacramental bond between a couple may be dissolved. This is contrary to the teaching of the Catholic Church, as we have seen, on the indissolubility of a valid sacramental marriage. As a consequence, it allows persons who divorce civilly to remarry in the church with the permission of the bishop upon the recommendation of the priest who provided the couple's premarital counseling.

The Episcopal Church also permits same-sex marriage. Not all Episcopalians agree with this teaching; some affirm, as the Catholic Church does, that in the divine plan of creation marriage is between one man and one woman. In response to the Episcopal Churches allowing same-sex marriage, Anglican leaders in 2016 temporarily suspended the United States Episcopal Church's full participation in the Anglican Communion. This included the suspension of its right to vote on doctrinal and polity matters (the latter concerning the governance of the Church) for a period of three years.

⊙ **Homosexuality**: The Catholic Church and the Anglican (Episcopalian) Communion respect the dignity of every person, including persons with homosexual and lesbian tendencies, as children of God. The Catholic Church makes a distinction between a person's dignity as a child of God and the behaviors of individuals. Based on the teachings of Sacred Scripture and Sacred Tradition, the Catholic Churches teaches that sexual intercourse and related sexual acts outside of marriage are grave moral evils.

⊙ **Marriage**: Sacred Scripture and the Sacred Tradition reveal that in the divine plan marriage is ordered to be between a man and a woman. Based on these truths the Catholic Church teaches that two persons of the same sex cannot enter a true and valid marriage—even when civil law permits them to marry. Some mainline Episcopalian groups, though not all, do not see marriage as being only between a man and a woman. Therefore, these Episcopalian communities both permit and welcome same-sex couples to marry in their churches, and their clergy to officiate at those marriages. The local Episcopalian bishop has the authority to implement or not to implement this polity in his diocese. The local congregation, with the approval of its bishop, in turn, may choose to implement or not to implement this polity. Some Episcopalian dioceses and congregations and other members of the Anglican Communion have chosen not to implement this polity.

⊙ **Abortion**: The Catholic Church and the Anglican Communion teach that every human life is a gift from God and is sacred from its inception until death. The Episcopal Church acknowledges that the direct abortion of an unborn child is a tragedy; but it also maintains, unlike the Catholic Church, that there may be circumstances that even necessitate the decision for a direct abortion where this loss of an unborn life is the greater good. It is to be noted that the Catholic Church teaches that it morally permissible for a pregnant woman to undergo surgery to correct a condition that threatens her life,

and as a consequence may *indirectly abort* the unborn child.

⊙ **Social justice**: Catholics and Episcopalians share a deep commitment to the work of social justice and building the Kingdom of God. Both Catholics and Episcopalians teach that grace inspires and Christian faith requires our good works.

COMPARE AND SHARE
⊙ Work with a partner.
⊙ Create a two-column chart to summarize both the common ties that foster unity and the differences that are obstacles to the full communion of Episcopal and other Anglican Christians with the Catholic Church. List the common ties in one column and the differences in the other column.
⊙ Share and discuss charts as a class.

OVER TO YOU
⊙ Has your study given you a clearer understanding of the beliefs and practices of the Catholic Church? Give some examples of Catholic beliefs and practices that are now clearer to you.
⊙ How can you join with Episcopal young people in working together to bring about the Kingdom of God? Give examples.

How can you join with Episcopal young people in working together to bring about the Kingdom of God?

Protestant Reformed Christianity

MR. ROGERS' NEIGHBORHOOD

Fred Rogers (1928–2003) is best known for his long-running television show, *Mr. Rogers' Neighborhood* (1968–2001). Rogers was an ordained Presbyterian minister whose faith informed the message of love of self and neighbor that he promoted on his television show. *Mr. Rogers' Neighborhood* modeled ways to be loving and caring to all our neighbors—all the people whom we encounter every day. Rogers summed his message up this way: "I believe that appreciation is a holy thing—that when we look for what's best in a person we happen to be with at the moment, we're doing what God does all the time. So in loving and appreciating our neighbor, we're participating in something sacred."

OPENING REFLECTION

- ◉ Compare Fred Rogers' statement on "appreciation" with the teaching of Jesus on the Great Commandments in Matthew 22:37–39.
- ◉ Why is loving one's neighbors a sign of appreciation, or gratitude, to God?
- ◉ What are some of the ways you live the Great Commandments in your daily life?

THE REFORMED FAMILY OF CHURCHES

Protestant Reformed Christianity includes many denominations. Presbyterians constitute the largest denomination in the Reformed family of churches in the United States of America. Other denominations in the United States that identify themselves as belonging to Protestant Reformed Christianity include: the Reformed Church in America, the Christian Reformed Church, the United Church of Christ, Congregationalists, the Christian Church (Disciples of Christ), the Church of Christ and the Dutch Reformed Church.

JOHN CALVIN AND "REFORMED" CHRISTIANITY

John Calvin (1509–64) was a French Protestant theologian and pastor who is considered the founder of Protestant Reformed Christianity. His teachings, known as Calvinism, are central to Protestant Reformed Christianity. Calvin believed that the Catholic Church had strayed from the Gospel in many of its doctrines and practices. He and his followers wanted *to purify* Christianity.

Calvin, even more so than Luther, emphasized *human sinfulness* and *the human incapacity* to contribute anything to one's own salvation (see Philippians 2:12). This opinion of Calvin gave birth to his erroneous interpretation of the New Testament teachings on predestination. (Check out Romans 8:15, 19; Ephesians 1:4–5, 9; 1 Thessalonians 5:1–11; 2 Timothy 1:9–10.)

The origin of Presbyterianism is rooted in the teachings and work of John Knox

JOHN KNOX | 19TH-CENTURY ENGRAVING

Calvinism spread rapidly through northern Europe—especially in Switzerland, the Netherlands, Germany and Scotland. Colonists from Scotland—as well as Dutch and German settlers—brought Protestant Reformed Christianity to the colonies.

PRESBYTERIAN CHRISTIANITY

Presbyterians are part of the Protestant Reformed Christian family. Their origin is rooted in the teachings and work of John Knox (1514–72). Knox was a Roman Catholic priest who left the Church and joined with Protestant Reformers in Scotland. Knox taught that the Mass was a form of idolatry. In 1560 the Scottish Parliament joined in Knox's efforts. It outlawed the celebration of Mass, rejected the pope's authority over the Church in Scotland, and began other wide-ranging changes. For example, worship was simplified and based on reading, preaching and singing from God's Word in Scripture.

The very name "Presbyterian" reflects a key tenet of Presbyterian belief and governance. The name "Presbyterian" has its roots in the Greek *presbyteros,* which can mean "elder." Local Presbyterian congregations are led by *elders* (not priests) who represent the community. This leadership puts into practice the teaching that all the baptized constitute the *one* "priesthood of all believers." There is no need for a ministerial, or ordained, priesthood that is essentially different from the priesthood shared in by all the baptized and that exercises authority over all the baptized.

The first Presbyterian Church was organized in America in the early 1700s in Philadelphia. Today there is a diversity of Presbyterian denominations in the United States. The Presbyterian Church (U.S.A.) and the Presbyterian Church in America (PCA, or PC) are the two main denominations. In 1973, the PCA separated itself from the Presbyterian Church (U.S.A.) because of disagreement over theological issues. The Reformed Presbyterian Church (RPC) and Orthodox Presbyterian Church (OPC) adhere more closely to Calvin's thought.

REFLECT, COMPARE AND SHARE

- Are you aware of Presbyterian or other Reformed congregations in your community?
- What do you know about the beliefs and practices of these congregations?
- Compare those beliefs and practices with the beliefs and practices of the Catholic Church.
- Share reflections as a class.

PREDESTINATION

The term "predestination" does not have the same meaning in the writings of John Calvin and other Reformers as it does in the teachings of the Catholic Church. First, let's take a look at Calvin. In his *Institutes of the Christian Religion* Calvin taught that God only offers the grace of salvation to a select few and not to all people. He based this view on his belief in the utter sinfulness and total depravity of our fallen human nature. Human nature and its faculties of free will and intellect have become so depraved by Original Sin that they are incapable of freely responding to God's offer of grace or to do good. This and other teachings of Calvin were refuted and declared by the Council of Trent to be contrary to the teaching of the Catholic Church.

The Catholic Church teaches that the essential goodness of our fallen human nature has not been destroyed as a consequence of Original Sin. Human nature and its faculties of free will and intellect have been *wounded*; but they are not totally depraved. God destined us to be his sons and daughters, and desires *all human beings* to become one with him in Christ, now and forever.

God always gives us the grace to live a holy life. The human person can choose whether to cooperate or not to cooperate with God's grace to grow in holiness of life and come to eternal life. The human person, however, can knowingly and freely choose to say or do what is gravely evil (mortal sin) over what is good. When we knowingly and freely make such a choice we are choosing to live separated from God for eternity. The Church names this eternal state of living "hell." The Catholic Church teaches: "God predestines no one to hell" (CCC, no. 1037).

No person is conceived or born destined to hell. Original Sin did not change the divinely given destiny of all humanity, namely, eternal life and communion with God. Original Sin did not take away or limit God's love for all people. God destined, or it is God's *unchanging will and desire*, that *all people* would live in communion and friendship with him now and eternally. It is in this context that the Catholic Church uses the term "predestination."

SCRIPTURE ACTIVITY

- ⊙ Work in small groups.
- ⊙ Read and reflect on these New Testament passages: Romans 8:28–30; Ephesians 1:4–5, 9–11; 1 Thessalonians 5:1–11; 2 Timothy 1:9–10.
- ⊙ Discuss: How do these passages contribute to and clarify your understanding of the New Testament's and the Catholic Church's teaching that God *destines* the salvation of all persons?

JOHN CALVIN | ENGRAVING BY KONRAD MEYER

FAITH WORD

Predestination

God desires and destines salvation and eternal life for all people. God destines and desires all people to become one with him in Christ, now and forever. "To God, all moments of time are present in their immediacy. When therefore he establishes his eternal plan of 'predestination,' he includes in it each person's free response to his grace" (CCC, no. 600).

⊙ Are all people basically good, some of whom knowingly and freely choose to sin? Or are some people just basically bad?

WHAT ABOUT YOU PERSONALLY?

⊙ Is the Catholic Church's teaching that God created you and all people with a divine destiny, and God gives you the grace to live in communion with him now and forever, a source of hope for you as you struggle for holiness of life?

COMMON TIES AND DIFFERENCES

The Presbyterian *Book of Order: The Constitution of the Presbyterian Church (U.S.A.)* contains its beliefs, practices, worship rites and disciplines. Several elements are unifying agents and others are obstacles to full communion of Presbyterians and other members of the Protestant Reformed family of churches with the Catholic Church. We have already explored predestination. Other common ties and differences include:

⊙ **Baptism**: Representatives of the United States Conference of Catholic Bishops and four Reformed Christian denominations signed an agreement that a valid Baptism includes flowing water and the use of the Trinitarian formula. "The agreement affirmed that all of the churches involved recognize the validity of each other's baptisms" (*www.usccb.org*). The hope was expressed that this would be a model for similar agreements.

⊙ **Church**: The Catholic–Reformed dialogue is currently focusing on the nature and meaning of the Church. Reformed Christianity has no "Magisterium" or centralized governing authority and does not accept the teaching of the Catholic Church on the teaching, sanctifying and governing office of the bishops and their co-workers, the priests, in the Church.

There is no universal teaching and governing authority in the Presbyterian ecclesial communities. The Presbyterian Church (U.S.A.), as do all Presbyterians, utilizes a system of elders and elected councils to govern. Each local Presbyterian congregation is governed by a council that guides and makes decisions, such as the hiring of its minister. Each congregation belongs to a presbytery to which it sends elected representatives and its ministers. Presbyteries meet together in synods. These synods send elected representatives to the general assembly of the denomination. The

Catholic–Reformed Dialogue and Consultations

In 1965 four denominations of the Reformed family of churches and representatives of the National Conference of Catholic Bishops (now the United States Conference of Catholic Bishops) launched an official conversation in the United States. The Presbyterian denominations included the United Presbyterian Church (U.S.A.), the Presbyterian Church (U.S.), the Reformed Church in America and the United Church of Christ. Since then other members of the Reformed family, such as the Cumberland Presbyterian Church, the Christian Reformed Church and the Hungarian Reformed Church, have joined in the process.

—*United States Conference of Catholic Bishops (USCCB) website, www.usccb.org*

PRESBYTERIAN CHURCH, BAY OF FUNDY, MAINE

Jesus began his public ministry declaring, "[R]epent, and believe in the good news" (Mark 1:15)

JESUS CALLS THE FISHERMEN | WOODCUT, C. 16TH CENTURY

presbytery, synod and general assembly have no binding authority over the local congregations.

⊙ **Sacramental economy and practice**: Catholics and Presbyterians agree that Jesus Christ gave us sacraments and that the sacraments connect us to Christ. There is ongoing dialogue on how we encounter Christ and his saving grace in the sacraments.

Presbyterians, as other Protestants, limit the number of sacraments Christ gave his Church to two, namely, Baptism and the Lord's Supper. Current Presbyterian ecclesial communities uphold the relationship between Baptism and Communion by asserting that the Lord's Supper is a sacramental meal to be shared by baptized believers. The Presbyterian understanding of "sacramental meal" differs in essence from the teaching of the Catholic Church.

The Presbyterian *Book of Order* contains other rituals for the celebration of marriage, ordination and others. These rituals are not considered to rise to the level of a sacrament in the same way as Baptism and the Lord's Supper.

⊙ **Sanctity of life**: Catholics and Reformed Christians believe in the dignity of human life. Presbyterians, however, allow for the abortion of an unborn human life in certain circumstances when the choice is made with an informed conscience as they understand the meaning of an "informed conscience." The Catholic Church holds that a properly formed conscience will know that direct abortion of a human life is an intrinsic evil; it is the unjust killing of an innocent human being and is never permissible. (St. Pope John Paul II, Encyclical Letter *The Gospel of Life* [*Evangelium Vitae*], no. 58.)

REFLECT AND DISCUSS

⊙ John Calvin and his followers called on the Church to "purify" itself.
⊙ How do the Magisterium and the sacraments guide and enable the Catholic Church to engage in an authentic "purification"?

JOURNAL EXERCISE

⊙ "Repent" is another way of saying "purify oneself." Jesus began his public ministry declaring, "[R]epent, and believe in the good news" (Mark 1:15).
⊙ What is the connection between repentance and purification?
⊙ How do you go about the work of purification and repentance?

REVIEW AND SHARE WHAT YOU HAVE LEARNED

Review what you have learned in this chapter about the beliefs and practices of Lutherans, Anglicans (Episcopalians), and Reformed Christians. Share the teachings of the Catholic Church that you have learned in this chapter on these statements:

- The Sacrament of Baptism constitutes the foundation of communion among all Christians.
- The Catholic Church shares common ties with the Lutheran tradition.
- The Catholic Church shares common ties with the Anglican (Episcopalian) tradition.
- The Catholic Church shares common ties with the Reformed Christian tradition.
- There are beliefs and practices that are obstacles to the full communion of the Lutheran, Anglican (Episcopalian) and Reformed Christian ecclesial communities with the Roman Catholic Church.
- The Catholic Church is in ecumenical dialogue with each of the Lutheran, Anglican (Episcopalian) and Reformed Christian ecclesial communities.

DRAFTING THE DECLARATION OF INDEPENDENCE | ALONZO CHAPPEL

OVER TO YOU

- Name some of the key commonalities and fundamental differences between the Lutheran, Anglican (Episcopalian) and Reformed Christians traditions and the Catholic Church.
- What new insights and understanding did you gain about the beliefs and practices of the Lutheran, Anglican (Episcopalian) and Reformed Christian traditions from your study of this chapter?

WORKING FOR THE KINGDOM OF GOD

All Christians are called to work together for the establishment of justice in the world. Catholics, Episcopalians, Lutherans and Presbyterians often collaborate on a variety of justice issues. For example, Catholics will band together with other Christians to serve homeless people in their area. Where one parish or congregation might not have enough resources to help, Christians in partnership can and do make a real difference. Together, they encounter Christ when they work to feed the hungry, to give drink to the thirsty, to welcome the stranger (immigrant), to clothe the naked and to care for the sick. Together, they will hear the fulfillment of the promise of Jesus, "Come, you that are blessed by my Father, inherit the kingdom prepared for you from the foundation of the world" (Matthew 25:34b). Dietrich Bonhoeffer took this teaching of Jesus very seriously and it cost him his life.

Culture Note

The signatories of the Declaration of Independence included patriots from major Christian denominations. Charles Carroll was the only Catholic signatory; thirty-two were Episcopalian, including Thomas Jefferson and Benjamin Franklin; twelve were Presbyterian. While there were no Lutherans among the signatories, three Lutherans participated in the Constitutional Convention.

Dietrich Bonhoeffer, Lutheran pastor and martyr for his faith in Christ

Dietrich Bonhoeffer (1906–45) was a most courageous German Lutheran theologian and pastor. He lived in Germany during the Nazi regime and worked with other Christians to prevent the atrocities being committed by the Nazis.

Bonhoeffer was a founding member of the Confessing Church. This was an association of Christian denominations in Nazi Germany that opposed Nazi efforts to co-opt the churches to support the killing of Jews and others whom they deemed socially undesirable. In 1943 Bonhoeffer was arrested by the Nazis and sent to a concentration camp. He was executed in 1945, just two weeks before the camp was liberated.

Bonhoeffer saw the Gospel as an offer of "costly grace" and a call to a profound discipleship. In his classic book, *The Cost of Discipleship*, Bonhoeffer drew a distinction between "cheap" and "costly" grace. Cheap grace is "grace without discipleship, grace without the cross, grace without Jesus Christ."

Costly grace, on the other hand, "confronts us as a gracious call to follow Jesus. It comes as a word of forgiveness to the broken spirit and the contrite heart. Grace is costly because it compels [us] to submit to the yoke of Christ and follow him; it is grace because Jesus says: 'My yoke is easy and my burden is light.'"

OVER TO YOU

⊙ Make a list of what you consider to be the "costs" of discipleship for you.
⊙ What do you think of Bonhoeffer's distinction between *cheap grace* and *costly grace*?
⊙ How might you incorporate his ideas into your own life–faith–life journey and story?

JUDGE AND DECIDE

⊙ How can the witness of the many faithful Episcopalians, Lutherans, Presbyterians and other Reformed Christians inspire you to live your Catholic faith?
⊙ What might you do to encourage more collaboration, appreciation and friendship between your school, parish and these Christian denominations in your area?

SHARE FAITH WITH FAMILY AND FRIENDS

Members of Protestant communities meet regularly to read and study the Bible.

⊙ How can you and your family incorporate regular Bible study into your life together?
⊙ How can you gather with friends to read and study the Bible?
⊙ What might regular Bible study contribute to your family life? To your friendships?

[A]ll have sinned and fall short of the glory of God; they are now justified by his grace as a gift, through the redemption that is in Christ Jesus.

ROMANS 3:23–24

All pray the Sign of the Cross together.

Opening Prayer

LEADER

O God, who have united many nations in
confessing your name,
grant us we pray,
the grace to will and to do what you command,
that the people called to your Kingdom
may be one in the faith of their hearts
and the homage of their deeds.
Through our Lord Jesus Christ, your Son,
who lives and reigns with you in the unity of the
   Holy Spirit,
one God, for ever and ever.

RESPONSE

Amen.

> —*The Roman Missal*, Masses and Prayers for
> Various Needs and Occasions, 18B: For the Unity
> of Christians, Collect

Proclamation of the Word

READER

A reading from the Old Testament Book of
Zechariah.
Proclaim Zechariah 8:20–23.
The word of the Lord.

ALL

Thanks be to God.

Psalm Response

ALL

It was said among the nations,
   "The Lord has done great things for them."

SIDE A

When the LORD restored the fortunes of Zion,
   we were like those who dream.

SIDE B

Then our mouth was filled with laughter,
   and our tongue with shouts of joy.

SIDE A

then it was said among the nations,
   "The Lord has done great things for them."

SIDE B

The Lord has done great things for us,
   and we rejoiced.

SIDE A

Restore our fortunes, O LORD,
   like the watercourses in the Negeb.

SIDE B

May those who sow in tears,
   reap with shouts of joy.

SIDE A

Those who go out weeping,
   bearing the seed for sowing,

SIDE B

shall come home with shouts of joy,
   carrying their sheaves.

ALL

It was said among the nations,
   "The Lord has done great things for them."

READER

A reading from the holy Gospel according to John.

ALL

Glory to you, O Lord.

READER

Proclaim John 17:11, 20–24.
The Gospel of the Lord.

ALL

Praise to you, Lord Jesus Christ.

*All reflect on and apply the readings to their
participation in the Church's work of ecumenism.*

LEADER

Let us join in praying the prayer Jesus taught all
his disciples to pray.

All pray the Lord's Prayer together.

Concluding Prayer

LEADER

Almighty ever-living God,
who gather what is scattered
and keep together what you have gathered,
look kindly on the flock of your Son,
that those whom Baptism has consecrated
may be joined together by integrity of faith
and united in the bond of charity.

Through our Lord Jesus Christ, your Son,
who lives and reigns with you in the unity of the
    Holy Spirit,
one God, for ever and ever.

RESPONSE

Amen.

—*The Roman Missal*, Liturgy for *Friday of
the Passion of the Lord [Good Friday]*, Solemn
Intercession V: For the Unity of Christians

THE BAPTISM OF JESUS | JAMES TISSOT

CHAPTER 6

The Methodist, Baptist and Congregationalist Traditions

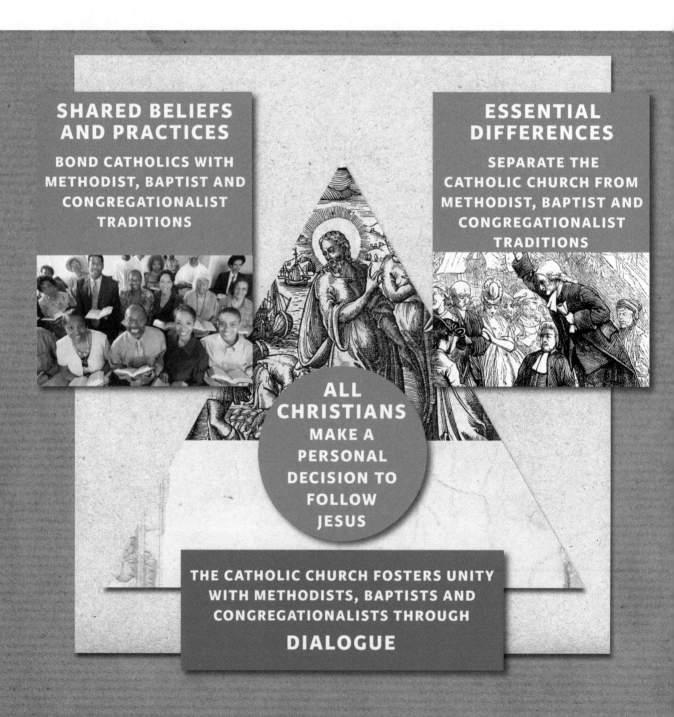

SHARED BELIEFS AND PRACTICES

BOND CATHOLICS WITH METHODIST, BAPTIST AND CONGREGATIONALIST TRADITIONS

ESSENTIAL DIFFERENCES

SEPARATE THE CATHOLIC CHURCH FROM METHODIST, BAPTIST AND CONGREGATIONALIST TRADITIONS

ALL CHRISTIANS MAKE A PERSONAL DECISION TO FOLLOW JESUS

THE CATHOLIC CHURCH FOSTERS UNITY WITH METHODISTS, BAPTISTS AND CONGREGATIONALISTS THROUGH **DIALOGUE**

THE PROTESTANT REFORMATION GAVE BIRTH TO several Christian denominations whose founders desired further reforms in the Church of England. These diverse traditions include the Methodist, Baptist and Congregationalist traditions, which collectively represent more than 20 percent of Protestants in the United States of America. In this chapter we examine the origins, beliefs and practices of those traditions and their common ties with and differences from the Catholic Church.

REFORM IN THE CATHOLIC CHURCH BOTH *PRESERVES* THE ESSENTIALS OF THE FAITH AND *ADAPTS* THE FAITH TO THE "SIGNS OF THE TIMES"

Faith Focus: These teachings of the Catholic Church are the primary focus of the doctrinal content presented in this chapter:

- The Church founded by Jesus Christ is a worldwide hierarchical society that is governed by the pope, the Bishop of Rome, and the bishops in communion with him.
- The divine plan of salvation is being accomplished through the Church, the Body of Christ.
- Ecclesial communities separated from the Catholic Church do not celebrate the Eucharist in its fullness, particularly because they do not have validly ordained ministers.
- Only a baptized man may validly receive the Sacrament of Holy Orders.
- Marriage by its very nature is ordered to be between a man and a woman. Remarriage of a person who is validly married is contrary to "the law and plan of God" (*Catechism of the Catholic Church*, no. 1665).
- The life of every person is sacred, from the moment of conception to natural death.

Discipleship Formation: As a result of studying this chapter and discovering the meaning of the faith of the Catholic Church for your life, you should be better able to:

- understand and articulate some of the commonalities between the Catholic Church and the Methodist, Baptist and Congregationalist traditions;
- understand and articulate some of the obstacles to communion between the Catholic Church and the Methodist, Baptist and Congregationalist traditions;
- discover and integrate true and authentic dialogue into your relationships with non-Catholic Christians.

Scripture References: These scripture references are quoted or referred to in this chapter:
OLD TESTAMENT: Jeremiah 8:18–22
NEW TESTAMENT: Matthew 16:13–20, 28:19; **Luke** 11:28; **John** 8:1–11, 21:15–17; **Acts of the Apostles** 16:13–15 and 26–33, 18:7-8, 28:19; **1 Corinthians** 1:16

Faith Glossary: Familiarize yourself with or recall the meaning of these key terms. Definitions are found in the Glossary: **biblical fundamentalism, economy of salvation, faith, grace, hierarchy, holiness, inerrancy, justification, Magisterium, obedience of faith, predestination, Real Presence, salvation, senses of Scripture, transubstantiation**

Faith Word: obedience of faith
Learn by Heart: Acts of the Apostles 16:31
Learn by Example: Rosa Parks

Why might reform be either unifying or divisive?

OPENING REFLECTION

⊙ How many Protestant friends or neighbors do you have?
  - Can you name the churches they attend?
  - How many different Protestant denominations do they represent?
⊙ What other Protestant denominations are in your community?

THE ONGOING REFORMATION OF PROTESTANTISM

The history of Protestantism is a story of ongoing reform and fragmentation. It is estimated that there are more than 30,000 Protestant denominations in the world today.

In the United States of America, Protestants make up over 51 percent of the Christian population. This population consists of hundreds of different denominations. These denominations are marked by great diversity and internal tension. At the heart of this tension are the efforts within each community to *preserve* the traditions of the faith community and, simultaneously, to *reform* doctrines and practices in keeping with contemporary insights and opinions.

REFORM IN THE CATHOLIC CHURCH

The Catholic Church has a long history of reform and change. In an address to Italian Catholics in Florence, Italy, in 2015, Pope Francis spoke of the openness of the Catholic Church to reform and change. The Pope said, in part, "Let it be a Church that is free and open to the challenges of the present, never on the defensive for fear of losing something."

Reform in the Church both *preserves* the essentials of the faith of the Church, the Tradition of the Church, and, simultaneously, under the guidance of the Holy Spirit, *adapts* the faith to the "signs of the times." In the words of Pope Francis, it "does not auction off" the faith of the Church.

Reform in the Catholic Church takes place under the watchful eye of the **Magisterium**. The Magisterium is the living teaching office of the Catholic Church. It has the divine authority to interpret authentically the Word of God. The Magisterium teaches only what is handed on and it exercises its office and authority in union with, and not above, the whole Church. It passes on the Word of God authoritatively and demands the **obedience of faith**. Reform in the Catholic Church is ordered to give clarity to our Catholic identity and helps us to proclaim the Gospel in a way that makes it easier for people to understand.

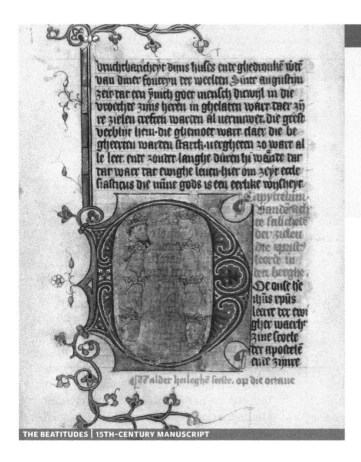

THE BEATITUDES | 15TH-CENTURY MANUSCRIPT

FAITH WORD

Obedience of Faith

Faith is hearing the Word of God and resolving to obey what God is asking of us. Jesus said, "Blessed are those who hear the word of God and observe it" (Luke 11:28).

—*United States Catholic Catechism for Adults* (USCCA), 521–22

REFLECT AND SHARE

◉ Why does both preserving *and* adapting the faith of the Church promote valuable reform within the Church?

◉ In what ways can reform efforts within the Catholic Church strengthen the identity and mission of the Church?

◉ Share your responses as a class

LACK OF AUTHORITY LEADS TO DIVISION AND FRAGMENTATION

The reforms of the Church carried out during the Protestant Reformation were based on the three teachings that are named *sola scriptura* (Scripture alone), *sola gratia* (grace alone) and *sola fide* (faith alone). Protestant Reformers sought to restore doctrines and practices within the Catholic Church that they judged had no basis in Sacred Scripture and were the result of the Church's misuse of its authority. Recall for a moment what you learned about *sola scriptura* in the previous chapter.

The many Protestant denominations to which the Reformation gave rise had no recognized central authority. Different reformers and their followers, as we have seen, interpreted *sola scriptura* in a variety of ways. This lack of an agreed unifying authority led to continuing fragmentation among the reformers.

REFLECT, ANALYZE AND SHARE

◉ What happens in an organization when there is no authentic and accepted unifying authority?

◉ What problems can arise within Christianity when interpretations of Sacred Scripture that are contrary to one another are presented as authentic?

◉ How does the authority of the pope and bishops within the Catholic Church contribute to the unity of the Church?

◉ Share reflections as a class.

The Methodist tradition

MOTHER'S DAY

Anna Jarvis (1864–1948), a Methodist, was born in Webster, Virginia and taught Sunday School for many years. Inspired by her faith, Jarvis lobbied businesses and the Government to establish a day to honor mothers for their contributions to families and society. Her efforts led to the celebration of the first Mother's Day in 1908. President Woodrow Wilson proclaimed Mother's Day a national holiday in 1914.

OPENING REFLECTION

⊙ Do you know anyone who "stands out" for you as an example of a person whose faith in Christ moves them to make a difference in the lives of others?

⊙ How might Anna Jarvis' example inspire you to take action on behalf of others? In what areas might you be inspired to take action?

JOHN WESLEY AND THE ORIGINS OF METHODISM

There are more than fourteen million Methodists and other Wesleyan bodies worldwide. The largest of these is the United Methodist Church (UMC). The United Methodist Church has members in more than 125 countries, with seven million members in the United States of America. In our brief examination of Methodism we will focus on the beliefs and practices of the United Methodist Church, which has been in dialogue with the Catholic Church in the United States of America since 1966.

Descendants from the Church of England

⊙ Methodists; Holiness Churches; Assemblies of God; Pentecostal Churches
⊙ Baptists; Church of God in Christ
⊙ Congregationalists; Quakers; United Church of Christ

As with the Lutheran, Anglican (Episcopalian) and Reformed Christian traditions, the Methodist, Baptist and Congregationalist traditions do not share in Apostolic Succession and thus are designated as ecclesial communities and not "churches," as the Catholic Church understands the meaning of "Church." When engaging in dialogue, Catholic participants use these bodies' formal titles, for example, the United Methodist Church, as a courtesy and to show respect for their fellow participants.

THE CHURCH OF ENGLAND DATES TO THE REIGN OF HENRY VIII

FOUNDERS OF METHODISM, BROTHERS JOHN AND CHARLES WESLEY, PREACHING IN BRISTOL, ENGLAND

Origins of Methodism: Methodism has its roots in the efforts of John Wesley (1703–91) and his brother Charles Wesley (1707–88) to reform the Church of England. The Wesley brothers were priests of the Church of England. They did not set out to create a separate Church from the Church of England; in fact, John and Charles Wesley remained members and priests of the Church of England throughout their lives.

The initial reform efforts of the Wesley brothers led to the establishment of Christian fellowship groups, which became known as United Societies. The brothers established these societies at Oxford University to help members of the Church of England enrich their understanding and living of their Christian faith in a *methodical* and systematic way. This "method" included the frequent reception of Holy Communion, disciplined study and prayer, and helping the poor and others in need. Members of the United Societies were eventually named "Methodists."

Methodism as a *distinct reform movement* within the Church of England began in 1738. On May 24, 1738 John Wesley attended a service of the Moravian Church of the Brethren at Aldersgate Street in London at the invitation of George Whitefield, an Anglican priest and evangelistic, charismatic preacher. During the service Wesley experienced an inner transformation. He joined with Whitefield in preaching a message of conversion and holiness of life. Methodism spread and eventually became its own separate religion in 1744.

Methodism in America: From his reading of the New Testament, Wesley believed that priests, and not only bishops, had the power to authorize men to preach the Gospel. Seeing the need for a more widespread preaching of the Gospel in England, Wesley appointed lay preachers to support the preaching efforts of Anglican priests. This belief and practice would eventually lead Methodism out of the Anglican Church. John Wesley himself, however, would die an Anglican.

THE FIRST METHODIST CHURCH IN THE USA, BUILT IN 1768 IN NEW YORK

This same commitment to evangelistic preaching kindled Wesley's desire to preach Christ in the colonies. He himself had undertaken this work in 1735 but failed and returned to England. Wesley continued to desire to preach Christ in America. To fulfill that desire he ordained two men who arrived in America in 1760. In 1777 Wesley named Thomas Coke superintendent to oversee the Methodist mission in North America. Ten years later Coke would become the first Methodist bishop in America.

Lay preachers travelled throughout the new nation preaching enthusiastic evangelical sermons. They often preached in fields and town squares or in tents. They urged their listeners to follow the "method" of Jesus. These charismatic preachers moved large numbers of people to commit themselves to live the Gospel as Methodists.

Lay preachers remain a characteristic of Methodism today. Some lay preachers today who receive the required education and training are also authorized by their bishop to serve as lay pastors. The ministry of lay pastors, as named in the Book of Discipline, includes the performance of the duties of Methodist elders, or ordained ministers. This includes the authority to preside over worship, including Holy Communion.

BELIEFS AND PRACTICES OF UNITED METHODISTS

The *Book of Discipline* of the United Methodist Church is the official agreed-upon statement of the beliefs and practices of United Methodists. The content of the *Book of Discipline* is neither infallible nor in any way sacrosanct for United Methodists. United Methodists can disagree on the interpretation of the content in the *Book of Discipline*. Elements in the *Book of Discipline* are reviewed, discussed and can by revised by a majority vote of the delegates to the General, or Quadrennial, Conference, the central governing authority of the United Methodist Church; the delegates are made up of an equal number of clergy and lay faithful.

Some beliefs and practices of the United Methodist Church share commonalities with beliefs and practices of Catholicism. Other beliefs and practices are obstacles to full communion between Catholics and Methodists. These commonalities and differences are the focus of the ongoing Catholic–Methodist dialogue that officially began in 1967. In the document *Methodist–Catholic Dialogues: Thirty Years of Mission and Witness* (United States Catholic Conference, copyright 2001), we read:

As Roman Catholics and as Methodists we live from the same Gospel, the apostolic message of God's saving acts in Jesus Christ, and we share the same faith. This faith is rooted in the Scriptures, which are the common ground of our preaching and teaching as Christian churches. It is summarized by the creeds of the early church, especially the Apostles' Creed and the Nicene Creed, which we confess regularly in our worship.

—*Methodist and Catholic Dialogues*, page 16

Creeds: Methodism acknowledges the importance of the creedal statements of Nicaea and Chalcedon in helping to "preserve the integrity of the church's witness, set boundaries for acceptable Christian doctrine, and proclaim the basic elements of the enduring Christian message. These statements of faith, along with the Apostles' Creed, contain the most prominent features of our ecumenical heritage" (*The Book of Discipline of the United Methodist Church*, copyright 2016).

God, the Holy Trinity: United Methodists believe, as the Church professes in the Creeds, that God has revealed himself in Jesus Christ to be a Triune God, who is God the Father, God the Son and God the Holy Spirit.

- God is the Father and Creator; he remains in history caring for his creation and working to bring about the Kingdom of God.
- The Son of God became incarnate in Jesus Christ. Jesus Christ is truly God and truly man; he is the only begotten Son of the Father, born of the Virgin Mary by the power of the Holy Spirit. He is the eternal Savior and Mediator by whom all people will be judged.
- The Holy Spirit proceeds from and is one being with the Father and the Son. He is the Comforter and Sustainer. The Holy Spirit empowers the faithful with his grace and guides them into all truth and holiness of life.

Sacred Scripture: United Methodists believe that Sacred Scripture is the divinely revealed Word of God and is the authority "in matters of faith" (*The Book of Discipline of the United Methodist Church*). The faithful come to know the truth of Scripture for their life through the writings of the Fathers of the Church, the early creeds, the writings of the Reformers and contemporary spiritual writers, through personal and communal experiences, and human reason. There is no divinely given teaching office that has the authority to interpret the Word of God in either its written or spoken form.

United Methodists believe that Sacred Scripture is the authority "in matters of faith"

Church: United Methodists profess "the essential oneness of the church in Christ Jesus. . . . Our unity is affirmed in the historic creeds as we confess one holy catholic and apostolic church" (*The Book of Discipline of the United Methodist Church*, copyright 2016). The Church is the community of all true believers under the lordship of Jesus Christ. Through Baptism a person is incorporated into the Church, becomes an adopted child of God and receives the transforming grace of the Holy Spirit.

There is no single person who is the universal head of or who has authority over the United Methodist Church. The General, or Quadrennial, Conference is the primary and central governing authority of the United Methodist Church. Ordained elders and lay persons elected by their Annual Conferences (Annual Conferences are similar to dioceses in the Catholic Church) or other jurisdictions are the decision-makers for the United Methodist Church. Decisions on doctrine and policy are made democratically by vote.

Bishops of the United Methodist Church are elected, appointed and ordained by other Methodist bishops. They participate in the

General Conference as non-voting members. They have the responsibility to implement the decisions of the General Conference and appoint pastors in the areas under their jurisdiction. Bishops in one jurisdiction may differ in their interpretation and implementation of Methodist polity.

LET'S PROBE DEEPER

- ⊙ Review the summary of the beliefs and practices of the United Methodist Church in relation to God, Scripture and the Church.
- ⊙ What have you learned that helps to clarify or has given you a new understanding of Methodism? Of Methodism's relationship to Catholicism?
- ⊙ Share small group discussions as a class.

Divine worship and sacraments: The proclamation of Scripture and preaching are part of every Methodist worship service. The celebration of the Lord's Supper (Eucharist, or Holy Communion) is not. This practice has its roots in the origins of Methodism in America, when ordained clergy were few in number and lay pastors and lay preachers were the primary Methodist ministers.

United Methodists accept only Baptism and the Lord's Supper as sacraments "ordained by Christ." Methodists believe that "the sacraments are symbols and pledges of the Christian's profession and God's love for us" (*The Book of Discipline of the United Methodist Church*, Article VI). Methodist teachings on the sacraments and

Celebration of the Eucharist (or the Lord's Supper) is not a part of every Methodist worship service

Some members of the United Methodist Church support same-sex marriages and seek to revise its *Book of Discipline*

A STOCK PHOTO OF THE METHODIST CENTRAL HALL IN CENTRAL LONDON WITH RAINBOW FLAG. PHOTOGRAPH TAKEN OTHEA ANOTROS DESIGN, LONDON, ENGLAND

their role in the **economy of salvation** differ substantially from the teachings of the Catholic Church. Here are several key differences:

⊙ **Lord's Supper:** For Methodists, the Lord's Supper is a *representation* of the redemption of humankind. Methodism does not teach, as the Catholic Church does, that the liturgical celebration of the Lord's Supper, or Eucharist, is the memorial of Christ's Passover which *makes present again* the one sacrifice of Christ. Methodists truly believe in the mystery of Jesus Christ's presence in Holy Communion but their understanding of this mystery of the Lord's presence does not include the teaching that the bread and wine truly and really become the Body and the Blood of Christ, as taught by the Catholic doctrine of **transubstantiation**.

⊙ **Holy Orders:** The bishops of the Methodist ecclesial communities are also not in direct historical line of succession from the Apostles. They do not share in the authority of validly ordained bishops to ordain a baptized man to the priesthood or diaconate, or to celebrate the Sacrament of the Eucharist. Methodists, contrary to the teaching and practice of the Catholic Church, "ordain" both men and women as bishops and elders and deacons.

Methodists, contrary to tradition, also permit deacons and non-ordained lay pastors to preside over the celebration of the Lord's Supper.

⊙ **Christian Marriage:** The *Book of Discipline of the United Methodist Church* teaches that marriage is ordained by God to be a lifelong faithful commitment between one man and one woman. This teaching of the *Book of Discipline* is currently under debate within the United Methodist Church. Some members of the United Methodist Church support same-sex marriages and seek to revise its *Book of Discipline*. Christian marriage is a "sacred covenant reflecting the Baptismal Covenant" ("A Service of Christian Marriage I," *The United Methodist Book of Worship*).

Divorce is permitted when a marriage is so broken that reconciliation and healing are not possible. An ordained elder or lay pastor may remarry the divorced in a Christian marriage. Same-sex marriage is contrary to the Gospel.

Grace and faith: United Methodists believe that **justification** and **holiness** (sanctification) are the work of **faith** and **grace** alone. Grace precedes holiness of life as it empowers a person to strive for holiness of life through living one's faith in Jesus Christ. Good works, in the Methodist tradition, are the fruits of grace and faith, which follow upon a person's being reborn of the Holy Spirit. Good works give evidence of one's faith; they do not remove one's sins or free one from the power of sin.

REVIEW, COMPARE AND SHARE

- ⊙ Review the teachings of the Catholic Church on the sacraments and justification in chapter 5.
- ⊙ Review the summary of the beliefs and practices of the United Methodist Church in relation to the sacraments.
- ⊙ Has what you learned clarified or given you a new understanding of Methodism? Of Methodism's relationship to Catholicism?
- ⊙ Share responses as a class.

Social teachings and practices: Methodists have a strong and longstanding tradition of working for social justice rooted in the Great Commandment of love. The United Methodist

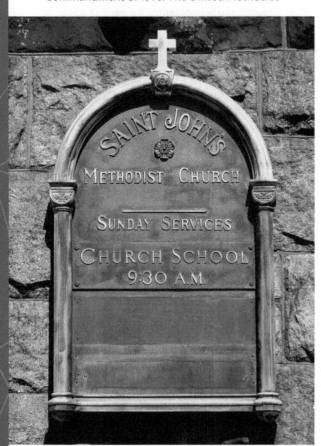

Church teaches that "personal salvation always involves Christian mission and service to the world. By joining heart and hand, we assert that personal religion, evangelical witness, and Christian social action are reciprocal and mutually reinforcing" (*The Book of Discipline of the United Methodist Church*).

The teachings of the United Methodist Church on moral and ethical issues share commonalities with the social teachings of the Catholic Church. There are also differences that prevent full communion between the Catholic Church and Methodism. Here are some key examples:

- ⊙ The Catholic Church teaches that all human life, unborn and born, is sacred. This sacredness, or inherent sanctity, of all human life means that a human person from the *very moment* of her or his conception to the end of his or her natural life has the right to life. All direct abortion of an unborn child, therefore, is a grave moral evil. Methodist teaching, on the other hand, permits a woman, under certain circumstances, to choose to directly end the natural life of her unborn child. The Methodist teaching permits a woman to choose "the legal option of abortion under proper medical procedures"; but only "after thoughtful and prayerful consideration . . . and pastoral, and other appropriate counsel" (*The Book of Discipline of the United Methodist Church*). Note: You will recall that there is an essential difference between *direct abortion* and *indirect abortion*. The Catholic Church teaches that it is morally permissible for a pregnant woman to choose to undergo a

Good works, in the Methodist tradition, are the fruits of grace and faith, which follow upon a person's being reborn of the Holy Spirit

John Wesley's Letter to a Roman Catholic

In his *Letter to a Roman Catholic*, written in 1749, John Wesley invited Methodists and Catholics to "help each other in whatever we are agreed leads to the Kingdom." Wesley proposed that "if we cannot as yet think alike in all things, at least we may love alike" (quoted in "Homily of Cardinal Walter Kasper on the 300th anniversary of the birth of John Wesley," June 22, 2003).

surgery to correct a condition that threatens her life, even when that the surgery may indirectly abort the unborn child.

⊙ Human sexuality is a sacred gift of God. God created humanity male and female. Homosexual persons no less than heterosexual persons are individuals of sacred worth. The current *Book of Discipline* states that homosexual activity is contrary to the God-given nature of the human person. The teaching on homosexuality in the *Book of Discipline* is a source of controversy and division within the United Methodist Church.

⊙ Marriage and the family are the foundation of society. God ordered marriage to be between one man and one woman. Same-sex marriages are contrary to the law of God. This teaching in the *Book of Discipline* is a source of division within the United Methodist Church and is being debated along with the authority of the clergy to officiate at same-sex weddings.

⊙ Care for the environment is a mutual concern of United Methodists and Catholics. In 2009 the Council of United Methodist Bishops issued the pastoral letter, *God's Renewed Creation: Call to Hope and Action*. In this letter they stated: "We cannot help the world until we change our way of being in it." In the 2012 joint statement *Heaven and Earth Are Full of Your Glory: A United Methodist and Roman Catholic Statement on the Eucharist and Ecology*, Roman Catholics and United Methodists affirmed and supported their mutual concern: "We believe that we can and should offer a joint prophetic witness on a significant challenge facing both our communions regarding the relation of humanity to the rest of the natural world" (no. 3).

REVIEW, COMPARE AND SHARE

⊙ Review the summary of the social teachings of the Catholic Church at the end of the "Catholic Prayers, Devotions and Practices" section of this text.

⊙ What have you learned about the teachings of Methodism that gives you a new understanding of Methodism? Of Methodism's relationship to Catholicism?

⊙ Share as a class some of the ways Catholic and Methodist youth can work together to build a just and compassionate world rooted in the love for God and neighbor.

CATHOLIC—METHODIST DIALOGUES

The *Book of Discipline of the United Methodist Church* states the Methodist commitment to ecumenical dialogue:

Christian unity is founded on the theological understanding that through faith in Jesus Christ we are made members-in-common of the one body of Christ. Christian unity is not an option; it is a gift to be received and expressed. . . .

CHARLES WESLEY | WILLIAM THOMAS FRY

Charles Wesley was a prolific hymn-writer. Page through your parish hymnal and identify any hymns written by Wesley

(We) welcome and celebrate the rich experience of United Methodist leadership in church councils and consultations, in multilateral and bilateral dialogues, as well as in other forms of ecumenical convergence that have led to the healing of churches and nations.

We see the Holy Spirit at work in making the unity among us more visible.

Catholics and Methodists have been in dialogue on a global level since 1967. Participants in these dialogues are members of the Joint International Commission of the Methodist World Council and the Pontifical Council for Promoting Christian Unity of the Catholic Church. In the United States of America these dialogues between Catholics and the United Methodist Church were established in 1966.

The seventh round of these dialogues was held between 2008 and 2011. A joint Catholic–Methodist statement on the connection between Eucharist and environmental stewardship was the result of this dialogue. The statement reads, in part: "The Eucharist is regarded as the central form of Christian worship because it orchestrates all that humans are and can be on this earth—our senses, abilities, talents, gifts, and intelligence—and offers them back to God the Father in thanksgiving for the Paschal victory of his Son." Again, although dialogues are not official teaching statements of the Catholic Church, they show progress toward achieving the unity Christ wills and desires among his followers.

REFLECT, PAIR AND SHARE

- ⊙ Charles Wesley was a prolific hymn-writer. Many of his hymns have been approved for use during the celebration of Mass. Page through your parish hymnal and identify any hymns written by Wesley. Do you remember singing any of these hymns during Mass?
- ⊙ Discuss with a partner how Wesley's hymns might be used as a starting point for Catholics and Methodists to share their faith.

OVER TO YOU

- ⊙ Summarize the insights this brief exploration has given you into the Methodist tradition.
- ⊙ How will this new knowledge and insight help you to dialogue and share your faith with friends who are Methodist? To work with Methodist youth to bring about God's kingdom?

The Baptist tradition

MARTIN LUTHER KING, JR., BAPTIST PASTOR AND CIVIL RIGHTS ACTIVIST

Martin Luther King, Jr. (1929–68) was the co-pastor of the Ebenezer Baptist Church in Atlanta, Georgia. Throughout his ministry King's faith in Jesus was the inspiration and driving force behind his work for civil rights, first for black people and eventually for all people. Dr. King's commitment to living his faith cost him his life. On April 4, 1968 King was assassinated while he was standing on the balcony of his motel room in Memphis, Tennessee, as he waited to join a peaceful protest by garbage workers.

OPENING REFLECTION

- ⦿ Do you know someone who willingly suffered because of their decision to live their faith in Christ?
- ⦿ Have you chosen to accept suffering as part of living your faith?

JOHN SMYTH AND THE ORIGINS OF THE BAPTIST TRADITION

Baptist Christianity has its roots in the efforts of those who believed that the Church of England did not go far enough in "purifying" itself from the beliefs and practices of the Catholic Church. One group of reformers who sought further reform of the Church of England became known as the English Separatists. John Smyth (1570–1612) was among the Separatists. In 1606, after renouncing his ties with the Church of England, Smyth became a minister to a group of Separatists in England. He then fled to Amsterdam to escape persecution, where he ministered with pilgrims.

Smyth taught that *only* adults could be baptized and that Baptism could take place *only after* a person had *personally* professed faith in Jesus Christ. Smyth also taught that Baptism by immersion was the only "real" baptism. Hence,

Baptists in America

There are more than fifty million Baptists in the United States of America. The Southern Baptist Convention (SBC) and the American Baptist Convention (also called the American Baptist Churches USA) are the two major groups of Baptists in America. The Southern Baptist Convention, which was founded in 1845, is the world's largest Baptist denomination.

EBENEZER BAPTIST CHURCH, ATLANTA, GEORGIA

the name "Baptists" has come to designate this reform movement. Baptists were originally called Anabaptists, or re-baptizers, and were later given the name Baptists by the Catholic Church. On the other hand, the Catholic Church teaches:

Born with a fallen human nature and tainted by original sin, children also have need of the new birth in Baptism to be freed from the power of darkness and brought into the realm of the freedom of the children of God, to which all men are called. The sheer gratuitousness of the grace of salvation is particularly manifest in infant Baptism. The Church and the parents would deny a child the priceless grace of becoming a child of God were they not to confer Baptism shortly after birth.

—CCC, no. 1250

LET'S PROBE DEEPER: A SCRIPTURE ACTIVITY

◉ Work in small groups.
◉ Look up, read and discuss these accounts about Baptism in the early Church: Acts of the Apostles 16:13–15, 16:26–33, 18:7–8; 1 Corinthians 1:16.
  – What do the passages say about the practice of Baptism in the apostolic Church?

  – How is your understanding of the baptizing of all members of a "household" deepened by these passages? How does it contribute to your understanding of the baptizing of infants "shortly after birth"?
◉ Share group discussions as a class.

OVER TO YOU

◉ At what age were you baptized?
◉ How have members of your family, your godparents and your church community helped you grow in your understanding of living out your faith in Jesus Christ?

ROGER WILLIAMS AND THE PURITANS

Roger Williams (1603–83) was a priest of the Church of England who became a Puritan and then a Separatist. The Puritans were heavily influenced by the teachings and "purifying" efforts of Calvinism. The Calvinist teaching on predestination, for example, led Puritans to consider themselves to be an elected or chosen people in God's plan of salvation.

Williams and his followers emigrated to the Massachusetts Bay Colony (later New England) in 1631 in search of religious freedom. Williams advocated for the separation of church and state and for freedom from all religious coercion. He established the Rhode Island colony as a place

BAPTISM NEAR THE WHITE FORT, HUDSON RIVER, NEW YORK | 19TH-CENTURY LITHOGRAPH

Catholic–Baptist Dialogue

The United States Conference of Catholic Bishops' Committee for Ecumenical and Interreligious Affairs held conversations with the Southern Baptist Convention from 1978 to 2001. The Southern Baptist Convention–Catholic Conversations discussed issues such as the environment, poverty, racism, life, and sickness, disability, and healing. Its last round, which began in 1995, discussed issues pertaining to scripture and salvation.

Although no official dialogue exists at this time, the Conference remains open to dialogue and welcomes a collaborative relationship on ad hoc projects of common interest.

—Website of the United States Conference of Catholic Bishops, *www.usccb.org*

BEECH STREET FIRST BAPTIST CHURCH, TEXARKANA, ARKANSAS

of religious freedom and he founded the first Baptist Church there in 1638.

Puritan teachings and practices played a significant role in the life of the colonies in America. Puritans established a *congregational* form of church governance, which Baptists practice. Congregationalists reject an episcopal or ordained hierarchical authority and leadership; instead, each congregation independently and autonomously runs its own affairs. (*We will explore the Congregationalist tradition in more detail in the next section of this chapter.*)

REFLECT, DISCUSS AND SHARE

⦿ Recall and reflect on what you have learned about:
  – the role of the teaching, sanctifying and governing offices of the pope and the bishops in union with him in the Catholic Church;
  – the role of the laity and the hierarchy in the Catholic Church;
  – the relationship between the laity and hierarchy in the Catholic Church.
⦿ Share reflections as a class.

CORE BELIEFS AND PRACTICES OF BAPTISTS

We will now take a brief look at some of the key beliefs and practices of Baptists and examine some of the commonalities shared by Catholics and Baptists, and the obstacles to full communion of Catholics and Baptists. As we probe these commonalities and differences, we need to remember that while both Catholics and Baptists use similar terms to name the mysteries of faith, the Baptist understanding of these terms often does not mirror and, indeed, is sometimes contrary to Catholic teaching.

God and salvation: Baptists believe that there is one God who is Father, Son and the Holy Spirit. Jesus Christ is truly and fully God and truly and fully man. He is our Lord and Redeemer who was conceived of the Holy Spirit and born of the Virgin Mary. He rose from the dead and ascended to heaven, and he will come, at any moment, to *claim his own*. This latter belief in a future event when all true believers will be taken by God into heaven is known as the "Rapture."

Baptists believe Scripture alone is the "authoritative" guide for knowing and serving God

Living and walking with God through a close personal relationship with Jesus Christ is the center of Baptist life. The Holy Spirit is the Sustainer who enlightens and empowers all believers to come to know the mind of Christ and to live their faith in him. Salvation is a pure and total gift of God given through the Death of Jesus Christ. Baptism and good works are seen as having no role in a person's salvation. They are seen as things one does in obedience to God.

Sacred Scripture: Baptists are sometimes called "people of the Book." Scripture *alone* is the "authoritative" guide for knowing God (doctrine), serving God (morality), and worshiping God (sacraments). For this reason, Baptists do not consider Sacred Tradition and creedal statements as *authoritative* expressions of and guides for one's faith.

Catholics and Baptists both hold that Sacred Scripture is divinely inspired and has been written without *any* error. While Baptists do hold that the Bible is the *inerrant* revealed Word of God, their

understanding of biblical inerrancy differs from the teaching of the Catholic Church. Baptists do not recognize that the Holy Spirit guides any ecclesial authority (such as the Magisterium of the Catholic Church) to interpret Revelation authentically. As a consequence, the understanding of biblical inerrancy varies among Baptists.

Some Baptists understand the inerrancy of Scripture to include the literal interpretation of all scientific and historical content of the Bible. This teaching is contrary to the teaching of the Catholic Church. On the inerrancy of Scripture, the Catholic Church teaches: "The inspired books teach the truth. 'Since therefore all that the inspired authors or sacred writers affirm should be regarded as affirmed by the Holy Spirit, we must acknowledge that *the books of Scripture firmly, faithfully, and without error teach that truth which God, for the sake of our salvation, wished to see confided to the Sacred Scriptures'* [emphases added]" (Vatican II, *Dogmatic Constitution on Divine Revelation*, no. 11; quoted in CCC, no. 107).

The Catholic Church teaches that there are two senses of Scripture: the literal and the spiritual. "The *literal* sense is the meaning conveyed by the words of Scripture and discovered by exegesis, following the rules of sound interpretation: 'All other senses of Sacred Scripture are based on the literal' " [St. Thomas Aquinas, *Summa Theologiae*, I, 1, 10, ad I; quoted in CCC, no. 116). "The spiritual senses: 'Thanks to the unity of God's plan, not only the text of Scripture but also the realities and events about which it [Scripture] speaks can be signs" (CCC, no. 117). Understanding the *layers of meaning,* or *spiritual senses*, buried beneath the literal meaning of the words enables the Church both to come to know more fully the truths of faith God wishes to reveal, and to apply those truths to living the Christian faith.

The extension of the literal interpretation of Sacred Scripture to include *all scientific and historical content* of the Bible is a form of biblical fundamentalism. Biblical fundamentalism is not unique to the Baptist tradition. Members of a variety of Protestant denominations assert some form of biblical fundamentalism. Biblical fundamentalism is contrary to the teachings of the Catholic Church.

RECALL, REFLECT AND SHARE

⊙ Check out "Senses of Scripture" in the Faith Glossary of this text.
- What is the Catholic teaching on the *literal senses* of Scripture?
- What is the Catholic teaching on the *spiritual senses* of Scripture?
⊙ How does this teaching differ from the Baptist teaching on the interpretation of biblical texts?
⊙ Share reflections as a class.

While some Baptist congregations choose to elect women as pastors, most limit the office of pastor to men

Church governance: Baptists practice a congregationalist form of church governance. Baptists do not have nor do they recognize a central, universal governing and teaching authority equivalent to the Magisterium of the Catholic Church. Authority is centered in the local leadership of the pastors and deacons whom they have elected. Pastors are independent of any external authority beyond the local congregation, such as the Southern Baptist Convention or the American Baptist Convention. These gatherings simply provide fellowship and shared resources. While some Baptist congregations choose to elect women as pastors, most limit the office of pastor to men.

Sacraments: Baptists practice "ordinances" (commands) and not sacraments. They teach that only Baptism and the Lord's Supper are specifically commanded in the New Testament. Baptism and the Lord's Supper are testimonies of God's great love for them. Baptists reject the teaching that Jesus Christ instituted and gave the Church seven sacraments which are "efficacious signs of grace" through which the Holy Spirit "dispenses divine life" (CCC, no. 1131).

THE BAPTISM OF CHRIST | FANOLI AFTER JÄGER

Baptists emphasize that God's grace cannot be mediated and cannot be confined or harnessed by human activity, such as in the celebration of sacraments. As a consequence of this understanding, the Baptist tradition also rejects the need for ordained priests to act as mediators of God's grace for others.

⊙ **Baptism:** Baptism is an act of obedience to the command (ordinance) of Jesus in Matthew 28:19. Baptists baptize only by full immersion, since the word "baptism" means "a burial." While the Catholic Church teaches the same mystery of faith about Baptism, the Catholic rite of Baptism permits Baptism by either a threefold immersion in water or a threefold pouring of water over the head of the person.

⊙ **The Lord's Supper:** Baptists believe that at the Lord's Supper the bread and cup *symbolize* Jesus' broken body and the blood that Jesus shed and offered to his Father for humanity. Christ's broken body and his blood *give testimony* of the saving Death of Jesus for the atonement of sins. Baptists do not hold that the bread and wine become the Body and Blood of Christ. They reject the Catholic doctrine of transubstantiation, which teaches

that "By the consecration, the substance of bread and wine is changed into the substance of Christ's Body and Blood" (USCCA, Glossary, "Transubstantiation," 530).

Social teachings and practices: Baptists teach that God has a plan for everyone. Every Christian is to walk with God, to glorify God by the witness of their life, and to spread the Gospel of Jesus Christ. Christians are to work for the good of all and treat everyone with Christian love, as Christ commanded.

A number of key general principles guide Baptist pastors in carrying out their ministry in their local congregations. The implementation of these practices varies among Baptists. These principles include:

⊙ The life of every person is sacred. Human life from conception to natural death must be protected. Direct abortion, assisted suicide and other forms of euthanasia are grave moral evils. Not all Baptists agree on this teaching. Some Baptists are pro-choice (favoring legal abortion); others are pro-life (favoring making direct abortion illegal).

⊙ Marriage is ordered by God to be between one man and one woman. It is a lifelong and permanent covenant and a reflection of our relationship with Jesus Christ. Teachings in relation to remarriage after divorce are specific to each congregation.

⊙ The practice of homosexuality is not a valid alternative lifestyle. Sexual intimacy is a gift from God to be shared by a man and a woman in a "biblically sanctioned marriage." Same-sex marriages are contrary to the Law of God. (Some Baptist congregations permit pastors to marry same-sex couples.) The ordaining of gays and lesbians is prohibited.

REFLECT, ANALYZE AND SHARE
⊙ Work in small groups.
⊙ What insights has this brief exploration given you into the Baptist Christian tradition?
⊙ How might those insights guide you in:
   – sharing your faith with Baptist youth?
   – working with Baptist youth to bring about God's kingdom?
⊙ Share reflections as a class.

The Congregationalist tradition

HARRIET BEECHER STOWE

Harriet Beecher Stowe (1811–96) was an American abolitionist and author who lived her Christian faith as a Congregationalist. Her father and seven brothers were preachers. Harriet believed she could preach the Gospel through her writing. In her lifetime she published more than thirty books on a wide range of topics, including children's textbooks, advice books on homemaking and childrearing, biographies and religious studies, as well as collections of articles and letters. The most famous of her books is undoubtedly the novel *Uncle Tom's Cabin*, in which she exposed the evil of human slavery. She described her reasons for writing: "I wrote what I did because as a woman, as a mother, I was oppressed and broken-hearted with the sorrow and injustice I saw, because as a Christian I felt the dishonor to Christianity—because as a lover of my country, I trembled at the coming day of wrath."

HARRIET BEECHER STOWE, C. 1880

OPENING REFLECTION

- Whom do you know personally or whom have you learned about whose faith in Christ inspired them to work for justice for oppressed people? What did they do?
- Has your faith in Christ ever inspired you to act or speak out against injustice?

ORIGINS OF CONGREGATIONALISM: A QUESTION OF FREEDOM AND AUTHORITY

Congregationalism is part of the Protestant Reformed Christian tradition. Its origins are in the "Free Churches" movement in England. The structure of Congregationalism is based on the belief that the local church (the local congregation) is answerable directly to God and not to any person or human organization, ecclesial or civil.

The establishment of Congregationalist congregations became widespread in New England, especially in Massachusetts and Connecticut. In the 1630s and 1640s thousands of Puritans left England and settled in the Massachusetts Bay Colony. The Puritans separated themselves from all forms of episcopal or hierarchical government and authority. Their beliefs and practices were closely connected to Presbyterians and Anabaptists.

Puritans, who became known as Independents, eventually used Congregationalism as their form of governance. In the late eighteenth century these local congregations began to merge with the other Christian denominations. Their *denominational* organization came in 1871 with the formation of the National Council of Congregational Churches. These efforts continued well into the twentieth century.

There are numerous Congregationalist denominations in the United States. They include members of the National Association of Congregational Christian Churches, the Conservative Congregational Christian Conference, and the United Church of Christ. In 1957 the Congregational Christian Churches and the Evangelical and Reformed Church united to become the United Church of Christ.

ROMAN CATHOLIC—UNITED CHURCH OF CHRIST DIALOGUE

The United Church of Christ (UCC) has been in dialogue with the Catholic Church in the United States of America for more than forty years. This dialogue is part of an ongoing dialogue between representatives of the United States Conference of Catholic Bishops, the United Church of Christ and three other Reformed Christian denominations, namely, the Presbyterian Church (USA), the Christian Reformed Church, and the Reformed Church in America.

In 2013 participants in the dialogue, as you learned in chapter 5 of this text, signed an agreement that recognized the validity of the Baptism of their members. Members of the United Church of Christ and other Congregationalists are brothers and sisters to members of the Catholic Church, as are all baptized persons. Future dialogues will include issues such as church unity and diversity, ministry and ordination, the nature and role of authority and the episcopacy.

THE UNITED CHURCH OF CHRIST: SOME KEY BELIEFS AND PRACTICES

The United Church of Christ (UCC) states its mission to be threefold: (1) To proclaim in word and action the Gospel of Jesus Christ; (2) To work for reconciliation and the unity of the Body of Christ; and (3) To seek justice and liberation for all.

The doctrinal teachings of the United Church of Christ are rooted in Scripture, in the Apostles' Creed and Nicene Creed, and in the confessions of the Reformation. These creeds and confessions of the past are *testimonies* to the faith of Christians; they are not dogmatic tests of the authenticity of one's faith. Why is that? Congregationalists hold that God is still *speaking to humanity today*, and the meaning of Scripture and of these testimonies is to be continually opened up.

The Roman Catholic Church and the United Church of Christ share some commonalities in beliefs and practices; but there are also serious obstacles to full communion with the Catholic Church. Key beliefs and practices of the United Church of Christ include, among others:

WESTCHESTER CONGREGATIONAL CHURCH, COLCHESTER, CONNECTICUT

Congregationalists hold that God is still speaking to humanity today

The United Church of Christ teaches that the Bible alone is the "sufficient rule of faith and practice." It is the only authoritative witness to the Word of God

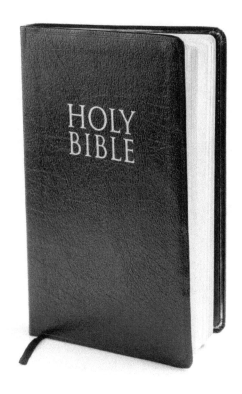

Trinity: There is one God who is a Trinity of Divine Persons—Father, Son and Holy Spirit. The UCC begins its original *Statement of Faith*: "We believe in God, the Eternal Spirit, Father of our Lord Jesus Christ and our Father, and to his deeds we testify" (*UCC Statement of Faith*, 1959).

Jesus Christ: Jesus Christ is the center of all creation. He is the image of the invisible God, the first born of all creation. He is the only begotten Son of the Father. He is truly God and truly human. Jesus Christ is our Redeemer. Through his blood and according to the riches of his grace we have forgiveness of sins. "In Jesus Christ, the man of Nazareth, our crucified and risen Lord, he has come to us and shared our common lot, conquering sin and death and reconciling the world to himself" (*UCC Statement of Faith*, 1959).

Sacred Scripture: The United Church of Christ teaches that the Bible alone (*sola scriptura*) is the "sufficient rule of faith and practice" (Principles of the Christian Church—United Church of Christ, no. 3). The UCC teaches that there is "no centralized authority or hierarchy that can impose any doctrine or form of worship on its members" (*Statement of Beliefs*, United Church of Christ, copyright 2017). This belief, which we have seen, is contrary to the teaching of the Catholic Church. It flows from the teaching of Congregationalism that private judgment and liberty of conscience is a right and a privilege that should be accorded to and exercised by all members.

Church: God destined humanity before time to be his own adopted sons and daughters through Jesus Christ. "He calls us into his church to accept the cost and joy of discipleship, to be his servants in the service of men, to proclaim the gospel to all the world and resist the powers of evil, to share in Christ's baptism and eat at his table, to join him in his passion and victory" (*UCC Statement of Faith*, 1959).

Jesus Christ is the *one and only head* of the Body of Christ, the whole Church, both on earth and in heaven. The United Church of Christ understands this revealed truth of faith differently than the Catholic Church. The United Church of Christ does not agree with the Catholic doctrine that Jesus Christ chose St. Peter and his successors, the popes, to be the visible head and sign of the unity of the Church on earth. The Gospel of Matthew gives this account of Jesus choosing St. Peter the Apostle to be the foundation of his Church on earth:

Now when Jesus came into the district of Caesarea Philippi, he asked his disciples, "Who do people say that the Son of Man is?" And they said, "Some say John the Baptist, but others

JESUS INSTRUCTS PETER TO 'FEED MY LAMBS' | ROBERT AND LESUEUR AFTER RAPHAEL

Jesus said to [Peter], "Feed my sheep."

JOHN 21:17

Elijah, and still others Jeremiah or one of the prophets." He said to them, "But who do you say that I am?" Simon Peter answered, "You are the Messiah, the Son of the living God." And Jesus answered him, "Blessed are you, Simon son of Jonah! For flesh and blood has not revealed this to you, but my Father in heaven. And I tell you, you are Peter, and on this rock I will build my church, and the gates of Hades will not prevail against it. I will give you the keys of the kingdom of heaven, and whatever you bind on earth will be bound in heaven, and whatever you loose on earth will be loosed in heaven."

—Matthew 16:13–20

The Gospel according to John, in turn, gives the following account of the risen Jesus appointing St. Peter to shepherd the Church on earth in his name. Jesus had invited his disciples to share breakfast with him on the shore of the Sea of Tiberias.

When they had finished breakfast, Jesus said to Simon Peter, "Simon son of John, do you love me more than these?" He said to him, "Yes, Lord; you know that I love you." Jesus said to him, "Feed my lambs." A second time he said to him, "Simon son of John, do you love me?" He said to him, "Yes, Lord; you know that I love you." Jesus said to him, "Tend my sheep." He said to him the third time, "Simon son of John, do you love me?" Peter felt hurt because he said

to him the third time, "Do you love me?" And he said to him, "Lord, you know everything; you know that I love you." Jesus said to him, "Feed my sheep."

—John 21:15-17

Jesus, the one true head of the whole Church, gave St. Peter the authority to teach and govern (shepherd) the Church on earth *in his name*. Both Sacred Scripture and Sacred Tradition teach that this authority has been passed on to St. Peter's successors. The doctrine of the Catholic Church on the authority of the popes, the direct successors of St. Peter, is rooted in Sacred Scripture and Sacred Tradition.

Scripture and Tradition also teach that the other Apostles both recognized the authority of Peter and worked collegially (together) with him to lead the Church. Hence the Catholic Church teaches: "The Roman Pontiff and the bishops are 'authentic teachers . . . endowed with the authority of Christ, who preach the faith to the people entrusted to them, the faith to be believed and put into practice' [Vatican II, *Dogmatic Constitution on the Church*, 25]" (CCC, no. 2034).

The United Church of Christ does not acknowledge the pope or any human head to be the visible head of the Church on earth. The basic unit of the UCC is the local congregation, whose members "covenant" with God and with one another to live their faith. Congregationalists do not view the Church as a worldwide communion, as does the Catholic Church. They do not profess that Jesus appointed Peter and his successors to be the foundation and the shepherd of his entire flock, the whole Church, on earth.

Local congregations of the United Church of Christ "covenant" with one another to form larger covenant groups. Members of these covenant groups are not "juridically" bound to one another. No member of the UCC is acknowledged to have universal juridical authority over any individual local congregation or group of congregations.

Sacraments: The United Church of Christ sees sacraments as ritual actions instituted by Christ. "Sacraments are ritual actions in worship which, according to Scripture, were instituted by Jesus. In the sacraments of baptism and communion we ask the Holy Spirit to use water, bread, and wine to make visible the grace, forgiveness, and presence of God in Christ" (*Holy Communion: A Practice of Faith in the United Church of Christ*, United Church of Christ, copyright 2017). They consider Baptism and the Lord's Supper, or Holy Communion, to be the only sacraments instituted by Jesus. The United Church of Christ does not accept Confirmation, Penance, Anointing of the Sick, Marriage, and Holy Orders to be sacraments instituted by Christ and given to his Church.

⊙ **Baptism:** The United Church of Christ teaches: "The sacrament of baptism is an outward and visible sign of the grace of God. Through baptism a person is joined with the universal church, the body of Christ. In baptism, God works in us the power of forgiveness, the renewal of the spirit, and the knowledge of the call to be God's people always" (*Baptism: A Practice of Faith in the United Church of Christ*, United Church of Christ, copyright 2017). The UCC administers Baptism to infants, youth and adults. The United Church of Christ, as the Catholic Church does, recognizes all valid Baptisms and does not re-baptize any validly baptized person.

⊙ **Holy Communion (The Lord's Supper):** The United Church of Christ and the Catholic Church both use the terms "Lord's Supper" and "Holy Communion." The teaching of the UCC does not reflect the Catholic Church's teaching on the full meaning of these terms and, as a consequence, presents serious obstacles to the full communion of the UCC with the Catholic Church.

First, the UCC teaches that the celebration of the Lord's Supper is a *memorial meal* of thanksgiving with the risen Christ. The Catholic Church also teaches that the Eucharistic celebration is a "memorial" meal of thanksgiving. The English noun "Eucharist" comes from a Greek verb meaning "to give

The UCC teaches that the celebration of the Lord's Supper is a memorial meal of thanksgiving with the risen Christ

CELEBRATION OF COMMUNION AT FIRST CONGREGATION UCC, YARMOUTH, MAINE

thanks." The UCC's understanding of the meaning of "memorial," however, differs essentially from the teaching of the Catholic Church.

The United Church of Christ teaches: "The wheat gathered to bake one loaf and the grapes pressed to make one cup *remind* (emphasis added) participants that they are one body in Christ, while the breaking and pouring *announce* (emphasis added) the costliness of Christ's sacrifice for the forgiveness of sin" (*Holy Communion: A Practice of Faith in the United Church of Christ*, United Church of Christ, copyright 2017).

This UCC teaching differs from the Catholic doctrine that the Eucharist memorial meal is a true sacrifice: "The Eucharist is the memorial of Christ's Passover, the making present and the sacramental offering of his unique sacrifice, in the liturgy of the Church which is his Body" (CCC, no. 1362). The Eucharist *makes present* the one sacrifice of Christ. "The Eucharist is thus a sacrifice because it *re-presents* (makes present) the sacrifice of the cross, because it is its *memorial* and because it *applies* its fruit" (CCC, no. 1366).

Second, the United Church of Christ teaches that the bread and wine shared at the celebration of the Lord's Supper do not truly become the Body and Blood of Jesus Christ. This UCC teaching is contrary to the Catholic doctrine of transubstantiation. Sharing the bread and wine in Holy Communion is not receiving the Body and Blood of Christ. The UCC teaches that the reception of Holy Communion only *reminds* those who receive the bread and wine that they are "one body in Christ." The Catholic Church teaches that one of the effects, or graces, of receiving Holy Communion is the deepening of the recipient's communion, or union, with Christ and the members of the Church.

Third, the UCC also welcomes all Christians, regardless of denomination, to receive Holy Communion. This practice is contrary to Catholic teaching: "Ecclesial communities derived from the Reformation and separated from the Catholic Church 'have not preserved the proper reality of the Eucharistic mystery in its fullness, especially because of the absence of the sacrament of Holy Orders' (Vatican II, *Decree on Ecumenism* [*Unitatis Redintegratio*], no. 22§3). It is for this reason that, for the Catholic Church, Eucharistic intercommunion with these communities is not possible. However these ecclesial communities, 'when they commemorate the Lord's death and

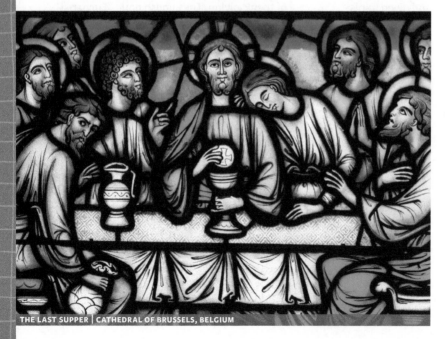

THE LAST SUPPER | CATHEDRAL OF BRUSSELS, BELGIUM

The Catholic Church teaches that the Eucharist *makes present* the one sacrifice of Christ

The ordaining of both men and women has been the practice of the United Church of Christ since 1853

resurrection in the Holy Supper . . . profess that it signifies life in communion with Christ and await his coming in glory' (*Decree on Ecumenism*, no. 22§3)" (CCC, no. 1400).

Ordained clergy: Ordination is not a sacrament. A local congregation selects members to be ordained to serve as ordained pastors and administrators of the rites of the church. "An ordained minister is a representative minister of the United Church of Christ and is in covenant with the local church where (s)he holds UCC membership" (*Authorized Ministry*, United Church of Christ, copyright 2017). The ordaining of both men and women has been the practice of the United Church of Christ since 1853.

Social teachings and practices: The United Church of Christ is committed to work for the justice of the Kingdom of God that Jesus Christ proclaimed for all people. Members of the UCC undertake this commitment in a wide variety of ways. The following examples include some of the teachings and practices that the UCC holds in common with the Catholic Church, and other examples that are serious obstacles to full communion of the UCC with the Roman Catholic Church.

- ⊙ **Human dignity:** The United Church of Christ teaches, as does the Catholic Church, that every person has the sacred dignity of being created in the image and likeness of God. Because of that inherent dignity, every person, without exception, deserves respect.
- ⊙ **Homosexuality:** Some, but not all, congregations of the United Church of Christ welcome gay and lesbian partners *living an active homosexual lifestyle* to participate fully in the life of the congregation. This participation includes the right of those persons to share in Holy Communion, to marry and to serve the local UCC congregation as "ordained" ministers. The UCC ordained its first gay person into ministry in 1985. Such practices and their underlying teachings are contrary to the teaching and practice of the Catholic Church.

  The Catholic Church teaches that there is a clear distinction between the dignity of every human being and the sinful choices and actions of a person, such as choosing to live an active homosexual lifestyle. Based on Sacred Scripture and the constant teaching of the Church's Tradition, the Catholic Church teaches that sexual intercourse and related

The Catholic Church teaches that the direct abortion of an unborn child is always a grave evil

sexual acts outside of marriage (which in God's plan is between a man and a woman), are grave sins. Such acts between gay and lesbian partners, just as other grave sins, hinder their unity with the Church. Having the inclination to homosexual tendencies on its own in no way separates a person from the Church.

The Gospels give several accounts of where Jesus himself showed respect to sinners, condemned their sins and told them to go and sin no more. Take a moment and read John's account of Jesus' treatment of the adulterous woman in John 8:1–11. This and numerous other passages in Sacred Scripture have been summarized in the adage "Love the sinner, hate the sin."

⊙ **Sanctity of life /Abortion:** The United Church of Christ promotes the legal right of a woman to choose abortion under certain circumstances. This includes the right of a woman to choose to directly end the life of an unborn person. This UCC teaching is contrary to the teaching of the Catholic Church. The Catholic Church, as you have already learned, teaches that every person, both born and unborn, has the right to life and to have that right protected from conception to natural death.

The Catholic Church holds that teaching "because the human person has been willed

for its own sake in the image and likeness of the living and holy God" (CCC, no. 2319). The direct abortion of an unborn child is always a grave evil. Vatican II also taught: "Direct abortion, that is, abortion willed as an end or as a means, is a 'criminal' practice (Vatican II, *Pastoral Constitution on the Church in the Modern World* [*Guadium et Spes*], no. 27 §3), gravely contrary to the moral law" (CCC, no. 2322). All human laws that allow direct abortion of an unborn child at any stage of his or her development are, therefore, "evil."

⊙ **Family life and marriage:** The United Church of Christ and the Catholic Church teach that marriage is a covenantal relationship. The UCC teaches: "Marriage is a divine institution, ordained of God, designed to be a loving, rewarding, continuously enriching, lifelong union. As such, St. Paul explained that it transcends the human plane, and is actually a reflection of the relationship Christ has with the Church (see Ephesians 5:22–33)" (Statement of Belief paper, "Divorce and Remarriage," page 9).

The United Church of Christ advocates that believers are to *refrain* from divorcing and remarrying. Spouses are to strive to repair their relationship. While the UCC strongly advocates that married persons refrain from divorce and remarriage, it does permit divorce in cases of sexual immorality or fraud. This latter UCC teaching and practice is contrary to the teachings of the Church from apostolic times on the indissolubility of every valid sacramental marriage. For the Catholic Church, fraud is grounds for an annulment, which renders the judgment that there was never a true and valid marriage.

The United Church of Christ, which follows the Protestant tradition of interpreting Scripture outside the authority of the Magisterium and outside of Sacred Tradition, teaches that persons of the same gender can marry. Some, but not all, congregations of the UCC permit their pastor to officiate at ceremonies at which persons of the same gender marry.

- **Stewardship of the environment:** Care for and responsible use of the environment has been a longstanding social justice practice of the United Church of Christ. Environment justice arose in the 1970s as a distinct social justice issue of the UCC's Commission for Racial Justice. The Commission addressed toxic waste dumping in a North Carolina county populated predominantly by Blacks. The United Church of Christ today advocates for urgent action against climate change.

REFLECT, ANALYZE AND SHARE

- Work in small groups. Discuss: What insights has this brief exploration of some of the beliefs and practices of the United Church of Christ given you into the United Church of Christ tradition?
- How might those insights guide you in:
  - sharing your faith with youth of the United Church of Christ tradition?
  - working with youth of the United Church of Christ tradition to bring about God's kingdom of "justice and liberation" for all?
- Share group discussions as a class.

Care for and responsible use of the environment is a social justice practice of the United Church of Christ

JUDGE AND ACT

REVIEW AND SHARE WHAT YOU HAVE LEARNED

Review what you have learned in this chapter about the beliefs and practices of the Methodist, Baptist and Congregationalist traditions. Share the teachings of the Catholic Church that you have learned in this chapter on these statements:

⊙ The Catholic Church has a history of authentic reform.
⊙ The lack of authentic authority wounds the unity of the Church.
⊙ The Methodist, Baptist and Congregationalist traditions originated as attempts to reform the Church of England.
⊙ The Catholic Church shares common ties with the Methodist tradition.
⊙ The Catholic Church shares common ties with the Baptist tradition.
⊙ The Catholic Church shares common ties with the Congregationalist tradition.
⊙ There are beliefs and practices that are obstacles to the full communion of the Methodist, Baptist and Congregationalist ecclesial communities with the Roman Catholic Church.

OVER TO YOU

⊙ Name some of the key commonalities and fundamental differences between the Methodist, Baptist and Congregationalist traditions and the Catholic Church.
⊙ What new insights and understanding did you gain about the beliefs and practices of the Methodist, Baptist and Congregationalist traditions from your study of this chapter?

The Evangelical Community

The fulfillment of the gospel mandate of evangelization is undertaken in a variety of ways. Christians in the Third Millennium number 1.7 billion. This number includes about 1 billion Catholics and 300 million Evangelicals. In the United States the name "Evangelicals" identifies the community of Christian believers from a diversity of Protestant denominations.

The National Association of Evangelicals (NAE), which was formed in 1942, represents "more than 45,000 local churches from almost 40 different denominations." The NAE answers the question "What is an Evangelical?" in this way: "Evangelicals are a vibrant and diverse group, including believers found in many churches, denominations and nations. Our community brings together Reformed, Holiness, Anabaptist, Pentecostal, Charismatic and other traditions."

Four main characteristics have been identified to summarize the distinctiveness of the Evangelical community. They are:

⊙ *"Conversionism*: the belief that lives need to be transformed through a "born again" experience and a lifelong process of following Jesus.
⊙ *Activism*: the expression and demonstration of the gospel in missionary and social reform efforts.
⊙ *Biblicism*: a high regard for and obedience

PENTECOSTAL YOUTH SERVICE, BRUNSSUM, NETHERLANDS

Catholics and Evangelicals come together to promote a just political, economic and social order

REV. TIMOTHY TYLER PREACHING AT THE AFRICAN METHODIST EPISCOPAL CHURCH, DENVER

to the Bible as the ultimate authority.

⊙ "*Crucicentrism*: a stress on the sacrifice of Jesus Christ on the cross as making possible the redemption of humanity."

The NAE goes on to say, "These distinctives and theological convictions define us—not political, social or cultural trends. In fact, many evangelicals rarely use the term 'evangelical' to describe themselves, focusing simply on the core convictions of the triune God, the Bible, faith, Jesus, salvation, evangelism and discipleship."

There are both commonalities and differences in doctrine and practices that unite and separate Catholics and Evangelicals. Both faith traditions are united by an ardent desire and effort to fulfill the mission of evangelization. Teachings on the Bible, Baptism and Eucharist, ordained priesthood and the hierarchical nature of the Church, and the practice of evangelization are among those differences.

Catholics and Evangelicals have come together to give common witness to Christ. This witness includes promoting a just political, economic and social order. In the United States, both Catholics and Evangelicals advocate respect for all human life, unborn and born; marriage and family life; commitment to the poor and elimination of poverty; religious liberty; immigration; and responsible care of the environment.

The United States Conference of Catholic Bishops began formal dialogue with the Evangelical Community in 2003. Dialogue between Catholics and Evangelicals continues today at both national and local levels.

REFLECT AND SHARE

⊙ Reflect: Black Christian congregations and denominations were successful in inspiring and empowering African American enslaved people in their fight for justice and freedom.

⊙ Discuss with a partner:
  – What black Christian Americans, both Catholic and non-Catholic, can you name who led or continue to lead black people in their struggle for justice and freedom from oppression?
  – What Black spirituals do you know or have you sung during worship? What do they express about the role the Christian faith has played and continues to play in the life and work of black people?

⊙ Share discussions as a class.

Rosa Parks (1913–2005), Methodist and civil rights activist

From my upbringing and the Bible I learned people should stand up for rights just as the children of Israel stood up to the Pharaoh.

From her earliest days, the singing and music in church became part of the fiber of her very being. "The church," Parks recalled, "with its musical rhythms and echoes of Africa, thrilled me when I was young." The "thrill" of the music contributed to her spiritual formation as a courageous promoter of justice for blacks and all people suffering from oppression.

Parks carried on the legacy of working against injustice that was a central dimension of John Wesley's faith. In the last letter that John Wesley wrote—to William Wilberforce, a Methodist and member of Parliament who fought successfully for the ending of England's participation in the slave trade— Wesley wrote, in part:

On December 1, 1955 in Montgomery, Alabama, a black woman, Rosa Parks, refused an order to give up her seat on a bus to make room for a white person. This action led to the Montgomery Bus Boycott, which eventually resulted in the ending of the practice of racial segregation on public transport. It also catapulted Reverend Martin Luther King Jr. to the forefront of the Civil Rights Movement. In her book, *Quiet Strength: The Faith, the Hope and the Heart of a Woman Who Changed a Nation*, Parks revealed that her decision to refuse to give up her seat on the bus that day was an *act of faith*.

Parks was a Methodist and her religion shaped her life. She had been raised in the African Methodist Episcopal Church and she found her inspiration in the Bible.

I remember finding such comfort and peace while reading the Bible. Its teaching became a way of life and helped me in dealing with my day-to-day problems. . . .

O be not weary of well doing! Go on, in the name of God and in the power of his might, till even American slavery (the vilest that ever saw the sun) shall vanish away before it.

Reading this morning a tract wrote by a poor African, I was particularly struck by that circumstance that a man who has a black skin, being wronged or outraged by a white man, can have no redress; it being a "law" in our colonies that the *oath* of a black against a white goes for nothing. What villainy is this?

The work of Rosa Park has the same message: "Be not weary of well doing!"

TALK IT OVER
- In what ways does your faith inform your response to situations of injustice or oppression?
- Do you grow weary of "well doing"? How do you work against that weariness?

- How might Rosa Parks inspire you to work against that weariness?

SHARE FAITH WITH FAMILY AND FRIENDS
All Christians must make a personal decision to follow Jesus. Each year at the Easter liturgy,

Catholics are given the opportunity to renew their baptismal profession of faith and promises.

- Talk with members of your family about how you can support one another in renewing your personal commitment to live as disciples of Jesus.
- Talk with your friends about how you can support one another in renewing your personal commitment to live as disciples of Jesus.

JUDGE AND DECIDE

The Methodist, Baptist and Congregationalist traditions, as the Roman Catholic Church does, have a significant commitment to learn about and dialogue with other faith traditions.

- How can you deepen your own commitment to learn more about your Catholic faith and how best to live it?

- How might interacting and dialoging with non-Catholic Christians lead to respect of one another?
- What joint efforts can and will you undertake with non-Catholic Christian youth to help bring about the Kingdom of God inaugurated by Jesus Christ?

LEARN BY HEART

"Believe on the Lord Jesus, and you will be saved, you and your household."

ACTS OF THE APOSTLES 16:31

LEADER

The African American spiritual is a particular type of Christian folksong that is characteristic of black Christians. In our prayer time today we will reflect on the spiritual "There Is a Balm in Gilead."

Let us first place ourselves in the presence of God and then listen to a reading from the Old Testament. (*Pause*)

The grace of the Lord Jesus Christ,
and the love of God,
and the communion of the Holy Spirit
be with you all.
> —The *Roman Missal*, "The Introductory Rites"

READER

A reading from the Book of the Prophet Jeremiah.
Read Jeremiah 8:18–22.
The word of the Lord.
ALL
Thanks be to God.

LEADER

We will now listen to and reflect on the spiritual "There Is a Balm in Gilead." Balm is "an oily substance that has a pleasant smell and that is used for healing, smoothing, or protecting the skin; something that gives comfort or support" (Merriam-Webster). Gilead was a mountainous area east of the River Jordan, which corresponds today to the northwestern part of the Kingdom of Jordan.

Refrain
There is a balm in Gilead
to make the wounded whole;
there is a balm in Gilead
to heal the sin-sick soul.

Sometimes I feel discouraged
and think my work's in vain,
but then the Holy Spirit
revives my soul again.
Refrain

If you cannot preach like Peter,
if you cannot pray like Paul,
just tell the love of Jesus
and say, "He died for all."
Refrain

Reflect:
- ⊙ What is God's message of hope and liberation from oppression?
- ⊙ How does that apply to your life?
- ⊙ What is your response?

Reflect in silence. All who wish to do so share their reflections.

LEADER

Let us join together to express our needs and concerns, confident that God hears and responds to all our prayers.

All pray in silence. Those who wish to do so share their petitions. All respond, "Lord, hear our prayers," after each petition.

LEADER

God of mercy and compassion,
we offer you our joys and our sorrows.
Send your Holy Spirit to fire us up with your love
so that we may offer our lives as testimonies
to the liberating power
of the life, Death and Resurrection
of your Word, Jesus Christ,
who lives and reigns with you
in the unity of the Holy Spirit,
one God, for ever and ever.
ALL
Amen.

A QUEEN ADMINISTERING A HEALING BALM TO A LEPER | 15TH-CENTURY WALL PAINTING, ETON COLLEGE, ENGLAND

CHAPTER 7

Judaism and the Jewish People

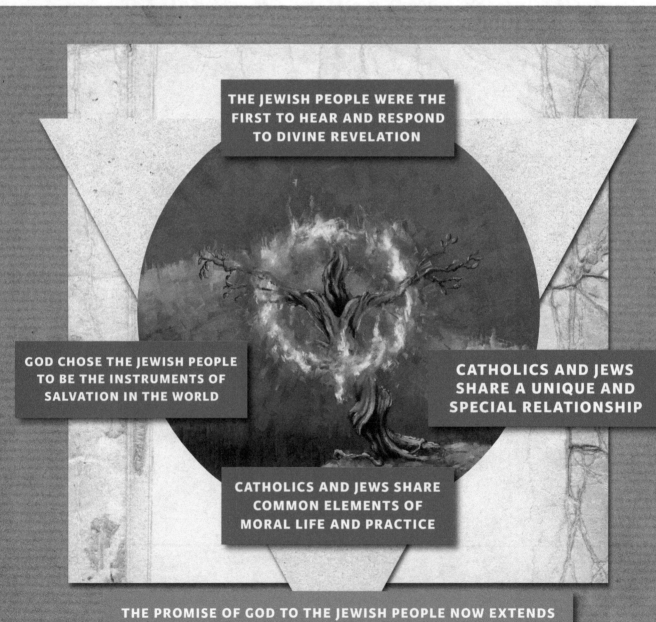

THE JEWISH PEOPLE WERE THE FIRST TO HEAR AND RESPOND TO DIVINE REVELATION

GOD CHOSE THE JEWISH PEOPLE TO BE THE INSTRUMENTS OF SALVATION IN THE WORLD

CATHOLICS AND JEWS SHARE A UNIQUE AND SPECIAL RELATIONSHIP

CATHOLICS AND JEWS SHARE COMMON ELEMENTS OF MORAL LIFE AND PRACTICE

THE PROMISE OF GOD TO THE JEWISH PEOPLE NOW EXTENDS TO ALL PEOPLE THROUGH JESUS, THE SAVIOR OF THE WORLD

THE JEWISH PEOPLE ARE THE ORIGINAL CHOSEN
People of God; they are our "elder brothers" in faith
(St. John Paul II). The Jewish people were the first
to hear the Word of God through explicit Divine
Revelation. God entered an everlasting covenant
with Abraham and chose the descendants of
Abraham to be the first instruments of the divine
plan of salvation for humanity. In this and the next
chapter we explore in some detail the relationship of
the Catholic Church, the new People of God, to the
Jewish people.

**JEWISH PEOPLE ARE THE
CHOSEN PEOPLE OF GOD**

**CHRISTIANS ARE THE NEW
PEOPLE OF GOD**

Faith Focus: These teachings of the Catholic Church are
the primary focus of the doctrinal content presented in this
chapter:

- ⊙ The link between the Catholic Church and the Jewish
  people is special.
- ⊙ The Jewish people are the original Chosen People of God;
  Christians are the new People of God.
- ⊙ God chose the Jewish people to be the instruments of
  salvation in the world.
- ⊙ The Jewish people were the first to hear and respond to
  Divine Revelation.
- ⊙ The patriarchs of the Jewish people—Abraham, Isaac,
  Jacob and Moses—are also the ancestors in faith for
  members of the Catholic Church.
- ⊙ Catholics and Jews share common elements of moral life
  and practice.
- ⊙ The New Covenant with Jesus Christ is the fulfillment of
  the promises of the first covenant between God and the
  Jewish people.
- ⊙ The Catholic Church condemns anti-Judaism or anti-
  Semitism and all forms of unjust discrimination.

Discipleship Formation: As a result of studying this chapter
and discovering the meaning of the faith of the Catholic
Church for your life, you should be better able to:

- ⊙ understand and value your ancestral spiritual roots in
  Judaism;
- ⊙ respect the Jewish people as the first Chosen People of
  God and an instrument of salvation;
- ⊙ grow in mutual respect for one another as sons and
  daughters of God;
- ⊙ reject and speak out against all expressions of anti-
  Judaism, or anti-Semitism;
- ⊙ talk with your Jewish friends about your spiritual
  connections;
- ⊙ give common witness on matters of peace and justice;
- ⊙ deepen your mutual understanding of the one God and
  his plan for the world.

Scripture References: These scripture references are quoted
or referred to in this chapter:
OLD TESTAMENT: Genesis 3:15, 9:9–16, 12:1–4, 14:13 and
17–20, 15:3–4, 17:1–8 and 15–22, 18:1–15, 21:1–7, 22:1–2, 32:28;
Exodus 3:6–10 , 12 and 14, 12, 12:14–20, 13:3–10, 19:3–8a;
Leviticus 19:18; **Deuteronomy** 6:4–5; **Psalms** 27:1, 4, 7–9 and
13–14, 98:3, 139:13–14; **Isaiah** 2:1–4, 11:1–9; **Jeremiah** 33:14–18;
Ezekiel 34
NEW TESTAMENT: Matthew 1:1–2 and 6, 5:17–41, 22:36–40,
23:7–8 and 34–40, 26:17, 28:19; **Mark** 6:2, 16:15; **Luke** 2:41–51,
4:4–22; **John** 1:38–39, 3:2 and 26, 6:25, 13:31–35, 15:13; **Acts of
the Apostles** 2:14–42, 10:35; **Romans** 8:18–25, 9:4–5, 11:29; **2
Corinthians** 11:22; **Hebrews** 9:5, 12 and 26, 11:17–19

Faith Glossary: Familiarize yourself with or recall the
meaning of these key terms. Definitions are found in the
Glossary: **Chosen People of God, covenant, Hebrews,
Israelites, Jews, Passover, People of God, Revelation,
sacrament, salvation, salvation history, supersessionism,
Tanakh, twelve tribes of Israel**

Faith Word: covenant
Learn by Heart: Genesis 17:7
Learn by Example: Abraham Heschel

When have you been chosen unexpectedly?

Do you worry about being accepted by your friends and fear being left out? Have you ever been chosen unexpectedly to be a member or a leader of a group? People of all ages are chosen by teachers, coaches, managers, employers and others for jobs, for opportunities, for promotion, for awards and honors. Presidents and prime ministers and leaders of countries go before the public to be elected or rejected, chosen or not chosen.

OPENING REFLECTION

- ◉ Have you ever had an experience of being chosen? Recall one such experience and describe what happened.
- ◉ What responsibilities came with your being chosen? How did you exercise those responsibilities?
- ◉ Have you ever had an experience of being left out? Describe what happened.
- ◉ What did you learn from such experiences? How did they help you to live your faith in Jesus Christ?

GOD'S CHOSEN PEOPLE

Sometimes we can be chosen "out of the blue," completely unexpectedly. This is precisely what happened to Abraham and his descendants, the Jewish people, also known as the Hebrews or the Israelites. Judaism and Christianity (as well as Islam) attest that the first person to hear God's word was not one of the great ones of this world, not a king or queen, general or emperor, but a pagan nomad named Abram, whose name God would change to Abraham.

Abraham was truly "a chosen one." God chose Abraham over all others to be the one to whom God would reveal himself. God's choice of Abraham has established him as the "father in faith" of all believers in the one true God. It also marks the beginning of God's explicit **Revelation** of himself and the divine plan of **salvation** for the human race.

The Bible also reveals that God entered an everlasting covenant with Abraham and his descendants, the Jewish people, and chose them to be the first instruments for God's saving work within human history. God assured Abraham that he and his descendants would be a source of blessing for all other peoples. *(We will return to the call of Abraham in the next section of this chapter.)*

DIFFERENT NAMES FOR THE "CHOSEN PEOPLE"

Jews, Israelites and Hebrews are one and the same people. The Bible, both the Old Testament and the New Testament, uses these three names to identify God's original Chosen People.

Hebrews: The word *Hebrews* means "people beyond." "Hebrews" is used in the Bible to distinguish the Israelites from other peoples. For example, in the Pentateuch it is used to distinguish God's people from the Egyptians and Philistines. In Genesis 14:13 we read "Abram the Hebrew." The designation means "Abram, the man of the region beyond" (Emil G. Hirsch, John P. Peters, "Hebrew: The Name and Its Use," *Jewish Encyclopedia*).

Israelites: The name *Israelites* identifies the Chosen People as descendants of Jacob, whose name God changed to Israel. (Check out Genesis 32:28.) According to the *Jewish Encyclopedia*, the names "Hebrews" and "Israelites" usually describe the same people; they were called Hebrews before the conquest of the Land of Canaan and called Israelites after the conquest. In the New Testament the term "Hebrew" is most often used to identify the language of the Jews. St. Paul also uses the term "Hebrews" to identify the Jewish people. (Check out 2 Corinthians 11:22.) The New Testament Letter to the Hebrews was probably written for Jewish Christians.

Jews: The name *Jew* (*Yehudi* in Hebrew) or *Jews* (*Yehudim* in Hebrew) refers to the descendants of Judah, the fourth son of Jacob. Judah was one of the twelve sons of Jacob and one of the **twelve tribes of Israel**. The use of the names "Jew" and "Jews" developed over time and is associated with the name of the land in which the people dwelt.

For example, at the time of Jesus it was the Roman Province of Judea. "Jew" or "Jews" has come to designate not only the religious faith of the Chosen People, but also their cultural and political heritage. The name "Jew" or "Jews" is now the most common name for the descendants of the original Chosen People of God.

WHAT ABOUT YOU PERSONALLY?

⊙ What does it mean that the identity of the Jewish people is rooted in their being the Chosen People of God?

⊙ What does it mean that Christ has chosen you to be a member of his Church, the new People of God?

FIRST RESPONDENTS TO DIVINE REVELATION

The revealed Word of God contained in the Old Testament, which houses the Sacred Scriptures of the Jewish people, can be traced to God's Chosen People, the Israelites, through whom God's Revelation first came to humankind. Unlike other non-Christian religions, the Jewish faith is a response to God's Revelation in the Old Covenant. This teaching of the Catholic Church is vital to coming to an understanding of the unique and special relationship between the Catholic Church and the Jewish people.

Judah was one of the twelve sons of Jacob and one of the twelve tribes of Israel

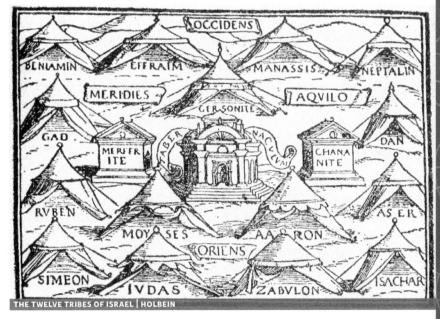

THE TWELVE TRIBES OF ISRAEL | HOLBEIN

The Tanakh, the Jewish Scriptures

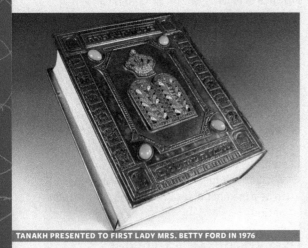

TANAKH PRESENTED TO FIRST LADY MRS. BETTY FORD IN 1976

The **Tanakh** contains the Scriptures the Jewish people believe to be the inspired Word of God. The word word "Tanakh" is an acronym for **T**orah (or teachings), **N**evi'im (or prophets) and **K**etuvim (or writings). For our Jewish brothers and sisters these Sacred Scriptures are truly the Word of God that reveals God's purpose for them and how they are to live the **covenant** that they and God have entered. The thirty-nine books of the Tanakh were passed on by each generation and, according to rabbinic tradition, they were accompanied by an oral tradition, called the Oral Torah. The Oral Torah has a unique place in the Jewish interpretation of Scripture and their applying the meaning of the Word of God to each generation.

These Scriptures, which are among the forty-seven books in the Old Testament of the Catholic Bible, continue to be sacred to Christians today, as they have been since apostolic times. "Christians venerate the Old Testament as true Word of God. The Church has always vigorously opposed the idea of rejecting the Old Testament under the pretext that the New has rendered it void (Marcionism)" (*Catechism of the Catholic Church* [CCC], no. 123).

Marcionism is a heresy that arose in the mid-second century. This heresy arose from the teachings of Marcion of Sinope. Marcion (b. c. 85–d.c. 160) was an assistant bishop to the Bishop of Sinope in the eastern Black Sea area of modern-day Turkey. Marcionism "rejected the writings of the Old Testament and taught that Christ was not the Son of the God of the Jews, but the Son of the good God, who was different from the God of the Ancient Covenant" ("Marcionites," New Advent *Catholic Encyclopedia*).

When she delves into her own mystery, the Church, the People of God in the New Covenant, discovers her link with the Jewish people (see Vatican II, *Declaration on the Relation of the Church to Non-Christian Religions* [*Nostra Aetate*], no. 4), "the first to hear the Word of God" (*The Roman Missal*, Good Friday 13, "General Intercessions," VI). The Jewish faith, unlike other non-Christian religions, is already a response to God's revelation in the Old Covenant. To the Jews "belong the sonship, the glory, the covenants, the giving of the law, the worship, and the promises; to them belong the patriarchs, and of their race, according to the flesh, is the Christ" (Romans 9:4–5), "for the gifts and the call of God are irrevocable" (Romans 11:29).

—CCC, no. 839

Thus, the descendants of the patriarchs of the Jewish people—Abraham, Isaac, Jacob and Moses—are ancestors in faith for members of the Catholic Church. Both Jews and Christians, each in their unique way and in response to their unique calling, are instruments for the salvation of the world. *We will continue our discussion of the patriarchs in the next section of this chapter.*

JOURNAL EXERCISE

- Describe how you understand the mystery that God speaks to you in your daily life. For example, through what people or things?
- How often do you turn to the Scriptures to listen to God's word?
- What biblical passage reassures you about God's unconditional love for you? Write about it in your journal.

Our elder brothers and sisters in faith

THE IMPORTANCE OF DISCOVERING OUR ROOTS

Researching one's family history is a widespread practice. Perhaps you began that search in elementary school when you created a family tree using names and pictures. That simple activity reflects the desire of people throughout the world to know their family roots—their ancestors and history.

We all "belong" to a family. Understanding one's "roots" is an invaluable source for coming to know one's identity. This also applies to our identity as Christians. Pope Francis has said that "to be a good Christian it is necessary to understand Jewish history and traditions." Pope Francis has also reminded us that Jews and Christians share the same roots and that dialogue is the key to building a common future (*News.va,* "Meeting with Jewish Leaders," September 3, 2013).

OPENING REFLECTION

⊙ How far back can you trace your family's ancestors? What do you know of your family's history?

⊙ Do you gather in your home to remember and celebrate your family?
- Who do you remember and celebrate? What do you remember and celebrate? When do you gather?
- Does taking part in those family celebrations deepen your bond with your family? Your identity as a member of your family?

⊙ Take a moment and write your reflections in your journal.

GOD'S ORIGINAL CHOSEN PEOPLE

Judaism is first and foremost a *people of faith* gathered by the Word of God, who are bonded in the spirit of God's saving word to them. Unlike other non-Christian religions, the Jewish faith is a response to God's Revelation in the Old Covenant. Jewish religious life is sustained by this communal spirit and extraordinarily confident familiarity with God. The Jewish people are the original **Chosen People of God**. This is what inspires them to pass on their story, the tradition of God's word and saving will being revealed to them, from generation to generation.

Jesus, our Savior and Lord, was born and raised as a Jew (as were Mary, Joseph, the Apostles and the first disciples). In his genealogy of Jesus, the Evangelist Matthew writes: "An account of the genealogy of Jesus the Messiah, the son of David, the son of Abraham. Abraham was the father of Isaac, and Isaac the father of Jacob, and Jacob the father of Judah and his brothers, . . . Joseph the husband of Mary, of

The People of God

At all times and in every nation, anyone who fears God and does what is right has been acceptable to him (see Acts of the Apostles 10:35). He has, however, willed to make women and men holy and to save them, not as individuals without any bond between them, but rather to make them into a people who might acknowledge him and serve him in holiness. He therefore chose the people of Israel to be his own people and established a covenant with them. He instructed them gradually, making both himself and his intentions known in the course of their history, and made them holy for himself. All these things, however, happened as a preparation and figure of that new and perfect covenant which was to be ratified in Christ, and of the fuller revelation which was to be given through the Word of God made flesh.
—Vatican II, *Dogmatic Constitution on the Church* (*Lumen Gentium*), no. 9

MOSES | 3RD-CENTURY FRESCO, SYRIA

whom Jesus was born, who is called the Messiah" (Matthew 1:1–2, 16).

Jesus, Mary and Joseph took part in the religious life of the Jews during Jesus' youth. (Check out Luke 2:41–51.) Later, as an adult, Jesus continued to practice the Jewish faith he learned in the Holy Family. (Check out Matthew 26:17, Mark 6:2, and Luke 4:14–16.) Jesus knew, lived and fulfilled the Torah. In the Sermon on the Mount he declared: "Do not think that I have come to abolish the law or the prophets; I have come not to abolish but to fulfill" (Matthew 5:17).

Jesus knew the Jewish Scriptures and traditions well. He drew on the Decalogue, or Ten Commandments, and the teachings of the prophets in his teaching on self-giving love and moral living. (Check out John 13:31–35, 15:13; Matthew 5:18–41, 23:34–40.) His followers and enemies alike acknowledged him to be a wise rabbi, a teacher of the Law. (Check out Matthew 23:7–8; John 1:38 and 39, 3:2 and 26, 6:25.) And he inaugurated the Kingdom of God foretold by the prophets of his people. (Check out Luke 4:4–22.)

The Catholic Church teaches that the Jewish people were the first people to come to faith in the one true God. She also teaches that Jesus Christ, the Incarnate Word of God, is the final and fullest Revelation of God and of his saving plan for humanity. The four accounts of the Gospel and the other New Testament writings clearly pass on this faith of the apostolic Church.

The Church is rooted in the heritage and faith of the people of Ancient Israel. The New Covenant with Jesus Christ is the fulfillment of the promises of the first covenant between God and the Jewish people. The Church is the new **People of God**. "Already prefigured at the beginning of the world, this church was prepared in marvelous fashion in the history of the people of Israel and in the ancient alliance. . . . it will be brought to glorious completion at the end of time" (Vatican II, *Dogmatic Constitution on the Church*, no. 2).

OVER TO YOU

- At Mass we sometimes name Abraham as "our father in faith" (*The Roman Missal*, Eucharistic Prayer I).
- How aware were you up to now of the Jewish background and identity of Jesus?
- What difference might this knowledge make to your understanding of your Catholic faith?

Covenant

A solemn agreement between human beings or between God and a human being involving mutual commitments or guarantees. The Bible refers to God's covenants with Noah, Abraham, and Moses as the leader of the chosen people, Israel.

—CCC, Glossary

GOD'S COVENANT WITH ABRAM | 20TH-CENTURY ILLUSTRATION

PEOPLE OF THE COVENANT

Abraham, Isaac, Jacob and Moses, the patriarchs of the Jewish people, are the spiritual ancestors for the members of the Catholic Church. The patriarchs received God's promise that they would be his people and a source of blessing for the human race. The biblical stories, or narratives, of the patriarchs form the background to the history of salvation, or **salvation history**. The Church uses the term "salvation history" to describe the story of God's reaching out to humanity to fulfill the divine plan of salvation, and also of humanity's response to God.

Jesus Christ is "the Messiah, the son of David, the son of Abraham" (Matthew 1:1). The story of God's gathering for himself a people to be the instrument of salvation in the world begins with Abraham. We will now briefly review the role of the patriarchs Abraham, Isaac and Jacob. (*We will explore the covenant God entered into with Moses and the Israelites in the desert at Sinai in the next section of this chapter.*)

Abraham, our father in faith

During the celebration of Mass, the Catholic Church proclaims Abraham to be "our father in faith" (*The Roman Missal,* Eucharistic Prayer I).

Abraham and his descendants are ancestors in faith for the members of the Catholic Church. (Take a moment to recall Abraham's encounter with God. Read Genesis 12:1–4 and Genesis 17:1–8.)

Abram and Sarai and their family were polytheists; in other words, they believed in many gods. What a difficult choice this "God" offered Abram. If he would gather his family and possessions, leave his native land and move to the land God would show him, Abram would eventually have a large and powerful and prosperous family—though he and his wife Sarai were already old and far beyond child-bearing age. God invited Abram:

"Go from your country and your kindred and your father's house to the land that I will show you. I will make of you a great nation, and I will bless you, and make your name great, so that you will be a blessing. I will bless those who bless you, and the one who curses you I will curse; and in you all the families of the earth shall be blessed."

—Genesis 12:1–3

Abram responded by placing his faith and trust in God. God, true to his word, entered a covenant with Abram and his descendants "throughout their generations":

When Abram was ninety-nine years old, the Lord appeared to Abram, and said to him, "I am God Almighty; walk before me, and be blameless. And I will make my covenant between me and you, and will make you exceedingly numerous." Then Abram fell on his face; and God said to him, "As for me, this is my covenant with you: You shall be the ancestor of a multitude of nations. No longer shall your name be Abram, but your name shall be Abraham; for I have made you the ancestor of a multitude of nations. I will make you exceedingly fruitful; and I will make nations of you, and kings shall come from you. I will establish my covenant between me and you, and your offspring after you throughout their generations, for an everlasting covenant, to be God to you and to your offspring after you. And I will give to you, and to your offspring after you, the land where you are now an alien, all the land of Canaan, for a perpetual holding; and I will be their God."

—Genesis 17:1–8

ABRAHAM AND HIS VISITORS | 12TH-CENTURY STONE CARVING

As the divine plan of salvation continued to unfold and move forward, God would always be faithful to his people. For God's part, the relationship would always be one of "steadfast love and faithfulness" (Psalm 98:3). As St. Paul explained, "the gifts and the calling of God are irrevocable" (Romans 11:29). For this reason, the Catholic Church teaches that "the Old Covenant has never been revoked" (CCC, no. 121). The special relationship that God established with the Jewish people is "an everlasting covenant" (Genesis 17:7).

TALK IT OVER

⊙ The Catholic Church teaches that the covenant God entered into with Abraham and the Israelites prepared the way for the Church. It was an everlasting covenant. The Old Covenant continues and did not end with the New Covenant instituted by Christ. (See *Catechism of the Catholic Church*, no. 762.)
⊙ How does that impact the connection between the Jewish people and Catholics?
⊙ Share discussions as a class.

Isaac, the son of Abraham and Sarah

The Lord appeared again to Abraham on the journey to the land God promised him and his descendants and assured him that Sarah would conceive and give birth to a son. (Check out Genesis 15:3–4, 17:15–22.) Then Abraham and Sarah received visitors who affirmed the Lord's promise. (Read Genesis 18:1–15 carefully and savor the details.) It is a charming tale of hospitality.

Strangers visit with Abraham and Sarah, whom they welcome and care for. In return, Abraham and Sarah are once again taken by surprise. They receive an amazing promise, that Sarah shall have a son, which Scripture records made Sarah and her neighbors laugh.

Abraham and Sarah were well advanced in age, far beyond child-bearing years. But it was precisely in this "surprise" that God was faithful to his covenant.

The LORD dealt with Sarah as he had said, and the LORD did for Sarah as he had promised. Sarah conceived and bore Abraham a son in his old age, at the time of which God had spoken to him. Abraham gave the name Isaac to his son whom Sarah bore him. . . . Now Sarah said, "God has brought laughter for me; everyone who hears will laugh with me." And she said, "Who would ever have said to Abraham that Sarah would nurse children? Yet I have borne him a son in his old age."

—Genesis 21:1–3, 6–7

Abraham and Sarah named their son Isaac. The Hebrew name *Isaac* is derived from a Hebrew verb meaning "to laugh." The birth of Isaac would begin another phase of Abraham and Sarah's faith journey. The faith of Abraham would be tested again. Imagine Abraham's initial response to God's command to him to sacrifice Isaac! (Check out Genesis 22:1–2.) Sacrificing children to the gods was not unusual in those times.

Abraham lived at a time when people feared the power of their gods to do them good and to bring evil upon them; for example, to bless the people with a bountiful harvest or to inflict their land with a crop-destroying drought. To win favor of their gods, the Canaanites and people of other ancient world cultures tried to appease their gods. This included the abhorrent practice of sacrificing children. Abraham and Sarah lived and breathed that culture. They could have erroneously believed it was reasonable that God was testing them; and so they prepared to obey God's command.

Abraham bound Isaac, placed his son on the pyre he had constructed, and prepared to sacrifice Isaac. An angel of the Lord intervened. The angel appeared to Abraham and ordered him not to sacrifice Isaac.

Abraham's faith and trust in God grew stronger. Abraham came to believe that the one true God was unlike the gods of Abraham's pagan neighbors. The Lord God would remain faithful to him, and Abraham to God. Through the intervention of an angel, Isaac lived and became the father of Jacob.

Reflecting on this Old Testament passage, the author of the New Testament Letter to the Hebrews wrote, in part:

THE SACRIFICE OF ISAAC | ENGRAVING AFTER RUBENS

He who had received the promises was ready to offer up his only son, of whom he had been told, "It is through Isaac that descendants shall be named for you." He considered the fact that God is able even to raise someone from the dead—and figuratively speaking, he did receive him back.

—Hebrews 11:17–19

READ, REFLECT AND SHARE

- ⊙ Read Genesis 17:19–22. God tells Abraham that he will name his son Isaac, a Hebrew name that means "he laughs."
- ⊙ Why were Abraham and Sarah surprised at the prediction of the visitors in Genesis 18:10?
- ⊙ Share what this story says to you about God working in your life and in the life of the Church.

ESAU AND JACOB | A.N. MIRONOV

Jacob (Israel) and the Twelve Tribes of Israel

The divine plan of salvation continues through Jacob, the grandson of Abraham, and his descendants. Isaac and his wife Rebekah became the parents of twin sons, Esau and Jacob, whom an angel of God would later rename Israel (check out Genesis 32:28). With the help of his mother, Rebekah, Jacob deceived his father in order to claim Esau's birthright. It was through Jacob and his twelve sons that the **twelve tribes of Israel** would take shape and the covenant God made with Abraham and his descendants would continue to be fulfilled.

Around 1300–1200 BC famine struck. Jacob sent several of his sons to Egypt to buy grain for their survival. Joseph was one of the sons of Jacob. His brothers, out of jealousy, had sold Joseph to slave traders who took him to Egypt. (Check out Genesis 37.) Joseph, whom Pharaoh had made one of his highest ranking advisers and confidants, recognized, aided and eventually reconciled with his brothers. Joseph also became reunited with his father, Jacob, who called his twelve sons to his deathbed and blessed them. Jacob's story images the story of the spiritual journey of all people of faith—the story of imperfect people striving for perfection, as Jesus commands of us.

TALK IT OVER
⊙ Review the definition of covenant.
⊙ What do you recall about the covenant at creation? With Noah? (Check out Genesis 3:15 and Genesis 9:9–16.)
⊙ How did God's covenant with Abraham, Isaac and Jacob build on these previous covenants?

OVER TO YOU
⊙ What insights into the connection between the Jewish people and the Catholic Church did you receive from studying this section of the chapter?
⊙ How do these insights help you understand and live your faith as a disciple of Jesus and a member of the Catholic Church, the new People of God?

The liberating power of living the Torah

PASSOVER

The Passover festival "commemorates the deliverance of Israel's first-born from the judgment wrought on those of the Egyptians [see Exodus 12:12-13; also Exodus 13:2, 12 and following], and the wondrous liberation of the Hebrews from Egyptian bondage [see Exodus 12:14-17]" (Emil G. Hirsch, "PASSOVER," *Jewish Encyclopedia*).

Exodus 13:8 "You shalt tell your children on that day, 'It is because of what the LORD did for me, when I came forth out of Egypt'" is the foundation of the Passover celebration. "On the basis of that passage it was considered a duty to narrate the story of the Exodus on the eve of Passover" (Gotthard Deutsch, Joseph Jacobs, "HAGGADAH (SHEL PESAH)," *Jewish Encyclopedia*).

OPENING REFLECTION

- ◉ Have you ever been liberated from someone or something that was oppressing you? Did you call upon God during that time of oppression?
- ◉ Did that experience of oppression and liberation call you to a deeper faith in God and his liberating presence in your life?

Every year Jews celebrate a special Passover meal, known as a Seder meal, to commemorate the Exodus of their ancestors from Egypt. This ritual event includes reading from the Haggadah, eating symbolic foods and answering the Four Questions, or the Haggadah Questions.

THE HAGGADAH

The ritual actions of the Passover or Seder meal include the youngest child at table asking four questions, to which those present respond. The asking and answering of these questions brings the memory of the Exodus event into the lives of those present at the meal.

Before asking the Four Questions, [all present] recite: There arose in Egypt a Pharaoh who knew not of the good deeds that Joseph had done for that country. Thus he enslaved the Jews and made their lives harsh through servitude and humiliation. This is the basis for the Passover holiday which we commemorate with these different rituals tonight.

The youngest child (or any individual) asks (or sings): Why is this night different from all other nights? 1. On all other nights we eat either bread or matzah; on this night, why only matzah? 2. On all other nights we eat herbs or vegetables of any kind; on this night why bitter herbs? 3. On all other nights we do not dip even once; on this night why do we dip twice? 4. On all other nights we eat our meals in any manner; on this night why do we sit around the table together in a reclining position?

The rest of the participants at the Seder answer: We were slaves to Pharaoh in Egypt, and God brought us out with a strong hand and an outstretched arm. And if God had not brought our ancestors out of Egypt, we and our children and our children's children would still be subjugated to Pharaoh in Egypt. Even if we were all old and wise and learned in Torah, we would still be commanded to tell the story of the Exodus from Egypt. And the more we talk about the Exodus from Egypt, the more praiseworthy we are.

—*The Passover Haggadah: A Guide to the Seder*, The Jewish Federation of North America, pages 4-5

THE LIFE-GIVING POWER OF REMEMBERING

The annual Passover celebration invites Jews to deepen their faith and trust in the God who not only freed their ancestors in the past but who continues to guide them in the present to live in freedom as his Chosen People.

We tell the story through ritual, food and song. And we conclude with the experience of redemption. This ancient experience of redemption gives us hope for today. Just as God redeemed our ancestors, so may he deliver us, wherever we are. This ultimate victory—of life over death—is our eternal promise.

—Rabbi Evan Moffic, *What Every Christian Needs to Know About Passover*, 130

In the retelling of the biblical Exodus narrative, the Exodus journey becomes the Jews' journey, as it speaks to the lives of individuals and families, communities and nations in each generation.

At the Last Supper Jesus celebrated the Passover meal with his disciples. At that celebration Jesus transformed the Passover meal into a **sacrament** and instituted the Sacrament of the Eucharist. "When Jesus instituted the Eucharist, he gave a new and definitive meaning to the blessing of the bread and the cup" (CCC, no. 1334).

WHAT ABOUT YOU PERSONALLY?

⊙ Have you ever participated in a Seder meal? What was the occasion?

⊙ What do you remember about the celebration? About its connection with our Catholic faith?

FROM SLAVERY TO FREEDOM

During that same period in the Israelites' history when they were enslaved in Egypt, God remained true to his covenant with Abraham, Isaac and Jacob. God called Moses to free his people from their oppression under Pharaoh. The *Exodus* (literally "going out") from Egypt is the central happening of the Jewish Scriptures and the defining moment in the identity of the Jewish people.

The annual Passover celebration invites Jews to deepen their faith and trust in the God who freed their ancestors and continues to guide them today

This epoch freedom journey begins with the response of Moses to "the God of Abraham, the God of Isaac, and the God of Jacob" (Exodus 3:6), who revealed his name , "I AM WHO I AM" (Exodus 3:14), and his fidelity to his Chosen People in the desert at Mount Horeb. After Moses approached a bush that was blazing but not being consumed by the flames, the Lord said to Moses:

> "I have observed the misery of my people who are in Egypt; I have heard their cry on account of their taskmasters. Indeed, I know their sufferings, and I have come down to deliver them from the Egyptians, and to bring them up out of that land to a good and broad land, a land flowing with milk and honey, to the country of the Canaanites, the Hittites, the Amorites, the Perizzites, the Hivites, and the Jebusites. The cry of the Israelites has now come to me; I have also seen how the Egyptians oppress them. So come, I will send you to Pharaoh to bring my people, the Israelites, out of Egypt. . . . I will be with you; and this shall be the sign for you that it is I who sent you: when you have brought the people out of Egypt, you shall worship God on this mountain."
>
> —Exodus 3:7–10, 12

GOD SPOKE TO MOSES THROUGH A BURNING BUSH

God revealed to Moses that he not only opposes slavery and oppression but also is willing to intervene in human history to set people free. God not only favors freedom and justice for all who are oppressed but he is also abundantly generous in the freedom that follows. God promised Moses and the Israelites that they would live in "a land flowing with milk and honey." In the world of the time, these words symbolized "the best of everything." Later, when the Israelites were oppressed by others or were oppressing one another, the prophets reminded them of this saving and liberating action of God. (Check out Isaiah 2:1–4 and 11:1–9.)

The Jewish people today, as they have always done, recognize and trust that God always raises up people to guide them to live in freedom from oppression and with justice with all people. The Exodus established for all humankind that God is always on the side of the oppressed, the poor, the vulnerable and the marginalized.

Jesus fulfilled this prophetic faith in the God as revealed in the Torah and the history of the Chosen People. Jesus' teachings and life, his Passion, Death and Resurrection, are the foundation and source of the salvation of all people and for all people to live in the freedom of the children of God. This faith is the basis of our commitment to strive for justice and peace rooted in love. (Check out Romans 8:18–25.)

LET'S PROBE DEEPER: A RESEARCH ACTIVITY

- ⦿ Reflect: God desires that all people "live with liberty and justice" (from the Pledge of Allegiance). The Exodus was a source of inspiration for Benjamin Franklin and other founders of our nation. It was a source of hope for the enslaved Black people and indentured peoples who worked the land of the wealthy.

At Sinai God revealed the Decalogue and entered a covenant with the Israelites

- ◉ Research the impact of the Exodus on the values established as the guiding principles of our nation. How are those values reflected in the Pledge of Allegiance?
- ◉ How does the Exodus continue to be a universal source of hope for all oppressed peoples today?
- ◉ Share your research as a class.

OVER TO YOU

- ◉ Read, reflect and analyze carefully Exodus 3:7–10. How does it affirm or challenge your own image of God?
- ◉ How is one's free response to God the source of true freedom?

THE COVENANT AT SINAI

God revealed himself once again to his people during their journey to freedom in the land of Canaan. Upon their arrival at Sinai God revealed the Decalogue and entered a covenant with the Israelites. He gave them a code of both worship and morality.

At Sinai God reaffirmed his relationship with the Israelites as his Chosen People, and they reaffirmed their covenantal relationship with the God of Abraham, Isaac and Jacob. In the Book of Exodus we read:

Then Moses went up to God; the LORD called to him from the mountain, saying, "Thus you shall say to the house of Jacob, and tell the Israelites: You have seen what I did to the Egyptians, and how I bore you on eagles' wings and brought you to myself. Now therefore, if you obey my voice and keep my covenant, you shall be my treasured possession out of all the peoples. Indeed, the whole earth is mine, but you shall be for me a priestly kingdom and a holy nation. These are the words that you shall speak to the Israelites."

So Moses came, summoned the elders of the people, and set before them all these words that the LORD had commanded him. The people all answered as one: "Everything that the LORD has spoken we will do."

—Exodus 19:3–8a

THE DECALOGUE

The Decalogue, which God revealed to Moses at Sinai, reminded the Israelites of the foundational moral laws at the heart of their living their covenant with God and with one another as the community of God's Chosen People. These Commandments summarized the ways the Israelites were to faithfully live just lives rooted in the love of God and neighbor. They spelled out in some detail the two inseparable commands in Deuteronomy 6:4–5 and Leviticus 19:18. These laws are at the heart of living in true freedom as the Chosen People of God for both Jews and Catholics. (Take a moment and recall Jesus' teaching on these two Old Testament precepts in Matthew 22:36–40.)

Moses continued to lead the Israelites through the desert, but the task of bringing them into the Promised Land would fall to Joshua. Ever since then, the Israelites have suffered internal division or external invasion. They would next be governed by judges (1250–1050 BC), and then, following their own request to God, by kings (1020–599 BC). The first three kings, and the most significant in the history of salvation, were Saul, David and Solomon. Solomon, David's son, ruled the Israelites from about 1020 BC through 922 BC. It was from the family of David, as we have seen, that Jesus would be born.

REFLECT AND SHARE

- What great truth can you take to heart for your own life from the story of the Exodus?

- What oppressions or injustices do you recognize in the life of the People of God, both Jews and Christians, right now?
- How might your faith and trust in God inspire you to respond to these?
- Share reflections as a class.

JEWISH RELIGIOUS PERSPECTIVE: GOD'S PROMISES ARE FOR ALL

The Jewish people still live in a special and lasting covenantal relationship with God. Their covenant with God is an everlasting covenant. The memory of Abraham, Isaac, Jacob and Moses shapes the Jewish world view. The reigns of David and Solomon and the teachings of the prophets afford a glimpse of the peace (*shalom*) and the blessings that God desires for Israel and all nations—that all people would live in justice and holiness of life, which is at the root of the divine plans of creation and salvation.

The prophets spoke constantly of God's special promise to send a messiah—a Hebrew word that means "anointed one"—to re-establish that kingdom and bring about those

Moses continued to lead the Israelites through the desert, but the task of bringing them into the Promised Land would fall to Joshua

JOSHUA AND CALEB WITH THE GRAPES OF CANAAN | QUIMPER CATHEDRAL, FRANCE blessings. This Messiah would free the people, re-establish their nation and bring about the new and everlasting covenant. He would usher in the coming of God's reign, when all nations will worship the Lord God.

At God's appointed time God sent his Incarnate Son, Jesus Christ, and established the new and everlasting covenant that he had first promised to Abraham. Luke tells us that when Jesus entered the synagogue at Nazareth and announced that he was the Messiah, Jesus' Jewish contemporaries rejected his claim. (Read Luke 4:14–30.) The Jewish people today do not acknowledge Jesus to be either the Messiah or a Divine Person, the Son of God. Nor do they accept the revealed truth of the Triune God, which is unique to Christian Revelation.

The Word of God for the Israelites is a word of hope and of promise, a divine life-giving word for them and for the world. The teachings and celebrations of the Jewish religion remind people of the power of God, the divine demands on human beings, the faithfulness of God, and the values God has placed at the heart of every person. The Jewish people continue to live with the hope and trust that God, at his own appointed time, will raise up a messiah and inaugurate a permanent era of justice and peace as foretold by the prophets.

WHAT ABOUT YOU PERSONALLY?

⊙ Do you feel that you have been chosen by God? For what?

⊙ Do you believe that God cares for every single person in the world?

⊙ Do you consider your faith in God to be a source of hope and promise in your life?

Jesus entered the synagogue at Nazareth and announced that he was the Messiah

JESUS IN THE SYNAGOGUE AT JERUSALEM (DETAIL) | ENGRAVING AFTER ALEXANDRE BIDA

The first covenant has never been revoked

AFFIRMING THE ORIGINAL COVENANT

Pope Francis' relationship with the Jewish people is well known and documented. He gave witness to this relationship in his written reply to the founder of the Italian newspaper *La Repubblica*. The Pope wrote, in part:

"You ask me, . . . what we should say to our Jewish brothers about the promise made to them by God: has it all come to nothing? Believe me, this is a question that challenges us radically as Christians, because, with the help of God, especially since Vatican Council II, we have rediscovered that the Jewish people are still for us the holy root from which Jesus germinated. . . . What I can say to you, with the Apostle Paul, is that God's fidelity to the close covenant with Israel never failed and that, through the terrible trials of these centuries, the Jews have kept their faith in God."

—Pope Francis, "Letter to the Founder of *La Repubblica*," September 11, 2013

OPENING REFLECTION

⊙ In light of what you have been learning in this chapter, how would you respond to someone who asks you, "Hasn't Christianity taken over from Judaism?"

⊙ Share responses as a class.

The Jewish World Population

Most estimates suggest that there are 13–14 million Jews in the world. Eighty percent of the world's Jews live in two countries, the United States of America and Israel. Six million European Jews died in the Holocaust, also called the *Shoah*. The devastating effect of the Nazi slaughter of the Jewish population, then and since, must commit all peoples to say, "Never again."

INTERNATIONAL HOLOCAUST REMEMBRANCE DAY 2015, AUSCHWITZ, POLAND

GOD'S COVENANT WITH THE JEWISH PEOPLE HAS NEVER BEEN REVOKED

Pius XI, who was pope from February 6, 1922 until his death on February 10, 1939, addressed a Belgian group as the world was on the brink of the Second World War: "Through Christ and in Christ we are the spiritual progeny of Abraham. Spiritually we are all Semites."

The Apostles and the other first disciples of Jesus, as we have seen, were Jews who came to profess their faith in Jesus to be their Lord and Messiah but who never gave up their identity as Jews. Recall the teaching of St. Peter on Pentecost in Acts of the Apostles 2:14–42. On that day over three thousand Jews from many nations became believers and followers of Jesus.

The fact that these first followers never gave up their Jewish identity is attested to by the early controversy in the Church as to whether Gentiles (non-Jews) had to become Jews before being baptized. The Church in apostolic times believed that God was always faithful to his promises and covenants and God did not revoke his covenant with the Jews nor reject the Jewish people. St. Paul could not be clearer on this point; he taught: "for the gifts and the calling of God are irrevocable" (Romans 11:29).

The promise of God to the Jewish people now extends to all people through Jesus, the Savior of the world. Through Jesus God has fulfilled both the first promise of salvation (see Genesis 3:15) and also the covenant he first made to Abraham, our father in faith, that "all the families of the earth shall be blessed" (Genesis 12:3).

Certainly, there is no place for arrogance or prejudice among Christians toward Jews. The Second Vatican Council made this clear, and taught: "Since Christians and Jews have such a common spiritual heritage, this sacred council wishes to encourage and further mutual understanding and appreciation. This can be achieved, especially, by way of biblical and theological enquiry and through friendly discussions" (*Declaration on the Relation of the Church to Non-Christian Religions*, no. 4). The Jewish people are still beloved of God, as the New Testament attests. "The Old Covenant has never been revoked" (CCC, no. 121).

When she delves into her own mystery, the Church, the People of God in the New Covenant, discovers her link with the Jewish

POPE PIUS XI PHOTOGRAPHED IN 1930

"Through Christ and in Christ we are the spiritual progeny of Abraham. Spiritually we are all Semites."

POPE PIUS XI

Judaism is the root and fountain-head of Christian faith

People, "the first to hear the Word of God" (*The Roman Missal*, Good Friday: General Intercessions, VI). The Jewish faith, unlike other non-Christian religions, is already a response to God's revelation in the Old Covenant. To the Jews "belong the sonship, the glory, the covenants, the giving of the law, the worship, and the promises; to them belong the patriarchs, and of their race, according to the flesh, is the Christ" (Romans 9:4-5) "for the gifts and the call of God are irrevocable" (Romans 11:29).

—CCC, no. 839

The Church is the sacrament of salvation in the world. This revealed truth does not negate that the Jewish people still have a unique role as an instrument of salvation in the world. The Jews, in God's own time and in God's own way, will be part of the full flowering of the Kingdom of God foretold by the prophets and inaugurated by Jesus Christ. Both Jews and Christians aim to give common witness on matters of peace and justice as they work together for the full realization of God's reign "on earth as it is in heaven."

CHRISTIANS *HAVE NOT* REPLACED JEWS
From the earliest days of the Church many Christians have wrongly considered Jews to have been "rejected by God." They believed that Christians were now the only "Chosen People," whom God chose to replace the Jews. As you have already learned, the cardinals and bishops of the Catholic Church assembled in a great worldwide (Ecumenical) Council from 1962 to 1965. Among other things, they reviewed what should be the proper relationship between Jews and Christians and addressed the question of the relevance of Judaism for Catholics today. The Council's response, titled *Declaration on the Relation of the Church to Non-Christian Religions* (*Nostra Aetate*), signaled a profound change of direction for the Catholic Church in her acknowledgment of the true nature of the relationship between the Jewish people and the Church.

The largest part of *Nostra Aetate* is devoted to Judaism. The Council reiterated that Judaism is the root and fountain-head of Christian faith. The declaration taught that Christian believers are like wild grafts spliced onto the cultivated plant of Judaism. The declaration referred to St. Paul's teaching about Jews: "They are Israelites, and to them belong the adoption, the glory, the covenants, the giving of the law, the worship, and the promises; to them belong the patriarchs, and from them, according to the flesh, comes the Messiah, who is over all, God blessed for ever. Amen" (Romans 9:4–5). St. Paul is referred to in the document as the zealous Pharisee who came to believe in Jesus to be his Lord and the Messiah.

The unique and special relationship between Christians and Jews evolved as time moved on into mutual estrangement and hostility. This eventually led to contempt of and, at times, outright persecution of the Jews in the West. This contempt and hostility, or anti-Semitism or anti-Judaism, emerged in the eleventh and twelfth centuries. Forgetting God's faithfulness to the Jews, many Christians thought that God had revoked or cancelled the covenant he entered into with the Jews. Christians erroneously came to believe that Christianity had superseded, or replaced, Judaism. This teaching is called "supersessionism" (from the verb "supersede," which means "to replace").

THE FULFILLMENT OF THE PROMISES GOD MADE TO THE JEWISH PEOPLE

If the New Covenant in Christ does not supersede the Jewish covenants, what does it do? Catholicism believes and teaches that Jesus Christ is the Messiah whom God promised. He is the new King in the line of King David (Jeremiah 33:14–18 and Matthew 1:6). Jesus Christ is the High Priest in the order of Melchizedek (Genesis 14:17–20) who sacrifices himself (Hebrews 9:26) and brings about a new covenant (Ezekiel 34) that would make atonement and bring forgiveness for sins (Hebrews 9:15) and acquire an eternal redemption (Hebrews 9:12). The Church believes Jesus Christ *fulfills*, but does not supersede (replace or revoke), God's irrevocable promises to and everlasting covenant with the Jews (Genesis 17:17).

The Catholic Church, in *Nostra Aetate*, roundly condemned supersessionism and taught that the first covenant has never been revoked. *Nostra Aetate* called Christians to respect the Jewish faith which teaches that Jews *still await* the coming of the Messiah whom God promised to send them. "God's People of the Old Covenant and the new People of God tend toward similar goals: expectation of the coming (or the return) of the Messiah" (CCC, no. 840). This teaching reflects the teachings of the Apostles and the early Church.

THE CHURCH CONDEMNS ANTI-JUDAISM OR ANTI-SEMITISM

The Gospel accounts of the response of some of the Jewish leaders to Jesus and of the arrest and trial of Jesus have led many Christians to falsely

St. John Paul II's historic apology

St. John Paul II, when he was pope, made an historic apology on behalf of the Church to the Jewish people. He placed this signed handwritten note in the Wailing Wall during his visit to Jerusalem in March 2000:

> God of our Fathers, you chose Abraham and his descendants to bring your Name to the nations: we are deeply saddened by the behavior of those who in the course of history have caused these your children to suffer, and asking your forgiveness we wish to commit ourselves to genuine brotherhood with the people of the Covenant.

ST. JOHN PAUL II AT THE WAILING WALL IN MARCH 2000

The sins of all humanity were the cause of Jesus' death

ECCE HOMO | HONORÉ DAUMIER

accuse the Jewish people as a whole of being responsible for Jesus' death.

This false judgment among Catholics and other Christians has been used as an excuse to justify the oppression and persecution of Jews for many centuries. All we can reasonably conclude from the Gospel accounts is that *some* Jewish religious leaders and the Roman authorities in Jerusalem cooperated in accusing, trying, condemning and crucifying Jesus. The vast majority of the Jewish people of that time, and all Jews since then, are guiltless of Jesus' death. (See CCC, no. 597.) The Second Vatican Council taught:

> neither all Jews indiscriminately at that time, nor Jews today, can be charged with the crimes committed during [Jesus'] passion.

And it explicitly condemned:

> all hatreds, persecutions [and] displays of anti-Semitism leveled at any time or from any source against the Jews.
> —*Declaration on the Relation of the Church to Non-Christian Religions*, no. 4

Never again should Christians have even the faintest trace of prejudice toward their Jewish brothers and sisters.

The truth is that the sins of *all humanity* were the cause of Jesus' death by crucifixion. "Taking into account the fact that our sins affect Christ himself, the Church does not hesitate to impute to Christians the gravest responsibility for the torments inflicted upon Jesus, a responsibility with which they have all too often burdened the Jews alone" (CCC, no. 598). One example of the Catholic Church implementing this teaching of the Council was when she dropped from her liturgy any reference to the Jewish people as a whole being responsible for the Death of Jesus.

LET'S PROBE DEEPER: A RESEARCH ACTIVITY

- ⊙ Since the close of Vatican II in 1965, every pope has given witness to this teaching of the Council condemning anti-Judaism or anti-Semitism.
- ⊙ Work in teams of four. Each member takes one of these four popes: Pope Paul VI, St. John Paul II, Pope Benedict XVI and Pope Francis, and researches their teachings on the unique and special relationship that unites the Catholic Church and the Jewish people.
- ⊙ Each team shares its research with the class.

Benedict XVI on Catholic–Jewish Relations

BENEDICT XVI DURING HIS VISIT TO THE USA IN 2008

During his apostolic visitation to the United States in April of 2008, Pope Benedict XVI addressed the Jewish community of New York City's Park East Synagogue. Speaking in tones of deep respect marked by fraternal warmth and affection, he stated:

> In addressing myself to you I wish to re-affirm the Second Vatican Council's teaching on Catholic–Jewish relations and reiterate the Church's commitment to the dialogue that in the past forty years has fundamentally changed our relationship for the better. . . . Because of that growth in trust and friendship, Christians and Jews can rejoice together in the deep spiritual ethos of the Passover.

DIALOGUE: SHARING OUR ROOTS OF FAITH

The words of Benedict XVI on Catholic–Jewish relations, to which Pope Francis has given witness, point to the importance of dialogue with our Jewish brothers and sisters. Such dialogue requires that Catholics and Jews remain faithful to the teachings and practices of their faith. For example, both Catholics and Jews need to acknowledge the differences in beliefs and in sacramental understanding and practice between the two faiths.

The United States Conference of Catholic Bishops (USCCB) is in dialogue with the leaders of the Jewish people. The aims of this dialogue, as outlined by the Church, include:

- growing in mutual respect for one another as sons and daughters of God;
- giving common witness on matters of peace and justice;
- deepening our mutual understanding of the one God and his plan for the world.

The USCCB website states: "The dialogues continue to meet once or twice a year, and have addressed such topics as moral education in public schools, pornography, holocaust revisionism, the death penalty, religious hatred, children and the environment, and the tragic events of September 11, 2001. . . .

The USCCB's Secretariat for Catholic–Jewish Relations, which later merged into the Secretariat for Ecumenical and Interreligious Affairs, has produced many documents on the development of Catholic–Jewish Relations in the United States" ("Our Catholic–Jewish Dialogues," *www.usccb.org*).

TALK IT OVER

- Why can prejudice based on religion be so destructive?
- Why should people of faith reject prejudice of every kind?
- How does open and honest dialogue work to overcome prejudice and the harm that prejudice can give rise to?

WHAT ABOUT YOU PERSONALLY?

- How might you reach out in friendship and love to Jewish people in your community?

A BRIEF SUMMARY: THE JEWISH–CATHOLIC CONNECTION

While there are, as we have seen, fundamental differences between the Catholic faith and the Jewish faith, our connection with the Jewish faith is special and unique. This similarity and difference is seen in a number of ways.

Sacred Scripture: You have already learned in the first section of this chapter that: (1) for Jews and Catholics and other Christians, the Scriptures are the revealed Word of God; (2) there is an unbreakable connection between the revealed and inspired Word of God contained in the Jewish Scriptures and the Old Testament: "The unity of the [Old and New Testaments] proceeds from the unity of God's plan and his Revelation. The Old Testament prepares for the New and the New Testament fulfills the Old; the two shed light on each other" (CCC, no. 140); (3) the Tanakh, or Jewish Scriptures, contains thirty-nine books. This differs from the forty-six books included in the Catholic Scriptures.

In addition to the above, it is to be noted that the arrangement or classification of sacred texts in the canonical books in the Jewish Scriptures and the Old Testament books in the Catholic Bible differs. The thirty-nine canonical books in the TaNaK are collected and arranged in three main sections: "T (**Torah**)," "N (**Nevi'im**)," and "K (**Ketuvim**)." The forty-six canonical texts in the Old Testament of the Catholic Bible are gathered into four sections: the Pentateuch or Torah, Historical Books, Wisdom Books, and the Books of the Prophets.

Messiah and a hope-filled future: Judaism and Christianity both look forward to a similar future: the *coming* of the Messiah (Judaism) or the *return* of the Messiah (Christianity), when the Kingdom of God will come about. This belief in the future is common to both traditions of the People of God, as well as containing a difference within it.

Judaism today, as we have seen, does not accept that the Messiah has already come in Jesus and it still awaits the fulfillment of that promise of God. Judaism also does not acknowledge Jesus to be a Divine Person, the Son of God, or the promised Messiah, nor does Judaism accept the revealed truth of the Triune God, which is unique to Christian Revelation. Christians believe that Jesus is the Messiah promised in the Old Testament, who inaugurated the kingdom that will come about in its fullness when he returns in glory.

Cyclical celebration of the liturgy: Jews and Catholics both celebrate their faith in a yearly cycle of liturgical celebrations. The proclamation of Sacred Scripture is central to both Jewish and Catholic celebrations. The Jewish people, however, have no sacramental economy; they continue to rely on the ritual prescriptions of the first covenant, which have been reinterpreted for post-Temple Judaism.

Moral life: Catholics and Jews share common elements of moral life and practice. The Decalogue is a strong part of Catholic moral teaching and tradition. Jesus drew on the Decalogue and the teaching of the prophets in his teaching on self-giving love and moral living. The rabbinic tradition within Judaism interprets and applies the Decalogue for the lives of Jews; the Magisterium of the Church reads the signs of the times and applies the Law of God, revealed in both Sacred Scripture and Sacred Tradition, to the life of Christians.

JOURNAL EXERCISE

⊙ Write your reflections on how dialogue and cooperation between Jews and Christians can deepen understanding and respect for both faith traditions.

⊙ Mention how you can and will participate in that dialogue.

SYMBOLS OF THE DECALOGUE AND EUCHARIST, TURIN, ITALY

REVIEW AND SHARE WHAT YOU HAVE LEARNED

Review what you have learned in this chapter about the beliefs and religious practices of the Jewish people and about the connection between those beliefs and practices and those of the Catholic Church. Use these statements as the focus of your responses:

⊙ The relationship between the Catholic Church and the Jewish people is unique and special.

⊙ The Jewish people are the original Chosen People of God; Christians are the new People of God.

⊙ The New Covenant with Jesus Christ is the fulfillment of the promises of the first covenant between God and the Jewish people.

⊙ "The Old Covenant has never been revoked" (CCC, no. 121).

⊙ Catholics and Jews share common elements of moral life and practice.

⊙ There are fundamental differences between Judaism and Catholicism.

⊙ The Catholic Church condemns anti-Judaism or anti-Semitism.

OVER TO YOU

⊙ Name some of the key commonalities and fundamental differences between Judaism and the Catholic Church.

⊙ What new insights and understanding about the beliefs and practices of Judaism have you gained from your study of this chapter?

LEARN BY EXAMPLE

Abraham Heschel (1907–72), Jewish scholar and gifted interfaith bridge builder

Abraham Heschel was a Jewish scholar who escaped the Holocaust because he fled from Poland to London and then to the United States in 1939. Heschel said that he was

"plucked from the fire of an altar of Satan on which millions of human lives were exterminated." Like a torch, he sought to set others alight with the truth, but he was intensely aware of those who perished in the ashes of the Holocaust—also called the *Shoah*, or "The Catastrophe." Among the victims of the *Shoah* were members of his family.

Heschel spent his life speaking out against injustice and oppression of all kinds. In New York he taught at the Jewish Theological Seminary for twenty-six years until his death in 1972. His abiding interest was in the call of the prophets to social action and justice for all. He accompanied Martin Luther King, Jr. on the March to Selma in 1962 during the Civil Rights Movement, remarking: "My feet were praying." Heschel argued that God had compassion (*pathos*) for human beings in pain and, indeed, that God becomes angry when people ignore the prophetic call.

Abraham Heschel played a crucial role at the time of the Second Vatican Council, as a theological representative of the AJC, the American Jewish Committee. He consulted with the Vatican Secretariat as they crafted the document that became *Nostra Aetate* (*Declaration on the Relation of the Church to Non-Christian Religions*). Charismatic, prayerful and spiritual, he was gifted in building bridges with others. The eventual vote in favor of *Nostra Aetate* is a tribute, among others, to Heschel's prophetic language. Abraham Heschel once said of his approach: "Don't be old. Don't be stale. See life as all doors. Some are open, some are closed. You have to know how to open them."

TALK IT OVER

⊙ What inspiration do you take from the life and work of Abraham Heschel?

⊙ What doors do you recognize as being unjustly "closed"? How can you help to open them?

SHARE FAITH WITH FAMILY AND FRIENDS

⊙ Reflect: Israel and the Jewish religion continue to play a decisive role in religion and the world.

⊙ Discuss:
   – Why should Catholics continue to cherish the values and commitments of the Jewish faith?
   – Why should Catholics join with their Jewish neighbors and friends to work for the coming of God's kingdom of peace and justice?

JUDGE AND DECIDE

⊙ Discuss with your group the possibility of reaching out to a Jewish teenager, perhaps someone who has just celebrated their Bar Mitzvah or Bat Mitzvah.

⊙ Draw up a list of questions you would like to ask him or her about the teachings or practices of the Jewish religion.

⊙ Contact a rabbi at the local synagogue or temple and set up the meeting.

JOURNAL EXERCISE

⊙ Reflect in your journal on your encounters with Judaism and Jewish people. Do you have friends or neighbors who are Jewish? Do you see them as your "brothers and sisters in faith"? How do you demonstrate this?

⊙ Can you recall when you first heard about the killing of millions of Jewish people by Adolf Hitler's Nazi regime and its collaborators during the Second World War? How did you respond?

⊙ Is there something that you think God may be calling you to do or change in your life as a result of what you have learned this week?

LEARN BY HEART

I will establish my covenant between me and you, and your offspring after you throughout their generations, for an everlasting covenant, to be God to you and to your offspring after you.

GENESIS 17:7

LEADER

We will use the *lectio divina* prayer format for today's Prayer Reflection. *Lectio divina* is a way of praying with Sacred Scripture and other texts that involves reading, meditation and contemplation. We read, reflect, try to understand, and listen to hear what God may be communicating to us, right here and right now, and we then act on what we have heard God calling us to do.

The Scripture passage for the prayer is from Psalm 27. The praying of the Psalms is central to the prayer life of both Jews and Christians. "Though a given psalm may reflect an event of the past, it still possesses such direct simplicity that it can be prayed in truth by men of all times and conditions" (CCC, no. 2588).

Read and Reflect

Quiet your mind and heart. Place yourself in the presence of God as you pray these verses from Psalm 27:

The LORD is my light and my salvation;
 whom shall I fear?
The LORD is the stronghold of my life;
 of whom shall I be afraid? . . .

One thing I asked of the LORD,
 that will I seek after:
to live in the house of the LORD
 all the days of my life,
to behold the beauty of the LORD,
 and to inquire in his temple. . . .

Hear, O LORD, when I cry aloud,
 be gracious to me and answer me!
"Come," my heart says, "seek his face!"
 Your face, LORD, do I seek.
 Do not hide your face from me. . . .

I believe that I shall see the goodness of the LORD
 in the land of the living.

Wait for the LORD;
 be strong, and let your heart take courage;
 wait for the LORD!
 —Psalm 27:1, 4, 7–9, 13–14

Now, silently and slowly pray the prayer once again, being alert for what stands out for you or seems significant for your life right now.

Meditate

Pray the psalm verses again, pausing and talking silently in your heart to God the Father, Son and Holy Spirit about what you are hearing.

Contemplate

Pray the psalm verses once again, as you listen to hear what God may be saying to you.

Pray

Acknowledge God's presence and pray for whatever may be the deepest desire of your heart.

Act

LEADER

Respond in the silence of your heart to these questions to help you decide what you can and will do to put your prayer into action. Then, if you wish, share your reflections on these questions with a partner:

⊙ What does this study and prayer time call me to do?
⊙ How will I take it to heart in my life now?

Let us share a sign of peace and go forth and glorify God by our lives.

All share a sign of peace and then pray the Sign of the Cross together.

CHAPTER 8

Islam and the Muslim People

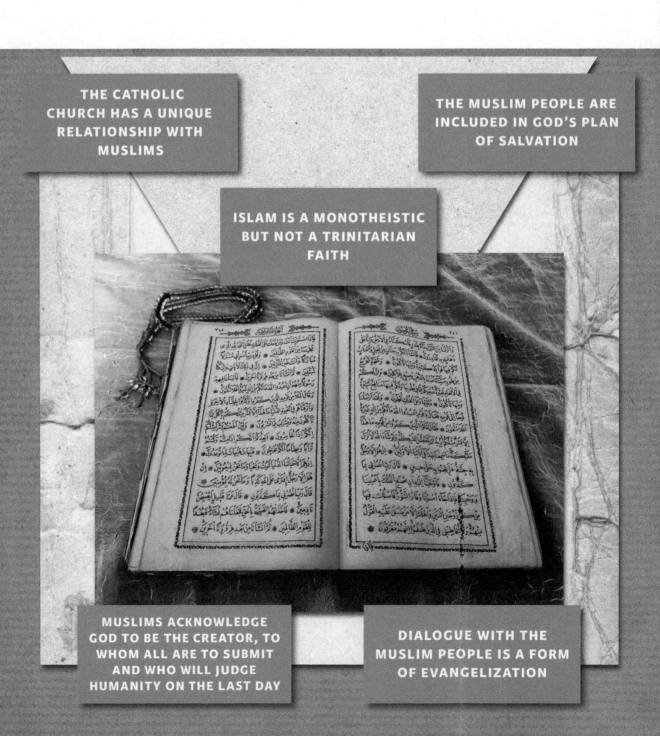

THE CATHOLIC CHURCH HAS A UNIQUE RELATIONSHIP WITH MUSLIMS

THE MUSLIM PEOPLE ARE INCLUDED IN GOD'S PLAN OF SALVATION

ISLAM IS A MONOTHEISTIC BUT NOT A TRINITARIAN FAITH

MUSLIMS ACKNOWLEDGE GOD TO BE THE CREATOR, TO WHOM ALL ARE TO SUBMIT AND WHO WILL JUDGE HUMANITY ON THE LAST DAY

DIALOGUE WITH THE MUSLIM PEOPLE IS A FORM OF EVANGELIZATION

THE CATHOLIC CHURCH "RECOGNIZES THAT SHE HAS A unique relationship to Muslims" (*United States Catholic Catechism for Adults* [USCCA], 131). Like Jews and Christians, Muslims acknowledge God to be the Creator and they "profess to hold the faith of Abraham, and together with us they adore the one, merciful God, who will judge humanity on the last day" (*Dogmatic Constitution on the Church* [*Lumen Gentium*], no. 16). Catholics and Muslims share many common elements of moral life and practice, including a similar outlook on the importance of prayer, care of the poor, self-discipline, personal sacrifice and seeking the will of God above all things.

FIVE PILLARS OF ISLAM

SHAHADA (CREED)
SALAT (PRAYER)
ZAKAT (POOR TAX)
SAWM (FASTING)
HAJJ (PILGRIMAGE)

Faith Focus: These teachings of the Catholic Church are the primary focus of the doctrinal content presented in this chapter:
- "The Church . . . recognizes that she has a unique relationship to Muslims" (USCCA, 131).
- The Muslim people are included in God's plan of salvation.
- Islam is a monotheistic faith that claims ties to the faith of Abraham, but it is not a Trinitarian faith.
- Islam does not acknowledge God to be the Father of Jesus Christ, or Jesus to be the Divine Son of God.
- Catholics and Muslims acknowledge God to be the Creator.
- Catholics and Muslims acknowledge that God will judge humanity on the last day.
- "Dialogue [with the Muslim people] is a form of evangelization" (USCCA, 131).

Discipleship Formation: As a result of studying this chapter and discovering the meaning of the faith of the Catholic Church for your life, you should be better able to:
- describe the origins of Islam;
- understand and articulate the common ties between the teachings and practices of Islam and those of the Catholic Church;
- understand and articulate the differences between the teachings and practices of Islam and those of the Catholic Church;
- dialogue with Muslim friends and neighbors;
- speak out against prejudice toward Islam and the Muslim people;
- work cooperatively with Muslim friends and neighbors to bring about God's kingdom of peace, justice and charity.

Scripture References: These scripture references are quoted or referred to in this chapter:
OLD TESTAMENT: Genesis 16:7–16
NEW TESTAMENT: Matthew 4:10, 28:16–20; **Acts of the Apostles** 17:16–34; **Romans** 12:18

Faith Glossary: Familiarize yourself with or recall the meaning of these key terms. Definitions are found in the Glossary: **common good, evangelization, Incarnation, Islam, miracles, monotheism, Muslim, Original Sin, polytheism, Qur'an, Shariah, Trinity**

Learn by Heart: Matthew 4:10
Learn by Example: Malala Yousafzai

How does a person's faith impact their decisions and actions?

Some Basic Facts About Islam

Founder: Muhammad
Belief about God: There is one God (Monotheism)
Holy Writings: Qur'an (Koran)
Five Pillars of the Faith: Profession of Faith, Prayer, Almsgiving, Fasting, Pilgrimage to Mecca
Types: Sunnis (the majority); Shiites, or Shias

OPENING REFLECTION

⊙ Review the feature box "Some Basic Facts About Islam."
⊙ Brainstorm, as a class, other facts you know about Islam and the Muslim people.
⊙ List the information on a chart. Add and clarify information as you continue your study of Islam and its unique relationship to the Catholic Church.

ISLAM: A GROWING RELIGION

Islam, with more than 1.3 billion members worldwide, is the second largest religion. Those who profess Islam are called Muslims. There are over 900 million Muslim people in Eastern Asia, 300 million in the Middle East and North Africa, 200 million in Africa south of the Sahara, 43 million in Europe, and about 4 million in the Western Hemisphere. Some project that by 2070 Islam will have the largest number of believers worldwide.

The number of Muslims in the United States of America has been growing steadily. Attitudes of Catholics and other Christians in the United States toward the Muslim people range from hostile to welcoming. These attitudes are often founded on fear and erroneous, prejudicial information about Islam.

REFLECT AND SHARE

⊙ Where do you get your knowledge about Islam and the religious beliefs of Muslim people?
⊙ What negative attitudes toward Muslims have you encountered, and where?
⊙ Share as a class how your interactions with Muslim friends or neighbors may have caused you to question or dismiss any of the negative things you have heard about Muslims and the Islamic faith.

The Catholic Church's relationship with Islam

The Church . . . recognizes that she has a unique relationship to Muslims. "The plan of salvation also includes those who acknowledge the Creator, in the first place amongst whom are the Muslims; these profess to hold the faith of Abraham, and together with us they adore the one, merciful God, mankind's judge on the last day" (*Catechism of the Catholic Church* [CCC], no. 841, citing Vatican II, *Dogmatic Constitution on the Church* [*Lumen Gentium*], no. 16).

—*United States Catholic Catechism for Adults* (USCCA), 131

THE LIFE—FAITH—LIFE STORY OF MUHAMMAD YUNUS

Muhammad Yunus, a devout Muslim, was teaching economics in 1974 at Chittagong University in Bangladesh when he began to have doubts about being a university teacher: "All of a sudden, I started having an empty feeling. What good were all these elegant theories when people died of starvation on pavements and on doorsteps?"

Muhammad decided to go and look at what was happening in the neighboring village. He tells the story himself:

I was shocked to discover a woman in the village, borrowing less than a dollar from the money-lender, on the condition that he would have the exclusive right to buy all she produces at the price he decides. . . . I decided to make a list of the victims of this money-lending "business" in the village next door to our campus. When my list was done, it had the names of 42 victims who borrowed a total amount of US $27. I offered US $27 from my own pocket to get these victims out of the clutches of those money-lenders. The excitement that was created among the people by this small action got me further involved in it. If I could make so many people so happy with such a tiny amount of money, why not do more of it?

Muhammad Yunus learned a number of very important things about poverty from this experience. He learned that a small amount of money given as a loan was enough to start a small enterprise. He learned that women are often more adventurous in seeking to improve their situation than men. He learned that poor people are prepared to work hard. He learned that the poor repay loans when they have the necessary resources. And he learned that banks are badly organized and generally unwilling to change in order to help poor and illiterate people with loans.

So Muhammad set up his own bank, called the Grameen Bank. *Grameen* means "rural" or "village" in the Bangla language. In its first twenty years the Grameen Bank loaned six billion US dollars to 7.6 million people. Women received 97 percent of the loans in 73,000 Bangladeshi villages, and 99 percent of those loans were repaid.

TALK IT OVER

⊙ What insights do the decisions and actions of Muhammad Yunus give you into the values of Islam?

"An authentic faith always involves a profound desire to change the world. Here is the question we must ask ourselves: do we also have great vision and impulse? Are we also daring? Do our dreams fly high? Does zeal consume us?"

POPE FRANCIS, JANUARY 3, 2014

THE LIFE—FAITH—LIFE STORY OF MUHAMMAD YUNUS *CONTINUED*

Where did Muhammad Yunus get his enthusiasm to change the world? Why was he so keenly alert to the causes of poverty in the villages? Yunus answers that question by telling us about his upbringing in a devout Muslim home:

> My father was a devout Muslim all his life, and made three pilgrimages to Mecca. . . . He usually dressed all in white, white slippers, white *paijama* pants, a white tunic and a white prayer cap. He divided his time between his work, his prayers and his family life. . . .
>
> My mother, Sofia Khatun, was a strong and decisive woman. . . . She was full of compassion and kindness, and probably the strongest influence on me. She always had money put away for any poor relations who visited us from distant villages. It was she, through her concern for the poor and the disadvantaged, who helped me discover my destiny, and she who most shaped my personality.

In 2006 Muhammad Yunus and the Grameen Bank were awarded the Nobel Peace Prize. They were the first Muslims to receive that recognition and honor.

TALK IT OVER

- What impact did Muhammad's family have on the formation of his religious beliefs? How did the faith of his parents influence his personal life choices as an adult?
- What other insights does Muhammad's life—faith—life story give you into Islam?

WHAT ABOUT YOU PERSONALLY?

- The Christian home is a domestic church, a church of the home.
- How has your family influenced your living the Catholic faith? Give specific examples.
- What is the connection between practicing your Catholic faith and being a responsible citizen? Give concrete examples.

The origins of Islam

OPENING REFLECTION
- ⊙ What do you know about the origins of Islam and the life and work of Muhammad?
- ⊙ What are the sources of your knowledge of Islam and of its founder, Muhammad?

THE ROOTS OF ISLAM

The Arabic term *islām* literally means "surrender." The true Muslim is one who obeys or submits or surrenders to the will of Allah. *Allāh* is the Arabic word for God.

Islam has its roots in the life and teachings of Muhammad (c. 570–632), whom the Muslim people revere, considering him to be the last of the prophets and messengers of God. Muhammad's name means "The Glorified One," though Islam does not confess Muhammad to be divine. Muslims add the phrase "Peace be upon him," which often appears in print as PBUH, when they speak Muhammad's name. The Muslim people revere but do not worship Muhammad. It is offensive, therefore, to call Muslims "Muhammadans," as this implies that Muslims worship Muhammad as divine.

Muhammad was born in Mecca in Arabia (today Saudi Arabia) sometime shortly before or after AD 570. The economy of Mecca was rooted in trade, transport and finance and in the pilgrimages to the shrine of the Ka'aba, a cube-like mosque. (*Ka'aba* is an Arabic word that means "cube.") Muslim tradition teaches that Abraham (whom Muslims name Ibrahim and revere as a prophet) and his son Ishmael built the Ka'aba as a place where they could worship the one true God. The Bible does not teach that Abraham and Ishmael went to Arabia

THE KA'ABA IN MECCA

and built the Ka'aba. But Muslims read Genesis 16:7–16, in which an angel of the Lord tells Hagar, Ishmael's mother, that his descendants would be innumerable, as a text supportive of this belief.

The **Qur'an**, the holy writings of Islam, often attests to the importance for Muslims of Abraham's faith in the one true God. For example, we read: "Who can be better in religion than one who submits his whole self to Allah, does good, and follows the way of Abraham the True in Faith? For Allah did take Abraham for a friend" (Qur'an 4:125). In another place we read: "Follow the ways of Abraham the True in Faith" (Qur'an 16:123). Like Jews and Christians, Muslims believe that faith in one transcendent God (**monotheism**) begins with the faith of Abraham. We will explore in detail in the "Embrace the Vision" section of this chapter Islam's teachings on monotheism and how they differ from the teachings of Christianity as professed in the creeds of the Church.

THE MESSAGE TO MUHAMMAD ON MOUNT HIRA

When Muhammad was a child, all the members of his immediate family died. An uncle, Abu Talib, cared for him. At the age of twenty-five Muhammad married Khadijah, a rich widow. He worked in the transportation business in Mecca. Because of his honesty and business acumen he earned the title El Amin, which means "The Reliable One."

Muhammad's life changed when he was forty years old. According to Islamic belief, one night in AD 610 while he was praying in a cave on Mount Hira, which is about two miles outside of Mecca, Muhammad received a mystical vision of the Angel Gabriel and the first of many messages. The angel told Muhammad to *recite* the words of the message he had for him. Muslims call this event "the Night of Power."

For the rest of his life Muhammad would continue to receive other messages; and, as he did so, he would recite and dictate the words to a scribe. These written messages were collected to form the Muslim sacred book of holy writings, the Qur'an. (*Qur'ān* is an Arabic word meaning "Recite.") Muslims believe that the Qur'an is a

miracle. They believe this because Muhammad, an illiterate man, could not have written on his own the words that have the power to transform and give direction to the lives of so many Muslim people.

The Catholic Church teaches: "Christian faith cannot accept 'revelations' that claim to surpass or correct the Revelation of which Christ is the fulfillment, as is the case in certain non-Christian religions and also in certain recent sects which base themselves on such 'revelations' " (CCC, no. 67). We will explore this and other teachings and practices of Islam in the remaining sections of this chapter.

REFLECT AND SHARE

⊙ Muhammad lived in an area of Arabia that during his life had a significant Christian and Jewish population. Reflect:
  - What impact might Muhammad's interaction with Jews and Christians have had on the origins of Islam?
  - What similarities and what differences do you see between the origins of Islam, Judaism and Christianity?
⊙ Share reflections as a class.

THE HOLY QU'RAN

PILGRIMS AT THE SITE OF THE BATTLE OF UHUD, WHICH WAS FOUGHT BETWEEN CITIZENS OF MECCA AND MEDINA IN 625

THE HIJRA AND THE PREACHING OF MUHAMMAD

In AD 613 Muhammad began to preach in Mecca. By then the Ka'aba had become both a profitable enterprise and the center of worship for pagan Arabs who believed in and worshiped many gods. Muhammad called on his fellow citizens to return to obedience to the one true God, moral living, honesty in business, righteous conduct and charity toward the poor. He warned people not to ignore God's message, for the time of judgment was approaching. God would, however, be merciful if they changed their lives now.

The wealthy and powerful turned a deaf ear and closed their minds and hearts to Muhammad's preaching. Acceptance of his message came slowly. After ten years his followers numbered only about two hundred.

In 622 the city of Yathrib, which lies two hundred miles north of Mecca, was torn with conflict. Some of the citizens invited Muhammad to help them settle their disputes; so he and his followers moved to Yathrib. The journey to that city, which is known in Islamic history as the *Hijra*, or "emigration," marks the beginning of Islam as a religion.

Yathrib is now called Medina, or "the city," to mark its status in Islam. The year AD 622 is designated 1 AH (*Anno Hegirae*, or "in the year of the Hijra"—the first year of the Muslim calendar). Many people accepted the teachings of Muhammad and professed their faith in and worshiped Allah alone. Muhammad built the first mosque in Medina and established the first Muslim constitution.

Citizens of Mecca attacked Medina three times between 622 and 630. The people of Medina defended their city successfully and it grew in power and prestige. These battles ensured the success of Islam. Some of the fighting between Medina and Mecca was bloody and cruel.

In 628 Muhammad negotiated peace with Mecca. Under the terms of this agreement he would return to the city of his birth in 630. Upon his return Muhammad offered reconciliation and he did not seek revenge or retribution. Pagan practices were discontinued, and worship of the one true God was restored at the Ka'aba.

PROBE MORE DEEPLY

⊙ Mecca is Islam's holy city. Every year Muslims from around the world make a pilgrimage to Mecca.

⊙ What role does Mecca play in Islam today? How do Muslims express their reverence for Mecca? Why do you think they do so?

DOMES ABOVE THE PROPHET'S TOMB, MEDINA

DEATH OF MUHAMMAD AND CONTROVERSY OVER HIS SUCCESSORS

Muhammad had just returned from his first and only *Hajj*, or pilgrimage to Mecca, when he became ill and died at the age of sixty-two, on June 8, AD 632 (10 AH). The group around Muhammad chose Abu Bakr, the father of Muhammad's wife Aisha, to be the caliph, or successor of Muhammad.

Controversy then arose as to who was the true successor of Muhammad. Other Muslims believed that Muhammad divinely ordained his cousin and son-in-law Ali, who was the son of Abu Talib and the husband of Muhammad's daughter Fatimah, to be the next caliph, and Ali became the fourth caliph after a battle in 656. This led to the division of Islam into several branches, of which Sunnis and Shiites are the major two.

Shia is a shortened Arabic word meaning "the party of Ali." Shia Muslims, or Shiites, assert that Ali was divinely chosen to succeed Muhammad, and they discount the legitimacy of the first three caliphs who ruled after the death of Muhammad. Shias maintain that the successor of Muhammad ought to be a member of the Prophet's family, and that Ali and his descendants are the sole legitimate Islamic leaders. The Sunni, on the other hand, maintain that the caliph should be chosen by the leading group of Muslims. The majority of Muslims today are Sunni.

All Muslim people, despite their divisions and diverse understandings and interpretations of the Qur'an and other Islamic teachings, consider Islam to be an *Ummah*, a single community bound and united as one by a common faith.

JOURNAL EXERCISE

⊙ How does what you are learning about Islam and the Muslim people prepare you to share faith experiences and engage in a more meaningful way with Muslim friends and neighbors?

⊙ How might you work cooperatively with Muslim friends, neighbors and others to build a more just world rooted in charity, or love?

Discovering what is true and holy in Islamic teachings

Acknowledging what is true and holy

The Catholic Church rejects nothing of what is true and holy in these [non-Christian] religions. . . . The church has also a high regard for the Muslims. They worship God, who is one, living and subsistent, merciful and almighty, the Creator of heaven and earth, who has also spoken to humanity. They endeavor to submit themselves without reserve to the hidden decrees of God, just as Abraham submitted himself to God's plan, to whose faith Muslims eagerly link their own. Although not acknowledging him as God, they venerate Jesus as a prophet; his virgin Mother they also honor, and even at times devoutly invoke. Further, they await the day of judgment and the reward of God following the resurrection of the dead. For this reason they highly esteem an upright life

and worship God, especially by way of prayer, alms-deeds and fasting.

—Vatican II, *Declaration on the Relation of the Church to Non-Christian Religions (Nostra Aetate)*, no. 2

OPENING REFLECTION

⊙ Carefully read and reflect on "Acknowledging What Is True and Holy" to prepare for our exploration of some of the key beliefs and practices of Islam.

⊙ Write down any questions that arise as you reflect on the teachings of the Catholic Church summarized in that excerpt from *Nostra Aetate*.

THE HOLY BOOK, THE QUR'AN (KORAN)

The Qur'an, as we have seen in the "Attend and Reflect" section of this chapter, is the holy book, or holy writings, of Islam. Muslims reverence the original language of the Qur'an. For the Muslim people, the Arabic words are the very words of Allah, which they strive to memorize and recite

by heart. Translations are not regarded as the true Qur'an; they are only *versions* of the Qur'an.

Muslims treat the Qur'an with great reverence and respect. For example, a Muslim would not place anything on the holy book, nor leave it on the floor, nor allow it to be abused in any way. Muslims also differ among themselves in their interpretation of the Qur'an. These differences arise because in Islam, unlike in the Catholic Church, there is no central figure of authority who has been given the authority to authentically interpret the Qur'an.

RECALL, REFLECT AND SHARE

⊙ Recall what you have already learned about Sacred Scripture, Sacred Tradition, and the Magisterium during this course of study.

- How would you explain to a Muslim friend the teachings of the Catholic Church on:
  - the Bible as the revealed, inspired written Word of God?
  - authentically interpreting the Sacred Scriptures?
- Share reflections as a class.

OVER TO YOU
- Where is your copy of the Bible right now? Is it well-used, or neglected or even abused? What does the condition of your Bible say to you about your respect for the Bible as the inspired written Word of God?
- What are your favorite passages in the Bible? Have you memorized any of them?
- How might learning biblical passages guide you in living your Christian faith?

THE FIVE PILLARS OF ISLAM
Muhammad, when asked to summarize his teaching, answered by listing the Five Pillars of Islam, or the five things that every Muslim must *do* to express their faith: creed or declaration of faith, prayer, almsgiving, fasting and pilgrimage. He then listed the Six Articles of Muslim faith as the things all Muslims should *believe:* faith in one God, in angels, in the holy books, in the prophets, in the last day and in God's decree and will.

Islamic faith does not hold to the Catholic teaching on the role of the sacraments in the divine plan of salvation. It has no sacramental economy, that is, "the communication (or 'dispensation') of the fruits of Christ's paschal Mystery in the celebration of the Church's 'sacramental' liturgy" (CCC, no. 1076).

Islamic law requires a Muslim's *testimony* of faith through works, prayer, fasting, almsgiving and pilgrimage as expressions of living their faith. This testimony is summarized in the Five Pillars of Islam, which are:
- **Shahada (creed)**. The First Pillar is the Islamic creed that affirms the one God (Allah) and the divine truth of the prophecies given to Muhammad.

What does the condition of your Bible say to you about your respect for the Bible as the inspired written Word of God?

MUSLIMS AT PRAYER IN THE MASJID MOSQUE OF FATEHPUR SIKRI NEAR AGRA, INDIA

- **Salat (prayer)**. The Second Pillar is the daily prayer. The central action is prostration, as the worshiper faces Mecca, kneels and bows forward; this daily prayer is performed five times a day.
- **Zakat (poor tax)**. The Third Pillar is the poor tax, or almsgiving. The levy, or tithe, is usually 2.5 percent of one's wealth.
- **Sawm (fasting)**. The Fourth Pillar is the fast. Muslims fast during daytime throughout the month of Ramadan. Only when darkness falls can one eat and drink.
- **Hajj (pilgrimage)**. The Fifth Pillar is the pilgrimage to Mecca, known as the Hajj. Every Muslim who is physically and financially able should make a pilgrimage to Mecca once in their lifetime. Over two million people participate in the Hajj each year.

RECALL, REFLECT AND SHARE
- Muslims and Christians are to worship God in both words and deeds. Islamic law, as we have seen, requires good works, prayer, fasting, almsgiving and pilgrimage as expressions of a Muslim's testimony to living their faith.
- Does Sacred Scripture and the laws of the Catholic Church require Catholics to worship God in a similar manner? Brainstorm examples; for instance, the Precepts of the Church in the "Catholic Prayers, Devotions and Practices" section of this text.

WHAT ABOUT YOU PERSONALLY?
- Do you set aside times each day to share your thoughts and feelings with God in prayer? How often?
- Do you value your blessings as gifts from God to be shared? How generous are you toward other people, especially toward people who are living in poverty?
- In our culture we fast and train to promote bodily health and well-being. How might fasting or denying yourself some pleasure contribute to your spiritual fitness?
- Did you ever take part in a religious pilgrimage? If so, share how you felt about it.

THE SHAHADA
Muslims believe that one becomes a Muslim by the recitation of the *Shahada* before a witness. The Shahada, which means "Testimony," summarizes the heart of Islamic belief. Devout Muslims recite the Shahada more than twenty times each day. The words of the Shadada are:

> There is no God but God; Muhammad is the messenger of God.
> *La ilaha ill Allah; Muhammadur Rasul Allah.*

The words of the Shahada are the first and last words that a Muslim hears. The Shahada is recited over a newly born Muslim and whispered into the ear of a dying Muslim. There are no pictures or statues in a mosque. You will see only intricate designs called Arabesques. Some are the script of the Shahada. The flags of Muslim countries often depict the Shahada.

GOD IS ONE: ISLAM'S TEACHINGS ON MONOTHEISM

The Shahada professes the oneness (tawhid) of God. Islam, like Christianity and Judaism, is a monotheistic religion. Monotheism is the belief in one God. The Muslim people believe, as do Christians and Jews, that there is one Lord God to whom all owe obedience, as Abraham also believed.

Islam professes Allah to be the one almighty and infinite God, who is the the creator of all that is seen and unseen, which, for Muslims, as for Christians, includes angels. This monotheistic Islamic faith is in direct contrast to the polytheism that was practiced in Mecca at the time of Muhammad, when people worshiped some 360 pagan idols.

The monotheism taught by Islam excludes the belief that the one God has revealed himself to be a Trinity of Divine Persons. This is a fundamental difference that separates the monotheism taught by Christianity from that taught by Islam.

ISLAM'S TEACHINGS ON JESUS

Jesus is mentioned more than fifty times in the Qu'ran. He is identified as a Prophet-Messenger and servant of Allah. The Qu'ran has Jesus saying, "I am indeed a servant of Allah: he hath given me revelation and made me a prophet" (Qu'ran 19:30). Islam, as Mormonism does, proposes a new revelation that supersedes, or supplants, the unsurpassable Revelation in Christ, which is realized most fully in Jesus Christ and ended with the death of the last Apostle.

Islam rejects the Christian dogma of the Incarnation, that is, "the Second Person of the Holy Trinity assumed our human nature, taking flesh in the womb of the Virgin Mary" (USCCA, Glossary, 515) without giving up his identity as God. Islam rejects the Christian belief that Jesus is a divine Person who has "two natures, a human one and a divine one" (USCCA, Glossary,

TILE WITH PART OF THE SHAHADA IN KUFIC CALLIGRAPHY, IRAN, 14TH CENTURY

STREET SIGN FOR THE VIA DOLOROSA, JERUSALEM, IN HEBREW, ARABIC AND ROMAN CHARACTERS

515). Islam teaches that Jesus is a human person whom Allah created and who prepared the way for Muhammad and for Allah's revelations to Muhammad.

Mary, *Maryam* in Arabic, is named in several chapters of the Qu'ran, and the whole of chapter 19 is named after her. The Qu'ran teaches that Jesus had no human father and was born miraculously of the Virgin Mary, whom Allah had "chosen above all the women of the worlds" (Qu'ran 3:42). Islam reveres Mary as the virgin mother of Jesus and rejects the Christian belief that Mary is the Mother of God. Islam also interprets Jesus' many miracles and other works of compassion as signs of the infinite mercy of Allah and not signs that Jesus was divine. (*Take a moment and review the definition of "miracle" in the Faith Glossary of this text.*)

Islam rejects the Christian dogma on Original Sin and that Jesus is the Savior of the world. It denies that Jesus freely gave his life and was crucified to redeem humanity. Islam holds that Allah spared Jesus from death itself and took him up to heaven, from where he will return on Judgment Day.

RECALL, REFLECT AND SHARE

⊙ Recall and reflect on this teaching of the Catholic Church: "Whatever of good or truth is found amongst them [those who, through no fault of their own, do not know the Gospel of Christ and his Church] is considered by the church to be a preparation for the Gospel and given by him who enlightens all men and women that they may at length have life" (Vatican II, *Dogmatic Constitution on the Church* [*Lumen Gentium*], no. 16).

⊙ Discuss with a partner: What teachings of Islam would you consider "a preparation for the Gospel"? (*Note: Use the Apostles' Creed and the Nicene Creed as your guide.*)

⊙ Share discussions as a class.

JOURNAL EXERCISE

⊙ Does the teaching of Islam on Jesus and Mary surprise you?

⊙ Where would you begin a dialogue with a Muslim high school student about the meaning of your faith in Jesus and your reverence for Mary?

⊙ Write your thoughts in your journal in the form of a conversation.

Understanding and promoting the will of God

"Live peaceably with all" (Romans 12:18)

Over the centuries many quarrels and dissensions have arisen between Christians and Muslims. The sacred council now pleads with all to forget the past, and urges that a sincere effort be made to achieve mutual understanding; for the benefit of all, let them together preserve and promote peace, liberty, social justice and moral values.

[T]he church reproves, as foreign to the mind of Christ, any discrimination against people or any harassment of them on the basis of their race, color, condition in life or religion.

—*Declaration on the Relation of the Church to Non-Christian Religions*, nos. 3 & 5

OPENING REFLECTION

⊙ Read and reflect on the excerpts in "Live Peaceably with All" from the Vatican II document *Declaration on the Relation of the Church to Non-Christian Religions*.

⊙ Does your experience of the general attitude toward and treatment of Muslims by Christians and of Christians by Muslims in your community and throughout the United States of America reflect this teaching of the Catholic Church?

⊙ Do the words and actions of some Christians and some Muslims work against achieving the vision of the Catholic Church in "Live Peaceably with All"?

OVER TO YOU

⊙ What about your own own attitude and actions?

⊙ What is the source of these attitudes and actions?

⊙ Do you need to work at bringing them into harmony with the Church?

VIOLENCE IN THE NAME OF GOD

Believers are often guilty of acts of violence and creating division in the name of God, quite as much as they can be credited with working for peace, justice and reconciliation. Historians sometimes apply the term "The Clash of Civilizations" to such conflicts.

Christians and Muslims are no exception to this reality. For example, the *force* of Arab arms impelled the early expansion of Islam. The early Muslim governors and commanders saw themselves as enlightened conquerors and benevolent dictators. Christian armies during the Crusades, with the blessing of popes, invaded the Holy Land in their efforts to recapture it. As Islam spread across the Mediterranean, Christian forces won victories at Constantinople in modern Turkey and Tours in France to halt the Muslim advance into Europe from Asia Minor and from Spain.

THE CRUSADES

There were nine crusades to the Holy Land between 1095 and 1291. The title "Crusade," or "Taking the Cross," came to be applied to these military campaigns, and the Christian armies painted the cross on their banners. While the religious intent of these military expeditions was clear—to recapture Jerusalem and the other "holy" Christian sites and protect Christian pilgrims—economic, political and social goals also played a part.

In the long run, the Crusades provoked a strong Muslim reaction. Muslim armies drove the Europeans from the Holy Land. Saladin, a Sunni leader, summoned his army in 1182—between the Second Crusade (1147–49) and the Third Crusade (1189–92)—with a call to *jihad*, or "holy war," against the crusaders.

During the Fifth Crusade St. Francis of Assisi and one of his friars visited with the Sultan in Egypt in 1219 to preach the Gospel. It was a time when "bitter and long battles were being waged daily between Christians and pagans" (Thomas of Celano, the first biographer of Francis of Assisi).

The Sultan received Francis and his companion courteously; but he sent them back to the crusaders' camp.

Since 1790, Europeans in search of building an empire and enriched by colonial expansion in the New World, Africa and Asia, have returned to the Middle East. The Muslim populations saw these Christian Europeans as the *crusaders returning to continue their holy war.*

Many Muslims today see the use of force in Muslim countries by western nations for political, economic and social reasons to be a holy war, or jihad, between Islam and Christianity. For example, Al Qaeda, ISIS and other extremist Islamic groups have issued their own call for a holy war.

JIHAD, OR HOLY WAR

"Holy war" is not a good translation for the Arabic *jihad*. At its root, this Arabic word means "struggle" and can refer to either a personal effort to live well or a communal battle. Muhammad distinguished between the "greater jihad," an inner spiritual struggle, and the "lesser jihad," an outer conflict with non-believers. Many Muslims will emphasize the greater jihad, the personal struggle against evil temptations that every religious person faces in life.

CRUSADER GODFREY OF BOUILLON AT THE SIEGE OF JERUSALEM IN 1099

Nowadays, on the other hand, jihad is more often promoted and presented as *violent and terroristic combat* against the enemies of religion—identified as oppressive western (Christian) cultures. Radical Islamic groups promote jihad as a rallying cry to fight what they see as liberal and immoral western society. Some Muslim groups refer to jihad as the Sixth Pillar of Islam.

Christian and Muslim theologians maintain that neither Islam nor Christianity condones the killing of innocent civilians. Muslim scholars state that the Qur'an allows only defensive war, similar to the just war doctrine in Christian theology. This similarity is captured by this classic Islamic quotation: "Fight for the sake of Allah those who fight against you, but do not attack them first. Allah does not like aggressors" (Qur'an 2:19).

TALK IT OVER
- Hearing the word "crusade" evokes bitter memories for Muslims. The word "jihad" threatens westerners.
- Is there ever a holy war? Why or why not?

OVER TO YOU
- St. Francis of Assisi lived during a time of intense conflict and animosity between Christians and Muslims. Does reflecting on the visit of St. Francis and the Sultan of Egypt in 1219 provide a model for building relationships between Christians and Muslims?
- Share as a class how a similar initiative might have a positive impact today.

SHARIAH, OR ISLAMIC LAW
Shariah (sometimes Sharia) is the name of the Islamic legal system, or law of Islam. It is a body of moral and religious law based on the teachings of the Qur'an and the traditions of the Prophet recorded in the Hadith and Sunna. Here is how the Islamic Supreme Council of America describes Shariah, in part:

Shariah is the Islamic Law—the disciplines and principles that govern the behavior of a Muslim individual towards his or herself, family, neighbors, community, city, nation and the Muslim polity as a whole, the Ummah. Similarly Shariah governs the interactions between communities, groups and social and economic organizations. Shariah establishes the criteria by which all social actions are classified, categorized and administered within the overall governance of the state.

Shariah first establishes the patterns believers should follow in worshipping Allah: prayers, charity, fasting and pilgrimage.

Muslim scholars state that the Qur'an allows only defensive war, similar to the just war doctrine in Christian theology

MINARET IN THE MÉDINA OF TUNIS, TUNISIA

Islam's law comprises a comprehensive outlook on life. As one looks from a satellite at this planet, the Shariah conceives of the earth as a single "city" with diverse inhabitants—in modern parlance, a "global village." Islam looks to the benefit of the society as a whole from a general perspective and presents a theoretical model that if followed provides safety and protection for society.

Shariah literally means "a well-trodden path to water," the source of all life, representing the Path to Allah, as given by Allah, the Originator of all life.

Shariah is Arabic for "a way to the water." In the desert, water is a primary necessity. For Muslims, social order and religious obedience are necessities for the present and for eternity. Islamic law indicates a path for society, public affairs and everyday life.

In today's society the term Shariah has become a source of division and controversy and often of violence. Many non-Muslims associate Shariah law with extremism. The Islamic Supreme Council of America cautions against taking aspects of Islamic faith and culture out of context:

Islam is a complete package—a complete message and way of life. To fraction it into its components, then examine them individually, will yield little or no understanding of Islam's holistic whole. Inevitably aspects of Islam examined separately, without a wide-ranging grasp of its totality, will be taken in a fragmented context, in which case aspects may take on the appearance of extremism. However, when viewed from a comprehensive perspective by any fair person, Islam will be found sensible in all its aspects and practices.

AUTHORITY IN ISLAM

Muslims do not have a central figure of authority on matters of faith and morals. For example, they have no pope or college of bishops or magisterium that has been given the authority to authentically interpret the Qur'an. Thus, there is considerable diversity within Islam. Indeed, one may be forgiven for thinking that some Muslim practices are products of particular cultures. Nevertheless, all Muslims justify religious practice under Islamic law, or Shariah.

There are different sources for Islamic Law: the Qur'an, the Hadith, Muslim consensus and rational thinking. The Hadith (recorded sayings of the Prophet Muhammad) give expression to the Qur'an. Different regions and traditions and periods of history used these sources with varying emphases. All Muslims agree, however, that the Qur'an and Hadith outweigh individual thinking and the majority vote.

There are major differences between the Muslim approach to civil law and the attitude to civil law in much of the Christian West. Western culture tends to separate the sacred from the secular—the Church from the State. Western culture and law tend to emphasize personal freedoms and to define the common good from the perspective of individual rights. Islam applies a more holistic principle to its interpretation of the common good.

REVIEW, ANALYZE AND DISCUSS

⊙ The foundation and legitimacy of all civil laws is the eternal moral law. The Catholic Church teaches:

– "There is no authority except from God, and those authorities that exist have been instituted by God" (CCC, no. 1918).

– "There are different expressions of the moral law, all of them interrelated: eternal law—the source, in God, of all law; natural law; revealed law, comprising the Old Law and the New Law, or Law of the Gospel; finally, civil and ecclesiastical laws" (CCC, no. 1952).

⊙ What happens when a civil law conflicts with the eternal moral law?

⊙ How is that conflict resolved? Discuss by taking specific examples.

THE UMMAH, THE MUSLIM WORLD COMMUNITY

Muhammad's efforts in Medina consolidated Islam, and his followers grew in faith and in action. Tribal divisions were gradually removed in favor of the Ummah, the world community of Muslims. *Ummah* is an Arabic word meaning "nation" or "community." The principles underlying the Ummah remain an essential quality of Islam today, demanding respect and tolerance for all Muslims, as well as care for the poor, the sick and orphans.

The details governing the Ummah are laid down by the Sunna, or Sunnah. "The Arabic word *sunnah* lexically means "road" or "practice." In the language of the Prophet and the Companions it denotes the whole of licit [lawful] practices followed in the Religion [*din*], particularly the pristine [*hanîf*] path of Prophets, whether pertaining to belief, religious and social practice, or ethics generally speaking" (Dr. G.F. Haddad, "The Meaning of Sunna").

Islam integrates both religious *and* civil matters, as we have seen, as part of "a complete package"

Islam promotes the transformation of society and the world so as to be obedient to God's will

for both the good of the individual person and the common good of society. Islam sees reality as a unified, interrelated whole. It promotes the transformation of society and the world so as to be obedient to God's will. The message of Muhammad is simple, straightforward and clear. It can be put into practice everywhere for all times by the peoples of the world.

REFLECT AND SHARE

- ⊙ What insights does the teaching on the Ummah give you into the nature of Islam?
- ⊙ Does the Islamic teaching on the Ummah resonate with the universal human desire to live in community? With the Judaic and Christian teaching on the People of God?
- ⊙ Share responses as a class.

CATHOLIC–MUSLIM DIALOGUE

The Gospel clearly commands Christians to engage sincerely in religious dialogue. Interreligious dialogue is a form of **evangelization**. The Committee on Ecumenical and Interreligious affairs (CEIA) of the United States Conference of Catholic Bishops (USCCB) is in dialogue with several Muslim organizations. Our bishops are steadfast in fulfilling the gospel mandate, the teaching of *Nostra Aetate*, and the example of the recent popes.

In October 2007 one hundred and thirty-eight Islamic leaders from a diversity of countries around the world issued the letter "A Common Word Between Us and You," which they addressed to all the leaders of Christianity. The Islamic leaders wrote: "So let our differences not cause hatred and strife between us. Let us vie with each other only in righteousness and good works. Let us respect each other, be fair, just and kind to another and live in sincere peace, harmony and mutual goodwill."

Acknowledging the violence that continues to characterize Muslim–Christian relations, our bishops have stated:

Still, it is our belief that the most efficient way to work toward ending or at least curtailing such violence and prejudice is through building networks of dialogue that can overcome

POPE BENEDICT XVI IN 2007

ignorance, extremism, and discrimination and so lead to friendship and trust with Muslims. . . .

Perhaps most importantly, our work together has forged true bonds of friendship that are supported by mutual esteem and an ever-growing trust that enables us to speak candidly with one another in an atmosphere of respect. . . .

Our path is therefore to proceed confidently in our Christian faith with an openness to receive intimations of truth wherever it is found in other traditions, including Islam.

—USCCB, "Dialogue with Muslims Committee Statement"

REFLECT, DECIDE AND SHARE

- ⊙ Name three things you can do to promote mutual esteem and trust between Muslims and Christians.
- ⊙ Share responses as a class.

JOURNAL EXERCISE

- ⊙ How has your understanding of Islam and your attitude to Muslims and their way of life changed as a result of studying this chapter?
- ⊙ What have you learned about Islam and Muslim life that would deepen your own commitment to the Catholic faith?

JUDGE AND ACT

REVIEW AND SHARE WHAT YOU HAVE LEARNED

Review and share what you have learned in this chapter about the beliefs and religious practices of Islam. Use these statements as the focus of your responses:

⊙ The Catholic Church has a unique relationship to Islam and the Muslim people.
⊙ The Catholic Church respects what is holy and truthful in Islam.
⊙ The Muslim people have a monotheistic but non-Trinitarian faith.
⊙ The Qur'an reveres Jesus and the Virgin Mary.
⊙ There are many common elements of moral life and practices between Catholics and Muslims.

⊙ The Islamic pathway to holiness of life is non-sacramental but requires Muslims to give testimony to their faith in five ways.
⊙ Islam has no central figure of authority on matters of faith and morals.
⊙ The Catholic Church seeks to engage the Muslim community in dialogue to advance human solidarity.

OVER TO YOU

⊙ Name some of the key commonalities and fundamental differences between the Catholic Church and Islam.
⊙ What new insights and understanding did you gain about the beliefs and practices of Islam from your study of this chapter?

LEARN BY EXAMPLE

The story of Malala Yousafzai, Sunni Muslim and advocate for girls' right to education

Malala Yousafzai (1997–), a Sunni Muslim, experienced firsthand and responded to the unjust social structure of her native Pakistan. Malala, in her blog, described the desire for the opportunity for an education for herself and all Pakistani girls—a right denied by the Taliban. Malala, who used the pseudonym Gul Makai, the name of the heroine of a Pakistani folktale, was only eleven years old when her voice became public.

This excerpt, which Malala posted in 2009 as schools were closing for the winter holidays, captures her passionate determination to speak out for the right of Pakistani girls to an education:

> The girls were not too excited about vacations because they knew if the Taliban implemented their edict [banning girls' education] they would not be able to come to school again. I am of the view that the school will one day reopen but while leaving I looked at the building as if I would not come here again.

Malala's blog became a voice for young Pakistani girls—a voice the Taliban leadership did not welcome. On October 9, 2012 a Taliban gunman shot Malala and two of her friends as they rode the school bus. Malala, who was shot in the head, was flown to the United Kingdom while still unconscious, along with her family, where she received treatment and eventually recovered.

Three days after the shooting, on October 12, fifty Islamic clerics issued a joint declaration against the Taliban who had attempted to assassinate Malala, but the Taliban reiterated their intent to kill her and her father. And so Malala and her family were forced to live in exile in Birmingham, England.

The attempt on her life did not silence Malala, and as soon as she was well again she resumed her schooling and her efforts to promote girls' right to education. She spoke before audiences all over the world, including the United Nations. Her example and efforts have inspired people around the globe.

Malala was the youngest person ever to be named a Noble Prize laureate

In 2012 the Pakistani government awarded Malala the National Peace Award, now the National Malala Peace Prize for those under eighteen years of age. In 2013 the European Parliament awarded her its Sakharov prize for Freedom of Thought; and the *New York Times* included her on its list of "The 100 Most Influential People in the World." In 2014, at the age of seventeen, Malala was a co-recipient of the Nobel Peace Prize—she was the youngest person ever to be named a Nobel Prize laureate. She received the news that she was to become a Nobel laureate while in class with her fellow students.

TALK IT OVER

- ⊙ What can young Christians learn from the inspirational life and efforts of Malala Yousafzai?
- ⊙ What similarities can you see between Malala's efforts and the efforts of Christians to bring about the Kingdom of God?

SHARE FAITH WITH FAMILY AND FRIENDS

- ⊙ Watch and listen to the news carefully. Analyze what you see and hear.
- ⊙ Do the messages about Islam that you see and hear reflect what you have been learning in this chapter?
- ⊙ Share your responses and the reasons behind them with family and friends.

JUDGE AND DECIDE

- ⊙ What opportunities might there be for you to engage in interreligious activity with Muslims that puts the Great Commandment into action?
- ⊙ Come up with and implement a plan.

LEARN BY HEART

"Worship the Lord your God,
and serve only him."

MATTHEW 4:10

All pray the Sign of the Cross together.

Opening Prayer

LEADER

Let us thank God for making us instruments of the Gospel in the world. *(Pause)*
Let us acknowledge the times when we have not accepted that responsibility. *(Pause)*

O God, who sent your Son into the world as the
    true light,
pour out, we pray, the Spirit he promised
to sow seeds of truth constantly in people's
    hearts
and to awaken in them the obedience to the faith,
so that, being born to new life through Baptism,
all may become part of your one people.
Through our Lord Jesus Christ, your Son,
who lives and reigns with you in the unity of the
    Holy Spirit,
one God, for ever and ever.

RESPONSE

Amen.

—*The Roman Missal*, Masses and Prayers
for Various Needs and Occasions, For the
Evangelization of Peoples (18A), Collect

Proclamation of the Word of God

READER

A reading from the Acts of the Apostles.
Proclaim Acts 17:16–34.
The word of the Lord.

ALL

Thanks be to God.

READER

A reading from the holy Gospel according to Matthew.

ALL

Glory to you, O Lord.

READER

Proclaim Matthew 28:16–20.
The Gospel of the Lord.

ALL

Praise to you, Lord Jesus Christ.

All reflect on the readings: How am I a true witness to the love of God in the world? What do my words and actions tell non-believers about the Person I believe Jesus to be? Do my words and actions invite non-believers to come to know Jesus Christ?

Intercessory Prayer

LEADER

Jesus gave his Church the command to preach
the Good News of the Gospel to all people.
Let us pray for those who do not believe in Christ,
that, enlightened by the Holy Spirit,
they, too, may embark on the journey that leads
to salvation.

All pray in silence.

LEADER

Almighty ever-living God,
grant to those who do not confess Christ
that, by walking before you with a sincere heart,
they may find the truth
and that we ourselves, being constant in mutual
    love
and striving to understand more fully the
    mystery of your life,
may be made more perfect witnesses to your
    love in the world.
Through Christ our Lord.

RESPONSE

Amen.

—*The Roman Missal*, Liturgy for Friday of the
Passion of the Lord [Good Friday], Solemn
Intercession VII: For Those Who Do Not Believe
in Christ

Concluding Blessing

O God, be gracious and bless us
and let your face shed its light upon us, and have
    mercy.
So will your ways be known upon earth
and all nations learn your salvation.

ALL
Amen.

— *The Roman Missal*, Masses and Prayers
for Various Needs and Occasions, For the
Evangelization of Peoples (18A), Entrance
Antiphon

CHURCH OF ALL NATIONS, MOUNT OF OLIVES, JERUSALEM

CHAPTER 9

Eastern Religions

—Hinduism, Buddhism and Confucianism

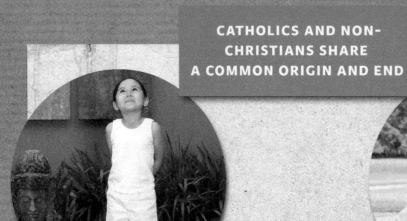

CATHOLICS AND NON-CHRISTIANS SHARE A COMMON ORIGIN AND END

THE WORLD—ALL THAT IS SEEN, AND ALL THAT IS UNSEEN—WAS CREATED AND EXISTS FOR THE GLORY OF GOD

THERE ARE IN NON-CHRISTIAN RELIGIONS ELEMENTS OF THE TRUTH THAT WAS FULLY REVEALED IN JESUS CHRIST

HINDUISM, BUDDHISM AND CONFUCIANISM CONTAIN ELEMENTS OF TRUTH AND VIRTUE THAT ECHO THE TEACHINGS OF THE CATHOLIC CHURCH

GOD DESIRES THE SALVATION OF ALL PEOPLE IN CHRIST

THE CATHOLIC CHURCH HAS LONG TAUGHT THAT MANY non-revealed religions have truths they share with us about the origin, purpose and destiny of human life. At Vatican II the Church taught: "[O]ther religions which are found throughout the world attempt in different ways to overcome the restlessness of people's hearts by outlining a program of life covering doctrine, moral precepts and sacred rites" (*Declaration on the Relation of the Church to Non-Christian Religions* [*Nostra Aetate*], no. 2). In this chapter we explore Hinduism, Buddhism and Confucianism.

"INCULTURATION" IS A DIMENSION OF THE CHURCH'S WORK OF EVANGELIZATION

Faith Focus: These teachings of the Catholic Church are the primary focus of the doctrinal content presented in this chapter:

◉ God is one and God is triune.
◉ We can know God with certainty from his works by the use of our reason.
◉ God has revealed other truths about himself that can only be known through Divine Revelation.
◉ Belief in and love of God has consequences for one's life.
◉ The world was created and exists for the glory of God, who cares for all creation and guides it toward perfection.
◉ Sanctification for human beings means to participate in the love of God now and eternally.
◉ Salvation is a gift of grace available through faith in Jesus Christ.
◉ Christ will judge every person individually at the moment of their death.
◉ At the end of time the just will reign with Christ forever, glorified in body and soul.

Discipleship Formation: As a result of studying this chapter and discovering the meaning of the faith of the Catholic Church for your life, you should be better able to:

◉ apply the teachings of the Catholic Church on the connection between non-Catholic religions and the Catholic Church to Hinduism, Buddhism and Confucianism;
◉ identify elements of truth and virtue that echo Christian values in the key teachings and practices of Hinduism, Buddhism and Confucianism;
◉ identify teachings from Hinduism, Buddhism and Confucianism that are contrary to the teachings of the Catholic Church.

Scripture References: These scripture references are quoted or referred to in this chapter:
OLD TESTAMENT: Genesis 1:1—2:25; **Psalms** 145
NEW TESTAMENT: Matthew 5:14–16; **Mark** 13:34; **Acts of the Apostles** 17:22–28; **1 Corinthians** 1:30, 15:28

Faith Glossary: Familiarize yourself with or recall the meaning of these key terms. Definitions are found in the Glossary: **asceticism, charity (love), compassion, divination, divine providence, Divine Revelation, eternal life, evangelization, gifts of the Holy Spirit, heaven, hell, human virtues, idolatry, inculturation (of the Gospel), justice, particular judgment, Purgatory, reincarnation, religion, salvation, social doctrine of the Catholic Church, superstition, wisdom**

Faith Word: Inculturation (of the Gospel)
Learn by Heart: James 1:27
Learn by Example: Matteo Ricci

Do non-Christian religions give us insight in our quest for truth?

NON-CHRISTIAN RELIGIONS IN NORTH AMERICA

Members of non-Christian religions make up about 6 percent of the population of the United States. A 2015 report from the Pew Research Center on Religion and Public Life measured the size of non-Christian religions in North America. Jews, Buddhists, Muslims, and Hindus, in that order, account for the largest number of members. Other non-Christian religions mentioned in the report include the Bahá'í religion, Jainism, Shintoism, Sikhism, Taoism, Tenrikyo, Wicca, and Zoroastrianism.

OPENING REFLECTION

◉ Name the non-Christian religions, in addition to Judaism and Islam, in your community.

◉ Are any of your neighbors or friends members of those religions?

◉ Have you ever shared your faith with them? If so, what did you learn about their beliefs and practices?

THE MYSTERY OF LIFE'S JOURNEY

The diversity of religions throughout the globe attests to the continuing quest of humanity to discover the meaning of life and humanity's own purpose within creation. Architectural evidence confirms that all advanced peoples have paused and wondered with awe before the immensity of the universe and the power of nature.

The human responses to the ultimate questions concerning the meaning and purpose of life have sometimes, though not always, brought people to believe in a Supreme Being. When people came to a common understanding and acceptance of such a belief, it gave rise to a **religion**, or a system of spiritually based beliefs,

Seeking Answers to Life's Questions

Throughout history, to the present day, there is found among different peoples a certain awareness of a hidden power, which lies behind the course of nature and the events of human life. At times, there is present even a recognition of a supreme being, or still more of a Father. This awareness and recognition results in a way of life that is imbued with a deep religious sense. The religions which are found in more advanced civilizations endeavor by way of well-defined concepts and exact language to answer these questions.

—Vatican II, *Declaration on the Relation of the Church to Non-Christian Religions* (*Nostra Aetate*), no. 2

Pope Francis on Interreligious Dialogue

"Interreligious dialogue, before being a discussion of the main themes of faith, is a 'conversation about human existence' *(The Joy of the Gospel [Evangelii Gaudium]*, no. 250). This conversation shares the experiences of daily life in all its concreteness, with its joys and sufferings, its struggles and hopes; it takes on shared responsibilities; it plans a better future for all. We learn to live together, respecting each other's differences freely; we know and accept one another's identity."

—Address to Ecumenical and Interreligious Representatives at the Franciscan International Study Center in Sarajevo (Bosnia and Herzegovina), June 6, 2015

THE MIXED RELIGIOUS HERITAGE OF SARAJEVO SEEN IN ITS SKYLINE

morals and ritual practices that helped people to find and express meaning in life and to live it well. Some of the values and virtues of non-Christian religions, as we will explore in this and the next chapter, are similar to what the Catholic Church proclaims.

ELEMENTS OF TRUTH IN NON-CHRISTIAN RELIGIONS

The Church, following the command and example of Jesus Christ, has always reached out to non-believers. In so doing, the Church takes areas of agreement as the starting point of dialogue. Recall for a moment the dialogue of St. Paul, the Apostle to the Gentiles, with the pagan Greeks at the Areopagus in Athens:

Then Paul stood in front of the Areopagus and said, "Athenians, I see how extremely religious you are in every way. For as I went through the city and looked carefully at the objects of your worship, I found among them an altar with the inscription, 'To an unknown god.' What therefore you worship as unknown, this I proclaim to you. The God who made the world and everything in it, he who is Lord of heaven and earth, does not live in shrines made by human hands, nor is he served by human hands, as though he needed anything, since he himself gives to all mortals life and breath and all things. From one ancestor he made all nations to inhabit the whole earth, and he allotted the times of their existence and the boundaries of the places where they would live, so that they would search for God and perhaps grope for him and find him—though indeed he is not far from each one of us. For 'In him we live and move and have our being'; as even some of your own poets have said, 'For we too are his offspring.'"

—Acts of the Apostles 17:22–28

REFLECT, READ AND SHARE

⊙ What truth did St. Paul use as a starting point in his dialogue with the pagan Athenians?
⊙ Was this an effective way to dialogue with the pagan Greeks? Read Acts of the Apostles 17:32–34 before responding.
⊙ Share reflections as a class.

The Catholic Church passes on and teaches the Apostolic Tradition, as found in the above passage from Acts of the Apostles, that there are in non-Christian religions *elements of the*

ST. PAUL PREACHING IN ATHENS | BOLOGNA, ITALY

truth that was fully revealed in Jesus Christ for the salvation of humanity. This teaching mirrors the heart of St. Paul the Apostle's dialogue with the Greek pagans at the Areopagus in Athens. The Catholic Church has long taught that God desires the salvation of all people in Christ. The Second Vatican Council passed on this apostolic teaching:

> Those who, through no fault of their own, do not know the Gospel of Christ or his church, but who nevertheless seek God with a sincere heart, and, moved by grace, try in their actions to do his will as they know it through the dictates of their conscience—these too may attain eternal salvation. Nor will divine providence deny the assistance necessary for salvation to those who, without any fault of theirs, have not yet arrived at an explicit knowledge of God, and who, not without grace, strive to lead a good life. Whatever of good or truth is found amongst them is considered by the church to be a preparation for the Gospel and given by him who enlightens all men and women that they may at length have life.
> —*Dogmatic Constitution on the Church* (*Lumen Gentium*), no. 16

THINK, PAIR AND SHARE

- ⊙ Work with a partner.
- ⊙ Recall the teaching of the Catholic Church on salvation outside the Church that you explored in chapter 6 of this course of study.
- ⊙ Discuss: Does the teaching of the *Dogmatic Constitution on the Church*:
  - – echo St. Paul's message to the pagan Greeks?
  - – guide us to discern elements of truth in non-Christian religions?
- ⊙ Give reasons for your responses based on what you have learned in this course of study and also throughout your study of the teachings of the Catholic Church in your other theology courses.
- ⊙ Share discussion as a class.

LET'S PROBE DEEPER: A RESEARCH ACTIVITY

- ⊙ Look up and read the subsection "Interreligious Dialogue" in Pope Francis' Apostolic Exhortation *Evangelii Gaudium*, nos. 250–254.
- ⊙ Use the Pope's teaching as your guide as you continue your study of Hinduism, Buddhism and Confucianism in this chapter.

Hinduism: The way of experience

SPIRITUAL SOLIDARITY

The first Parliament of the World's Religions was convened in Chicago in 1893. Swami Vivekananda (1863–1902), a young Hindu monk from India, was among those who addressed the participants. He began: "Brothers and Sisters of America." Those present immediately affirmed the young monk's greeting of solidarity with them by a two-minute standing ovation. In his address, Vivekananda said: "I am proud to belong to a religion which has taught the world both tolerance and universal acceptance. We believe not only in universal toleration, but we accept all religions as true."

OPENING REFLECTION

⊙ Are tolerance and universal acceptance of difference virtues to be practiced by all people regardless of their religion?

⊙ Vivekananda asserted that Hindus "accept all religions as true." Compare this with what you learned in chapter 3 about the Catholic Church's teaching on other religions in the Vatican II document *Declaration on the Relation of the Church to Non-Christian Religions* (*Nostra Aetate*).

THE WORLD FACE OF HINDUISM

Hinduism is considered to be the oldest of the great world belief and moral systems. The name "Hindu" means "at the Indus River." The Indus River in North India is an entry way into the subcontinent. Hinduism, then, is simply "the religion of India."

Hinduism is the world's third largest religion. Hindus number about 1 billion, or 15 percent of the world population. India is the most populous Hindu country, with more than 900 million Hindus, which is about 80 percent of India's population. Hindus number 4 million in Indonesia, 3 million in Sri Lanka, 3 million in Africa, 2 million in North America, and 1 million in Europe.

Exploring the Divine Mystery

In Hinduism people explore the divine mystery and express it both in the limitless riches of myth and the accurately defined insights of philosophy. They seek release from the trials of the present life by ascetical practices, profound meditation and recourse to God in confidence and love.

—Vatican II, *Declaration on the Relation of the Church to Non-Christian Religions*, no. 2

HINDU *DEVI* (GODDESS) AT THE BHULESHWAR TEMPLE, INDIA

HINDU SACRED WRITINGS

The Vedas, Bhagavad Gita and Agamas are three Hindu sacred writings. Hindus attribute a "divine" authority to their sacred writings. This authority is both similar to and yet very different from the Catholic teaching on **Divine Revelation** in Scripture and Sacred Tradition.

Vedas: The Vedas are the oldest of the Hindu sacred writings; their exact date is unknown. Hindus believe these hymns to be of non-human origin and they credit Brahman as their source. The Rigveda, one of the four great Vedas and considered to be the most sacred, contains these verses about the beginning of everything:

> Who really knows, and who can swear,
> How creation came, when or where!
> Even gods came after creation's day,
> Who really knows, who can truly say
> When and how did creation start?
> Did He do it? Or did He not?
> Only He, up there, knows, maybe;
> Or perhaps, not even He.
>
> —Rigveda 10:129.6–7

The Vedas also express, among other things, the Hindu belief in the existence of many kindly deities that issue from the "all-pervasive Supreme Being," Brahman.

Agamas: The Sanskrit word *Agama* is translated in several ways, including "tradition" or "received knowledge." The Agamas, which date to the eighth century BC, were written after the Vedas. They contain the beliefs and practices of many Hindu traditions; in particular, they include detailed information on temple building, image making, rituals and yoga. (*We will explore yoga in more detail later in this section of the chapter.*)

Bhagavad Gita: The Bhagavad Gita ("The Song of the Lord") is commonly referred to as the Gita. Written between 200 and 100 BC, the Gita is probably the best known and most influential of the Hindu scriptures. The Gita teaches that life is an illusion because nothing is as it seems. The Gita represents the synthesis of the impersonal and personal strands in Hindu thinking about Brahman and is a great summary of *bhakti*, the Hindu devotion to the deities and to fellow creatures. It stresses bhakti yoga, one of the four kinds of yoga, as the way of devotion and love.

STATUE OF BRAHMAN ON AN ELEPHANT | GUJARAT, INDIA

Do you see any elements of truth in the main teachings of the Hindu sacred scriptures that echo or relate in any way to the teachings of the Catholic Church?

REVIEW, COMPARE AND SHARE

- ⊙ Recall the teachings of:
  - – the creation stories in Genesis 1:1—2:25;
  - – the Creeds of the Church: God the Father is "Creator of heaven and earth" (Apostles' Creed); "of all things visible and invisible" (Nicene Creed).
- ⊙ Compare the teachings of the Hindu sacred writings on God with the teachings of Genesis and the Creeds of the Catholic Church.
- ⊙ Do you see any elements of truth in the main teachings of the Hindu sacred writings that echo or relate in any way to the teachings of the Catholic Church? Where are the similarities?
- ⊙ Share and discuss comparisons as a class.

KEY BELIEFS OF HINDUISM

Hinduism is a cosmic monotheistic religion. Hindus call their way of life *sanatana dharma*, or "the eternal religion." The Sanskrit word *dharma* has many layers of meaning. One of those meanings is "path," which is similar in meaning to "religion." Hinduism is essentially a spiritually inspired path, or way, of life, forged over centuries by a succession of religious seers, poets, philosophers, thinkers and teachers.

There is no universally fixed set of Hindu beliefs and practices. The teachings and practices of Hinduism are tied to particular places and local traditions. Hindus believe in "one, all-pervasive Supreme Being"; they also believe in and worship many deities who are creations of the one Supreme Being. They trust that these lesser deities care directly for humanity during their time on earth. This devotion is known as *bhakti*.

The Himalayan Academy at Kauai's Hindu Monastery names nine beliefs that form a broad, but not exhaustive, summary of Hindu spirituality:

1. Hindus believe in a one, all-pervasive Supreme Being who is both immanent and transcendent, both Creator and Unmanifest Reality.
2. Hindus believe in the divinity of the four Vedas, the world's most ancient scripture, and venerate the Agamas as equally revealed. These primordial hymns are God's word and the bedrock of *Sanatana Dharma*, the eternal religion.
3. Hindus believe that the universe undergoes endless cycles of creation, preservation and dissolution.
4. Hindus believe in *karma*, the law of cause and effect by which each individual creates his own destiny by his thoughts, words and deeds.

Hindus believe that the soul reincarnates, until liberation from the cycle of rebirth is attained

5. Hindus believe that the soul reincarnates, evolving through many births until all karmas have been resolved, and *moksha*, liberation from the cycle of rebirth, is attained. Not a single soul will be deprived of this destiny.

6. Hindus believe that divine beings exist in unseen worlds and that temple worship, rituals, sacraments and personal devotionals create a communion with these devas and gods.

7. Hindus believe that an enlightened master, or *satguru*, is essential to know the Transcendent Absolute, as are personal discipline, good conduct, purification, pilgrimage, self-inquiry, meditation and surrender in God.

8. Hindus believe that all life is sacred, to be loved and revered, and therefore practice *ahimsa*, non-injury, in thought, word and deed.

9. Hindus believe that no religion teaches the only way to salvation above all others, but that all genuine paths are facets of God's Light, deserving tolerance and understanding.

REVIEW, COMPARE AND SHARE

⊙ Reflect on each of the nine statements of Hindu belief:
  – Where do you see elements of truth in these statements that echo or relate in any way to the teachings of the Catholic Church?
  – Are any of the teachings of Hinduism contrary to the teachings of the Catholic Church?

⊙ Give examples of appropriate Catholic teachings and share responses as a class.

BRAHMAN, THE FOUNDATION AND ESSENCE OF REALITY

For Hindus, Brahman is the Absolute Reality, the Ultimate Source, the foundation and essence of Reality, of all that is. Brahman alone exists and is. Brahman is deep within each person—beneath one's thoughts, one's feelings, one's body and brain, one's physicality and spirituality. Brahman is at the center of what a person might think is you and me. *Advaita* is the term that summarizes the Hindu teaching that everything is an expression of Brahman. We can translate *Advaita* as "non-dualism," meaning that the universe and Brahman are one.

There are two distinct Hindu belief traditions about Brahman. First, Brahman is impersonal, working in and through and beneath everything that exists. So Brahman is a great life-force that evolves toward sensation, relationship, communication and self-awareness. *Atman* is the Hindu term for the Brahman within people. What we see in the bright rush of the world is a shadow of the spiritual reality that lies beneath everything. Everything else is an illusion. Only Brahman is real.

Second, Brahman is a personal and caring being who brought the universe into existence and is ready to help humans cope with the cycle of births and deaths. The universe reflects a powerful, caring and eternal creator who brought us into existence, appreciates our struggles, enters into our lives and shapes our destiny.

Faithful Hindus choose particular, often local, gods to worship. They may have an altar at home for family prayer, and they will visit their god at the temple from time to time during the year. They seek a *darshan*, or a glance of the god, as visible proof of divine favor.

These Hindu teachings on Brahman contain elements of truth and relate in some way to these truths of faith that the Catholic Church proclaims: (1) God has revealed himself to be one God in three Divine Persons, Father, Son and Holy Spirit; (2) God creates the human person in the divine image and likeness; (3) all creation is a manifestation of the Creator; (4) the existence of the Creator can be known with certainty through his works; (5) the world—all that is seen, and all that is unseen—was created and exists for the glory of God; (6) **divine providence**, or God's loving care and concern for all he has made, sustains creation and presides over its development and destiny.

WHAT ABOUT YOU PERSONALLY?

- ◉ St. Ignatius of Loyola (1491–1556) had a deep sense of God's presence in the ordinary and everyday of life.
- ◉ Do you notice the presence of God in the things of creation and in the ordinary experiences of your life? How do you respond?

The Hindu Caste System

A deep feature of Hinduism is the notion that people are born into a certain social caste. The four castes are: *Brahmins*, priests and scholars; *Kshatriyas*, kings and warriors; *Vaishyas*, merchants and farmers; *Shudras*, unskilled laborers and workers. Outside and far below these four castes are the *Pariahs*, or "Untouchables," who carry out the most menial of functions and are looked down on by all. In contemporary India they are known as *Dalits*, or "oppressed." There is no marriage outside one's caste and people's work and station in life is dictated by their caste of origin.

STREET PORTER AT WORK IN RAJASTHAN, INDIA

KARMA

The Sanskrit word *karma* refers both to the deeds a person performs *and* to the consequences of those deeds upon a person's life. Karma is one of the three paths described in the Gita; the other two paths are knowledge and bhakti. Hindus believe that we can do good karma or bad karma. As one acts, so one becomes. We make ourselves what we are by our own good or bad karma—and we get whatever we deserve. We must take the inevitable consequences in this life and in the next life for what we do. Each individual creates their own destiny by their thoughts, words and deeds.

REINCARNATION: SAMSARA

The Sanskrit word *samsara* means "flowing together" and it describes the Hindu teaching on **reincarnation**—that every life is *déjà vu* (life all over again), a continuous cycle of death and rebirth. The *Atman* (soul) cannot die; it passes from one body to another upon death in a repeating cycle. All the dead will be reborn in another form over and over. By one's karma a person can reach to a higher form of life or caste, or be reduced to a lower state of life or caste.

Everyone longs to be released from the cycle of samsara, with its painful experiences of birth, illness, aging and death. The release from being eternally reborn is called *moksha*. Moksha is the ultimate goal in life. It is the liberation from samsara, or salvation from the human condition, to life as a union with Brahman through surrender and service to the Supreme Brahman.

YOGA AS A WAY TO LIBERATION

Good karma coupled with yoga is the key to moksha. The Sanskrit word *yoga* means "union." Yoga is a series of spiritual, mental and physical disciplines that can help a person achieve liberation from samsara. In the West, many non-Hindus, Christians included, practice yoga to maintain physical fitness or as a method of meditation that calms the mind and nurtures the spirit.

In 1989 the Congregation for the Doctrine of the Faith acknowledged the use of yoga and other practices of some eastern religions by Catholics in their practice of Christian meditation. "The expression 'eastern methods' is used to refer to methods which are inspired by Hinduism and Buddhism, such as 'Zen,' Transcendental Meditation' or 'Yoga.' Thus it indicates methods of meditation of the non-Christian Far East which today are not infrequently adopted by some Christians also in their meditation" (*Letter to the Bishops of the Catholic Church on some Aspects of Christian Meditation*, footnote no. 1).

The Sanskrit word *samsara* describes the Hindu teaching that life is a continuous cycle of death and rebirth

> The love of God, the sole object of Christian contemplation, is a reality which cannot be "mastered" by any method or technique

In their *Letter* the Congregation set forth "criteria of a doctrinal and pastoral character which might allow them to instruct others in prayer, in its numerous manifestations, while remaining faithful to the truth revealed in Jesus, by means of the genuine Tradition of the Church" (no. 1). The *Letter* reminds and, at the time, warns that through the history of the Catholic Church various forms of prayer have appeared. Some of these were contrary to the Catholic understanding of the nature of prayer and the method of praying. The *Letter* explains:

> To answer this question, one must first of all consider, even if only in a general way, in what does the intimate nature of Christian prayer consist. Then one can see if and how it might be enriched by meditation methods which have been developed in other religions and cultures. However, in order to achieve this, one needs to start with a certain clear premise. Christian prayer is always determined by the structure of the Christian faith, in which the very truth of God and creature shines forth. For this reason, it is defined, properly speaking, as a personal, intimate and profound dialogue between man and God. It expresses therefore the communion of redeemed creatures with the intimate life of the Persons of the Trinity. This communion, based on Baptism and the Eucharist, source and summit of the life of the Church, implies an attitude of conversion, a flight from "self" to the "You" of God. Thus Christian prayer is at the same time always authentically personal and communitarian. It flees from impersonal techniques or from concentrating on oneself, which can create a kind of rut, imprisoning the person praying in a spiritual privatism which is incapable of a free openness to the transcendental God. Within the Church, in the legitimate search for new methods of meditation it must always be borne in mind that the essential element of authentic Christian prayer is the meeting of two freedoms, the infinite freedom of God with the finite freedom of man.
>
> —*Letter to the Bishops of the Catholic Church on some Aspects of Christian Meditation*, no. 3

The *Letter* concludes, in part:

> The love of God, the sole object of Christian contemplation, is a reality which cannot be "mastered" by any method or technique. On the contrary, we must always have our sights fixed on Jesus Christ, in whom God's love went to the cross for us and there assumed even the condition of estrangement from the Father [see Mark 13:34]. (no. 31)

Raja Yoga is the way of contemplation that calms the mind, reaching for the soul or Atman within

FORMS OF YOGA

Hindus practice four different forms of yoga. All four ways require in-depth education in Hindu knowledge, something that is available only to the upper castes.

- *Karma Yoga* is about fulfilling the duties of one's particular caste.
- *Bhakti Yoga* is the way of devotion expressed through right action, which strives to honor the oneness of all things through union with Brahman.
- *Jnana Yoga* is the way of knowledge through insight that recognizes the real and eternal—Brahman—distinct from the illusory.
- *Raja Yoga* is the way of contemplation that calms the mind, reaching for the soul or Atman within.

The Hindu teachings on karma, samsara and yoga relate to and echo in some way these teachings of the Catholic Church:

- Human actions in themselves do not earn salvation.
- **Salvation** is the "forgiveness of sins and restoration of friendship with God, which can be done by God alone" (CCC, Glossary).
- The human person is responsible for acts which he knowingly and freely performs.
- "Moved by grace, man turns toward God and away from sin, and so accepts forgiveness and righteousness from on high" (CCC, no. 2018).

- The vocation to **eternal life** "is supernatural. It depends entirely on God's gratuitous initiative, for he alone can reveal and give himself. It surpasses the power of human intellect and will, as that of every other creature" (CCC, no. 1998).
- "Every man receives his eternal recompense in his immortal soul from the moment of his death in a **particular judgment** (*bold type added*) by Christ" (CCC, no. 1051). That eternal recompense will be **heaven**, **Purgatory**, or **hell**.
- At the Final, or Last, Judgment "the souls of all those who die in the grace of Christ whether they must still be purified in purgatory, or whether from the moment they leave their bodies Jesus takes them to paradise as He did for the Good Thief, are the People of God in the eternity beyond death, which will be finally conquered on the day of the Resurrection when these souls will be reunited with their bodies" (Paul VI, Apostolic Letter *Credo of the People of God*, no. 28).

JOURNAL EXERCISE

- St. John Paul II in his first Encyclical Letter, *Redemptor Hominis* (*The Redeemer of Man*), suggested common activities that might take place between Catholics and representatives of non-Christian religions.
- Look up and read number 6 of *Redemptor Hominis*. The encyclical may be found on the Vatican website.
- What activities might Hindus and Catholics undertake together? How might those activities help both Catholics and Hindus to live their religion? Give specific examples.

Buddhism: The way of truth and wisdom

BUDDHIST DEVOTION TO SANCTITY OF LIFE

A headline in *The New York Times* on July 25, 2014 read: "In Scarred Chinese Tibetan City, Devotion to Sanctity of Life." A huge earthquake had left more than 100,000 people homeless in Yushu, China. The earthquake also caused the local Batang River to overflow, leaving huge deposits of mud beyond the river banks. The news story described the efforts of local Buddhist people to search for and rescue tiny river shrimp still buried in the mud. One digger described why she was digging so carefully with chopsticks, "Buddha has taught us that treating others with love and compassion is the right thing to do, no matter how tiny that life is."

The reporter summarized the motivations of these Buddhist people: "Buddhists are encouraged to demonstrate a reverence for all sentient beings; some believers spurn meat while others buy animals destined for slaughter and then set them free. Here in Yushu, a largely Tibetan city where more than 3,000 people died in an earthquake four years ago, the faithful have been flocking to the Batang River to rescue a minuscule aquatic crustacean that would hardly seem deserving of such attention."

OPENING REFLECTION

⊙ What is your immediate response to this story?
⊙ What connection between Christianity and Buddhism does this news report reveal?
⊙ What might you learn from this story for your own calling as a Christian to treat all life with reverence, compassion and love?

THE DALAI LAMA TEACHING IN DHARAMSALA, INDIA, SEPTEMBER 2014

Profile of Buddhism

Buddhism is the world's fourth largest religion. Its members number about 350 million worldwide. It is difficult to quantify the number of Buddhists in the United States but estimates range from about 3 to 4 million, of which 800,000 are American converts. The vast majority are Asian Americans.

There are many traditions of Buddhism. Theravada Buddhism, Mahayana Buddhism, Zen Buddhism and Vajrayana Buddhism are its major traditions. Zen Buddhism emphasizes meditation, while Vajrayana Buddhism emphasizes chanting mantras and the role of the guru in the search for wisdom. The Dalai Lama of Tibet, China, is perhaps the best-known Buddhist.

Prince Siddhartha's journeys outside the palace as a young adult led him to experience the reality of suffering, old age and death

THE GREAT DEPARTURE OF SIDDHARTHA GAUTAMA | 2ND-CENTURY RELIEF

CATHOLIC AND BUDDHIST DIALOGUE AND COOPERATION

The Second Vatican Council noted the Buddhist teaching that the path to true happiness is the spiritual quest for wisdom and not the quest for an accumulation of created goods. The Council taught:

> Buddhism in its various forms testifies to the essential inadequacy of this changing world. It proposes a way of life by which people can, with confidence and trust, attain a state of liberation and reach supreme illumination either through their own efforts or with divine help.
> —*Declaration on the Relation of the Church to Non-Christian Religions*, no. 2

Pope Francis met with participants at a meeting of Catholic and Buddhist religious and social action leaders at the Vatican on June 24, 2015. In his address the Pope reminded participants that Buddhists and Christians can work together to build a just world rooted in love. The Pope said: "It is a visit of fraternity, of dialogue, and of friendship. And this is good. This is healthy. And in these moments, which are wounded by war and hatred, these small gestures are seeds of peace and fraternity. I thank you for this and may God bless you."

ORIGINS OF BUDDHISM: THE QUEST FOR WISDOM AND TRUTH

The quest for **wisdom** to enlighten the way we live our life is a universal quest. It is the search for God. It is the search for Jesus Christ. "[God] is the source of your life in Christ Jesus, who became for us wisdom from God, and righteousness and sanctification and redemption" (1 Corinthians 1:30).

The quest for true wisdom and enlightenment is central to all the great world religions. The origins of Buddhism lie in the reflections and enlightenment of Prince Siddhartha Gautama, who lived in northern India in the sixth and fifth centuries BC. Siddhartha never claimed any direct revelation from an outside source for his knowledge and teachings. You may have read the classic story of his search for enlightenment as part of your literature curriculum.

In summary, Siddhartha enjoyed a privileged upbringing as a member of a ruling family. He lived within the protective walls of a palace, where he was sheltered from disheartening, saddening or demoralizing experiences. His journeys outside the palace as a young adult led him to experience the reality of suffering, old age and death and to think about how best to deal with such suffering in one's life.

During several of those journeys Siddhartha encountered monks and hermits who had renounced their worldly possessions for lives of simplicity and reflection. After coming upon one monk who was poor in possessions but tranquil and peaceful in demeanor, Siddhartha decided to divest himself of all his worldly possessions and begin a new life in search of true wisdom and enlightenment. He learned how to meditate and contemplate, to practice yoga, and to embrace a life of self-discipline and asceticism.

Through these life experiences Siddhartha became enlightened, or awakened, to reality as it really is. His own enlightenment marks the beginning of Buddhism. *Bodhi* is the Sanskrit word for "being enlightened" or "awakened." Siddhartha is known as the Buddha, or Enlightened One. *Dhamma* (also *darma*) is the Sanskrit word used to name the teachings of the Buddha. The word has various meanings including "cosmic law and order" and "truth and law."

The richest fruit of Siddhartha's enlightenment was his extraordinary compassion and care for all living things, especially for those who suffer. Compassion, the love for all sentient beings, is an essential aspect of the Buddhist path of life.

COMPARE AND SHARE

⊙ How does Siddhartha Gautama's journey in search of enlightenment relate to a Christian's journey to become a true and faithful disciple of Christ?

⊙ Pause for a moment and read Matthew 5:14–16.

⊙ What are the similarities? How are the two journeys different?

⊙ Share your responses as a class.

THE FOUR NOBLE TRUTHS

Enlightenment, according to the teachings of Buddha Siddhartha Gautama, is achieved through knowledge of the Four Noble Truths, which explain the nature and cause of suffering, and how to end it in order to achieve the freedom of *nirvana*. The Four Noble Truths are (1) *dukkha:* the reality or existence of suffering; (2) *tanha,* or "craving": the primary cause of suffering; (3) *nirhodha:* there is a way to end suffering; and (4) *magga:* the "path" that leads to liberation from suffering.

THE FIRST NOBLE TRUTH: THE REALITY OR EXISTENCE OF SUFFERING

The First Noble Truth of Buddhism is that suffering (*dukkha*) is the reality that defines life.

Nirvana

The Sanskrit word *nirvana* literally means to "extinguish." Nirvana is the hope and goal of Buddhists. Nirvana refers to the extinction of all cravings and false desires that cause suffering. It is liberation from perpetual wandering, from the illusion of self and from suffering, and it is reached through enlightenment.

Nirvana is the ultimate end of life, but not necessarily an "afterlife" following the physical death of a person who has reached full enlightenment. For some Buddhists, nirvana can be realized in the present life. For example, there are holy people—*Bodhisattvas,* or "Enlightened Ones"—within Mahayana Buddhism who, out of compassion for their fellow human beings, delay their final embrace of nirvana to help others share in it with them.

Only enlightenment can bring liberation from the cycle of endless suffering. Until people recognize and embrace this truth, enlightenment will always escape them.

As part of our suffering, life is marked by impermanence, or *annica*. Nothing is reliable or lasting. Even when we think we have found pleasure or happiness, it quickly passes away. Even the greatest moments of joy are fleeting, at best. Part of our impermanence is *annata*. Our "self" has no permanent or intrinsic identity. Everything about us is just appearance and illusion.

Buddhism teaches a form of reincarnation. Buddhist understanding of reincarnation, however, differs from that of Hinduism. The ultimate goal of the reincarnation cycle for Hindus is "oneing" with the Divine. In Buddhism the cycle of birth, life, death and rebirth (*samsara*) will continue until one is enlightened and achieves nirvana. Recognizing this truth is the first step toward reaching nirvana.

REVIEW, REFLECT AND SHARE

⊙ Review these teachings of the Catholic Church:

– Salvation is a gift of grace that "comes from God alone" (CCC, no. 169).

– The Trinity, in God's own ways, invites all people to come to know, love and serve God. This divine work bears much fruit in the world: "The Catholic Church . . . has a high regard for the manner of life and conduct, the precepts and doctrines which, although differing in many ways from its own teaching, nevertheless often reflect a ray of that truth which enlightens all men and women" (Vatican II, *Declaration on the Relation of the Church to Non-Christian Religions*, no. 2).

– Sanctification for human beings is a participation in the love of God now and eternally. (See CCC, nos. 851, 1709.)

– Human work "can be a means of sanctification and a way of animating earthly realities with the Spirit of Christ" (CCC, no. 2427).

DHAMEKH STUPA, INDIA, WHERE THE BUDDHA GAVE THE FIRST SERMON ON THE FOUR NOBLE TRUTHS

- How do the insights of the First Noble Truth echo the teaching of the Gospel as it is passed on by the Catholic Church?
- Share and discuss reflections as a class.

THE SECOND NOBLE TRUTH: THE PRIMARY CAUSE OF SUFFERING

The Buddhist path to enlightenment involves the realization that unwholesome "cravings," such as sensuous lust, greed, aversion, ill will, sloth, restlessness, anxiety and doubt, hinder one from progressing to enlightenment. The constant craving for pleasure and success, and grasping for the acquisition of goods (which we name consumerism), separate us from other people and deny us happiness. These unwholesome cravings, which serve only the *self*, are the primary cause of our suffering.

THE THIRD NOBLE TRUTH: THE CESSATION OF SUFFERING

The way to freedom from suffering (*dukkha*) lies not in the scholarly study and understanding of these truths, but in "letting go" of our unwholesome cravings or thirsts. The truths must be lived. This takes constant practice, which includes keen observation, meditation, mindfulness and reflection, and making the Noble Truths one's own. This Third Noble Truth offers hope; it points to the example of Buddha, in whom nirvana has taken place.

REVIEW, REFLECT AND SHARE

- Review these teachings of the Catholic Church from the *Catechism of the Catholic Church*:
  - "Christ's faithful 'have crucified the flesh with its passions and desires' (Galatians 5:24); they are led by the Spirit and follow his desires" (CCC, no. 2555).
  - "Detachment from riches is necessary for entering the Kingdom of heaven. 'Blessed are the poor in spirit' " (CCC, no. 2556).
- Reflect:
  - Where do you see elements of truth in the Second and Third Noble Truths of Buddhism that echo or relate in some way to the teachings of the Catholic Church? Identify those elements and how they relate to Catholic Church teachings.

- Name the elements of these Buddhist teachings that are contrary to the teachings of the Catholic Church. Explain how they are contrary to Catholic Church teaching.
⊙ Share and discuss reflections as a class .

THE FOURTH NOBLE TRUTH: THE MIDDLE WAY

The Fourth Noble Truth is that there is a way out of suffering. It is the Buddha's "middle way," known as the Eightfold Path. Buddha Gautama pointed out that in following this path there are two extremes one should avoid: a life totally given to pleasure, and a life entirely devoted to self-denial. He had experienced each way of life and knew that both are fruitless. The person seeking enlightenment should avoid both extremes and, instead, find a middle way.

The Eightfold Path includes the integration of "right" ways into one's life (similar to the Christian understanding of the "human virtues"). Buddhism is above all else a system of spiritual practices. The Eightfold Path includes:

1. right understanding, or vision of life;
2. right thought and attitude;
3. right, or truthful, speech;
4. right action, or the practice of "letting go" and not exploiting or dehumanizing one's self or others;
5. right livelihood that flows from right action;
6. right effort, or diligence, in following the path to wholeness of life and freedom from suffering;
7. right mindfulness, or growth in full awareness of Reality;
8. right concentration, or reaching of the state of perfect enlightenment (Buddhahood).

The Eightfold Path is not a list of sequential steps, but rather interconnected practices to be constantly implemented. These practices represent a middle way that avoids extremes. They engage the person mentally, verbally and bodily. They involve three approaches to good, or Real, living: *Wisdom* (right understanding and

DHARMA WHEEL AT JOHKANG TEMPLE, TIBET

Buddhist Monks and Nuns

Buddhist monks and nuns live in community. Unlike Christian monks and nuns, their communal life is not "religious" in nature. Buddhism is agnostic. It does not claim any special revelation as its source. Logical and rational thinking is the source of its teachings and practices.

Buddhist monks and nuns depend on the surrounding community for their food and sustenance. Usually Buddhist monks and nuns do not marry, though in some Buddhist communities they may marry. There are 227 rules for Buddhist monks and nuns. The principal rules, which also apply to every Buddhist, are:

- Do not harm living beings.
- Do not take another's property.
- Do not engage in sexual misconduct.
- Do not offend by speech.
- Do not take alcohol or intoxicating substances.

A BUDDHIST MONK IN SUKHOTHAI, THAILAND

good purpose); *Morality* (in speech, action and livelihood); and *Contemplation* (mindfulness and concentration). Following the Eightfold Path is a lifelong program leading to Reality—the removal of illusion, the control of one's unwholesome desires (craving and thirsts), and the attainment of enlightenment and nirvana.

REVIEW, REFLECT AND SHARE

- Review the seven gifts of the Holy Spirit in the life of a Christian. (The gifts of the Holy Spirit are listed and explained in the "Prayers, Devotions and Practices" section of this text.)
- Reflect:
  - Do you see any elements of truth in the Eightfold Path that echo or relate in any way to the Church's teachings on the gifts of the Holy Spirit? Identify those elements.
  - Do you see any elements of the Eightfold Path that are contrary to the teachings of the Catholic Church? Identify those elements.
- Share and discuss reflections as a class.

THE *SANGHA* OR COMMUNITY AUTHORITY

The Buddha did not leave a pope, hierarchy or personal authority to guide his followers. Instead, when the Buddha was dying, he told the monks (*bhikkhus* or beggars) that, in the event of any question or doubt about his teaching, they should discuss the matter together as a community. This tradition of giving authority to the community of holy monks and nuns became known as the *Sangha* (literally "community"). In time the Sangha also came to include holy women and men, besides monks and nuns. Today the Sangha refers to any community of Buddhist practitioners. The Sangha is identified as one of the "three jewels of Buddhism." A Buddhist's daily prayer is: I take refuge in the Buddha. / I take refuge in the Dhamma. / I take refuge in the Sangha.

REVIEW, REFLECT AND SHARE

- Review these teachings of the Catholic Church which we have already explored in this course of study:

MONKS EATING AT MAHAGANDAYON MONASTERY IN MANDALAY, MYANMAR

Today the Sangha refers to any community of Buddhist practitioners

- The Church founded by Jesus Christ is a hierarchical society that is governed by the pope, the Bishop of Rome, and the bishops in communion with him.
- "Bishops, with priests as co-workers, have as their first task 'to preach the Gospel of God to all men,' in keeping with the Lord's command. [Vatican II, *Decree on the Ministry and Life of Priests*, no. 4]. They are 'heralds of faith, who draw new disciples to Christ; they are authentic teachers' of the apostolic faith 'endowed with the authority of Christ' [Vatican II, *Dogmatic Constitution on the Church*, no. 25]" (CCC, no. 888).
- "In order to preserve the Church in the purity of the faith handed on by the apostles, Christ who is the Truth willed to confer on her a share in his own infallibility. By a 'supernatural sense of faith' the People of God, under the guidance of the Church's living Magisterium, 'unfailingly adheres to this faith' [Vatican II, *Dogmatic Constitution on the Church*, no. 12]' " (CCC, no. 889).

⊙ Reflect:
  - Do you see any elements of truth in the Buddhist teachings on the Sangha that echo or relate in any way to the above teachings of the Catholic Church? Identify those elements.
  - Do you see any elements of the Buddhist teachings on the Sangha that are contrary to the teachings of the Catholic Church? Identify those elements.

⊙ Share and discuss reflections as a class.

JOURNAL EXERCISE

⊙ Revisit St. John Paul II's first Encyclical Letter, *Redemptor Hominis* (*The Redeemer of Man*), in which he suggested common activities that might take place between Catholics and representatives of non-Christian religions.

⊙ What activities might Buddhists and Catholics undertake together? How might those activities help both Catholics and Buddhists to live their religion? Give specific examples.

Confucianism: The way of order and harmony

CONFUCIUS SAYS. . .

You may have heard the expression, "Confucius says," followed by an aphorism such as "Life is really simple, but we insist on making it complicated"; or "Everything has beauty, but not everyone sees it"; or "Our greatest glory is not in never falling, but in rising every time we fall."

OPENING REFLECTION

◉ Can you recall any other aphorisms attributed to Confucius? What insights have you gained from those aphorisms?

◉ Do you have a favorite aphorism that helps you keep focused in living your Catholic faith?

CONFUCIUS AND THE ORIGINS OF CONFUCIANISM

Confucianism is fundamentally a philosophy of life and not a religion. Because of Confucius' significant contribution to the development of a moral philosophy of life, we will now examine his life and teachings.

At the same time as the enlightened Siddhartha Gautama was establishing Buddhism in the sixth century BC, poets and philosophers of Classical Greece were developing the seeds of European rational thought and human ethics. Confucius (c. 551–479 BC) and other sages of ancient China were also laying the foundations for Chinese, Korean, Japanese and East Asian cultures as we know them today.

Kong Fuzi (Kong the Teacher), or Confucius, was born into a poor noble family and he is probably the best known and most influential of the great sages of Chinese history. Confucius is the Latin form of his name, given to him by Jesuit missionaries in the sixteenth century.

Confucius the politician: Confucius' life was quite different from that of Siddhartha Gautama.

Confucius was not a royal member of society who renounced his wealth and privilege, nor did he seek and live the life of a monk. He earned his living and provided for his family as an administrator and civil servant in the small municipal government of Lu. Lu was an ancient state in today's Shandong Province in the eastern part of the People's Republic of China. Politics in Lu was turbulent and violent. In this political climate Confucius became increasingly respected for his character and advice. He urged reconciliation among people and, like many peace-keepers in the history of the world, he failed.

Confucius the advisor and consultant: Confucius could get nowhere in Lu with his program of national harmony. He resigned from his post and traveled to other city states to offer his services as an advisor and consultant. Though he had a reputation for wisdom, no other city government would hire him. He decided that his only course was to return home to Lu, gather followers and teach them the principles he had worked out for achieving peace and harmony.

Confucius the teacher: Legend tells us that Confucius spent the final years of his life instructing seventy followers. He wanted to ensure that, though he failed to achieve anything useful, his students would keep his ideas alive. When he died, around 479 BC, the ruler of Lu granted him a state funeral. The paradox was, as it so often is, that his ideas grew more powerful after his death than during his lifetime. Confucius' ideas were taken up by scholars and philosophers who created a system of thought that has lasted to the present day.

REFLECT AND SHARE

- Work with a partner. Draw up a list of peacemakers of our time. Include both Christian and non-Christian examples from countries around the world.

- How did the beliefs and practices or vision of life or religion of these peacemakers guide their efforts?
- Was their work successful? Or did it fall on deaf ears? Give reasons for your responses.
- Share reflections as a class.

KEY CONCEPTS OF CONFUCIANISM

Chinese thinkers have proposed a diversity of rational and religious answers to the mystery of life's journey. One school of thought advocates altruism; it argues for the spread of universal love. People should overcome self-preoccupation and act out of concern for others. A second school of thought advocates "law and order." It proposes adherence to detailed laws and strict punishments as a guide through life. For adherents of this philosophy, compliance to laws is their goal; coercion is their method for ensuring compliance.

Confucius proposed neither love nor law and order alone. He taught a third way: human society can be held together by mutual regard and a strong sense of community. Leaders should respect and be guided by a power beyond

TEMPLE OF CONFUCIUS, BEIJING, CHINA

themselves. People should be led by example, not driven by force. Social order is possible only if there is order in the city, order in the family, and order in the human heart.

The teachings and practices of Confucius have been passed down through more than two thousand years and have undergone much interpretation and development. We will now examine several key concepts of those teachings and practices. Confucius arrived at these concepts through logical and rational thinking; and he did not claim any special revelation as their source.

As you explore these concepts, try to discern what elements of the truths they contain have been revealed in Sacred Scripture and Tradition and are found in what the Catholic Church proclaims.

THE CHINESE CHARACTER 'HE' (HARMONY)

The Command of Heaven (*Tien*): Confucianism appears to possess a concept of non-personal supreme reality or transcendence that gives order to the world. Confucius spoke about the earth but based what he said on the designs of Heaven (*Tien*). Heaven commands that justice be done. Justice or good order is the rule of the universe. The sixteenth-century Jesuit missionaries explained God to the Confucians as "The Lord of Heaven" (*Tien Zhou*), emphasizing that God was different from heaven.

Harmony (*He*): Harmony (*He*) is the distinguishing feature of the design of Heaven. Everything has to be in balance. Nothing exists on its own. Everything grows in a web of relationships that ensures equilibrium. Confucius taught, "Heavens and humans are one." The beyond and the here-and-now, the past and the future, ancestors and posterity should all be in accord. The teaching entitled "Five Relationships" summarizes the areas in which human beings should strive to attain harmony and balance. They are: ruler to ruled, father to son, husband to wife, elder brother to younger brother, friend to friend.

Goodness (*De*): Humans are good by nature. We naturally try to develop this innate goodness, or *De*. We do this first in the family, then with our relatives and community, and finally, if the occasion arises, for the people and the nation.

We value good people. Everyone wants to do good. We hope to be known as good.

Benevolence (*Ren*): Goodness is benevolence. Benevolence, or *Ren*, is "human-heartedness," thinking and doing good for others, and is regarded by Confucians as the highest of human qualities. A good human is directed by Ren, which comes from one's inward spirit. Benevolence is first learned at home; it is directed first of all to one's family; then extended to one's superiors, one's followers, one's colleagues, one's fellow citizens and to all human beings.

Right rules and patterns (*Li*): *Li* embodies the emotions (human passions) and attitudes that should accompany Ren behaviors. Outwardly human actions are directed by appropriate conduct, politeness, consideration and proper behavior. Li, in its totality, refers to morality, rites and rituals, habitual gestures of respect, ranging from bowing to each other up to the elaborate sacrifices and ceremonials proper to state occasions.

"The Gentleman" (*Junzi*): *Junzi* embodies the Confucian ideal. It refers to the nobility of the moral character. Junzi is benevolence and right rules (Li) personified. Confucius described the good ruler as Junzi: "He leads them by means of virtue (Ren) and makes them equal by means of rites (Li).

- ⊙ The social doctrine of the Catholic Church is rooted in seeking justice based on charity (love). Review the seven key points of the social doctrine of the Catholic Church. (You will find a summary of those teachings in the "Prayers, Devotions and Practices" section of this text.)
- ⊙ Reflect:
  - Do you see any elements of truth in the teachings of Confucianism that echo or relate in any way to the social teachings of the Catholic Church? Identify those elements.
  - Do you see any of the teachings of Confucianism that do not reflect or are contrary to the teachings of the Catholic Church? Identify those teachings.
- ⊙ Share reflections as a class.

Other Chinese Teachers and "Ways"

Lao Tzu (b. 640 BC): A Chinese name that means "Old Master." Lao Tzu's writings, known as *Tao Te Ching,* or *Dao De Jing* in the new Chinese spelling, focus on the way of power and order in the universe. The source of Lao Tzu's writings is more intuitional than rational and logical.

Taoism (Daoism): The *Tao Te Ching* is the foundation of Daoism. The word *tao* means "way"; *dao* is the "way of nature." The way of nature is beyond knowing by the use of reason. It is the transcendent, non-personal, immanent force of all that is and it pervades nature. Taoism is a good fit with Confucianism. Its focus is the mandate of heaven and the virtue of naturalness, or behaving as nature dictates. Confucianism seeks the "way" (*dharma*) within the social relationships of human life. Daoism seeks the "way" (*tao*) in a mystical and intuitive grasp of reality.

Yin and Yang: The foundational insight of Daoism is that human beings and nature and the whole of the universe follow the same law. The key to this law is the division between *Yin* and *Yang*. These dual categories for everything are associated with the female (*Yin*) and male (*Yang*) principles; but these principles go far beyond gender. Yang is assertive and dominant, hard, bright and giving. Yin is retiring and submissive, soft, dark and receptive. The two exist in opposition; but they are not enemies. For example, day needs night; summer requires winter. Yin and Yang interface in harmonious communion. Daoism has been characterized as the Yin and Confucianism as the Yang of the pathways of life.

STATUE OF LAO TZU IN QUANZHOU, CHINA

CONFUCIANISM: RELIGION OR SOCIAL PHILOSOPHY

Recall what you have learned about the nature of religion from your ongoing study of theology, as well as from the definition of "religion" in the Faith Glossary of this text. What are the essential qualities of a religion?

Is Confucianism a religion? Confucius himself was ambivalent and ambiguous about that. While he professed not to pray for specific favorable outcomes in life, he advocated traditional ceremonies and sacrifices to preserve the harmony, or balance, between human life and the universe. In the second century AD, Confucianism was declared the state religion of a unified China, and Confucianism was deliberately transmitted to the whole of China for many generations. School children studied the Five Classics attributed to Confucius and the Four Books based on his ideas.

REVIEW, REFLECT AND SHARE

⊙ The Catholic Church teaches: "The first commandment summons man to believe in God, to hope in him, and to love him above all else" (CCC, no. 2134). Religion is a virtue rooted in the First Commandment.

⊙ Reflect:
  – Do you see any elements of truth in the teachings of Confucianism that echo or relate in any way to the teachings of the Catholic Church on the nature of religion? Identify those elements.
  – Do you see any of the teachings of Confucianism that do not reflect or are contrary to the teachings of the Catholic Church? Identify those teachings.
⊙ Share reflections as a class.

JOURNAL EXERCISE

⊙ Revisit St. John Paul II's *Redemptor Hominis* (*The Redeemer of Man*), in which he suggested common activities that might take place between Catholics and representatives of non-Christian religions.
⊙ What activities might followers of Confucianism and Catholics undertake together? How might those activities help both Catholics and followers of Confucianism to live their religion or philosophy of life? Give specific examples.

JUDGE AND ACT

REVIEW AND SHARE WHAT YOU HAVE LEARNED

Review and share what you have learned in this chapter about the beliefs and religious practices of Hinduism, Buddhism and Confucianism. Use these statements as the focus of your responses: Hinduism, Buddhism and Confucianism teach:

◉ all human beings share a common origin and end;

◉ to some degree, compassionate action, moral restraint, spiritual discipline and respect for human dignity;

◉ elements of truth and virtue, which can help orient their members toward reception of the Gospel;

◉ values and virtues similar to those which the Catholic Church proclaims.

OVER TO YOU

◉ What new insights and understanding did you gain from your study of this chapter about "the manner and life and conduct, the precepts and doctrines" of Hinduism, Buddhism and Confucianism?

INCULTURATION OF THE GOSPEL MESSAGE

Catholic missionaries and others have responded to Christ's command to proclaim the Gospel to all peoples. Catholic missionaries to Chinese and other peoples in the East had to address many practices that appeared to be superstition, idolatry and divination. These practices, which are contrary to the First Commandment, were woven into the very culture of the people. One response of the missioners was to demand that these practices be abandoned. A second response was to use the truths within these cultures as seeds that could be nurtured in the evangelization of peoples. This approach to evangelization, which the Jesuit missioner Matteo Ricci advocated, has come to be named the inculturation of the Gospel message. The Church teaches:

> In this work of inculturation, . . . the Christian community must discern, on the one hand, which riches to "take" up as compatible with the faith; on the other, it must seek to "purify" and "transform" those criteria, modes of thought and lifestyles which are contrary to the Kingdom of God. . . . All of the people of God must be involved in this process. . . .
> —*General Directory for Catechesis*, no. 109

St. John XXIII, St. John Paul II and Pope Benedict XVI have each praised Ricci's approach to evangelization.

FAITH WORD

Inculturation

A two-way process whereby the Gospel is woven into the various dimensions of human culture and experience, both personal and social, and authentic cultural values are in turn integrated into the Christian life. Inculturation is a dimension of the Church's work of evangelization.

Matteo Ricci (1552–1610), Jesuit priest and missioner to Chinese people

Matteo Ricci (1552–1610) was an Italian Jesuit priest. In 1582 on his arrival as a missioner at Macau, an island near Hong Kong, he worked at becoming fluent in Chinese and familiar with China's history and culture. Ricci astonished the Chinese people with his prodigious feats of memory using his own mnemonic system. He and his companions introduced the Chinese to geographical maps of the world and to scientific astronomical calculations. They intrigued Chinese scholars by predicting solar eclipses accurately.

In 1601 Ricci and some other Jesuits were invited by the Emperor to reside in Beijing. They dressed like Chinese scholars and took part in local cultural practices, such as those that involved showing reverence toward Chinese ancestors. Their respect for Chinese culture drew many Chinese to Christianity.

When Ricci died in 1610, the Emperor allowed him the privilege of burial in Beijing. Ricci's grave can be visited at the Beijing Administrative College to this day. In 2010, on the four hundredth anniversary of his birth, Ricci's home diocese began the process for his canonization.

TALK IT OVER

⊙ How does Matteo Ricci's openness to discover and respond to the truth in non-Christian cultures reflect the teachings of Vatican II's, *Declaration on the Relation of the Church to Non-Christian Religions*?

SHARE FAITH WITH FAMILY AND FRIENDS

⊙ Share with family and friends these words of St. John Paul II describing the religious and cultural values that are important to Asian people:

The people of Asia take pride in their religious and cultural values, such as love of silence and contemplation, simplicity, harmony, detachment, non-violence, the spirit of hard work, discipline, frugal living, the thirst for learning and philosophical enquiry. They hold dear the values of respect for life, compassion for all beings, closeness to nature, filial piety towards parents, elders and ancestors, and a highly developed sense of community. In particular, they hold the family to be a vital source of strength, a closely knit community with a powerful sense of solidarity. Asian peoples are known for their spirit of religious tolerance and peaceful co-existence.... All this indicates an innate spiritual insight and moral wisdom

WORSHIPERS AT THE CATHEDRAL OF THE IMMACULATE CONCEPTION, BEIJING, CHINA

in the Asian soul. . . . In this framework of complementarity and harmony, the Church can communicate the Gospel in a way which is faithful both to her own Tradition and to the Asian soul.

—*Ecclesia in Asia*, no. 6

⊙ Discuss whether any or all of these values could also be described as Christian values.
⊙ How well do you and other Christians whom you know live these values?
⊙ Share how you might put such values into greater practice in your daily life.

JUDGE AND DECIDE
⊙ Has your exploration of Hinduism, Buddhism and Confucianism deepened your commitment to listen openly and respectfully to people of other religions?
⊙ How might you put that commitment into practice?

LEADER

In our prayer today we will use the *lectio divina* prayer technique. *Lectio divina* includes vocal prayer, meditation and contemplation. We read and reflect on Sacred Scripture, and listen and seek to understand how God might be speaking to us, right here and right now. We then act on what the Lord is asking of us.

Read

Quiet your mind and heart. Place yourself in the presence of God. Pray Psalm 145.

I will extol you, my God and King,
    and bless your name for ever and ever.
Every day I will bless you,
    and praise your name for ever and ever.
Great is the LORD, and greatly to be praised;
    his greatness is unsearchable.

One generation shall laud your works to another,
    and shall declare your mighty acts.
On the glorious splendor of your majesty,
    and on your wondrous works, I will meditate.
The might of your awesome deeds shall be
      proclaimed,
    and I will declare your greatness.
They shall celebrate the fame of your abundant
      goodness,
    and shall sing aloud of your righteousness.

The LORD is gracious and merciful,
    slow to anger and abounding in steadfast
      love.
The LORD is good to all,
    and his compassion is over all that he has
      made.

All your works shall give thanks to you, O LORD,
    and all your faithful shall bless you.
They shall speak of the glory of your kingdom,
    and tell of your power,
to make known to all people your mighty deeds,
    and the glorious splendor of your kingdom.
Your kingdom is an everlasting kingdom,
    and your dominion endures throughout all
      generations.

The LORD is faithful in all his words,
    and gracious in all his deeds.
The LORD upholds all who are falling,
    and raises up all who are bowed down.
The eyes of all look to you,
    and you give them their food in due season.
You open your hand,
    satisfying the desire of every living thing.
The LORD is just in all his ways,
    and kind in all his doings.
The LORD is near to all who call on him,
    to all who call on him in truth.
He fulfills the desire of all who fear him;
    he also hears their cry, and saves them.
The LORD watches over all who love him,
    but all the wicked he will destroy.

My mouth will speak the praise of the LORD,
  and all flesh will bless his holy name for ever
      and ever.

Now, silently and slowly, read and pray the psalm once again. Be alert for what God might be calling you to understand and do to act upon what you have learned in this chapter.

Meditate

Quiet your mind and heart. Place yourself in the presence of God and pray the psalm again. Pause and talk silently in your heart to God the Father, Son and Holy Spirit. Ask for the grace to understand what you are hearing.

Contemplate

Quiet your mind and heart. Welcome God the Father, Son and Holy Spirit into the deepest place in your heart. Pray the psalm a third time, asking God to deepen your understanding of his word to you.

Act

Acknowledge God's presence. Pray for the wisdom and courage to act on his word.

LEADER

Let us respond to these questions to help us decide what we will do to act upon God's word to us.

⊙ What does this prayer time call you to do so as to integrate what you have learned in this chapter into your life?

⊙ How will you take it to heart right now?

Share a sign of peace and go forth to glorify God by our life.

All share a sign of peace and pray the Sign of the Cross together.

Sikhism, the Bahá'í Religion and Mormonism

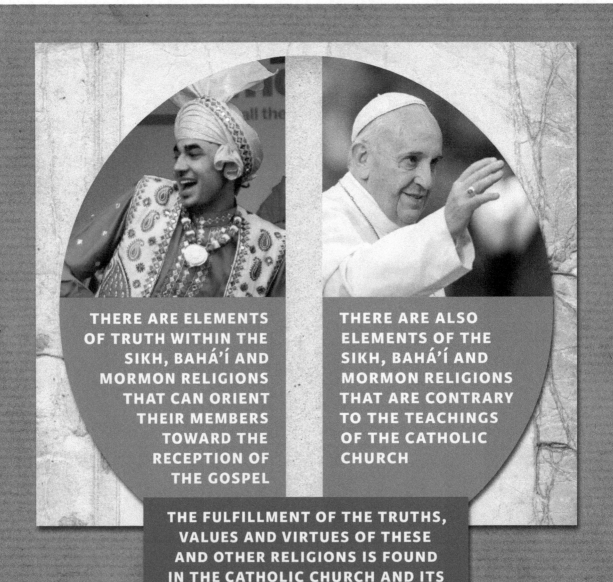

THERE ARE ELEMENTS OF TRUTH WITHIN THE SIKH, BAHÁ'Í AND MORMON RELIGIONS THAT CAN ORIENT THEIR MEMBERS TOWARD THE RECEPTION OF THE GOSPEL

THERE ARE ALSO ELEMENTS OF THE SIKH, BAHÁ'Í AND MORMON RELIGIONS THAT ARE CONTRARY TO THE TEACHINGS OF THE CATHOLIC CHURCH

THE FULFILLMENT OF THE TRUTHS, VALUES AND VIRTUES OF THESE AND OTHER RELIGIONS IS FOUND IN THE CATHOLIC CHURCH AND ITS TEACHINGS

IN CHAPTER 10 WE CONTINUE OUR STUDY OF THE CONNECTION of Christianity with other non-Christian religions by looking at the Sikh, the Bahá'í and the Mormon religions. We include Mormons here because, while they profess faith in Jesus Christ and identify themselves as The Church of Jesus Christ of Latter-day Saints, they reject the apostolic Christian doctrine of the Trinity, and therefore the Catholic Church teaches that Mormons are not validly baptized and cannot be called Christian. Mormons are *not in communion, even imperfect communion*, with Catholics and other Christian churches and ecclesial communities.

CHRISTIAN FAITH CANNOT ACCEPT "REVELATIONS" THAT CLAIM TO SURPASS OR CORRECT THE REVELATION OF WHICH CHRIST IS THE FULFILLMENT.

—CATECHISM OF THE CATHOLIC CHURCH, NO. 67

Faith Focus: These teachings of the Catholic Church are the primary focus of the doctrinal content presented in this chapter:

⊙ Non-Christian religions contain elements of truth and virtue, which can help orient their members toward reception of the Gospel.

⊙ The fulfillment of the truths, values and virtues of other religions is found in what the Catholic Church proclaims.

⊙ God is our Creator and destiny. As human beings we share a common origin and end.

⊙ God revealed himself to be a Triune God, one God in three Divine Persons.

⊙ Jesus Christ is the Incarnate Son of God; he is fully divine and fully human.

⊙ Jesus is the fullness of Revelation; there is no further Revelation after him.

⊙ Baptism is the bond of communion that unites all Christians as brothers and sisters in Christ. The valid celebration and reception of the Sacrament of Baptism gives a person the right to be called a Christian.

⊙ "Those who die in God's grace and friendship and are perfectly purified live for ever with Christ" (CCC, no. 1023).

Discipleship Formation: As a result of studying this chapter and discovering the meaning of the faith of the Catholic Church for your life, you should be better able to:

⊙ recognize and value elements of truth in the Sikh, Bahá'í and Mormon religions;

⊙ identify the teachings and practices of the Sikh, Bahá'í and Mormon religions that are contrary to the teachings of the Catholic Church;

⊙ share your Catholic faith with members of non-Christian religions.

Scripture References: These scripture references are quoted or referred to in this chapter:
OLD TESTAMENT: Psalm 67:1–5
NEW TESTAMENT: Matthew 28:19–20; **Mark** 16:16; **John** 1:1–9, 3:1–6, 8:12; **Acts of the Apostles** 2:37–42, 10:2 and 30–48

Faith Glossary: Familiarize yourself with or recall the meaning of these key terms. Definitions are found in the Glossary: **Apostolic Tradition, Baptism, Christian sect, Church, deacons, eternal life, evangelization, heaven, human person, Incarnation, Paschal Mystery, priest, Real Presence, Resurrection, resurrection of the body, Revelation (Divine), revelations (private), sacrament(s), sacramental economy, transubstantiation, Trinity**

Faith Word: Christian sect
Learn by Heart: Psalm 67:3
Learn by Example: St. Cornelius the Centurion

What helps us to know God's will?

OPENING REFLECTION

⊙ "What a revelation!" Have you ever heard or used that expression? What does it mean?

⊙ Compare your understanding of the word "revelation" with the Church's teaching on **Divine Revelation** that you explored in chapter 1 of this text.

DISCERNING GOD'S WILL FOR HUMANITY

The desire for a direct relationship and intimate communion with God is hardly a new or novel experience. "Man is made to live in communion with God in whom he finds happiness" (*Catechism of the Catholic Church* [CCC], no. 45). The thirst

and desire for God that is within all people comes from God. God desires and initiates a relationship with each one of us. Only through living in communion with God can lasting joy and peace be found in this life and the next.

In chapter 1 of this text we explored the Catholic Church's recognition of this desire and the role of religion in its fulfillment: "People look to their different religions for an answer to the unsolved riddles of human existence. . . . What is the meaning and purpose of life? . . . And finally, what is the ultimate mystery, beyond human explanation, which embraces our entire existence, from which we take our origin and toward which we tend?" (Vatican Council II, *Declaration on the Relation of the Church to Non-Christian Religions* [*Nostra Aetate*], no. 1).

The Catholic Church teaches that the **human person** has the God-given natural ability to gain insights into these riddles. This ability is based on the human person's "openness to truth and beauty, his sense of moral goodness, his freedom and the voice of his conscience, with his longings for the infinite and for happiness" (CCC, no. 33).

The Catholic Church also reminds us that the human ability is hindered in its attainment of these fundamental truths "by the activity of the senses and the imagination, and by evil passions arising from original sin" (Pope Pius XII, Encyclical Letter *Humani Generis* [Concerning some false opinions threatening to undermine the foundations of Catholic doctrine], no. 2).

This is why man stands in need of being enlightened by God's revelation, not only about those things that exceed his understanding, but also "about those religious and moral truths which of themselves are not beyond the grasp of human reason, so that even in the present

A WHITE HALO OF ROSES | A.N. MIRONOV

condition of the human race, they can be known by all men with ease, with firm certainty and with no admixture of error" (*Humani Generis*, no. 2).

—CCC, no. 38

THE ETERNAL WORD MADE FLESH ENLIGHTENS ALL HUMANKIND

God the Creator has not left humanity alone in our search for the path to communion with him. God in his goodness has revealed himself "to make known the mystery of his will, which was that people can draw near to the Father, through Christ, the Word made flesh, in the holy Spirit, and thus become sharers in the divine nature" (Vatican Council II, *Dogmatic Constitution on Divine Revelation* [*Dei Verbum*], no. 2).

Jesus Christ is the eternal Word of God; he is the true light who enlightens everyone. (Check out John 1:1–9.) He is the Incarnate Son of God, who declared, "I am the light of the world. Whoever follows me will never walk in darkness but will have the light of life" (John 8:12). He is the light who enlightens us on the true nature of our relationship with God and with one another. He alone is the One who makes us sharers in the love and the very life of God.

OVER TO YOU

⊙ What do the life and the **Paschal Mystery** of the Death, Resurrection and Ascension of Jesus reveal to you about the meaning of your life? Your relationship with God? Your relationship to the Church? Your relationship with non-Christians?

CLAIMS OF OTHER "REVELATIONS"

The founders of Islam, Hinduism, Buddhism, Sikhism, the Bahá'í religion, Mormonism and other non-Christian religions offer their followers answers to the "unsolved riddles" of human existence. These founders often claim that the source of their answers is a "revelation" from God. The Catholic Church teaches: "Christian faith cannot accept 'revelations' that claim to surpass or correct the Revelation of which Christ is the fulfillment, as is the case in certain non-Christian religions and also in certain recent sects which base themselves on such 'revelations'" (CCC, no. 67). We will explore the teachings and practices of the Sikh, Bahá'í and Mormon faith communities in this chapter.

The Sikh religion

SIKH WOMAN FINDS ENLIGHTENMENT IN JESUS

Nikky, a Sikh, attended a Catholic convent school in India, her native country. Later, as a young woman, she shared her memories of those days:

> I attended a convent school where we recited "Our Father" during the morning assembly, and we took courses on Moral Science. Most of all I loved going into the Convent where we sang psalms and collected beautiful images of Christ, and of Our Lady of Fatima, after whom my school was named. . . . The "question" of identity never came up: just as I knew my name, I knew I was a Sikh. But that did not stop me from participating excitedly in the religious space created by my Catholic teachers: it was mysterious and enchanting in its own way. I can still feel the fervor with which I would sing "The Lord is my shepherd, nothing shall I fear"—in spite of my desperately poor musical talents!

Nikky also acknowledged the impact of her learning about Jesus on her own identity as a Sikh. She wrote: "Jesus has been a wonderful mirror who in his unique form and vocabulary promoted my self-understanding. The image of Christ imbedded in my childhood has made the verses of the Gurus alive for me."

OPENING REFLECTION

◉ What do you think about Nikky's openness to embracing some of the truth and beauty of the Catholic faith, while at the same time remaining faithful to her identity as a Sikh?

◉ Has your study of other Christian and non-Christian religions strengthened your self-understanding as a Catholic?

THE SIKH COMMUNITY

The word "Sikh" in the Punjabi language means "disciple." Punjabi is the native language of what today is Western India and Eastern Pakistan. Sikhs identify themselves as disciples of God who follow the writings and teachings of the Ten Sikh Gurus.

There are more than 20 million followers of the Sikh religion worldwide. This makes Sikhism the fifth largest religion in the world. There are about 250 Sikh congregations serving about 500 thousand members in the United States of America.

Americans often mistake Sikhs for Muslims or Arabs. This

Sikhs honor the first Ten Gurus as the divinely enlightened teachers whom the one God blessed with great spiritual wisdom and other gifts

GURU NANAK | 19TH-CENTURY WATERCOLOR

"mistaken identity" often arises from Sikhs' physical appearance and dress; in particular from Sikh men not cutting their hair and wearing turbans and growing beards. This practice is an expression of the Sikh belief that hair is a gift from God, and not cutting one's hair is a sign of love of God and gratitude to God for his many blessings.

THE GURUS AND THE ORIGINS OF THE SIKH RELIGION

The Sikh religion, from one point of view, is a reformation of Hinduism and Islam. It began in the Punjab in India in the fifteenth century, at a time when the Muslim Mughal (Mogul) Empire ruled but the majority of the population was Hindu. Its origins lie with Guru Nanak (1469–1539), the first of the Ten Sikh Gurus. The nine Gurus who followed Guru Nanak from 1539 to 1708 passed on and built upon his teachings. The result was the creation of Sikhism.

The Gurus: The Sanskrit word *guru* has several meanings, including "teacher, enlightener" (Nikky-Guninder Kaur Singh, *Sikhism: An Introduction*, 236). Sikhs honor the first Ten Gurus as the divinely enlightened teachers whom the one God blessed with great spiritual wisdom and other gifts.

Sikhs also use the title Guru for the Sikh book of holy writings—the Guru Granth Sahib, or the Adi Granth. The Adi Granth is *the supreme spiritual guide and authority* for Sikhs. It contains hymns, poetry and other writings of the Gurus, as well as the writings of other people, both Sikhs and people of other religions, whom Sikhs revere as holy.

Guru Nanak and his successors: Guru Nanak was born into a Hindu family in a village in what is part of Pakistan today but, during his lifetime, was in a part of India ruled by the Muslim Mughal (Mogul) Empire.

Guru Nanak, a devout Hindu, became increasingly dissatisfied with both Hinduism and Islam. At around the age of thirty he had a life-changing mystical experience. He described this experience as an encounter with the one God, "whose name is Truth," who is neither Hindu nor Muslim. Guru Nanak committed himself totally to living and teaching that the only path (*dharma*) through life to salvation (*mukhti*), or the breaking of the cycle of births and rebirths, is a life lived in total obedience to the will of the one God, who is the origin and destiny of human beings.

Guru Nanak undertook many "missionary" journeys to share the message revealed to him. He traveled throughout India, Sri Lanka and Tibet, and visited Baghdad and Mecca. He taught through simple songs that he wrote and he established communities of his followers.

Guru Nanak's teachings openly challenged the foundational beliefs and practices of both Hinduism and Islam. On one occasion when he was asked whether Hinduism or Islam was the true religion, Guru Nanak replied: "If there is one God, then there is only His way to attain Him, not another."

Guru Granth Sahib: The Tenth Guru, Gobind Singh (1666–1708), came to believe that there was no longer a need for any further human Gurus. He declared that Sikhs could find all the spiritual wisdom they required for their path through life in the Guru Granth Sahib, the Sikh holy writings. Sikhs today revere these holy writings as they would revere a living Guru.

The Khalsa: Guru Gobind Singh also established the *Khalsa* in 1699. The term *Khalsa* means "pure ones" and is a collective term for the community of men and women who have undergone the *amrit sanskar*, the Sikh initiation ceremony, who vow to follow strictly Sikh teachings and disciplines, and to wear the "*kacha* (underwear), *kangla* (comb, tucked into the hair), *kara* (bracelet), *kesh* (uncut hair), and *kirpan* (sword)" (*Sikhism: An Introduction*, 236, 237)—the five symbols of their faith and of their membership of the Khalsa.

REVIEW, REFLECT AND SHARE
- ⊙ Work with a partner. Recall the Church's teaching on Divine Revelation.
- ⊙ How does the Church's use and understanding of the term "Divine Revelation" differ from the private and personal encounter with God, or "revelation," experienced by Guru Nanak?
- ⊙ Share reflections as a class.

KEY SIKH BELIEFS AND PRACTICES
"The Sikh religion is based entirely on Guru Nanak's revelation, '*Ikk Oan Kar*—One Being Is' " (*Sikhism: An Introduction*, 59). There is one transcendent, infinite and indivisible Reality who is the origin and the end of all things. Key Sikh teachings and practices flow from this foundational teaching.

Teachings

- ⊙ There is only one God. God is neither Hindu nor Muslim nor the God that any other religion professes. The God professed by any religion is that religion's particular understanding of the one eternal, infinite Being.
- ⊙ All religions are equal; the faith and beliefs of every religion are to be shown respect

PERFORMERS AT THE 2012 VAISAKHI FESTIVAL, LONDON, ENGLAND

Vaisakhi Day

Vaisakhi Day is the annual mid-April Sikh holiday. It commemorates the celebration of the first Sikh initiation ceremony and the establishment of Khalsa by Guru Gobind Singh.

THE "GOLDEN TEMPLE", AMRITSAR, PUNJAB, INDIA, IS THE HOLIEST *GURDWARA*, OR SIKH PLACE OF WORSHIP

and reverence. There is one God who is "comprehended and taught in different styles" (*Sikhism: An Introduction*, 64). Submission to the will of God is the heart of human life.

- Every human person, including Jesus Christ, is a manifestation of the Transcendent One, a child of God. All people, regardless of race, religion, gender or social status are equal.
- The soul exists and goes through cycles of births and deaths before it takes human form. Everyone regardless of their religion can achieve salvation. All knowledge that is necessary to attain salvation can be learned by every Sikh by reading the Guru Granth Sahib, the Sikh holy writings.
- Salvation, the goal of human life, is to *merge* with the Divine. "This union liberates the individual from the cycle of birth and death" (*Sikhism: An Introduction*, 65). This would be similar to **heaven**. Hell is being caught in the process of births and rebirths.
- Everyone is to be kind and generous toward others, especially to people in need, acting as individuals and with others in community. The free community kitchen (*langar*) found at every Sikh place of worship (*gurdwara*), which is open to people of all religions, is one expression of Sikh community service.
- "Without love, ablutions, charities, studies and rituals are only worthless" (*Sikhism: An Introduction*, 72).
- Pride, anger, lust, greed and inordinate worldly attachments are the five vices that hinder one from achieving salvation. "The root cause of the five vices is *haumani*, literally, 'I-Myself.' . . . The selfish person is called *manmukh*, 'turned toward the me,' in contrast to one who actualizes the Divine Oneness" (*Sikhism: An Introduction*, 71).

Practices

- There is no celebration of the **sacraments**.
- There is no priesthood, or order of priests.
- A person is initiated into the Sikh religion through the *Amrit sansar* ceremony, which is a non-sacramental initiation ritual. Those initiated, or *Amritdhari*, experience a "rebirth" that purifies and emancipates the soul from the cycle of births and death. "The initiation marks their new birth into the Khalsa family: they are now children of Guru Gobind Singh and his wife" (*Sikhism: An Introduction*, 95).
- The Amritdhari vow to:
  - worship only the one God and not worship

PARADE IN HONOR OF GURU NANEK, NEW DEHLI, INDIA

any created object or living thing;
- read the Sikh holy book, the Guru Granth Sahib;
- participate in the life of a Sikh congregation;
- serve others generously out of love.

⊙ There is no special sabbath-like day of worship. Sikh services of worship may take place at any time. The Guru Granth Sahib is the focal point of all Sikh services. "Kirtan is the basic Sikh ritual: the singing of scriptural verses" (*Sikhism: An Introduction*, 85). This ritual awakens one's sense of oneness with all Reality. It concludes with drinking of *karahprashad*, "the sweet sacrament consisting of equal portions of butter, flour, sugar and water" (*Sikhism: An Introduction*, 86).

LET'S PROBE DEEPER: ANALYZE AND COMPARE

There are many substantial differences that separate Catholics and Sikhs. There are also some elements of truth in Sikh beliefs and practices that *orient* Sikhs toward the reception of the Gospel.

⊙ Reflect on the items described above under "Key Sikh Beliefs and Practices."
⊙ Work with a partner and name:

- those elements of truth within Sikhism that can orient Sikhs toward the reception of the Gospel; for example, "There is one transcendent, infinite and indivisible Reality who is the origin and the end of all things" and "Without love, ablutions, charities, studies and rituals are only worthless" (*Sikhism: An Introduction*, 72). Then name the teachings of the Catholic Church that fulfill those teachings and practices;
- the differences between Catholic teachings and Sikh teachings; for example, the teachings on Divine Revelation, God, salvation, the sacraments, and **eternal life**.

⊙ Share and, with the guidance of your teacher, discuss as a class those teachings and the truths they contain.

WHAT ABOUT YOU PERSONALLY?

⊙ Reread the opening story, "Sikh Woman Finds Enlightenment in Jesus."
⊙ Has your study of Sikhism strengthened your understanding of and commitment to living your Catholic faith?
⊙ Has your study and reflection on Sikhism guided you to show more respect to people of other religions?

The Bahá'í religion

A Bahá'í's view of Pope Francis and his critics

"Speaking for myself, an average Bahá'í, on the initial period of Pope Francis' papacy, it is rather mystifying that his advocacy for the poor and his chastisement of those who wield economic power has resulted in a cascade of accusations.

What of these vociferous critics and their criticisms? They are mostly directed toward the pope's expressed views that money should be the servant of humanity, not the master. . . .

My sincere wish is that the pope's quest for economic justice jolts the world to look anew at what Jesus really taught."

—Christy Besozzi

POPE FRANCIS IN CENTRAL PARK, NEW YORK, 2015

OPENING REFLECTION

⊙ What impressed this Bahá'í most about Pope Francis?

⊙ Where in the Gospels does Jesus teach his followers to live in the way that Pope Francis advocates—building a world that promotes justice for all?

⊙ What do you think about this vision of the world? What role can you play, individually and with others, to promote such a way of life?

THE BAHÁ'Í COMMUNITY

The Bahá'í religion is "an independent religion with its own sacred scriptures which recognize the divine origin of all the world's religious systems, the oneness of the human race, the equality of men and women, the harmony of science and religion, and the importance of universal education. It eschews violence" (Kenneth E. Bowers, Secretary of the National Spiritual Assembly of the Bahá'ís of the United States, Testimony to the United States House of Representatives, May 22, 2014).

Bahá'í communities can be found in almost every country in the world. "Statistics on religious affiliation are difficult to gather and verify, but a conservative estimate of the number of Bahá'ís as of 2012 would be at least five million. Bahá'ís live in more than 100,000 localities around the world and represent more than 2,100 ethnic and tribal groups. The Bahá'í writings have been translated into more than 800 languages" (Frances Worthington, *Bahá'í Basics*, 3). The Bahá'í religion is the tenth largest religion in the United States of America.

THE ORIGINS OF THE BAHÁ'Í RELIGION: THE BABA AND BAHÁ'U'LLÁH

The Bahá'í religion originated in the nineteenth century in present-day Iran. Its roots are in the mission and teachings of the Bab (1819–50) and Bahá'u'lláh (1817–92). The Bab (a word meaning "gate" in Arabic) was a Muslim who claimed that he was divinely inspired to interpret the Qur'an. The Bab's mission was to prepare the way for a "Second Messenger of God." Bahá'ís believe that this Second Messenger was Bahá'u'lláh. The name Bahá'u'lláh means "the Glory of God." Both the Bab and Bahá'u'lláh suffered persecution, rejection and imprisonment throughout their lives. It was while he was in prison that Bahá'u'lláh had the mystical experience of his call to be the promised "Manifestation of God" (*Bahá'í Basics*, 61–63).

KEY BAHÁ'Í BELIEFS AND PRACTICES

The teachings of the Bab and Bahá'u'lláh are the foundation of the Bahá'í religion. These teachings have been passed on in a direct line of succession from Bahá'u'lláh's son and grandson

BAHÁ'U'LLÁH PHOTOGRAPHED IN 1868

and the Universal House of Justice. The Universal House of Justice is the international governing and law-making body of the Bahá'í.

Bahá'í teachings contain many elements, or seeds, of truths that were fully revealed in Sacred Scripture and Sacred Tradition and that are proclaimed by the Catholic Church. You will recall from your study of the Catholic Church's participation in interreligious dialogue that "the Catholic Church rejects nothing of what is true and holy" in these teachings (*Declaration on the Relation of the Church to Non-Christian Religions*, no. 2). Discerning, identifying, acknowledging and speaking to these truths is central to the Church's work of evangelization.

We will now take a brief look at some of the key Bahá'í teachings and practices. But before we begin, take a few moments to look at the subheadings for each of the teachings and recall what you have learned about the teachings of the Catholic Church on each of these faith concepts and practices.

God: Bahá'ís believe in one God who is infinite and transcendent and beyond human understanding. They believe we can come to a limited understanding of the one God from our experiences of love, goodness, beauty, mercy, and justice, which are attributes of the one transcendent God. "The name you use for him—Jehovah, Yahweh, Ahura, Mazda, Allah, Indra, or God—will depend on the language you speak" (*Bahá'í Basics*, 85).

Bahá'í teaching acknowledges the Christian teaching on the Trinity; but Bahá'í teaching on the Trinity is contrary to the Catholic Church's dogma on the mystery of the Trinity. Bahá'í teaching asserts that God the Creator, God the Son, and God the Holy Spirit are three different *reflections or forms of expression* of the one infinite and ineffable God. Bahá'ís do not believe that the one God is three distinct and inseparable Divine Persons, nor do they believe that Jesus Christ is the Incarnate Son of God and a Divine Person. *Pause for reflection and discussion on the elements of truth in these teachings and the differences from Catholic teachings.*

Revelation: "The fundamental principle enunciated by Bahá'u'lláh . . . is that religious truth is not absolute but relative, that Divine revelation is a continuous and progressive process" (Shoghi Effendi, *The Promised Day Is Come";* quoted in *Bahá'í Basics,* 33–34). This is contrary to the teaching of the Catholic Church that Divine Revelation ended with the death of the last Apostle. Bahá'ís also hold "that all the great religions of the world are divine in origin, that their basic principles are in complete harmony, that their aims and purposes are one and the same, that their teachings are but facets of one truth, that their functions are complementary, that they differ only in nonessential aspects of their doctrines, and that their missions represent successive stages in the spiritual evolution of human society" (Shoghi Effendi, *The Promised Day Is Come";* quoted in *Bahá'í Basics,* 33–34). Shoghi Effendi (1897–1957) was appointed Guardian of the Bahá'í Faith in 1921 to fulfill the will of his grandfather, 'Abdu'l-Bahá (1844–1921), the son of Bahá'u'lláh.

Sacred writings: The Bahá'í sacred writings include the writings of the Bab, of Bahá'u'lláh, of 'Abdu'l-Bahá, the son of Bahá'u'lláh, of Shoghi Effendi, and of the Universal House of Justice. The "reading of the scriptures and holy books is for no other purpose except to enable the reader to apprehend their meaning and unravel the innermost mysteries" (Bahá'u'lláh, Kitáb-i-Íqán, 185). The Bahá'í Universal House of Justice has the supreme authority to interpret and pass on but not change these teachings.
Pause for reflection and discussion on the elements of truth in these teachings and the differences from Catholic teachings.

Creation: Bahá'ís look at the beauty and goodness of the world as a manifestation of the Creator. "Man's capacity to know and love God is the primary purpose of creation. . . . Nature is a physical expression of the will of God, and each part of the natural world can be understood as reflecting one of His attributes" (*Bahá'í Basics,* 10, 11). Humanity is the steward of the planet's vast resources, which we are to use for the good of all peoples, present and future.

Humanity: Bahá'ís believe that the purpose of

'ABDU'L-BAHÁ, THE SON OF BAHÁ'U'LLÁH

human life is to know God, who is the common origin and destiny of human beings, and to attain his presence by serving our fellow human beings. True life is life of the spirit. The human person has two powers, material and spiritual. "A balance between material and spiritual progress is necessary to establish the happiness of the world" (*Bahá'í Basics,* 10, 11). Developing spiritual habits such as generosity, kindness and justice is essential to fostering harmony and peace with the human family. By developing these habits, or virtues, we acquire the divine qualities we will need in the life after death.

Life after death: Bahá'ís believe that we journey toward God, in this world and the next. The spirit world is timeless and placeless; it is an extension of the created world. Every human person is a unified body and an immortal soul. At death the physical body decays, but the soul continues on an *eternal journey* in the spirit world toward God. "Although each soul begins its path of growth and development through association with a physical body, its ultimate home lies within the

BAHÁ'U'LLÁH'S HOUSE IN ACRE, ISRAEL

Kingdom of God" (*Bahá'í Basics*, 10, 11).
Pause for reflection and discussion on the elements of truth in these teachings and the differences from Catholic teachings.

Jesus Christ and the Paschal Mystery: Bahá'ís believe that Jesus Christ was a "Manifestation of God," as were Abraham, Moses, Muhammad, the Bab, and Bahá'u'lláh. According to Bahá'í teaching, Jesus was a *bridge* between God and humanity, as were the founders of all the world's great religions. Jesus was not divine, or God, because God cannot become human. "In Jesus Christ God's attributes were perfectly reflected and expressed" ("Jesus Christ in the Bahá'í Writings" in *Bahá'í Studies Review*, 2:1).

Bahá'u'lláh acknowledged Jesus' Death on the Cross to be an atonement for humanity. He described Jesus' sacrifice in very specific terms:

Know thou that when the Son of Man yielded up His breath to God, the whole of Creation wept with a great weeping. By sacrificing Himself, however, a fresh capacity was infused into all created things. Its evidences, as witnessed in all the peoples of the earth, are now manifest before thee. The deepest wisdom which the sages have uttered, the profoundest learning which any mind hath unfolded, the arts which the ablest hands have produced, the

influence exerted by the most potent of rulers, are but manifestations of the quickening power released by His transcendent, His all-pervasive, and resplendent spirit. . . . He it is Who purified the world. Blessed is the man who, with a face beaming with light, hath turned towards Him.
— Bahá'u'lláh, *Gleanings*, 36

Bahá'ís also acknowledge Jesus' Resurrection and Ascension; but they reject the teaching of the Catholic Church on the Resurrection. "We do not believe that there was a bodily resurrection after the crucifixion of Christ, but that there was a time after His ascension when His disciples perceived spiritually His true greatness and realized He was eternal in being. This is what has been reported symbolically in the New Testament and been misunderstood. His eating with disciples after resurrection is the same thing" (Shoghi Effendi, *High Endeavors: Messages to Alaska*, 69–70).
Pause for reflection and discussion on the elements of truth in these teachings and the differences from Catholic teachings.

Prayer and worship: Prayer, the reading and study of Bahá'í sacred writings, and meditation are central to Bahá'í life. Bahá'ís are obligated to pray at least once daily, facing toward the place where Bahá'u'lláh is buried. The prayer life of

Bahá'ís includes personal prayer, family prayer and communal prayer. "The true worshipper, while praying, should endeavor not so much to ask God to fulfill his wishes and desires, but rather to adjust these and make them conform to the Divine Will" (from Letter written on behalf of Shoghi Effendi; quoted in *Bahá'í Basics,* 99). Bahá'í celebrations do not include rigid rituals; they focus primarily on reading scriptures and music that help to create an atmosphere of worship.

Bahá'ís do not have a sacramental economy. Bahá'ís gather for devotional and social gatherings to foster harmony and unity. These include celebrating nine holy days "on which Bahá'ís should suspend work. The nineteenth month of the year is devoted to fasting and ends with the beginning of the Bahá'í new year" (*Bahá'í Basics,* 108), which begins on March 21. If a Bahá'í is able, they should make at least one pilgrimage to the Shrine of Bab and to the houses in which Bahá'u'lláh lived.

Pause for reflection and discussion on the elements of truth in these teachings and the differences from Catholic teachings.

Organizational/administrative structure: Bahá'ís strive to fulfill their mission to bring about the unity of humankind under the guidance of the Bahá'í Administrative Order. "The purpose of the Administrative Order is to establish the Kingdom of God on earth by gradually bringing about and maintaining an entirely new mode of community life built on love, unity, and service to God" (*Bahá'í Basics,* 85).

"The Bahá'í Faith does not have any ministers, rabbis or clergy. Instead, Bahá'ís form self-governing bodies through elections. Local Spiritual Assemblies administer the affairs of individual communities, National Spiritual Assemblies cover a nation, and the Universal House of Justice is the final authority for the world" (*Bahá'í Basics,* 6). Membership of this governing body is limited to males.

Pause for reflection and discussion on the elements of truth in these teachings and the differences from Catholic teachings.

LET'S PROBE DEEPER: ANALYZE AND COMPARE

There are many substantial differences that separate Catholics and Bahá'ís. There are also some elements of truth in Bahá'í beliefs and practices that orient Bahá'ís toward the reception of the Gospel.

⊙ Reflect on the items described under "Key Bahá'í Beliefs and Practices."

⊙ Work with a partner and name:
- those elements of truth within the Bahá'í religion that can orient Bahá'ís toward the reception of the Gospel. Then name the teachings of the Catholic Church that fulfill those teachings and practices;
- the differences between Catholic teachings and Bahá'í teachings. Then name the teachings of the Catholic Church.

⊙ Share and, with the guidance of your teacher, discuss as a class those teachings.

HOW WOULD YOU RESPOND?

⊙ Work with a partner. One of you takes the role of a Bahá'í youth; the other, a Catholic high school student.

⊙ Choose and discuss ways you can work together for economic justice for all.

SHRINE OF THE BAB, HAIFA, ISRAEL

The Mormon religion

One Baptism, one faith, one Lord

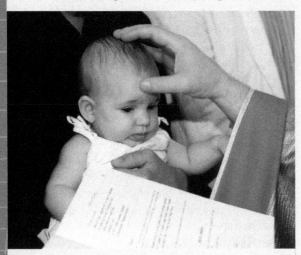

The Catholic Church teaches:

Baptism constitutes the foundation of communion among all Christians, including those who are not yet in full communion with the Catholic Church: "For men who believe in Christ and have been properly baptized are put in some, though imperfect, communion with the Catholic Church. Justified by faith in Baptism, [they] are incorporated into Christ; they therefore have a right to be called Christians, and with good reason are accepted as brothers by the children of the Catholic Church" (Vatican Council II, *Declaration on Ecumenism*, no. 3). "Baptism therefore constitutes *the sacramental bond of unity* existing among all who through it are reborn" (*Declaration on Ecumenism*, no. 22).

—CCC, no. 1271

OPENING REFLECTION

⊙ What is the significance of your having been baptized?

⊙ How does your Baptism connect you to other validly baptized Christians?

THE COMMUNION OF CHRIST'S DISCIPLES

Jesus taught that a person becomes a member of the disciples of Christ, the Church, through faith in Christ *and* Baptism. The practice of the Apostolic Church testifies clearly to this teaching of Jesus. (Check out Matthew 28:19; Mark 16:16; John 3:1–6; Acts of the Apostles 2:37–42.) This **Apostolic Tradition**, as we have seen, continues to be taught by the Catholic and Orthodox Churches and by the Anglican Church and other Protestant ecclesial communities. The valid celebration and reception of the Sacrament of Baptism gives a person the right to be called a

Christian. Baptism is the bond of communion that unites all Christians as brothers and sisters in Christ.

JOSEPH SMITH, THE FIRST PRESIDENT AND FOUNDER OF THE MORMONS

The term "Mormons" is used to designate the members of The Church of Jesus Christ of Latter-Day Saints (LDS), which was founded by Joseph Smith (1805–44).

Joseph Smith: Smith, who was born in Vermont, lived at a time when Christianity was becoming very diverse within the United States. New Christian faith communities were being founded everywhere.

In his desire "to know which of all the sects (churches) was right" (*Joseph Smith—History*, 1:19), Smith went off to pray in solitude. Smith

Christian sect

A group of people who profess Jesus Christ to be Lord and Savior but whose members are not validly baptized and whose teachings and practices are heretical, or contrary to the essential teachings and practices of Christianity that are part of the Apostolic Tradition of the Church.

THE SALVATION ARMY IS AN EXAMPLE OF A CHRISTIAN SECT

claimed that during that time of prayer and reflection he had a vision of God the Father and Jesus Christ, who revealed to him that all the churches were wrong and "all their creeds were an abomination in his sight" (*Joseph Smith—History*, 1:19). They called upon him to be a prophet, to preach the true Gospel and restore the true Church founded by Jesus Christ.

In relation to such visions, or "revelations," the Catholic Church teaches:

Christian faith cannot accept "revelations" that claim to surpass or correct the Revelation of which Christ is the fulfillment, as is the case in certain non-Christian religions and also in certain recent **sects** which base themselves on such "revelations."

—CCC, no. 67

The Book of Mormon: Smith claimed that, as part of the mission given to him, he was to translate the ancient Book of Mormon, which Mormons revere as the holy Word of God. For Mormons, the Book of Mormon does not replace the Bible. It is another "Testament of Jesus Christ." The Book of Mormon is the translation of the story of two ancient peoples who came to the Americas before the birth of Jesus Christ. It was given to a prophet

named Mormon on gold plates and buried by his son Moroni. Among other things, the Book of Mormon gives an account of the Risen Christ.

According to Smith, Moroni came back to earth as an angel in 1823 and appeared to him, and gave him the plates that were later translated by Smith and then printed for the first time in 1830. Mormons read the Book of Mormon as a companion to the Bible. They claim: "Almost all of the doctrines of the gospel are taught in the Book of Mormon *with much greater clarity and perfection* than those same doctrines are revealed in the Bible. Anyone who will place in parallel columns the teachings of these two great books on such subjects as atonement, plan of salvation, gathering of Israel, baptism, gifts of the Spirit, miracles, revelation, faith, charity, (or any of a hundred other subjects), will find conclusive proof of the *superiority* of the Book of Mormon teachings" (Bruce R. McConkie, *Mormon Doctrine* [2nd edition. Salt Lake City: Bookcraft, 1966], 99; italics added).

OVER TO YOU

⊙ Imagine you are sharing your Catholic faith with a friend who is Mormon. During the discussion, your friend says, "You really need to read and study the Book of Mormon. It will help you understand more clearly what Jesus taught."

⊙ Reflect on how you would respond.
⊙ Share responses as a class.

BAPTISM INTO THE BODY OF CHRIST

The risen Christ commanded his disciples, "Go therefore and make disciples of all nations, baptizing them in the name of the Father and of the Son and of the Holy Spirit, and teaching them to obey everything that I have commanded you" (Matthew 28:19–20). The Church has celebrated the Sacrament of Baptism from the day of Pentecost. (See Acts of the Apostles 2:41.)

You were joined to Christ and incorporated into the Body of Christ, the **Church**, at **Baptism**. You were baptized by a **priest** or a **deacon** obeying Christ's command. He baptized you in the name of the Father, and of the Son, and of the Holy Spirit as he immersed you in the water, or he poured water upon your head three times as he invoked the name of God, the Holy Trinity. Let us briefly review some of the key teachings of the Catholic Church on the Sacrament of Baptism:

⊙ "Baptism is birth into the new life in Christ. In accordance with the Lord's will, it is necessary for salvation, as is the Church herself, which we enter by Baptism" (CCC, no. 1277).
⊙ "The essential rite of Baptism consists in immersing the candidate in water or pouring water on his head, while pronouncing the invocation of the Most Holy Trinity: the Father, the Son, and the Holy Spirit" (CCC, no. 1278).
⊙ "The fruit of Baptism, or baptismal grace, is a rich reality that includes forgiveness of original sin and all personal sins, birth into the new life by which man becomes an adoptive son of the Father, a member of Christ and a temple of the Holy Spirit. By this very fact the person baptized is incorporated into the Church, the Body of Christ, and made a sharer in the priesthood of Christ" (CCC, no. 1279).
⊙ "Baptism imprints on the soul an indelible spiritual sign, the character, which consecrates the baptized person for Christian worship. Because of the character Baptism cannot be repeated" (CCC, no. 1280).

THE BAPTISM OF JESUS | ADI HOLZER

Catholic Teaching on the Sacrament of Baptism

Baptism is birth into the new life in Christ. In accordance with the Lord's will, it is necessary for salvation, as is the Church herself, which we enter by Baptism.

—CCC, no. 1277

The essential rite of Baptism consists in immersing the candidate in water or pouring water on his head, while pronouncing the invocation of the Most Holy Trinity: the Father, the Son, and the Holy Spirit.

—CCC, no. 1278

MORMON TEACHING ON THE "SACRAMENTS"

The Church of Jesus Christ of Latter-day Saints does not accept the doctrine of the Catholic Church on the sacraments. Contrary to the teaching of the Catholic Church, Mormonism teaches that Jesus did not institute or entrust to the Church any sacrament as an "efficacious sign of grace . . . by which divine life in dispensed to us by the work of the Holy Spirit" (USCCA, Glossary, "Sacrament," 526). Mormonism teaches that Baptism is not a sacrament; it is one of the two ordinances, or commands, that Jesus Christ gave his followers. The second ordinance is that his followers are to celebrate the Lord's Supper. In other words, the Church of Jesus Christ of Latter-day Saints rejects the need for the celebration of any of the Seven Sacraments as an essential element in the divine plan of salvation.

Baptism: According to Mormon teaching:

- Baptism is necessary for the remission of sins and "is essential for salvation" (Millet et al., *LDS Beliefs: A Doctrinal Reference* [Salt Lake City: Desert Book Company, 2011], 63).
- A Baptism is valid only if it is performed by immersion in water by an authorized Mormon male holding priesthood authority who says the words exactly and immerses the person's body and clothing completely according to Mormon specified procedures.
- At Baptism the person enters a sacred covenant with the Heavenly Father. "We covenant to keep His commandments, serve Him and His children, and take upon ourselves the name of Jesus Christ" (*Ensign* [Magazine of The Church of Jesus Christ of Latter-Day Saints], February 2013).
- Children are baptized only after they reach the age of eight.
- After a person is baptized they can receive the gift of the Holy Spirit and be confirmed as a member of The Church of Jesus Christ of the Latter-day Saints.
- A person baptized in another Christian denomination must be re-baptized.

Lord's Supper: Mormons celebrate the Lord's Supper (Communion or Eucharist) weekly in remembrance of the price Christ paid for the forgiveness of sins. A Mormon church manual says: "Today we partake of bread and water in remembrance of Jesus Christ's atoning sacrifice. This ordinance is an essential part of our worship

LDS TEMPLE IN ALBERTA, CANADA

and our spiritual development. The more we ponder its significance, the more sacred it becomes to us" (*True to the Faith: A Gospel Reference* [Salt Lake City: The Church of Jesus Christ of Latter-day Saints, copyright 2004], 147).

Mormons use bread and water (or wine) as the elements for Holy Communion. The elements are a *symbolic remembrance* of Christ's atoning sacrificial death. The celebration of the Lord's Supper is the recollection of past events and offers participants the opportunity *to reflect* on the sacrifice of Jesus. Mormons reject the Catholic dogma on the Eucharist as a memorial sacrifice and the Catholic doctrine on transubstantiation and the Real Presence of Jesus Christ. For Mormons, the one sacrifice of Christ is not made present again, and the elements do not become substantially, sacramentally, truly and really the Body and Blood of Jesus Christ.

LET'S PROBE DEEPER: BAPTIZING IN THE NAME OF THE HOLY TRINITY

⊙ Reflect: "The mystery of the Most Holy Trinity is the central mystery of the Christian faith and of Christian life. God alone can make it known to us by revealing himself as Father, Son and Holy Spirit" (CCC, no. 261).

⊙ Read the Nicene Creed, which succinctly states the Christian teaching on the Holy Trinity. You will find the Nicene Creed in the "Catholic Prayers, Devotions and Practices" section of this text. Then review the definition of "Trinity" in the Faith Glossary.

⊙ Mormon teaching rejects the Catholic dogma on the Trinity as taught in the early councils of the Church and professed in its Creeds. Mormons teach that the Father, the Son Jesus Christ and the Holy Spirit are three separate beings. The Divine Persons of the Trinity are not consubstantial, or of the same substance and one in being with each other.

⊙ For this reason the Catholic Church teaches that Mormons are not validly baptized. Since they do not profess faith in the Trinity, Mormons do not baptize by "pronouncing the invocation of the Most Holy Trinity." While they profess faith in Jesus Christ and identify themselves as a church of Jesus Christ, Mormons are *not in communion, even imperfect communion*, with Catholics and Protestants. They are not Christians as the Church has identified Christians since her earliest days.

OTHER COMMONALITIES AND DIFFERENCES BETWEEN CATHOLICS AND MORMONS

The body of Mormon teachings is very complex, and beyond the scope of this text to explore. We will instead look at the answers to some frequently asked questions about Mormon teachings.

⊙ **What is the Mormon teaching on human life?** The human person existed first as a spirit before their mortal life. This state of being is called the "first estate," or preexistence or premortality. Our personal individual identity is our spirit; we are eternal. Mortality is the "second estate" of human existence. During our mortal life on earth in a physical body we have the freedom to choose to love God or not to love God. *Reflect and compare with the teachings of the Catholic Church.*

MONUMENT TO JOSEPH SMITH AND HIS BROTHER HYRUM | LDS TEMPLE, NAUVOO, ILLINOIS

Mormons teach that God restored the priesthood authority, which Christ first gave to Peter and the other Apostles, to Joseph Smith

THE COMMISSION TO PETER | SAINT-GERVAIS-SAINT-PROTAIS, PARIS, FRANCE

- **What is the Mormon teaching on homosexuality?** Gays and lesbians are sons and daughters of God and deserve to be loved. "They may have certain inclinations which are powerful and which may be difficult to control. Most people have inclinations of one kind or another at various times. If they do not act upon these inclinations, then they can go forward as do all other members of the Church. If they violate the law of chastity and the moral standards of the Church, then they are subject to the discipline of the Church, just as others are" (*Doctrine and Covenants and Church History*). *Reflect and compare with the teachings of the Catholic Church.*

- **What is the Mormon teaching on abortion?** Human life is sacred. Choosing to have, performing, encouraging, paying for, or arranging an abortion is contrary to God's law. Extreme circumstances such as rape or incest may permit one to have an abortion after prayer and consultation with church leaders. *Reflect and compare with the teachings of the Catholic Church.*

- **What is the Mormon teaching on life after death?** Death is another step on our spiritual journey. Those who are judged worthy enjoy eternal celestial glory. For all others, spiritual opportunity to improve oneself continues in eternity. One's spirit will be reunited with one's body sometime after death and will never be separated again. Families will live together in heaven. *Reflect and compare with the teachings of the Catholic Church.*

- **What is the Mormon teaching on the priesthood?** God restored the priesthood authority, which Christ first gave to Peter and the other Apostles and which was lost after the death of the last Apostle, to Joseph Smith, who has passed it on to others in the Mormon church. The priesthood gives a man the authority, or "sealing power," to bind and loose on earth as Christ gave to Peter (Mark 3:14–15), to act in the name of God. A male member may be called to the priesthood by "foreordination," or from the foundation of the world by the foreknowledge of God; by lineage, from father to son; or by prophecy, or a call by God. The latter is the most common source of one's ordination to the priesthood. All male members who are in good standing may be ordained to the priesthood without regard for race or color. *Reflect and compare with the teachings of the Catholic Church.*

A POLYGAMIST MORMON FAMILY IN 1868 | 19TH-CENTURY ENGRAVING AFTER A PHOTOGRAPH BY CHARLES ROSCOE SAVAGE

Polygamy is not allowed by the Mormon church, though some groups have split from the Church and continue to practice it

⊙ **What is the Mormon teaching on marriage?**
Marriage performed in a Mormon temple is eternal and, in God's design, it is intended to last beyond death. Cohabitation prior to marriage and same-sex marriage are contrary to God's law and LDS teachings. Members can remarry after a divorce. Members married in a Mormon temple after obtaining a civil divorce can apply to have their temple marriage canceled with the approval of church leadership, and then remarry. *Reflect and compare with the teachings of the Catholic Church.*

⊙ **What is the Mormon teaching on polygamy?**
Polygamy, or one man having a plurality of wives, is not allowed. Marriage is a lifelong and faithful covenant between one man and one woman. Some groups have split from the Church of Jesus Christ of Latter-day Saints and continue to practice polygamy. *Reflect and compare with the teachings of the Catholic Church.*

LET'S PROBE DEEPER: ANALYZE AND COMPARE

There are many substantial differences that separate Catholics and Mormons. There are also some elements of truth in Mormon beliefs and practices that are shared by Catholics and Mormons.

⊙ Work with a partner and name:
- the beliefs and practices that separate Mormonism from Catholicism and all other Christian traditions;
- those elements of truth within Mormonism that can orient Mormons toward the reception of the Gospel.

⊙ Share and, with the guidance of your teacher, discuss responses as a class.

OVER TO YOU

⊙ If you were to share and talk about your Catholic faith with a Mormon youth, where would you begin. Why?

JUDGE AND ACT

REVIEW AND SHARE WHAT YOU HAVE LEARNED

Review and share what you have learned in this chapter about the beliefs and practices of the Sikh, Bahá'í and Mormon religions. Use these statements as the focus of your responses:

- ⊙ "Christian faith cannot accept 'revelations' that claim to surpass or correct the Revelation of which Christ is the fulfillment" (CCC, no. 67).
- ⊙ The Sikh religion contains practices and teachings that both separate it from the Catholic Church and also orient its members toward the reception of the Gospel.
- ⊙ The Bahá'í religion contains practices and teachings that both separate it from the Catholic Church and also orient its members toward the reception of the Gospel.
- ⊙ Mormonism cannot rightly be named a Christian religion.

OVER TO YOU

- ⊙ Describe the new insights and understanding you gained about "the manner and life and conduct, the precepts and doctrines" of the Sikh, Bahá'í and Mormon religions in this chapter.
- ⊙ How did these insights help you come to understand better the relationship between these three religions and the Catholic Church?

PROCLAIM THE GOOD NEWS

"Inter-religious dialogue is part of the Church's evangelizing mission. . . . In Christ, God calls all peoples to himself and he wishes to share with them the fullness of his revelation and love" (St. John Paul II, Encyclical Letter *The Mission of the Redeemer* [*Redemptoris Missio*], no. 55). In addressing the universality of the saving life, Death and Resurrection of Jesus Christ and the unique role of the Church in the divine plan of salvation, the Church at Vatican II taught:

[Jesus] completed and perfected revelation and confirmed it with divine guarantees. Everything to do with his presence and his manifestation of himself was involved in achieving this: his words and works, signs and miracles, but above all his death and glorious resurrection from the dead, and finally his sending of the Spirit of

Jesus Christ, "the Ultimate Truth"

In the Incarnation of the Son of God we see forged the enduring and definitive synthesis which the human mind of itself could not even have imagined: the Eternal enters time, the Whole lies hidden in the part, God takes on a human face. . . . Through this Revelation, men and women are offered the ultimate truth about their own life and about the goal of history.

—St. John Paul II, Encyclical Letter *Faith and Reason (Fides et ratio)*, no. 12

CRISTO REI OF DILI, EAST TIMOR

truth. . . . The Christian dispensation, therefore, since it is the new and definitive covenant, will never pass away; and no new public revelation is to be expected before the glorious manifestation of our Lord, Jesus Christ (see 1 Timothy 6:14 and Titus 2:13).

—*Dogmatic Constitution on Divine Revelation,* no. 4

During this course of study we have been exploring the Catholic Church's engagement in both ecumenical and interreligious dialogues, in which she openly and honestly proclaims the revealed truths handed on to her. The Church's conviction concerning the truth of the Catholic faith does not mean that Catholics should not show respect toward people of other faiths and religions. Catholics are to be respectful of people in their intrinsic dignity. Nor does it mean that Catholics are to reject, deny or water down the revealed truths of faith that the Church has received. To do so would be gravely wrong.

Honesty, openness and respect are essential characteristics of both interreligious, or interfaith, and ecumenical dialogues. Truth must be taken in its fullness; we need to subject ourselves to the whole truth, the fullness of truth revealed in Jesus Christ that is authentically passed on by the Catholic Church. Where beliefs are contrary to one another, that is, where there are intrinsic contradictions in belief, only one belief can be true—and so one must be false. That truth cannot be compromised. Serious respectful and loving pursuit of the whole truth can help us recapture the fullness of "God's communication of himself and his loving plan to save us" (USCCA, Glossary, "Revelation," 526).

The conversion and evangelizing efforts of the Roman centurion Cornelius serve as a model for open, honest and respectful proclaiming of the Gospel of Jesus Christ.

Saint Cornelius the Centurion—bishop and evangelizer

VISION OF CORNELIUS THE CENTURION | VAN DEN EECKHOUT

Cornelius was a Roman centurion stationed in Caesarea, who, according to church tradition, was the first Gentile convert to Christianity. St. Luke in his Acts of the Apostles describes Cornelius as "a devout man who feared God with all his household; he gave alms generously to the people and prayed constantly to God" (Acts of the Apostles 10:2).

Acts goes on to describe Cornelius's conversion from paganism to Christianity following St. Peter's proclamation of Jesus Christ to Cornelius and his household. We read, "While Peter was still speaking, the Holy Spirit fell upon all who heard the word. . . . Then Peter said, 'Can anyone withhold the water for baptizing these people who have received the Holy Spirit just as we have?' So he ordered them to be baptized in the name of Jesus Christ" (Acts of the Apostles 10:44–48). (*Read the full account of St. Peter's dialogue with Cornelius and his proclamation of the Gospel to Cornelius and his household in Acts of the Apostles 10:30–48.*)

Cornelius is revered by Catholics, Orthodox and Anglicans. According to several church traditions, Cornelius resigned from the Roman military after his Baptism. He became a companion to St. Peter, whom he accompanied along with St. Timothy in preaching the Gospel. St. Peter ordained Cornelius a bishop, and after learning about the widespread practice of idol worship in the city of Skepsis in present-day Turkey, he sent Cornelius to proclaim the Gospel there. Cornelius, himself a former pagan, addressed the yearnings of the pagans and the emptiness of worshiping false idols to fulfill those yearnings.

The local prince, Demetrius, responded by imprisoning Cornelius. While he was in prison, an earthquake destroyed the pagan temple. On hearing that Demetrius's wife and son were buried under the rubble, Cornelius prayed for their safety. Pagan priests, who witnessed Cornelius' praying, soon heard that the prince's son and wife had been found alive, and they reported to Demetrius all that they had witnessed. The prince now responded by asking for baptism for himself and his household.

The life and faith of St. Cornelius the Centurion is remembered and celebrated by Catholics on February 2, by the Episcopal Church in the United States on February 7, and by the Orthodox Churches on September 13.

TALK IT OVER

⊙ How does the story of Cornelius' conversion and his evangelization of the pagans in Skepsis reflect what you have been learning about the Catholic approach to interreligious dialogue?

SHARE FAITH WITH FAMILY AND FRIENDS

⊙ What opportunities might there be for you to engage with members of non-Christian religions to work toward building a community of respect and justice rooted in the love of God and neighbor?

⊙ Join with family and/or friends to come up with and implement a plan.

JUDGE AND DECIDE

⊙ Reflect: Pope Francis' prayer intention for January 2016 was that "sincere dialogue between men and women of different religions may yield fruits of peace and justice." The Pope concluded, "Within this multitude, in this wide range of religions and lack of religious, there is one certainty: we are all children of God" (Vatican Radio, January 7, 2016).

⊙ Why is prayer essential to both ecumenical and interreligious dialogue?

⊙ Will you respond to Pope Francis' prayer request and seek out ways to join with members of religions other than your own to bring about greater peace and justice in your community?

HOW WOULD YOU RESPOND?

⊙ Many people today are of the opinion that one religion is just as good as any other. They argue that it is more important to show tolerance and not say that one religion is better than any other.

⊙ How would you, a Catholic, respond with respect and charity to a non-Christian friend who made that claim? Base your response on what you have learned during this course of study.

LEARN BY HEART

Let the peoples praise you, O God; let all the peoples praise you.

PSALM 67:3

All gather around a bowl of sand, which has been placed in a central location in the learning space. Pray the Sign of the Cross together.

LEADER
If fire laws and school policy permit, light and hold up a lighted candle; if fire laws and school policy do not permit that, hold up an unlighted candle and proclaim:
Christ, be our light!
(*Pause and place the candle in the bowl of sand.*)

ALL
Thanks, be to God!

LEADER
God calls each of us to share the Good News of his Son, Jesus Christ, with all people. We believe that Jesus promised to send the Holy Spirit, the Spirit of truth, into the world. We believe that the Holy Spirit lives among us. We believe that the Holy Spirit constantly sows the seeds of truth, in his own way, in people's hearts—in the hearts of both believers and non-believers. The Holy Spirit inspires and strengthens us to openly and boldly proclaim Jesus Christ to others. We will now listen and respond to the Word of God. (*Pause*)

READER
A reading from the holy Gospel according to Matthew.
ALL
Glory to you, O Lord.

READER
Proclaim Matthew 28:19–20.
The Gospel of the Lord.
ALL
Praise to you, Lord Jesus Christ.

LEADER
May God be gracious to us and bless us
    and make his face to shine upon us,
that your way may be known upon the earth,
    your saving power among all nations.
ALL
Let the peoples praise you, O God;
    let all the peoples praise you.
LEADER
Let the nations be glad and sing for joy,
    for you judge the peoples with equity
and guide the nations upon earth.
ALL
Let the peoples praise you, O God;
    let all the peoples praise you.
—Psalm 67:1–5

LEADER
In the silence of our hearts we ask the Holy Spirit

to guide and strengthen us to be messengers of the Gospel, always honest and respectful of others. (*Pause*)

Let us pray for the Church that she may reveal the glory of Christ to all nations.
ALL
Christ, be our Light.

Let us pray for the pope and our other bishops, that they may enlighten the hearts and minds of all peoples with the light of Christ.
ALL
Christ, be our Light.

Let us pray for all our brothers and sisters who believe in Christ, that they may live the truth revealed by Christ.
ALL
Christ, be our Light.

Let us pray for the Jewish people to whom the Lord God first revealed himself.
ALL
Christ, be our Light.

Let us pray for all who do not believe in Christ, that they may come to know and believe in him, who is the way, the light and the truth.

ALL
Christ, be our Light.
—Based on the Solemn Intercessions from "Friday of the Passion of the Lord (Good Friday)"

LEADER
O God, who sent your Son into the world as the true light,
pour out we pray, the Spirit he promised
to sow seeds of truth constantly in people's hearts
and to awaken in them obedience to the faith,
so that, being born to new life through Baptism,
all may become part of your one people.
Through our Lord Jesus Christ, your Son,
who lives and reigns with you in the unity of the Holy Spirit,
one God, for ever and ever.
—*The Roman Missal*, "Mass A For the Evangelization of Peoples," Collect
ALL
Amen.

Pray the Sign of the Cross together.

Evangelize

—Proclaim Jesus Christ Far and Near!

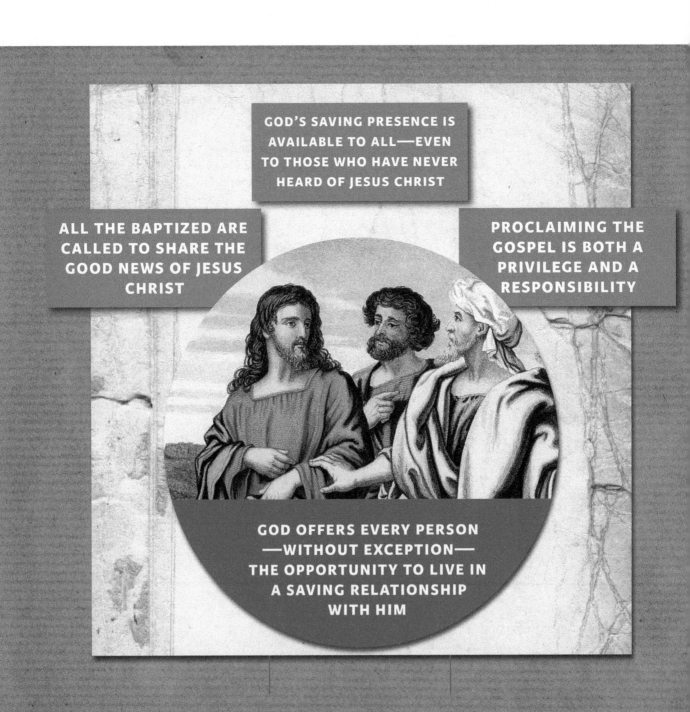

GOD'S SAVING PRESENCE IS AVAILABLE TO ALL—EVEN TO THOSE WHO HAVE NEVER HEARD OF JESUS CHRIST

ALL THE BAPTIZED ARE CALLED TO SHARE THE GOOD NEWS OF JESUS CHRIST

PROCLAIMING THE GOSPEL IS BOTH A PRIVILEGE AND A RESPONSIBILITY

GOD OFFERS EVERY PERSON —WITHOUT EXCEPTION— THE OPPORTUNITY TO LIVE IN A SAVING RELATIONSHIP WITH HIM

"THE CHURCH NEVER CEASES TO PROCLAIM HER FAITH in the one only God: Father, Son, and Holy Spirit" (*Catechism of the Catholic Church*, no. 152). In this epilogue we explore, in more detail, the Church's mandate to proclaim the Gospel to all peoples, and we connect that mandate with the gift of faith. We recall and examine the ways this course of study has prepared you to take part in the Church's mission of evangelization so that you and others can enjoy the benefits of God's saving work in Jesus Christ.

"GO THEREFORE AND MAKE DISCIPLES OF ALL NATIONS, BAPTIZING THEM IN THE NAME OF THE FATHER AND OF THE SON AND OF THE HOLY SPIRIT."
—MATTHEW 28:19

Faith Focus: These teachings of the Catholic Church are the primary focus of the doctrinal content presented in this chapter:

- ⊙ Jesus Christ gave his Church the mandate to proclaim the Gospel to all nations.
- ⊙ Proclaiming the Gospel is a privilege and a responsibility.
- ⊙ Jesus Christ wills that everyone be saved.
- ⊙ Evangelization is the primary mission of the Church.
- ⊙ The Catholic teaching on the New Evangelization includes the requirement that Catholics share their faith with one another.
- ⊙ Faith is a gift from God; it is one of the three theological virtues.
- ⊙ Faith is the beginning of eternal life with God, the goal of our earthly journey.

Discipleship Formation: As a result of studying this chapter and discovering the meaning of the faith of the Catholic Church for your life, you should be better able to:

- ⊙ share your faith in Jesus Christ and his Church;
- ⊙ meet your responsibilities to proclaim Jesus Christ;
- ⊙ discover ways to deepen your understanding and living of the faith of the Church into which you were baptized.

Scripture References: These scripture references are quoted or referred to in this chapter:
OLD TESTAMENT: Isaiah 9:6
NEW TESTAMENT: Matthew 1:23b, 16:13–20, 28:19–20; **Mark** 4:31–32; **Acts of the Apostles** 1:8, 17:25–28; **Romans** 8:32, 10:1–17; **1 Corinthians** 13:1–13; **Ephesians** 2:8, 4:4–6; **1 Timothy** 2:4–5; **Hebrews** 11:6; **1 Peter** 3:15, 16

Faith Glossary: Familiarize yourself with or recall the meaning of these key terms. Definitions are found in the Glossary: **Beatific Vision, evangelization, faith, grace, hope, New Evangelization, obedience of faith, salvation, theological virtues**

Faith Words: hope; salvation
Learn by Heart: Matthew 28:19–20
Learn by Example: Pope Francis

Why are humans driven to share good news?

SHARING GOOD NEWS

There seems to be something about us humans that we just love to share good news. How often do we say things like "I can't wait to tell you," or "I can't keep this to myself," or "I'm bursting to share this," and even, "I'm just dying to share this story." As the renowned American author Stephen King put it, "There is no bad time for good news." Indeed, life can bring bad news that we may need to share with someone, but it is never an easy thing to do. In contrast, it is always a joy to share good news.

OPENING REFLECTION

- ◉ Recall a personal story of sharing a piece of good news with a family member, friend or classmate. How did you share this news? How did you convey your enthusiasm? How did you get the other person interested in your news?
- ◉ Recall a time when you have been on the receiving end of someone else's good news? How did hearing it make you feel? How did you respond?

- ◉ Why do you think we want to share good news with our friends and family?
- ◉ Why is Jesus Christ and his Church good news that you want to share? Why would you want to share it, and with whom?

SHARE THE GOOD NEWS OF THE GOSPEL

The First Letter of Peter teaches us that our readiness to share the "Good News of Jesus Christ," the Gospel, with others is essential to our practice of the Christian faith. The Apostle says that you should always be ready to share "an account of the hope that is in you" (1 Peter 3:15). Christians are people of hope. St. Thomas Aquinas often said that hope is grounded in faith and should always lead to love.

Our faith in Jesus Christ is always the foundation of hope that leads to love. Thus, the Apostle Peter urges us to share the hope that we have and to do so out of love. We should always be willing to tell others about our Catholic faith and why we believe. Indeed, we should be "dying to share" the Good News of the Gospel.

Peter adds that when we share this "hope that is in us," we must do so "with gentleness and reverence" (1 Peter 3:16). In other words, we must do it with sensitivity and respect for other people. This gentleness and reverence does not mean watering down or compromising our faith. We are to approach others with an attitude that shows reverence for the Holy Spirit at work in their life and that respects where they are on their faith journey.

We are to share *what we believe,* realizing that it is the Holy Spirit who is at work inviting people to faith in Christ. We are to *evangelize* and not *proselytize.* Proselytizing is telling other people *what they should believe,* as if we are forcing our faith on them.

Hope

One of the three theological virtues "through which a person both desires and expects the fulfillment of God's promises of things to come" (*United States Catholic Catechism for Adults* [USCCA], Glossary, 515). Hope is the desire and expectation of the salvation God promised. It is based on God's unwavering fidelity to keeping and fulfilling his promises.

Salvation

The forgiveness of sins and restoration of friendship with God, which can be done by God alone.
—*Catechism of the Catholic Church* (CCC), Glossary

CHRIST AS SALVATOR MUNDI | JOHANN BAPTIST MODLER

We must always remember that faith is both a gift from God and a grace-filled free response to that gift. When sharing our faith, it is wisest to begin by listening to our conversation partners and inviting them to share their life experiences, issues and circumstances. When we know their faith story, we are likely to share our own story more effectively. We are called to be evangelizers who sow the seeds of faith in Jesus Christ.

THINK, PAIR AND SHARE

◉ Recall a time when you have had an opportunity to share your faith story with others. Share with a partner how that experience worked out for you. What did you learn about yourself from the experience? What did you learn about your faith?

◉ Have you ever had someone share their faith story with you? How was an attitude of gentleness and respect fostered or not fostered? What did you learn about yourself and your faith from this experience? Again, share your recollections of the experience and what you learned from it.

A FREE GIFT AND A BIG RESPONSIBILITY

The message and means of salvation is truly free, a grace. Nothing that we do can earn our salvation. As St. Paul wrote, "For by grace you have been saved through faith, and this is not your own doing; it is the gift of God" (Ephesians 2:8). God offers his grace to all people at all times. God offers every person—without exception—the opportunity to live in a saving relationship with him. This is an amazing gift flowing from God's unconditional love and desire for all people to live in communion with him.

The mandate for Christians to proclaim Jesus Christ (recall Matthew 28:19) and the divine plan of salvation is both a privilege and a responsibility. God's love for all people—believers and non-believers—is the root of that mandate. God's saving presence is available to all—even to those who have never heard of Jesus Christ.

THINK, PAIR AND SHARE

◉ What does it mean to be willing to share your faith with gentleness and reverence?

If you were going to talk about your Catholic faith with a person of another religion, what are the key points you would want to share?

⊙ Share ways you can put this New Testament mandate into practice.

A MESSAGE OF CONFIDENT HOPE

All the baptized are called to share the Good News of Jesus Christ. To share reverently and boldly our faith that the fullest message and means of salvation comes through Jesus Christ and his Church is an act of love, not judgment. To share that Jesus Christ is the Incarnate Son of God, the Lord and Savior of all, continues the work God himself announced in Jesus. Jesus, whose name means "God is with us" (Matthew 1:23b), lived, died and rose again so that all people might have the possibility of eternal life.

The abundance of God's gift of salvation in and through Christ and his Church is available to all people throughout the world. This is the Good News that the Catholic Church proclaims and shares. It is a message and invitation of confident hope, the seeds of which are bearing fruit in the lives of all who seek God with a sincere heart.

OVER TO YOU

⊙ If you were going to talk about your Catholic faith with a person of another religion, what are the key points you would want to share?

⊙ What are some practical ways that you can tell people about your faith— ways that seem natural and appropriate to you and respectful to others?

The hope of all nations

The Power of hope

From the movie The *Wizard of Oz*, the song "Somewhere Over the Rainbow" remains one of the most beloved and often sung American songs. Remember some of the lyrics:

Somewhere over the rainbow
Skies are blue
And the dreams that you dare to dream
Really do come true.
Some day I'll wish upon a star
And wake up where the clouds are far behind me.
Where troubles melt like lemon drops
Away above the chimney tops
That's where you'll find me.

OPENING REFLECTION
- Is chasing after rainbows a fantasy? Does it express a hope for the future?
- What "rainbows" do you chase?
- The Book of Genesis speaks of God placing a "bow" in the sky. What hope does that symbol signify for all people?

CHRIST WILLS EVERYONE TO BE SAVED
The Catholic Church clearly teaches, as we have already explored, that God's plan of salvation applies to everyone. The Church also believes and teaches that there are no limits to God's activity in the world. We do not and cannot know everything of the mystery of God's saving work among us.

In speaking of the mystery of "Christ the New Man," the Catholic Church at the Second Vatican Council taught:

All this holds true not only for Christians but also for all people of good will in whose hearts grace is active invisibly. For since Christ died for everyone (see Romans 8:32), and since all are in fact called to one and the same destiny, which is divine, we must hold that the holy Spirit offers to all the possibility of being made partners, in a way known to God, in the paschal mystery.
—*Pastoral Constitution on the Church in the Modern World (Gaudium et Spes)*, no. 22

And:

Nor is God remote from those who in shadows and images seek the unknown God, since he gives to everyone life and breath and all things (see Acts of the Apostles 17:25–28) and since the Savior wills everyone to be saved (see 1 Timothy 2:4). Those who, through no fault of their own, do not know the Gospel of Christ or his church, but who nevertheless seek God with a sincere heart, and, moved by grace, try in their actions to do his will as they know it through the dictates of their conscience—these too may attain salvation. . . . Whatever of good or truth is found amongst them is considered by the church to be a preparation for the Gospel and given by him who enlightens all men and women that they may at length have life.

—*Dogmatic Constitution on the Church (Lumen Gentium)*, no. 16

Well aware that her mandate to evangelize has been given to her by God, the Church undertakes her mission with both gentleness and reverence, as the Apostle Peter taught, and with the boldness and openness he modeled on that first Pentecost in the marketplace in Jerusalem.

HOW WOULD YOU RESPOND?

⊙ A non-Catholic Christian friend shares with you the belief of his denomination that only those people who are baptized can be saved.

⊙ From what you have learned during this course of study, how would you respond?

⊙ Share responses as a class. If time allows, two members of the class may role-play such a scenario. After the dialogue has concluded, the other members of the class give their input.

PROCLAIM TO ALL NATIONS—WITHOUT EXCEPTION

"Go therefore and make disciples of *all nations*, baptizing them in the name of the Father and of the Son and of the Holy Spirit, and teaching them to obey everything that I have commanded you. And remember, I am with you always, to the end of the age" (italics added; Matthew 28:19–20). Thus, God offers the gift of salvation to *all* people. The fact that some people may not know God, nor ever have heard the Good News of Jesus, does not relieve Christians of their calling, obligation and sacred right to share the Gospel with all nations. The Church reminds us of this responsibility:

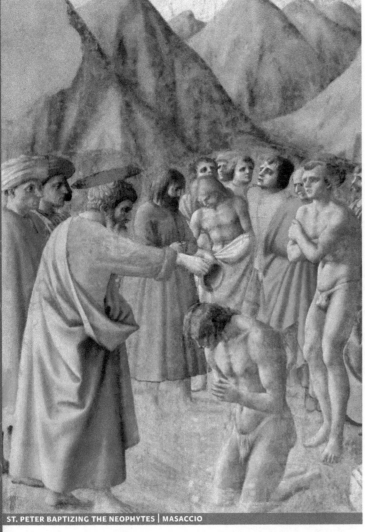

ST. PETER BAPTIZING THE NEOPHYTES | MASACCIO

> "Go therefore and make disciples of all nations, baptizing them in the name of the Father and of the Son and of the Holy Spirit."
>
> MATTHEW 28:19

"Don't be taken in by the messages of hatred or terror all around us. Instead, make new friends."

POPE FRANCIS

The reason for missionary activity lies in the will of God, "who wishes everyone to be saved and to come to the knowledge of the truth. For there is one God and one Mediator between God and humanity, himself a man, Jesus Christ, who gave himself as a ransom for all" (1 Timothy 2:4–5). . . . So, although in ways known to himself God can lead those who, through no fault of their own, are ignorant of the gospel, to that faith without which it is impossible to please him (Hebrews 11:6), the church, nevertheless, still has the obligation and also the sacred right to evangelize.

—Vatican II, *Decree on the Church's Missionary Activity (Ad Gentes Divinitus)*, no. 7

The obligation to share the Good News of Jesus Christ with all people is one of the fundamental privileges and responsibilities of all the baptized.

OVER TO YOU

- ⊙ What do you find most inspirational in these teachings of the Catholic Church for strengthening your commitment to witness to and proclaim the Gospel?
- ⊙ What elements of these teachings give you renewed hope for your faith journey?

REFLECT AND SHARE

- ⊙ Reflect: Pope Francis has often called young people not to lose hope and to stand up for their faith. At the opening of the Holy Year of Mercy (2016), during a celebration of Confirmation, the Pope spoke these words of encouragement to those being confirmed: "Remain steadfast in the journey of faith, with firm hope in the Lord. This is the secret of our journey! . . . Don't ever lose hope! The Lord has a great dream which, with your help, he wants to come true! . . . Don't be taken in by the messages of hatred or terror all around us. Instead, make new friends. Give of your time and always show concern for those who ask your help. Be brave and go against the tide; be friends of Jesus, who is the Prince of Peace [see Isaiah 9:6] (January 6, 2016).
- ⊙ Discuss as a class how Catholic youth can respond to the Pope's message and, in so doing, take to heart the Great Commission of Jesus. How would that be a work of **evangelization**?

WHAT ABOUT YOU PERSONALLY?

- ⊙ How can you be an evangelist today?
- ⊙ Decide on ways you can put into practice your responsibility to share the Gospel openly, honestly, respectfully and boldly?

The New Evangelization

POPE FRANCIS IN SRI LANKA, JANUARY 2015

RESPONDING TO OTHERS WITH RESPECT AND CONVICTION

Pope Francis visited the small Asian nation of Sri Lanka in January 2015. This small island nation has always been a religiously pluralist society and, for the last thirty years, the site of a civil war that has pitted Buddhists against Muslims and Hindus. The small Christian population has often been caught in the middle of this intractable conflict. Pope Francis called for dialogue based on respect, tolerance and mutual hospitality among the various religions. He emphasized that, as we engage one another in honest and open dialogue, we also need to know our own faith and stand firm on what we believe.

OPENING REFLECTION

- ⊙ When has your faith moved you to respond to a situation where you felt you could help, but where your decision to do so was questioned by others?
- ⊙ How did you respond to those who questioned your motives or actions?
- ⊙ What was the outcome of your dialogue?

EVANGELIZATION: THE PRIMARY MISSION OF THE CHURCH

The Church evangelizes, or "proclaims the Good News," first and foremost because Christ commanded her to do so. In their document *Go and Make Disciples,* our bishops outline why the Catholic Church evangelizes:

- ⊙ "so that the salvation of Christ Jesus, which transforms our lives even now, will bring as many as possible to the promised life of unending happiness in heaven" (no. 30);
- ⊙ "because salvation is offered to every person in him. . . . In Christ, all can come to know that the sin, the coldness, the indifference, the despair, and the doubt of our lives are overcome by God's taking on our human nature and leading us to new life. In him, and him alone, is the promise of resurrection and new life" (no. 29);
- ⊙ "in order to bring enlightenment and lift people from error. . . opening for us the wisdom that not only leads to life eternal but also leads to a human fulfillment that reflects the dignity and mystery of our nature. . . . Evangelization opens us to Christ's wisdom and personal union with God and others" (no. 31);
- ⊙ to make it known that "The Lord gave us a message that is unique. All faiths are not merely different versions of the same thing. Knowing Christ Jesus and belonging to his Church are not the same thing as believing anything else and belonging to any other community. Pope John Paul II has pointed out, 'While acknowledging that God loves all people and grants them the possibility of being saved (see 1 Timothy 2:4), the Church believes that God has established Christ as the one mediator and that she herself has been established as the universal sacrament

of salvation' (*On the Permanent Validity of the Church's Missionary Mandate*, no. 9). The unique claim of our message does not negate the sincerity and faith of others; likewise, the sincerity and faith of others do not take away from the clarity and truth of our message" (no. 32);

⊙ because "The Lord gave us yet another reason to evangelize: our love for every person, whatever his or her situation, language, physical, mental, or social condition. Because we have experienced the love of Christ, we want to share it. The gifts God has given to us are not gifts for ourselves. . . . As Jesus wanted to gather all Jerusalem . . . so also do we want to gather all people into God's kingdom, proclaiming the Gospel even 'to the ends of the earth' [Acts of the Apostles 1:8]" (no. 33).

REFLECT, COMPARE AND SHARE

⊙ Reflect on what you have been learning in this course of study.

⊙ How does what you have learned support this statement of the Church in *Go and Make Disciples*: "The unique claim of our message does not negate the sincerity and faith of others; likewise, the sincerity and faith of others do not take away from the clarity and truth of our message" (no. 32)?

⊙ Share reflections as a class.

THE NEW EVANGELIZATION: BRINGING THE GOSPEL TO THOSE FAR *AND* NEAR

The Catholic Church, as we have explored in detail during this course of study, has the mission to proclaim the Gospel and dialogue about the faith of the Church with non-Catholic Christians and with those who have never heard of Christ or who have never been baptized. The New Evangelization mandates the proclamation of the Gospel among Catholics:

The New Evangelization calls each of us to deepen our faith, believe in the Gospel message and go forth to proclaim the Gospel. The focus of the New Evangelization calls all Catholics to be evangelized and then go forth to evangelize. In a special way, the New Evangelization is focused on "re-proposing" the Gospel to those who have experienced a crisis of faith. Pope Benedict XVI called for the re-proposing of the Gospel "to those regions awaiting the first evangelization and to

---

FAITH WORD

New Evangelization

Proclaiming and witnessing Christ and his Gospel to those who have already been initiated into the Church but who have lost their deep sense of commitment to Jesus Christ and connection with the Christian community, as well as to those who have never heard the Gospel proclaimed.

ST. PAUL WRITING IN THE HOUSE OF AQUILA AND PRIS (DETAIL) | J. SADELER AFTER JODOCUS WINGHE

St. Paul in his Letter to the Romans taught about the necessity of proclaiming the Gospel

those regions where the roots of Christianity are deep but who have experienced a serious crisis of faith due to secularization" (Homily of First Vespers on the Solemnity of the Holy Apostles Peter and Paul). The New Evangelization invites each Catholic to renew their relationship with Jesus Christ and his Church.

— "New Evangelization," United States Conference of Catholic Bishops website

The New Evangelization calls us to awaken in Catholics the need to proclaim the Gospel among themselves. Catholics are to dialogue with one another in order to learn *about* and *from* the Gospel in a spirit of love and mutual respect. Catechesis, such as you are taking part in right now, is "an essential moment in the Church's mission of evangelization [*General Directory for Catechesis*, no. 63, citing *Catechesi Tradendae* (*On Catechesis in Our Time*), no, 18], [and] is a fundamental ecclesial service for the realization of the missionary mandate of Jesus here in the United States" (United States Conference of Catholic Bishops, *National Directory for Catechesis*, 53).

The New Evangelization calls the Church to reach out with gentleness and reverence toward the baptized who have become alienated from or have abandoned the Church, so as to initiate in them a re-awakening of the **obedience of**

faith. We are to offer one another the freedom and opportunity to describe our spiritual journey without fear of it being evaluated or judged. The New Evangelization calls all the baptized to provide opportunities for people to grow in faith—to come to know and love and serve God and to live in intimate communion with him now on earth and in eternal life.

LET'S PROBE DEEPER: A SCRIPTURE ACTIVITY

⊙ Read: St. Paul in his Letter to the Romans taught about the necessity of proclaiming the Gospel: "So faith comes from what is heard, and what is heard comes from the word of Christ" (Romans 10:17). Check out the whole passage in Romans 10:1–17.

⊙ Reflect: What does St. Paul teach about the responsibility of the Church to proclaim Christ? Does the Apostle's teaching deepen your own understanding of the Church's teaching on the New Evangelization?

⊙ Share reflections as a class.

WHAT ABOUT YOU PERSONALLY?

⊙ How well do your words and actions witness to your faith in Christ?

⊙ How well do they foster the Church's mission to evangelize?

⊙ How could you do better?

The gift of faith

ST. PETER'S CONFESSION OF FAITH

Recall Matthew 16:13–17, the gospel account of St. Peter's confession of faith in Jesus Christ to be the Messiah, the Son of the living God. Jesus and his disciples were in the Gentile community of Caesarea Philippi. Jesus began questioning his disciples, "Who do people say that the Son of Man is?" After the disciples shared what others were saying about him, Jesus directed the question to them, asking, "Who do you say that I am?" Peter, taking the lead, replied, "You are the Messiah, the Son of the living God." Jesus then opened up the meaning of the Apostle's reply, saying, "Blessed are you, Simon son of Jonah! For flesh and blood has not revealed this to you, but my Father in heaven." Faith in Jesus is a gift.

OPENING REFLECTION

◉ Why is it important to acknowledge that your faith in Christ to be the Son of the living God is a gift?

◉ How would that fact impact your sharing your Catholic faith with others?

THE GIFT OF FAITH

St. Peter's confession of faith in Christ to be "the Messiah, the Son of the living God" was his free grace-filled response to a Revelation from the "Father in heaven." Peter's response prompts our response to our invitation to faith in Jesus Christ. "For this faith to be accorded we need the grace of God, anticipating it and assisting it, as well as the interior helps of the holy Spirit, who moves the heart and converts it to God, and opens the eyes of the mind and 'makes it easy for all to accept and believe the truth' " (Vatican II, *Dogmatic Constitution on Divine Revelation* [*Dei Verbum*], no. 5).

Faith, hope and charity are the three theological virtues. "They dispose us to live in relationship with the Holy Trinity" (USCCA, 317).

"Who do you say that I am?"

"Even in our days, many people think that Jesus is a great prophet, a teacher of wisdom, a model of justice. . . . And even today, Jesus asks His disciples—that is, us, all of us—'But you, who do you say that I am?' A prophet? A teacher of wisdom? A model of justice? How will we answer? Let us think about it. But above all let us pray to God the Father, that He will give us the answer, and through the intercession of the Virgin Mary; let us pray that He will give us the gift to respond with sincere hearts: 'You are the Christ, the Son of the Living God.' This is a confession of faith; this is a creed."

—from Pope Francis' Angelus Address on Matthew 16:13–20, August 24, 2014

POPE FRANCIS GIVING AN ANGELUS ADDRESS IN 2014

They call us to believe in God the Father, Son and Holy Spirit and in all that God has revealed, to hope in the Triune God and his promises, and to love God above all else and our neighbor as ourselves because of our love for God. Faith in God "means coming to know God's greatness and majesty. It means living in thanksgiving. It means knowing the unity and true dignity of all men. It means making good use of created things. It means trusting in God, even in adversity" (USCCA, 59, see also CCC, nos. 222–227).

This faith is a supernatural gift and virtue from God. The supernatural gift and virtue of faith differs radically from the human virtue of faith that moves us to place our trust—and even our hopes and dreams—in another human person, group of people, or human institution. Such human faith is often betrayed. Supernatural faith is certain. For it is a gift and invitation from God, who is always true and faithful, who neither deceives nor can deceive.

LET'S PROBE DEEPER: A REFLECTION ON FAITH

⊙ At the Baptism of infants the celebrant asks the parents, "What do you ask of God's Church for (child's name)?" The parents may respond, "Baptism" or "Faith." The celebrant continues, in part: "You have asked to have your child baptized. In doing so you are accepting the responsibility of training him (her) in the practice of the faith. It will be your duty to bring him (her) up to keep God's commandments as Christ taught us, by loving God and our neighbor" (from *Rite of Baptism for One Child*).

⊙ "The Christian faith is, above all, conversion to Jesus Christ" (*General Directory for Catechesis* [GDC], no. 53). Now that you are older and accepting more personal responsibility for the gift of your faith, what are you doing to grow in and live your faith? What can you do to show that you value that gift?

FAITH AND THE NEW EVANGELIZATION

The Sacrament of Confirmation strengthens our baptismal graces to practice, grow in and give witness to our faith. We join the multitude of Christians who through the centuries have proclaimed Christ in "so many languages, cultures, peoples, and nations, . . . received from the one Lord, transmitted by one Baptism, and grounded in the conviction that all people have only one God and Father [see Ephesians 4:4–6]" (CCC, no. 171).

Evangelization can happen when people of good will come together in shared service to people who are suffering

VOLUNTEERS SORT RECYCLING IN GWINNETT COUNTY, GEORGIA

Whether we strive to give witness to our faith with other Christians who are not Catholic, or with members of non-Christian religions, or with non-believers, or with one another, we need to know our own faith well and be willing to listen to others. This respectful and honest engagement with others is not limited to theologians and scholars, nor does it have to happen around a table in a formal conversation. It can occur in the ordinary situations and contexts of daily living. For example, it can take place in the home or at a neighborhood or parish gathering, at school or in the workplace. It can occur wherever and whenever people of the same or different faiths or religions find the space and time to share their joys and sorrows, their successes and failures, their hopes and dreams. These everyday interactions, which may not be intentionally religious, offer an opportunity to give witness to Christ and engage in mutually honest and respectful conversation about one's faith or religion.

This evangelization can also happen when and where people of good will— youth, young adult or adult—come together in shared service to people who are suffering, such as from economic poverty, or from devastation caused by floods or fire or another natural disaster. When we work together to perform the works of mercy, the Spirit of God is at work in our midst. Working alongside others can remind us of the common human concerns that draw people to religious faith in the first place.

This evangelization also takes place when people share spiritual experiences—by praying together, in Bible study, on retreats and so forth—and when people seek guidance about their faith journey, or insights to resolve doubts about their faith. The formal conversations that happen in study groups about the teachings of the Church, or about the writings of scholars, theologians and spiritual masters, past and present, can provide insights that shape the ways that we all experience the Holy Spirit's invitation to faith.

OVER TO YOU

- Which of the various ways of engaging in the New Evangelization outlined above seem most appealing to you? Which of those ways of evangelizing have you engaged in? How did that impact your faith life? The faith life of others?
- What are some things you could do to seek out new opportunities for sharing your faith in Christ with others?

What does the parable of the mustard seed reveal about the potential that exists for you and other young people to engage with the Church's work of evangelization?

FAITH—THE BEGINNING OF ETERNAL LIFE

St. Paul encouraged the members of the Church at Corinth to deepen their conversion to Christ. The Apostle concluded his great hymn on love (1 Corinthians 13:1–13) with this statement: "For now we see in a mirror, dimly, but then we will see face to face. Now I know only in part; then I will know fully, even as I have been fully known. And now faith, hope, and love abide, these three; and the greatest of these is love."

The theological virtues empower us to share in the love and life of God, that is, in holiness of life, both now and forever in eternal life. "Faith makes us taste in advance the light of the Beatific Vision, the goal of our journey here below. Then we shall see God 'face-to-face,' 'as he is' [1 Corinthians 13:12]. So faith is already the beginning of eternal life" (CCC, no. 163).

LET'S PROBE DEEPER: A SCRIPTURE ACTIVITY

- ⊙ Read and reflect on these words of our Lord: "[The Kingdom of God] is like a mustard seed, which, when sown upon the ground, is the smallest of all the seeds on earth; yet when it is sown it grows up and becomes the greatest of all shrubs, and puts forth large branches, so that the birds of the air can make nests in its shade" (Mark 4:31–32).
- ⊙ Discuss with a partner: What does this parable of Jesus reveal about the potential and opportunities that exist for you and other young people to engage with the Church's work of evangelization?
- ⊙ Share responses as a class.

THINK, PAIR AND SHARE

- ⊙ Reflect:
  - How important is faith to our salvation? Why?
  - How and why is it important to share our faith with others?
- ⊙ Share your reflections with a partner.

WHAT ABOUT YOU PERSONALLY?

- ⊙ Has this course of study deepened your resolve to share your faith with others—with non-Catholic Christians, with non-Christians and with other Catholics?
- ⊙ Do you look upon the obligation to share your faith in Christ as a privilege? Why so?

REVIEW AND SHARE WHAT YOU HAVE LEARNED

Look back over this epilogue. Share what you learned from these teachings of the Catholic Church about the Church's mission to evangelize:

- ◉ The Church has the mission to proclaim Jesus Christ to all nations.
- ◉ Proclaiming the Gospel is a privilege and a responsibility; an act rooted in our love for God and for all people.
- ◉ Jesus Christ wills that everyone be saved.
- ◉ Catholics are to share their faith with one another.
- ◉ Faith is both a free gift of God and our free response to accept that gift. It is one of the three theological virtues.
- ◉ Faith is the beginning of eternal life with God, the goal of our earthly journey.

LEARN BY EXAMPLE

Pope Francis, evangelist for our times

Pope Francis, in his Apostolic Exhortation *The Joy of the Gospel* (*Evangelii Gaudium*), wrote: "We must never forget that we are pilgrims journeying alongside one another. This means that we must have sincere trust in our fellow pilgrims, putting aside all suspicion or mistrust, and turn our gaze to what we are all seeking: the radiant peace of God's face" (no. 244).

Pope Francis' generous actions and respect toward others give us an excellent example of how we can participate in the Church's ministry of evangelization. The Pope has called on Catholics to look deeply into their hearts and invited us to share our faith with one another to discover the true meaning of the Gospel message. At the end of his apostolic visit to South America in July 2015, the Pope encouraged a crowd of young people to "make a ruckus . . . a ruckus that brings a free heart, a ruckus that brings solidarity, a ruckus that brings us hope, a ruckus that comes from knowing Jesus and knowing that God, once I know him, is my strength. That is the kind of ruckus which you should make."

At a homily in 2013, the Pope reminded us that "the Lord has redeemed all of us, all of us, with the Blood of Christ: all of us, not just Catholics. Everyone!" To which he added: "Even the atheists." It is this spirit of trust in God and open hospitality and neighborliness to one another, to Christians and non-Christians, that God calls us to share—and that Pope Francis models so well in our time. Such reverence and respect, kindness and gentleness, openness and honesty will prepare the way for all to hear and respond to the Spirit of Christ.

TALK IT OVER

- Pope Francis leads the Church in her ministry of evangelization through both his words and his deeds. How can he inspire your own words and deeds in proclaiming Christ to others?

SHARE FAITH WITH FAMILY AND FRIENDS

- Talk with your family and friends about how you can proclaim Jesus Christ in a hospitable, respectful and honest way to people of faith traditions other than your own, as well as to people of your own faith tradition.
- Share why it is important for you to do so.

JUDGE AND DECIDE

- The United States is now rated the most religiously diverse nation in the world. On a scale of 1 to 10 (very committed), how ready are you to share your faith with others?
- What are some things you need to do to better prepare yourself?
- Discern and decide on one thing you will do to be a better evangelist.

LEARN BY HEART

"Go therefore and make disciples of all nations, baptizing them in the name of the Father and of the Son and of the Holy Spirit, and teaching them to obey everything that I have commanded you. And remember, I am with you always, to the end of the age."

MATTHEW 28:19–20

All pray the Sign of the Cross together.

Opening Prayer

LEADER

Holy God, Father, Son and Holy Spirit,
we thank you for the opportunity, over the
course of these months, to come to a deeper
understanding of our faith in your Son,
and to learn more about the religious beliefs,
traditions and practices of others.
Send your Holy Spirit to guide us as we search
out ways to know, love and serve you together,
and to cultivate the values that will enable us to
live out more faithfully our own faith.

ALL

Amen.

LEADER

The Church never ceases to proclaim her faith in
one God: Father, Son and Holy Spirit. We open
our minds and hearts to hear the Word of God so
that we may faithfully proclaim it in both words
and deeds.

*All pray the Sign of the Cross as they make a cross
on their forehead, lips and chest over their heart.*

Proclamation of the Word of God

READER

A reading from the holy Gospel according to
Matthew.

ALL

Glory to you, O Lord.

READER

Proclaim Matthew 16:13–20.
The Gospel of the Lord.

ALL

Praise to you, Lord Jesus Christ.

READER

Homily: Jesus Builds the Church on Faith
(*delivered by Pope Francis, August 24, 2014*)
The Gospel of this Sunday (Matthew 16:13–20)
is the celebrated passage, central to Matthew's
account, in which Simon, in the name of the
Twelve, professes his faith in Jesus as "the Christ,
the Son of the living God"; and Jesus calls Simon
"blessed" for his faith, recognizing in it a special
gift of the Father. He says to [Simon], "You are
Peter, and on this rock I will build my Church."

Let us pause for a moment to reflect on the
fact that Jesus bestows on Simon this new name,
"Peter," which in Jesus' language [Aramaic] was
"Kepha," a word meaning "rock." In the Bible,
this name, this term "rock," referred to God.
Jesus attributes this name to Simon not for his
own personal qualities or his human merits, but
on account of his genuine and firm faith, which
comes from on high.

Jesus feels a great joy in his heart, because
He recognizes in Simon the hand of the Father,
the action of the Holy Spirit. He recognizes that
God the Father has given Simon a "dependable"
faith, upon which He, Jesus, can build His Church,
that is, His community, that is, all of us. . . . Our
relationship with Jesus builds the Church. . . . . .

Brothers and sisters, what happened in a
unique way in Saint Peter, also takes place in every
Christian who develops a sincere faith in Jesus the
Christ, the Son of the living God. Today's Gospel
challenges each of us: How is your faith? Let each
of us answer in our heart. How is your faith? What
does the Lord find in our hearts: a firm heart,
like a rock? Or a heart like sand, that is doubtful,
mistrustful, unbelieving? . . . If the Lord finds in
our hearts a sincere faith—then He will see in
us, too, the living rocks on which He builds His
community. For this community, the foundation
stone is Christ, the unique cornerstone. For his
part, Peter is the rock, as the visible foundation
of the unity of the Church; but every baptized
person is called to offer to Jesus his or her own
faith, poor but sincere, so that He can continue to
build His Church, today, in every part of the world.

Even in our days, many people think that Jesus is a great prophet, a teacher of wisdom, a model of justice. . . . And even today, Jesus asks His disciples—that is, us, all of us—"But you, who do you say that I am?" A prophet? A teacher of wisdom? A model of justice? How will we answer? Let us think about it. But above all let us pray to God the Father, that He will give us the answer, and through the intercession of the Virgin Mary; let us pray that He will give us the gift to respond with sincere hearts: "You are the Christ, the Son of the Living God." This is a confession of faith, this is a creed. We will say it three times, together:

ALL
You are the Christ, the Son of the Living God.
You are the Christ, the Son of the Living God.
You are the Christ, the Son of the Living God.

All quietly reflect, asking, "Lord God, how might I faithfully and boldly proclaim your holy name?"

Concluding Prayer

LEADER
Let us raise up our minds, hearts and voices together in prayer.

Lord God,
set our hearts ablaze with a desire to live our faith fully and share it freely with others.
May we be eager to share our faith and transform our nation and,
with missionary dedication, the whole world.

Open our hearts to see the need for the Gospel in each life,
in our nation and on our planet.

We ask Mary, the one through whom Jesus entered our world,
to guide us as we present Jesus to those who live in our land.
May her prayers help us to share in her courage and faithfulness.
May they lead us to imitate her discipleship,
her turning to Jesus,
her love for God and for all.
May the compassion that Mary has always reflected be present in our hearts.

Like the disciples walking that Easter morning to Emmaus,
may all Catholics feel the presence of Jesus burn in their hearts.
As those two disciples felt the presence of Jesus in their journey,
we ask that our evangelization will help believers feel anew the presence of Jesus
and that it will help others discover his gracious presence.

We pray that the fire of Jesus enkindled in us by God's Spirit may lead
more and more people in our land to become disciples,
formed in the image of Christ our Savior.
Amen.
　　　—*Catholic Household Blessings & Prayers,* "For
　　　　Evangelization and Missions," 368–369

Dismissal
LEADER
Go and announce the Gospel of the Lord.
ALL
Thanks be to God.
　　　　　　　　　—*The Roman Missal*

CATHOLIC PRAYERS, DEVOTIONS AND PRACTICES

SIGN OF THE CROSS
In the name of the Father,
and of the Son,
and of the Holy Spirit. Amen.

OUR FATHER (LORD'S PRAYER)
Our Father who art in heaven,
hallowed be thy name;
thy kingdom come,
thy will be done
on earth as it is in heaven.
Give us this day our daily bread,
and forgive us our trespasses,
as we forgive those who trespass against us;
and lead us not into temptation,
but deliver us from evil. Amen.

GLORY PRAYER (DOXOLOGY)
Glory be to the Father,
and to the Son,
and to the Holy Spirit;
as it was in the beginning
is now, and ever shall be,
world without end. Amen.

PRAYER TO THE HOLY SPIRIT
Come, Holy Spirit, fill the hearts of your faithful.
Enkindle in them the fire of your love.
Send forth your Spirit and they shall be created.
And you shall renew the face of the earth.

O God, by the light of the Holy Spirit you have
    taught the hearts of your faithful.
In the same Spirit, help us to know what is truly
    right and always to rejoice in your consolation.
We ask this through Christ, our Lord. Amen.

HAIL MARY
Hail Mary, full of grace,
the Lord is with thee.
Blessed art thou among women
and blessed is the fruit of thy womb, Jesus.
Holy Mary, Mother of God,
pray for us sinners,
now and at the hour of our death. Amen.

APOSTLES' CREED
I believe in God,
the Father almighty,
Creator of heaven and earth,
and in Jesus Christ, his only Son, our Lord,
who was conceived by the Holy Spirit,
born of the Virgin Mary,
suffered under Pontius Pilate,
was crucified, died, and was buried;
he descended into hell;
on the third day he rose again from the dead;
he ascended into heaven,
and is seated at the right hand of God the Father
    almighty,
from there he will come to judge the living and
    the dead.

I believe in the Holy Spirit,
the holy catholic Church,
the communion of saints,
the forgiveness of sins,
the resurrection of the body,
and life everlasting. Amen.

NICENE CREED
I believe in one God,
the Father almighty,
maker of heaven and earth,
of all things visible and invisible.

I believe in one Lord Jesus Christ,
the Only Begotten Son of God,
born of the Father before all ages.
God from God, Light from Light,
true God from true God,
begotten, not made, consubstantial with the
    Father;
through him all things were made.
For us men and for our salvation
he came down from heaven,

and by the Holy Spirit was incarnate of the Virgin Mary,
and became man.

For our sake he was crucified under Pontius Pilate,
he suffered death and was buried,
and rose again on the third day
in accordance with the Scriptures.
He ascended into heaven
and is seated at the right hand of the Father.
He will come again in glory
to judge the living and the dead,
and his kingdom will have no end.

I believe in the Holy Spirit, the Lord, the giver of life,
who proceeds from the Father and the Son,
who with the Father and the Son is adored and glorified,
who has spoken through the prophets.

I believe in one, holy, catholic and apostolic Church.
I confess one Baptism for the forgiveness of sins
and I look forward to the resurrection of the dead
and the life of the world to come. Amen.

JESUS PRAYER
Lord Jesus Christ, Son of God, have mercy on me, a sinner. Amen.

ACT OF FAITH
O my God, I firmly believe that you are one God in three divine Persons, Father, Son, and Holy Spirit. I believe that your divine Son became man and died for our sins and that he will come to judge the living and the dead. I believe these and all the truths which the Holy Catholic Church teaches because you have revealed them, who are eternal truth and wisdom, who can neither deceive nor be deceived. In this faith I intend to live and die. Amen.

ACT OF HOPE
O Lord God, I hope by your grace for the pardon of all my sins and after life here to gain eternal happiness because you have promised it, who are infinitely powerful, faithful, kind, and merciful. In this hope I intend to live and die. Amen.

ACT OF LOVE
O Lord God, I love you above all things and I love my neighbor for your sake because you are the highest, infinite and perfect good, worthy of all my love. In this love I intend to live and die. Amen.

PRAYER FOR VOCATIONS
Loving Mother, Our Lady of Guadalupe,
you asked Juan Diego to help build a Church that would serve a new people in a new land.
You left your image upon his cloak as a visible sign of your love for us,
so that we may come to believe in your Son, Jesus the Christ.
Our Lady of Guadalupe and St. Juan Diego,
help us respond to God's call to build your Son's Church today.
Help us recognize our personal vocation to serve God as married or single persons or priests, brothers or sisters as our way to help extend the Reign of God here on earth.
Help us pay attention to the promptings of the Holy Spirit.
May all of us have the courage of Juan Diego to say "Yes" to our personal call!
May we encourage one another to follow Jesus, no matter where that path takes us. Amen.

Daily Prayers

Morning Prayer
CANTICLE OF ZECHARIAH (THE BENEDICTUS)
(based on Luke 1:67–79)
Blessed be the Lord, the God of Israel;
for he has come to his people and set them free.
He has raised up for us a mighty Savior,
born of the House of his servant David.
Through his prophets he promised of old
that he would save us from our enemies,
from the hands of all who hate us.
He promised to show mercy to our fathers
and to remember his holy covenant.
This was the oath he swore to our father Abraham:
to set us free from the hand of our enemies,
free to worship him without fear,
holy and righteous in his sight
all the days of our life.

You, my child, shall be called the prophet of the
    Most High,
for you will go before the Lord to prepare his way,
to give his people knowledge of salvation
by the forgiveness of their sins.
In the tender compassion of our God
the dawn from on high shall break upon us,
to shine on those who dwell in darkness and the
    shadow of death,
and to guide our feet into the way of peace.
Amen.

MORNING OFFERING

O Jesus, through the Immaculate Heart of Mary,
I offer you my prayers, works, joys and sufferings
    of this day
for all the intentions of your Sacred Heart,
in union with the Holy Sacrifice of the Mass
    throughout the world,
for the salvation of souls, the reparation for sins,
    the reunion of all Christians,
and in particular for the intentions of the Holy
    Father this month. Amen.

Evening Prayer
CANTICLE OF MARY (THE *MAGNIFICAT*)

My soul proclaims the greatness of the Lord;
my spirit rejoices in God my savior
for he has looked with favor on his lowly servant.
From this day all generations will call me blessed:
the Almighty has done great things for me
and holy is his name.
He has mercy on those who fear him
in every generation.
He has shown the strength of his arm,
and has scattered the proud in their conceit.
He has cast down the mighty from their thrones,
and has lifted up the lowly.
He has filled the hungry with good things,
and the rich he has sent away empty.
He has come to the help of his servant Israel
for he has remembered his promise of mercy,
the promise he made to our fathers,
to Abraham and his children forever. Amen.

GRACE BEFORE MEALS

Bless us, O Lord, and these your gifts,
which we are about to receive from your bounty,
through Christ our Lord. Amen.

GRACE AFTER MEALS

We give you thanks for all your benefits, almighty
    God, who lives and reigns forever.
And may the souls of the faithful departed,
    through the mercy of God, rest in peace.
    Amen.

PRAYER OF ST. FRANCIS (PEACE PRAYER)

Lord, make me an instrument of your peace:
where there is hatred, let me sow love;
where there is injury, pardon;
where there is doubt, faith;
where there is despair, hope;
where there is darkness, light;
where there is sadness, joy.

O divine Master, grant that I may not so much seek
to be consoled as to console,
to be understood, as to understand,
to be loved as to love.

For it is in giving that we receive,
it is in pardoning that we are pardoned,
it is in dying that we are born to eternal life.
Amen.

Contrition and Sorrow
CONFITEOR

I confess to almighty God
and to you, my brothers and sisters,
that I have greatly sinned,
in my thoughts and in my words,
in what I have done and in what I have failed to
    do,
through my fault, through my fault,
through my most grievous fault;
therefore I ask blessed Mary ever-Virgin,
all the Angels and Saints,
and you, my brothers and sisters,
to pray for me to the Lord our God. Amen.

ACT OF CONTRITION

O my God, I am heartily sorry for having offended
you, and I detest all my sins because of your
just punishments, but most of all because
they offend you, my God, who are all good and
deserving of all my love. I firmly resolve with the
help of your grace to sin no more and to avoid
the near occasion of sin. Amen.

Prayers before the Holy Eucharist

THE DIVINE PRAISES

Blessed be God.
Blessed be his holy name.
Blessed be Jesus Christ, true God and true man.
Blessed be the name of Jesus.
Blessed be his most Sacred Heart.
Blessed be his most precious Blood.
Blessed be Jesus in the most holy Sacrament of
the altar.
Blessed be the Holy Spirit, the Paraclete.
Blessed be the great Mother of God, Mary most
holy.
Blessed be her holy and Immaculate Conception.
Blessed be her glorious Assumption.
Blessed be the name of Mary, Virgin and Mother.
Blessed be St. Joseph, her most chaste spouse.
Blessed be God in his angels and in his saints.

ANIMA CHRISTI (SOUL OF CHRIST)

Soul of Christ, sanctify me.
Body of Christ, save me.
Blood of Christ, inebriate me.
Water from the side of Christ, wash me.
Passion of Christ, strengthen me.
O good Jesus, hear me.
Within your wounds hide me.
Permit me not to be separated from you.
From the malicious enemy defend me.
In the hour of my death call me.
And bid me come to you,
that with your saints I may praise you
forever and ever. Amen.

AN ACT OF SPIRITUAL COMMUNION

My Jesus, I believe that you are present in the
Most Blessed Sacrament.
I love you above all things, and I desire to receive
you into my soul.
Since I cannot at this moment receive you
sacramentally, come at least spiritually into
my heart.
I embrace you as if you were already there and
unite myself wholly to you.
Never permit me to be separated from you. Amen.

Prayers to Mary, Mother of God

ANGELUS

Verse: The Angel of the Lord declared unto
Mary.
Response: And she conceived of the Holy Spirit.
Hail Mary, full of grace,
the Lord is with thee.
Blessed art thou among women
and blessed is the fruit of thy womb,
Jesus.
Holy Mary, Mother of God,
pray for us sinners,
now and at the hour of our death.
Amen.
Verse: Behold the handmaid of the Lord.
Response: Be it done unto me according to your
Word.
Hail Mary. . . .
Verse: And the Word was made flesh,
Response: And dwelt among us.
Hail Mary. . . .
Verse: Pray for us, O holy Mother of God,
Response: That we may be made worthy of the
promises of Christ.

Let us pray. Pour forth, we beseech you, O Lord,
your grace into our hearts: that we, to whom the
Incarnation of Christ your Son was made known by
the message of an Angel, may by his Passion and
Cross be brought to the glory of his Resurrection.
Through the same Christ our Lord. Amen.

MEMORARE

Remember, O most gracious Virgin Mary, that
never was it known that anyone who fled to your
protection, implored your help, or sought your
intercession, was left unaided. Inspired by this
confidence, I fly unto you, O Virgin of virgins, my
mother; to you do I come, before you I stand,
sinful and sorrowful. O Mother of the Word
Incarnate, despise not my petitions, but in your
mercy hear and answer me. Amen.

REGINA CAELI (QUEEN OF HEAVEN)

Queen of Heaven, rejoice, alleluia:
for the Son you were privileged to bear, alleluia,
is risen as he said, alleluia.
Pray for us to God, alleluia.

Verse: Rejoice and be glad, O Virgin Mary, Alleluia!

Response: For the Lord is truly risen, Alleluia.

Let us pray. O God, who gave joy to the world through the resurrection of your Son, our Lord Jesus Christ, grant, we beseech you, that through the intercession of the Virgin Mary, his Mother, we may obtain the joys of everlasting life. Through the same Christ our Lord. Amen.

SALVE, REGINA (HAIL, HOLY QUEEN)

Hail, holy Queen, Mother of mercy: Hail, our life, our sweetness and our hope. To you do we cry, poor banished children of Eve. To you do we send up our sighs, mourning and weeping in this valley of tears. Turn then, most gracious advocate, your eyes of mercy toward us; and after this our exile show unto us the blessed fruit of your womb, Jesus. O clement, O loving, O sweet Virgin Mary. Amen.

PRAYER TO OUR LADY OF GUADALUPE

God of power and mercy,
you blessed the Americas at Tepeyac
with the presence of the Virgin Mary of
   Guadalupe.
May her prayers help all men and women
to accept each other as brothers and sisters.
Through your justice present in our hearts
may your peace reign in the world. Amen.

THE ROSARY

THE JOYFUL MYSTERIES: Traditionally prayed on Mondays and Saturdays and on Sundays of the Christmas Season.

1. The Annunciation (Luke 1:26–38)
2. The Visitation (Luke 2:39–56)
3. The Nativity (Luke 2:1–20)
4. The Presentation in the Temple (Luke 2:22–38)
5. The Finding of Jesus after Three Days in the Temple (Luke 2:41–50)

THE LUMINOUS MYSTERIES: Traditionally prayed on Thursdays.

1. The Baptism at the Jordan (Matthew 3:13–17)
2. The Miracle at Cana (John 2:1–11)
3. The Proclamation of the Kingdom and the Call to Conversion (Mark 1:14–15)
4. The Transfiguration (Matthew 17:1–13)
5. The Institution of the Eucharist (Matthew 26:26–28)

THE SORROWFUL MYSTERIES: Traditionally prayed on Tuesdays and Fridays and on the Sundays of Lent.

1. The Agony in the Garden (Matthew 26:36–56)
2. The Scourging at the Pillar (John 18:28—19:1)
3. The Crowning with Thorns (John 19:2–3)
4. The Carrying of the Cross (John 19:17)
5. The Crucifixion and Death (John 19:18–30)

THE GLORIOUS MYSTERIES: Traditionally prayed on Wednesdays and Sundays, except on the Sundays of Christmas and Lent.

1. The Resurrection (Matthew 28:1–8)
2. The Ascension (Matthew 28:16–20/Acts 1:1–11)
3. The Descent of the Holy Spirit at Pentecost (Acts 2:1–13)
4. The Assumption of Mary (See CCC, no. 966)
5. The Crowning of the Blessed Virgin as Queen of Heaven and Earth (See CCC, no. 966)

How to pray the Rosary

1. Pray the *Sign of the Cross* and pray the *Apostles' Creed* while holding the crucifix.
2. Touch the first bead after the crucifix and pray the *Our Father*, pray the *Hail Mary* on each of the next three beads, and pray the *Glory Prayer* on the next bead.
3. Go to the main part of your rosary. Say the name of the Mystery and quietly reflect on the meaning of the events of that Mystery. Pray the *Our Father*, and then, fingering each of the ten beads, pray ten *Hail Marys*. Then touch the next bead and pray the *Glory Prayer*. (Repeat the process for the next four decades.)
4. Pray the *Salve Regina (Hail, Holy Queen)* and conclude by praying:

Verse: Pray for us, O holy Mother of God.

Response: That we may be made worthy of the promises of Christ.

Let us pray. O God, whose only-begotten

Son, by his life, death and Resurrection, has purchased for us the rewards of eternal life, grant, we beseech you, that meditating on these mysteries of the most holy rosary of the Blessed Virgin Mary, we may imitate what they contain and obtain what they promise, through the same Christ our Lord. Amen.

5. Conclude by praying the *Sign of the Cross*.

STATIONS, OR WAY, OF THE CROSS

The tradition of praying the Stations, or Way, of the Cross dates from the fourteenth century. The tradition, which is attributed to the Franciscans, came about to satisfy the desire of Christians who were unable to make a pilgrimage to Jerusalem. The traditional Stations of the Cross are:

FIRST STATION: Jesus is condemned to death

SECOND STATION: Jesus is made to carry his Cross

THIRD STATION: Jesus falls the first time

FOURTH STATION: Jesus meets his mother

FIFTH STATION: Simon helps Jesus to carry his Cross

SIXTH STATION: Veronica wipes the face of Jesus

SEVENTH STATION: Jesus falls the second time

EIGHTH STATION: Jesus meets the women of Jerusalem

NINTH STATION: Jesus falls the third time

TENTH STATION: Jesus is stripped of his garments

ELEVENTH STATION: Jesus is nailed to the Cross

TWELFTH STATION: Jesus dies on the Cross

THIRTEENTH STATION: Jesus is taken down from the Cross

FOURTEENTH STATION: Jesus is laid in the tomb.

In 1991 St. John Paul II gave the Church a scriptural version of the Stations. The individual names given to these stations are:

FIRST STATION: Jesus in the Garden of Gethsemane—Matthew 25:36–41

SECOND STATION: Jesus, Betrayed by Judas, Is Arrested—Mark 14:43–46

THIRD STATION: Jesus Is Condemned by the Sanhedrin—Luke 22:66–71

FOURTH STATION: Jesus Is Denied by Peter—Matthew 26:69–75

FIFTH STATION: Jesus Is Judged by Pilate—Mark 15:1–5, 15

SIXTH STATION: Jesus Is Scourged and Crowned with Thorns—John 19:1–3

SEVENTH STATION: Jesus Bears the Cross—John 19:6, 15–17

EIGHTH STATION: Jesus Is Helped by Simon the Cyrenian to Carry the Cross—Mark 15:21

NINTH STATION: Jesus Meets the Women of Jerusalem—Luke 23:27–31

TENTH STATION: Jesus Is Crucified—Luke 23:33–34

ELEVENTH STATION: Jesus Promises His Kingdom to the Good Thief—Luke 23:39–43

TWELFTH STATION: Jesus Speaks to His Mother and the Disciple—John 19:25–27

THIRTEENTH STATION: Jesus Dies on the Cross—Luke 23:44–46

FOURTEENTH STATION: Jesus Is Placed in the Tomb—Matthew 27:57–60

Some parishes conclude the Stations with a prayerful meditation on the Resurrection.

The Way of Jesus: Catholic Practices

THE SEVEN SACRAMENTS

Sacraments of Christian Initiation

BAPTISM: The sacrament by which we are freed from all sin and are endowed with the gift of divine life, are made members of the Church, and are called to holiness and mission.

CONFIRMATION: The sacrament that completes the grace of Baptism by a special outpouring of the gifts of the Holy Spirit, which seals and confirms the baptized in union with Christ and calls them to a greater participation in the worship and apostolic life of the Church.

EUCHARIST: The ritual, sacramental action of thanksgiving to God which constitutes the principal Christian liturgical celebration of and communion in the Paschal Mystery of Christ. This liturgical action is also traditionally known as the Holy Sacrifice of the Mass.

Sacraments of Healing

PENANCE AND RECONCILIATION: The sacrament in which sins committed after Baptism are forgiven, which results in reconciliation with God and the Church. This sacrament is also called the Sacrament of Confession.

ANOINTING OF THE SICK: This sacrament is given to a person who is seriously ill or in danger of death or old age which strengthens the person with the special graces of healing and comfort and courage.

Sacraments at the Service of Communion

MARRIAGE (MATRIMONY): The sacrament in which a baptized man and a baptized woman enter the covenant partnership of the whole of life that by its nature is ordered toward the good of the spouses and the procreation and education of offspring.

HOLY ORDERS: The sacrament in which a bishop ordains a baptized man to be conformed to Jesus Christ by grace, to service and leadership in the Church as a bishop, priest, or deacon.

GIFTS OF THE HOLY SPIRIT

The seven gifts of the Holy Spirit are permanent dispositions which move us to respond to the guidance of the Spirit. The traditional list of these gifts is derived from Isaiah 11:1–3.

WISDOM: A spiritual gift which enables one to know the purpose and plan of God.

UNDERSTANDING: This gift stimulates us to work on knowing ourselves as part of our growth in knowing God.

COUNSEL (RIGHT JUDGMENT): This gift guides us to follow the teaching the Holy Spirit gives us about our moral life and the training of our conscience.

FORTITUDE (COURAGE): This gift strengthens us to choose courageously and firmly the good, despite difficulty, and also to persevere in doing what is right, despite temptation, fear or persecution.

KNOWLEDGE: This gift directs us to a contemplation, or thoughtful reflection, on the mystery of God and the mysteries of the Catholic faith.

PIETY (REVERENCE): This gift strengthens us to grow in respect for the Holy Trinity, for the Father who created us, for Jesus who saved us, and for the Holy Spirit who is sanctifying us.

FEAR OF THE LORD (WONDER AND AWE): This gift infuses honesty into our relationship with God.

FRUITS OF THE HOLY SPIRIT

The fruits of the Holy Spirit are the perfections that the Holy Spirit forms in us as the "first fruits" of eternal glory. The Tradition of the Church lists twelve fruits of the Holy Spirit. They are: love, joy, peace, patience, kindness, goodness, generosity, gentleness, faithfulness, modesty, self-control and chastity.

VIRTUES

The Theological Virtues

Gifts from God that enable us to choose to and to live in right relationship with the Holy Trinity.

FAITH: The virtue by which the believer gives personal adherence to God (who invites his or her response) and freely assents to the whole truth that God revealed.

HOPE: The virtue through which a person both desires and expects the fulfillment of God's promises of things to come.

CHARITY (LOVE): The virtue by which we give love to God for his own sake and love to our neighbor on account of God.

The Cardinal Moral Virtues

The four moral virtues on which all other human virtues hinge.

FORTITUDE: The virtue by which one courageously and firmly chooses the good despite difficulty and also perseveres in doing what is right despite temptation.

JUSTICE: The virtue by which one is able to give God and neighbor what is due to them.

PRUDENCE: The virtue by which one knows the true good in every circumstance and chooses the right means to reach that end.

TEMPERANCE: The virtue by which one moderates the desire for the attainment of and pleasure in earthly goods.

THE NEW LAW

The Great, or Greatest, Commandment

"You shall love the Lord your God with all your heart, and with all your soul, and with all your mind. . . . You shall love your neighbor as yourself."

—Matthew 22:37, 39, based on Deuteronomy 6:5 and Leviticus 19:18

THE NEW COMMANDMENT OF JESUS

"Love one another. Just as I have loved you, you also should love one another." John 13:34

THE BEATITUDES

Blessed are the poor in spirit, for theirs is the kingdom of heaven.

Blessed are those who mourn, for they will be comforted.

Blessed are the meek, for they will inherit the earth.

Blessed are those who hunger and thirst for righteousness, for they will be filled.

Blessed are the merciful, for they will receive mercy.

Blessed are the pure in heart, for they will see God.

Blessed are the peacemakers, for they shall be called children of God.

Blessed are those who are persecuted for righteousness' sake, for theirs is the kingdom of heaven.

Blessed are you when people revile you and persecute you and utter all kinds of evil against you falsely on my account. Rejoice and be glad, for your reward is great in heaven, for in the same way they persecuted the prophets who were before you.

—Matthew 5:3–11

SPIRITUAL WORKS OF MERCY

Admonish and help those who sin.
Teach those who are ignorant.
Advise those who have doubts.
Comfort those who suffer.
Be patient with all people.
Forgive those who trespass against you.
Pray for the living and the dead.

CORPORAL WORKS OF MERCY

Feed the hungry.
Give drink to the thirsty.
Shelter the homeless.
Clothe the naked.
Visit the sick and those in prison.
Bury the dead.
Give alms to the poor.

THE TEN COMMANDMENTS, OR THE DECALOGUE

Traditional Catechetical Formula

FIRST: I am the LORD your God: you shall not have strange gods before me.

SECOND: You shall not take the name of the LORD your God in vain.

THIRD: Remember to keep holy the LORD's Day.

FOURTH: Honor your father and mother.

FIFTH: You shall not kill.

SIXTH: You shall not commit adultery.

SEVENTH: You shall not steal.

EIGHTH: You shall not bear false witness against your neighbor.

NINTH: You shall not covet your neighbor's wife.

TENTH: You shall not covet your neighbor's goods.

Scriptural Formula

FIRST: I am the LORD your God, who brought you out of the land of Egypt, out of the house of slavery; you shall have no other gods before me.

SECOND: You shall not make wrongful use of the name of the LORD your God, for the LORD will not acquit anyone who misuses his name.

THIRD: Observe the sabbath day to keep it holy. . . .

FOURTH: Honor your father and your mother. . . .

FIFTH: You shall not murder.

SIXTH: Neither shall you commit adultery.

SEVENTH: Neither shall you steal.

EIGHTH: Neither shall you bear false witness against your neighbour.

NINTH: Neither shall you covet your neighbor's wife.

TENTH: Neither shall you desire . . . anything that belongs to your neighbor.

—From Deuteronomy 5:6–21

PRECEPTS OF THE CHURCH

The precepts of the Church are positive laws made by the Church that name the minimum in prayer and moral effort for the growth of the faithful in their love of God and neighbor.

FIRST PRECEPT: Participate in Mass on Sundays and on holy days of obligation and rest from work that impedes keeping these days holy.

SECOND PRECEPT: Confess serious sins at least once a year.

THIRD PRECEPT: Receive the Sacrament of the Eucharist at least during the Easter Season.

FOURTH PRECEPT: Fast and abstain on the days established by the Church.

FIFTH PRECEPT: Provide for the materials of the Church according to one's ability.

SOCIAL DOCTRINE OF THE CHURCH

These seven key principles are at the foundation of the social doctrine, or social teaching, of the Catholic Church:

1. *Life and dignity of the human person.* Human life is sacred and the dignity of the human person is the foundation of the moral life of individuals and of society.

2. *Call to family, community and participation.* The human person is social by nature and has the right to participate in family life and in the life of society.

3. *Rights and responsibilities.* The human person has the fundamental right to life and to the basic necessities that support life and human decency.

4. *Option for the poor and the vulnerable.* The Gospel commands us "to put the needs of the poor and the vulnerable first."

5. *Dignity of work and workers.* Work is a form of participating in God's work of creation. "The economy must serve people and not the other way around."

6. *Solidarity.* God is the Creator of all people. "We are one human family whatever our national, racial, ethnic, economic and ideological differences."

7. *Care for God's creation.* Care of the environment is a divine command and a requirement of our faith.

FAITH GLOSSARY

Abbreviations: CCC = *Catechism of the Catholic Church*; DB = *Dictionary of the Bible* (John L. McKenzie); USCCA = *United States Catholic Catechism for Adults*

A–B

abortion, direct: The intentional destruction of an unborn child; such an act is gravely contrary to the moral law and [to] the will of the Creator. (USCCA, Glossary, 503)

Anglican Communion: The Anglican Communion, or Anglican Episcopal family, is a worldwide communion of independently governed churches. The word "Anglican" comes from the thirteenth-century Latin term *ecclesia anglicana,* which means "English Church." The members of the Anglican Communion are descendants from the Church of England. Some Anglicans identify themselves as Episcopalian. The Anglican Communion describes itself as a "fellowship, within the one holy catholic and apostolic church, . . . in communion with the see of Canterbury." Members of the Anglican Communion can differ one from the other in their teachings and practices, for example, in the practice of marrying same-sex couples.

annulment (declaration of nullity of a marriage): The consent of the spouses entering into marriage must be a free act of the will, devoid of external or internal invalidating factors. If this freedom is absent, the marriage is invalid. For this reason, the Church, after an examination of the situation by a competent Church court, can declare the nullity of a marriage, i.e., that the sacramental marriage never existed. In this case, the contracting parties are free to marry, provided the natural obligations of the previous union are discharged (see CCC, 1628–1629; CIC, canons 1095–1107; CCEO, canons 1431–1449). (USCCA, Glossary, 503–04)

Apostle(s): "The title traditionally given to those specially chosen by Jesus to preach the Gospel and to whom he entrusted responsibility for guiding the early Church" (USCCA, Glossary, 504). The names of the first Apostles, also called the Twelve, are Peter, Andrew, James, John, Thomas, James, Philip, Bartholomew (also known as Nathaniel), Matthew, Judas, Simon, and Jude (also known as Thaddeus). After the Ascension of Jesus, Matthias, who replaced Judas Iscariot, and Paul were also called to be Apostles.

Apostolic Succession: The passing on of the office of bishop from the Apostles to bishops, and from them to other bishops down each generation, by means of ordination. (USCCA, Glossary, 504)

Apostolic Tradition: Jesus entrusted his revelation and teachings to his Apostles. They passed it on by their preaching and witness. Along with others, they began writing the message down in what became the New Testament. (USCCA, Glossary, 504)

ascesis: The practice of penance, mortification, and self-denial to promote greater self-mastery and to foster the way of perfection by embracing the way of the cross. (CCC, Glossary)

asceticism: *see* **ascesis.**

atonement: By his suffering and death on the Cross, Jesus freed us from our sins and brought about our reconciliation with God. (USCCA, Glossary, 506)

Baptism: The first Sacrament of Initiation by

which we are freed from all sin and are endowed with the gift of divine life, are made members of the Church, and are called to holiness and mission. (USCCA, Glossary, 505)

Beatific Vision: The seeing of God face to face; being and living in the presence of God in heavenly glory. "The contemplation of God in heavenly glory, a gift of God which is a constitutive element of the happiness (or beatitude) of heaven" (CCC, Glossary).

biblical fundamentalism: *see* **fundamentalism, biblical.**

Blessed Trinity: *see* **Trinity.**

Body of Christ: A name for the Holy Eucharist. It is also a title for the Church, with Christ as her head, sometimes referred to as the Mystical Body of Christ. The Holy Spirit provides the members with the gifts needed to live as Christ's Body. (USCCA, Glossary, 505)

C

Calvinism: John Calvin (1509–64) was a French Protestant theologian and pastor who is considered the founder of Protestant Reformed Christianity. His teachings, known as Calvinism, are central to Protestant Reformed Christianity. He emphasized human sinfulness and the human incapacity to contribute anything to one's own salvation (see Philippians 2:12). This opinion of Calvin gave birth to his erroneous interpretation of the New Testament teachings on predestination. *See also* **predestination.**

catholic: One of the four marks or notes of the Church, taken from the Nicene Creed. The Church is catholic or universal both because she possesses the fullness of Christ's presence and the means of salvation, and because she has been sent out by Christ on a mission to the whole of the human race. (CCC, Glossary)

Catholic Reformation, or Counter-Reformation: The Catholic Church responded to the Protestant Reformers with her own internal reformation.

These efforts have been named the Catholic Reformation, or the Counter-Reformation. The Council of Trent (1545–63) was the center of the Catholic Reformation. The council reasserted the Church's doctrinal teachings that Martin Luther had denied and also decreed the reformation of practices, in areas such as the education of clergy, that Luther rightly identified as harmful to the Church. *See also* **Protestant Reformation; Lutheranism.**

celibacy: The state or condition of those who have chosen to remain unmarried for the sake of the kingdom of heaven in order to give themselves entirely to God and to the service of his people. In the Latin Church, celibacy is obligatory for bishops and priests. In some Eastern Churches, celibacy is a prerequisite for the ordination only of bishops; priests may not marry after they have been ordained. (CCC, Glossary)

charity (love): The Theological Virtue by which we give love to God for his own sake and love to our neighbor on account of God. (USCCA, Glossary, 506)

Chosen People of God: Name given to the descendants of Abraham, the Jewish people, also known as the Hebrews or the Israelites. God chose Abraham over all others to be the one to whom he would reveal himself—and the descendants of Abraham, the Jewish people, to be the instruments for God's saving work within human history.

Christian sect: A group of people who profess Jesus Christ to be Lord and Savior but whose members are not validly baptized and whose teachings and practices are heretical, or contrary to the essential teachings and practices of Christianity that are part of the Apostolic Tradition of the Church.

Church: The name given the "convocation" or "assembly" of the People God has called together from "the ends of the earth." In Christian usage, the word "Church" has three inseparable meanings: the People that God gathers in the whole world; the particular or local church (diocese); and the liturgical (above all Eucharistic) assembly. The Church draws her life from the Word and the Body of Christ, and so herself becomes Christ's Body. In the Creed, the sole Church of Christ is professed to be one, holy, catholic, and apostolic. (CCC, Glossary) See *also* **Body of Christ; Eastern Churches; Western Churches.**

Code of Canon Law: The rules (canons or laws) which provide the norms for good order in the visible society of the Church. Those canon laws that apply universally are contained in the Codes of Canon Law. The most recent Code of Canon Law was promulgated in 1983 for the Latin (Western) Church and in 1991 for the Eastern Church. (CCC, Glossary)

college of bishops: All bishops, with the Pope as their head, form a single college [an organized body of persons], which succeeds in every generation the college of the Twelve Apostles, with Peter at their head. Christ instituted this college as the foundation of the Church. The college of bishops, together with—but never without—the pope, has the supreme and full authority over the universal Church. (USCCA, Glossary, 507)

collegiality: *see* **college of bishops.**

common good: "By common good is to be understood 'the sum total of social conditions which allow people, either as groups or as individuals, to reach their fulfillment more fully and more easily' " (CCC, no. 1906, quoting *Pastoral Constitution on the Church in the Modern World*, no. 26). "The common good consists of three essential elements: respect for and promotion of the fundamental rights of the person; prosperity, or the development of the spiritual and temporal goods of society; the peace and security of the group and of its members" (CCC, no. 1925).

Communion of Saints: This refers to members of the Church through all time—those now in the Church and those members who have already

gone before us and are either in Purgatory or heaven. (USCCA, Glossary, 507)

compassion: In the Bible, the English word "compassion" is a translation of a Greek word meaning "womb" and of a Hebrew word that is also translated as "mercy." Compassion is the quality of a person who so closely identifies with the suffering and condition of another person that the suffering of the other becomes their own, or "enters their womb." The Latin roots of the English word "compassion" are *cum* and *patior*, which mean "suffering with."

conscience: The interior voice of a human being, within whose heart the inner law of God is inscribed. Moral conscience is a judgment of practical reason about the moral quality of a human action. It moves a person at the appropriate moment to do good and to avoid evil. (CCC, Glossary)

covenant: A covenant is a solemn agreement made between human beings or between God and a human being involving mutual commitments or guarantees. The Bible speaks of covenants that God made with Noah and, through him, "with every living creature" (Genesis 9:10). Then God made the special covenant with Abraham and renewed it with Moses. The prophets constantly pointed to a new covenant that God would establish with all humankind through the promised Messiah— Jesus Christ.

creation: The act by which the eternal God gave a beginning to all that exists outside of himself. Creation also refers to the created universe or totality of what exists, as often expressed by the formula "the heavens and the earth." (CCC, Glossary)

creed: A brief, normative summary statement or profession of Christian faith, for example, the Apostles' Creed, the Nicene Creed. The word "Creed" comes from the Latin *Credo*, meaning "I believe," with which the Creed begins. Creeds are also called Symbols of Faith. (CCC, Glossary)

Cross (of Christ): The instrument of execution on which Christ died; a symbol of the unique sacrifice of Christ as sole mediator between God and man. Jesus invited his disciples to take up their cross and follow him, in order to associate with his redeeming sacrifice those who were to be its first beneficiaries. . . . A devotional cross with the figure of Jesus suspended on it is called a "crucifix." (CCC, Glossary)

D–E

deacons: Men ordained by the bishop to serve. They receive the Sacrament of Holy Orders but not the ministerial priesthood. Through ordination, the deacon is conformed to Christ who said he came to serve, not to be served. Deacons in the Latin Church may baptize, read the Gospel, preach the homily, assist the bishop or priest in the celebration of the Eucharist, assist at and bless marriages, and preside at funerals. They dedicate themselves to charitable endeavors, which was their ministerial role in New Testament times. (USCCA, Glossary, 509)

Decalogue: The Ten Commandments (literally, "ten words") given by God to Moses on Sinai. In order to be faithful to the teaching of Jesus, the Decalogue must be interpreted in the light of the great commandment of love of God and neighbor. (CCC, Glossary)

Deposit of Faith: The heritage of faith contained in Sacred Scripture and Tradition, handed on in the Church from the time of the Apostles, from which the Magisterium draws all that it proposes for belief as divinely revealed. (USCCA, Glossary, 509)

Diaspora: The lands outside of Palestine in which Jews settled and lived.

divination: "The art of knowing and declaring future events or hidden things by means of communication with occult forces" (*Catholic Dictionary*, John A. Hardon, SJ). "All forms of *divination* are to be rejected: . . . Consulting horoscopes, astrology, palm reading, interpretation of omens and lots, the phenomena

of clairvoyance, and recourse to mediums all conceal a desire for power over time, history, and, in the last analysis, other human beings, as well as a wish to conciliate hidden powers. They contradict the honor, respect, and loving fear that we owe to God alone" (CCC, 2116). Divination is contrary to the First Commandment.

Divine Person: The term used to describe the Father, Son, and Holy Spirit in their relation to and distinction from one another within the unity of the Trinity. Each of the three divine Persons is God in one divine nature. (USCCA, Glossary, 510)

divine providence: God's loving care and concern for all he has made; he continues to watch over creation, sustaining its existence and presiding over its development and destiny. (USCCA, Glossary, 510)

Divine Revelation: God's communication of himself and his loving plan to save us. This is a gift of self-communication, which is realized by deeds and words over time and most fully by his sending us his own divine Son, Jesus Christ. (USCCA, Glossary, "Revelation," 526) *See also* **natural revelation**.

divinization: A term that refers to the way we are made to be like God by grace. "Constituted in a state of holiness, man was destined to be fully 'divinized' by God in glory" (CCC, no. 398). The term "divinization" is not to be confused with the term "divination." *See also* **idolatry**.

divorce: The claim that the indissoluble marriage bond validly entered into between a man and a woman is broken. A civil dissolution of the marriage contract (divorce) does not free persons from a valid marriage before God; remarriage would not be morally licit. (CCC, Glossary)

Dogma/doctrine: The name given to divinely revealed truths proclaimed or taught by the Church's Magisterium; the faithful are obliged to believe these truths. (USCCA, Glossary, 510)

Eastern Churches: Churches of the East in union

with Rome (the Western Church), but not of [the] Roman rite, with their own liturgical, theological and administrative traditions, such as those of the Byzantine, Alexandrian or Coptic, Syriac, Armenian, Maronite, and Chaldean rites. The variety of particular churches with distinctive traditions witnesses to the catholicity of the one Church of Christ, which takes root in distinct cultures. (CCC, Glossary) *See also* **Eastern Churches and Western Churches**.

Eastern Churches and Western Churches: The Eastern Churches originated in that region of the world that was at one time part of the Eastern Roman Empire. These churches possess their own distinctive traditions that may be seen in their liturgy, theology, and law. The Western Church, focused in Rome, is sometimes called the Latin Church. All individual churches, Eastern or Western, that are in communion with the Apostolic See (Rome) are part of the Catholic Church. (USCCA, Glossary, 510–11)

ecclesial communities: This term is used in reference to non-Catholic denominations of baptized people "who are honored by the name of Christian, but do not profess the faith in its entirety or have not preserved unity of communion under the successor of Peter" (Vatican II, *Dogmatic Constitution on the Church*, no. 15). Lutherans, Anglicans and Episcopalians, and other Reformed Christians are among the ecclesial communities. The Catholic Church is committed to dialogue aimed at fostering fuller unity with these ecclesial communities.

economy of salvation: The economy of salvation . . . refers to God's activity in creating and governing the world, particularly with regard to his plan of salvation for the world in the person and work of Jesus Christ, a plan which is being accomplished through his Body the Church, in its life and sacraments; hence, the "sacramental economy." (CCC, Glossary)

Ecumenical Council: A gathering of all the bishops of the world, in the exercise of their collegial authority over the universal Church. An ecumenical council is usually called by the successor of St. Peter, the Pope, or at least confirmed and accepted by him. (CCC, Glossary, "Council, Ecumenical")

ecumenism: The efforts among all Christians to bring about the fulfillment of Christ's will for the unity of his followers. (USCCA, Glossary, 511)

eternal life: Living forever with God in the happiness of heaven, entered after death by the souls of those who die in the grace and friendship of God. (CCC, Glossary)

Eucharist: The ritual, sacramental action of thanksgiving to God which constitutes the principal Christian liturgical celebration of and communion in the paschal mystery of Christ. The liturgical action called the Eucharist is also traditionally known as the Holy Sacrifice of the Mass. It is one of the seven sacraments of the Church; the Holy Eucharist completes Christian initiation. The Sunday celebration of the Eucharist is at the heart of the Church's life. (CCC, Glossary)

evangelization: "This is the ministry and mission of proclaiming and witnessing Christ and his Gospel with the intention of deepening the faith of believers and inviting others to be baptized and initiated into the Church" (USCCA, Glossary, 512). Evangelization is the primary work of the Church.

Exodus: God's saving intervention in history by which he liberated the Hebrew people from slavery in Egypt, made a covenant with them, and brought them into the Promised Land. The Book of Exodus, the second of the Old Testament, narrates this saving history. The exodus is commemorated by the Jewish people at Passover, which for Christians is a foreshadowing of the "passover" of Jesus Christ from death to life and is celebrated in the memorial of the Eucharist. (CCC, Glossary)

F–G–H

faith: Faith is one of the three theological virtues. Faith "is both a gift of God and a human act by which the believer gives personal adherence to God (who invites his or her response) and freely assents to the whole truth that God has revealed" (USCCA, Glossary, 512).

Filioque: A word meaning "and (from) the Son," added to the Latin version of the Niceno–Constantinopolitan Creed, by which the Latin tradition of the Creed confesses that the Holy Spirit "proceeds from the Father *and the Son.*" (CCC, Glossary)

fruits of the Holy Spirit: The Tradition of the Church lists twelve fruits of the Holy Spirit: love, joy, peace, patience, kindness, goodness, generosity, gentleness, faithfulness, modesty, self-control and chastity. (USCCA, Glossary, 513)

fundamentalism, biblical: The literal interpretation of Scripture. "A . . . characteristic of biblical fundamentalism is that it tends to interpret the Bible as being always without error, or as literally true in a way quite different from the Catholic Church's teaching on the inerrancy of Scripture. For some Biblical Fundamentalists, inerrancy extends even to scientific and historical matters. The Bible is presented without regard for its historical context and development" (*Pastoral Statement for Catholics on Biblical Fundamentalism,* National Conference of Catholic Bishops, 1987).

Gentile(s): A non-Jew.

gifts of the Holy Spirit: These gifts are permanent dispositions that move us to respond to the guidance of the Spirit. The traditional list of these gifts is derived from Isaiah 11:1–3: wisdom, understanding, knowledge, counsel [right judgment], fortitude [courage], reverence (piety), and wonder and awe in God's presence (fear of the Lord). (USCCA, Glossary, 513)

God: The infinite divine being, one in being yet three Persons: Father, Son, and Holy Spirit. God has revealed himself as the "One who is," as truth and love, as creator of all that is, as the author of divine revelation, and as the source of salvation. (CCC, Glossary) *See also* **Trinity.**

Gospel: The good news of God's mercy and love revealed in the life, death, and resurrection of Christ. It is the *Gospel* or good news that the Apostles, and the Church following them, are to proclaim to the entire world. The *Gospel* is handed on in the apostolic tradition of the Church as the source of all-saving truth and moral discipline. (CCC, Glossary)

grace: The word "grace" comes from the Latin word *gratia,* which means "free." Grace is the "free and undeserved gift that God gives us to respond to our vocation to become his adopted children. As sanctifying grace, God shares his divine life and friendship with us in a habitual gift, a stable and supernatural disposition that enables the soul to live with God, to act by his love. As actual grace, God gives us the help to conform our lives to his will. Sacramental grace and special graces (charisms, the grace of one's state of life) are gifts of the Holy Spirit to help us live out our Christian vocation" (CCC, Glossary).

heaven: Eternal life with God; communion of life and love with the Trinity and all the blessed. Heaven is the state of supreme and definitive happiness, the goal of the deepest longings of humanity. (CCC, Glossary)

Hebrews: One of the names of the people of ancient Israel; the name appears in the Bible most frequently when applied to Israelites by foreigners or by Israelites when speaking to foreigners. (DB, 345) *See also* **Israel/Israelites; Jews.**

hell: The state of definitive self-exclusion from communion with God and the blessed, reserved for those who refuse by their own free choice to believe and be converted from sin, even to the end of their lives. (CCC, Glossary)

heresy: A religious teaching that denies or contradicts truths revealed by God. (USCCA, Glossary, 514)

hierarchy: The Apostles and their successors, the college of bishops, to whom Christ gave the authority to teach, sanctify, and rule the Church in his name. (CCC, Glossary)

hierarchy of truths: The order (hierarchy) of the truths in Catholic doctrine, insofar as they vary in their relation to the central mystery and foundation of Christian faith, the mystery of the Holy Trinity. (CCC, Glossary)

holiness: "A state of goodness in which a person—with the help of God's grace, the action of the Holy Spirit, and a life of prayer—is freed from sin and evil" (USCCA, Glossary, 514). A person in the state of holiness lives in communion with God, who is Father, Son and Holy Spirit. *See also* **original holiness.**

Holy Orders: The Sacrament in which a bishop ordains a [baptized] man to be conformed to Jesus Christ by grace, to service and leadership in the Church. A man can be ordained a deacon, priest, or bishop. Through this Sacrament, the mission entrusted by Christ to his Apostles continues to be exercised in the Church. The Sacrament confers a permanent mark or character on the one who receives it. (USCCA, Glossary, 514–15)

Holy See: The seat of the central administration of the worldwide Catholic Church; the name is taken from the seat or diocese of the Pope, Bishop of Rome and successor of St. Peter as Vicar of Christ and pastor of the universal Church. (CCC, Glossary) *See also* **Vatican.**

Holy Spirit: The Third Person of the Trinity who builds up, animates, and sanctifies the Church and her members. (CCC, Glossary)

homosexuality: Sexual attraction or orientation toward persons of the same sex and/or sexual acts between persons of the same sex. Homosexual acts are morally wrong because they violate God's purpose for human sexual activity. (CCC, Glossary)

hope: One of the three theological virtues "through which a person both desires and expects the fulfillment of God's promises of things to come" (USCCA, Glossary, 515). Hope is the desire and expectation of the salvation God promised. It is based on God's unwavering fidelity to keeping and fulfilling his promises. *See also* **charity.**

human person: The human individual, made in the image of God; not some thing but some one, a unity of spirit and matter, soul and body, capable of knowledge, self-possession, and freedom, who can enter into communion with other persons—and with God. The human person needs to live in society, which is a group of persons bound together organically by a principle of unity that goes beyond each one of them. (CCC, Glossary, "Person, human")

human virtues: "The human virtues are stable dispositions of the intellect and the will that govern our acts, order our passions, and guide our conduct in accordance with reason and faith. They can be grouped around the four cardinal virtues: prudence, justice, fortitude, and temperance" (CCC, no. 1834)

hypostatic union: The union of the divine and human natures in the one divine Person (Greek: *hypostasis*) of the Son of God, Jesus Christ. (CCC, Glossary).

I–J–K

idolatry: The divinization of a creature in place of God; the substitution of some one (or thing) for God; worshiping a creature (even money, pleasure, or power) instead of the Creator. (CCC, Glossary) *See also* **divinization.**

image of God: God has made us in his image by giving us the capacity for intelligence, love, freedom, and conscience. By Baptism, our bodies are made temples of the Holy Spirit. (USCCA, Glossary, 515)

Immaculate Conception: A dogma of the Church that teaches that Mary was conceived without Original Sin due to the anticipated redemptive graces of her Son, Jesus. (USCCA, Glossary, 515)

Incarnation: By the Incarnation, the Second

Person of the Holy Trinity assumed our human nature, taking flesh in the womb of the Virgin Mary. There is one Person in Jesus and that is the divine Person of the Son of God. Jesus has two natures, a human one and a divine one. (USCCA, Glossary, 515)

inculturation (of the Gospel): A two-way process whereby the Gospel is woven into the various dimensions of human culture and experience, both personal and social, and authentic cultural values are in turn integrated into the Christian life. *See also* **evangelization**; **Kingdom (Reign) of God/[Kingdom of Heaven].**

indefectibility: The Lord Jesus ensures that his Church will remain until the Kingdom is fully achieved. Indefectibility means that the Church does not and cannot depart from proclaiming the authentic Gospel without errors in spite of the defects of her members. (USCCA, Glossary, 515)

indissolubility of marriage: "What God has joined together, no human being must separate" (Mark 10:9). God's plan for marriage is a permanent covenant embraced by the spouses, hence the bond is indissoluble—not able to be dissolved. (USCCA, Glossary, 516)

indulgence/s: The remission of temporal punishment due to sin, granted to the faithful who recite specified prayers, visit a specified place of pilgrimage, or engage in a specified act of charity; punishment is remitted through the power of the Church and in the mutual exchanges of spiritual goods, particularly the merits of Christ and the saints. (USCCA, Glossary, 516)

inerrancy: Because the authors of Sacred Scripture were inspired by God, the saving meaning or truth found in the Scriptures cannot be wrong. (USCCA, Glossary, 516)

infallibility: This is the gift of the Holy Spirit to the Church whereby the pastors of the Church— the pope, and bishops in communion with him— can definitively proclaim a doctrine of faith and morals, which is divinely revealed for the belief of the faithful. This gift flows from the grace of the whole body of the faithful not to err in matters of faith and morals. The pope teaches infallibly when he declares that his teaching is *ex cathedra* (literally, "from the throne"); that is, he teaches as supreme pastor of the Church. (USCCA, Glossary, 516)

interreligious dialogue: Interreligious dialogue is a dimension of the Church's work of the New Evangelization. Unlike ecumenical dialogue, interreligious dialogue is not meant to lead to unity among the world's religions. Its immediate purpose is to increase knowledge and understanding and to build deeper relationships of friendship, mutual trust and respect between the different religions. *See also* **New Evangelization.**

Islam: Islam is the second largest religion in the world. It is a monotheistic faith. Those who profess Islam are called Muslims. The Arabic term *islām* literally means "surrender." The true Muslim is one who obeys or submits or surrenders to the will of Allah. *Allāh* is the Arabic word for God. Islam has its roots in the life and teachings of Muhammad (c. 570–632), whom the Muslim people revere as the last of the prophets and messengers of God.

Israel/Israelites: The Jewish people, chosen by God to be his people and named after Israel (Jacob), from whose twelve sons the tribes of Israel descend. God formed Israel into his priestly people in their exodus from the slavery of Egypt, when he made the first or Old Covenant with them and gave them his Law through Moses. (CCC, Glossary) *See also* **Hebrews**; **Jews.**

Jesus (name): The name given to the Son of God, the Second Person of the Trinity. This name, which means, "God Saves," was revealed to both the Blessed Virgin Mary and to St. Joseph [see Luke 1:31; Matthew 1:21]. (USCCA, Glossary, 516)

Jew(s): A name for God's chosen people; in the Scriptures, before the Exile it designates a member of the tribe of Judah; after the Exile, an inhabitant of the province of Judah. (DB)

justice: One of the four cardinal moral virtues "by which one is able to give to God and neighbor what is due to them" (USCCA, Glossary, 517). *See also* **original justice.**

justification: The term used to refer to the action of God by which we are freed from our sins and sanctified and renewed by the grace of God. (USCCA, Glossary, 517)

Kingdom [Reign] of God/[Kingdom of Heaven]: The actualization of God's will for human beings proclaimed by Jesus Christ as a community of justice, peace, mercy, and love, the seed of which is the Church on earth, and the fulfillment of which is in eternity. (USCCA, Glossary, 517)

L–M

Last Judgment: The moment at the end of time when everyone will appear before Christ and receive an eternal recompense in accord with their earthly life. (USCCA, Glossary, 517)

Last Supper: The last meal, a Passover supper, which Jesus ate with his disciples the night before he died. Jesus' passing over to his Father by his death and Resurrection, the new Passover, is anticipated in the Last Supper and celebrated in the Eucharist, which fulfills the Jewish Passover and anticipates the final Passover of the Church in the glory of the kingdom. Hence the Eucharist is called the "Lord's Supper." (CCC, Glossary)

Latin Church: *see* **Eastern Churches** and **Western Churches.**

law of love: The heart of God's Law revealed in Leviticus 19:18 and Deuteronomy 6:4–5 which was fulfilled in Jesus Christ and expressed in his teaching his disciples the new commandment in John 13:34–35.

Lord's Day, (the): A name used synonymously for Sunday, the day of the Lord Jesus' Resurrection. (USCCA, Glossary, 518)

Lord's Supper: The Eucharist. *See also* **Last Supper.**

Lutheranism: The roots of the Lutheran communion are founded in Martin Luther's calling the Catholic Church to reform itself. Luther (1483–1546) nailed his Ninety-five Theses, which outlined the reforms he sought, to the door of the cathedral church in Wittenberg, Germany on October 31, 1517 to promote his reform efforts. This event eventually became identified as the launching of the Protestant Reformation.

Magisterium: The living, teaching office of the Church, whose task it is to give authentic interpretation to the word of God, whether in its written form (Sacred Scripture) or in the form of Tradition. The Magisterium ensures the Church's fidelity to the teaching of the Apostles in matters of faith and morals. (CCC, Glossary

Marks of the Church: The name given to four singular characteristics of the Church: the Church is one, holy, catholic, and apostolic. (USCCA, Glossary, 519)

merit: The reward which God promises and gives to those who love him and by his grace perform good works. One cannot "merit" justification or eternal life, which are the free gift of God; the source of any merit we have before God is due to the grace of Christ in us. (CCC, Glossary)

miracle(s): Miracles are signs of the presence of God at work among us. "The miracles and other deeds of Jesus are acts of compassion and signs of the Kingdom and salvation" (USCCA, Glossary, 80).

Monophysitism: Eutyches (c. 380–c. 456), an Orthodox monastic priest from Constantinople who took part in the Council of Ephesus in AD 431, argued that there was only one nature in Christ, a divine nature. "The human nature had ceased to exist as such in Christ when the divine person of God's Son assumed it" (CCC, no. 467). Eutyches' heresy is called Monophysitism, a Greek term meaning "one nature." Those who believed the Monophysite heresy broke away from full communion with the Church and formed what are called Oriental Orthodox Churches.

monotheism: The belief in one God. Christianity, Judaism and Islam are monotheistic faiths.

morality: In one sense, this is the goodness or evil of particular actions. For a Catholic, it also refers to the manner of life and action formed according to the teaching laid down by Christ Jesus and authoritatively interpreted by the Church. (USCCA, Glossary, 520)

Muslim: A person who follows the religion of Islam. *See also* **Islam.**

N–O–P

natural revelation: The manifestation of God in his works, through which human beings can come to know God with certainty by natural reason. "The Church teaches that the one true God, our Creator and Lord, can be known with certainty from his works, by the natural light of human reason" (CCC, no. 47). *See also* **Divine Revelation.**

New Evangelization: Proclaiming and witnessing Christ and his Gospel either to those who have already been initiated into the Church but who have lost their deep sense of commitment to Jesus Christ and connection with the Christian community, or to those who have never heard the Gospel proclaimed.

obedience of faith: Faith is hearing the Word of God and resolving to obey what God is asking of us. Jesus said, "Blessed are those who hear the word of God and observe it" (Luke 11:28). (USCCA, Glossary, 521–22)

ordination: The rite of the Sacrament of Holy Orders by which the bishop, through the imposition of hands and the prayer of consecration, confers the order of bishop, priest, or deacon to exercise a sacred power which comes from Christ on behalf of the Church. (CCC, Glossary)

original holiness: "The grace of original holiness was to share in divine life (CCC, no. 375)" (USCCA, "Original Holiness and Justice," 522). The state of living in communion with God and sharing

in the gift of divine life enjoyed by our first parents from the moment of their creation until the Fall, when they freely chose to disobey God's command (Original Sin).

original justice: The inner harmony of the human person, the harmony between man and woman, and finally the harmony between the first couple and all creation, comprised the state of "original justice." (CCC, no. 376)

Original Sin: The personal sin of disobedience committed by the first human beings, resulting in the deprivation of original holiness and justice and the experience of suffering and death. (USCCA, Glossary, 522)

Orthodox Churches: The term "Orthodox Churches" refers to those Churches belonging to the two Orthodox families, namely the Eastern Orthodox Churches and the Oriental Orthodox Churches. The Eastern Orthodox Churches include those of the Byzantine tradition who are linked in some way to the Patriarchate of Constantinople. The Oriental Orthodox Churches are those who did not accept the Council of Chalcedon (AD 451) and now make up a communion of six churches. The Orthodox Churches while they "are separated from the Catholic Church (schism) ... are in an imperfect but deep communion with the Catholic Church by reason of our common Baptism, the profession of the Creed, and the possession of true sacraments by reason of apostolic succession of their priesthood" (CCC, Glossary).

parables: A characteristic feature of the teaching of Jesus. Parables are simple images or comparisons which confront the hearer or reader with a radical choice about his invitation to enter the Kingdom of God. (CCC, Glossary)

particular judgment: The eternal retribution received by each soul at the moment of death, in accordance with that person's faith and works. (CCC, Glossary)

Paschal Mystery: Christ's work of redemption accomplished principally by his Passion, death,

Resurrection, and glorious Ascension, whereby "dying he destroyed our death, rising he restored our life" (CCC, no. 1067). The Paschal Mystery is celebrated and made present in the liturgy of the Church, and its saving effects are communicated through the sacraments, especially the Eucharist, which renews the paschal sacrifice of Christ as the sacrifice offered by the Church. (CCC, Glossary) *See also* **redemption**; **salvation**.

Passover: The name of the Jewish feast that celebrates the deliverance of Israel from Egypt and from the Angel of Death who passed over their doors marked by the blood of the sacrificed lamb. (USCCA, Glossary, 523)

Patriarch(s): A title given to the venerable ancestors or "fathers" of the Semitic peoples, Abraham, Isaac, and Jacob, who received God's promise of election. In the Church hierarchy, and especially among the Churches of the East, a patriarch is a senior bishop with jurisdiction over a larger unit of particular churches (patriarchate) of a certain rite or region or liturgical tradition. (CCC, Glossary)

Pentecost: The "fiftieth" day at the end of the seven weeks following Passover (Easter in the Christian dispensation). At the first Pentecost after the Resurrection and Ascension of Jesus, the Holy Spirit was manifested, given and communicated as a divine Person to the Church, fulfilling the paschal mystery of Christ according to his promise. Annually the Church celebrates the memory of the Pentecost event as the beginning of the new "age of the Church," when Christ lives and acts in and with his Church. (CCC, Glossary)

People of God: A synonym for the Church, taken from the Old Testament people whom God chose, Israel. Christ instituted the new and eternal covenant by which a new priestly, prophetic, and royal People of God, the Church, participates in these offices of Christ and in the mission and service which flow from them. (CCC, Glossary)

Perpetual Virginity of Mary: Mary was a virgin in conceiving Jesus, in giving birth to him, and in remaining always a virgin ever after. (USCCA, 523)

polytheism: From the Greek *poly* meaning "many" and *theos* meaning "god"; the belief in many gods.

pope: The successor to St. Peter who serves as the Bishop of Rome and as the visible and juridical head of the Catholic Church. (USCCA, Glossary, 523)

predestination: God desires and destines salvation and eternal life for all people. God destines and desires all people to become one with him in Christ, now and forever. "To God, all moments of time are present in their immediacy. When therefore he establishes his eternal plan of 'predestination,' he includes in it each person's free response to his grace" (CCC, no. 600).

prejudice: Negative preconceived judgment of another; irrational suspicion or hatred of another because the person belongs to a particular race, religion, or group. (USCCA, Glossary, 524)

priest: A baptized man ordained through the Sacrament of Holy Orders. "Priests are united with the bishops in priestly dignity and at the same time depend on them in the exercise of their pastoral functions; they are called to be the bishops' prudent co-workers" (CCC, no. 1595). With the bishop, priests form a presbyteral (priestly) community and assume with him the pastoral mission for a particular parish. They serve God's People in the work of sanctification by their preaching, teaching, and offering the Sacraments, especially the Eucharist and the forgiving of sins. (USCCA, Glossary, 524)

Proselytism: Proselytism is a form of proclaiming the Gospel with the explicit intention of converting a non-believer to Christianity. Proselytism trusts in its arguments to persuade others to believe in Christ.

Protestant: A person who believes in Christ and has been baptized, but who does not profess the Catholic faith in its entirety, but rather is a member of a Protestant church or ecclesial community whose roots are in the Reformation, begun in the sixteenth century. (CCC, Glossary)

Protestant Reformation: A movement that sought reform of the Church in the West during the fifteenth and sixteenth centuries. John Calvin (1509-64) and Martin Luther (1483–1546), the founders of Calvinism and Lutheranism respectively, are among the best known of the Reformation leaders. Martin Luther's action of nailing his Ninety-five Theses to the door of the cathedral church in Wittenberg, Germany on October 31, 1517 to promote his reform efforts is seen as the launching of the Protestant Reformation. *See also* **Catholic Reformation, or Counter-Reformation; Calvinism; Lutheranism.**

Protoevangelium: The proto- or "first" Gospel: the passage in Genesis (3:15) that first mysteriously announces the promise of the Messiah and Redeemer. (CCC, Glossary)

providence: *see* **divine providence.**

Purgatory: A state of final purification after death and before entrance into heaven for those who died in God's friendship, but were only imperfectly purified; a final cleansing of human imperfection before one is able to enter the joy of heaven. (CCC, Glossary)

Q–R

Qur'an: The holy writings of Islam.

racism: Unjust discrimination on the basis of a person's race; a violation of human dignity, and a sin against justice. (CCC, Glossary)

Real Presence: The unique presence of Christ in the Eucharist. "When the bread is consecrated, it is changed into Christ's Body. When the wine is consecrated, it is changed into Christ's Blood. Jesus Christ is substantially present in a way that is entirely unique. This happens through the power of the Holy Spirit and the ministry of the priest or bishop acting in the person of Christ during the Eucharistic prayer" (USCCA, Glossary, 525). *See also* **transubstantiation.**

redemption: Redemption is the salvation won for us by Jesus by his paying "the price of his own sacrificial death on the Cross to ransom us, to set us free from the slavery of sin" (CCC, Glossary).

Reformation, Catholic: *see* **Catholic Reformation, or Counter-Reformation.**

Reformation, Protestant: *see* **Protestant Reformation.**

reincarnation: The false belief that a dead person's spirit returns to life in another body either of an animal or another person. This belief is not compatible with the Catholic faith, which teaches that every human person has only one body and one soul, and is unique and unrepeatable. (USCCA, Glossary, 525)

religion: A set of beliefs and practices followed by those committed to the service and worship of God. The first commandment requires us to believe in God, to worship and serve him, as the first duty of the virtue of religion. (CCC, Glossary)

Resurrection: "This is the triumph of Jesus over death on the third day after his crucifixion. Christ's risen body is real, but glorified, not restrained by space or time" (USCCA, Glossary, 525). The Resurrection confirms the "saving, "redeeming" and "liberating" power of Jesus and the truth of his divinity.

resurrection of the body (of the dead): The raising of the righteous, who will live forever with the risen Christ, on the last day. The eleventh article of the Christian creed states, "I believe in the resurrection of the body." The resurrection of the body means not only that the immortal soul will live on after death, but that even our "mortal bodies" (Romans 8:11) will come to life again. (CCC, Glossary)

Revelation (Divine): *see* **Divine Revelation; natural revelation.**

revelation, natural: *see* **natural revelation.**

revelation (private): Private revelations "add nothing to what was publicly revealed up and through Christ but can help inspire a more profound commitment to what has been revealed through public Revelation" (USCCA, 15). Private revelation is "intended only for the good of the person who receives it and does not need to be believed by others" (USCCA, Glossary, "Revelation," 526).

righteousness: In Scripture being in right relationship with God, others, and creation in accord with God's plan of justice. *See also* **original justice; salvation.**

rites: The diverse liturgical traditions in which the one catholic and apostolic faith has come to be expressed and celebrated in various cultures and lands; for example, in the West, the Roman and Ambrosian (Latin) rites; in the East, the Byzantine, Coptic (Alexandrian), Syriac, Armenian, Maronite, and Chaldean rites. "Rite" and "ritual" are sometimes interchanged, as in "the sacramental rite" or "the sacramental ritual." (CCC, Glossary)

S

sacrament: "An efficacious sign of grace, instituted by Christ and entrusted to the Church, by which divine life is dispensed to us by the work of the Holy Spirit" (USCCA, Glossary, 526). The Seven Sacraments of the Catholic Church are classified in three groups: the three Sacraments of Christian Initiation (Baptism, Confirmation, and Eucharist), the two Sacraments of Healing (Penance and Reconciliation, and Anointing of the Sick), and the two Sacraments at the Service of Communion (Marriage and Holy Orders).

sacramental economy: *see* **economy of salvation.**

Sacred Scripture: *see* **Scripture, Sacred.**

Sacred Tradition: *see* **Tradition, Sacred.**

salvation: The forgiveness of sins and restoration of friendship with God, which can be done by God alone. (CCC, Glossary)

salvation history: The story of God's reaching out to humanity to fulfill the divine plan of salvation, and also of humanity's response to God.

sanctifying grace: The word "sanctifying" means "that which makes holy." "Sanctifying grace is a habitual gift of God's own divine life, a stable and supernatural disposition that enables us to live with God and to act by his love" (USCCA, Glossary, "Grace," 514). *See also* **grace.**

schism: Refusal of submission to the Supreme Pontiff, or of communion with the members of the Church subject to him. (CCC, Glossary)

Scripture, Sacred (Bible): The inspired written Word of God. "The books that contain the truth of God's revelation and that were composed by human authors, inspired by the Holy Spirit, and recognized by the Church" (USCCA, Glossary, 527). *See also* **senses of Scripture.**

sect, Christian: *see* **Christian sect.**

senses of Scripture: "Tradition notes that there are two senses or aspects of Scripture—the literal and the spiritual. The literal meaning is that meaning conveyed by the words of Scripture and discovered by exegesis following the rules of sound interpretation. The spiritual meaning points to realities beyond the words themselves and is subdivided into three categories" (USCCA, Glossary, 527–528). These categories are the allegorical, the anagogical, and the moral.

Shariah: Shariah (sometimes Sharia) is the name of the Islamic legal system, or law of Islam. It is a body of moral and religious law based on the teachings of the Qur'an and the traditions of the Prophet Muhammad recorded in the Hadith and Sunna.

social justice: The respect for the human person and the rights which flow from human dignity and guarantee it. Society must provide the conditions that allow people to obtain what is their due, according to their nature and vocation. (CCC, Glossary)

social teaching (social doctrine) of the Catholic Church: The teaching (social doctrine) of the Church on the truth of revelation about human dignity, human solidarity, and the principles of justice and peace; the moral judgments about economic and social matters required by such truth and about the demands of justice and peace. (CCC, Glossary) – as SE8

Sola fide (Only faith): The Protestant reformer Martin Luther (1483–1546) taught that God saves through one's faith and trust in Jesus Christ *alone.* No good works a person performs can merit salvation and justification. This teaching is captured in the expression *sola fide* (only faith).

Sola gratia (Only grace): The Protestant reformer Martin Luther (1483–1546) asserted that forgiveness and salvation are pure gifts of God. Only the grace of God through the redeeming work of Jesus Christ can save a person. The expression *sola gratia* (only grace) summarizes this teaching of Luther.

sola scriptura (only Scripture): The teachings of the Protestant Reformers Martin Luther (1483–1546), John Calvin (1509-64) and others that "Scripture alone" is the guide to Christian faith and Christian living. They taught that all authority in the Church is subordinate to and under the authority of Scripture. They taught that each person, both "the learned and the unlearned," can come to a clear understanding of, and thus make up their own mind about, the meaning of Scripture. This teaching is still widely held by Protestant denominations today.

steward/stewardship: A steward is someone who has the responsibility of caring for what belongs to another person or group of people. In the biblical accounts of creation, God gives humanity dominion over creation. The root word for "dominion" is *domus,* which means household. God has entrusted creation, his household, to the care of humanity.

supersessionism: For a long time Christians mistakenly believed that the Jewish people had willfully refused to recognize Jesus as the Messiah and had him crucified. As a result, many Christians wrongly believed that the Jewish exile (*Diaspora*) was punishment for their rejection of the Messiah. Forgetting God's faithfulness, many thought that God had revoked or cancelled the first covenant, and that Christians had superseded, or replaced, the Jews. This teaching is called "supersessionism" (from the verb "supersede," which means "to replace").

superstition: The attribution of a kind of magical power to certain practices or objects, like charms or omens. Reliance on such power, rather than on trust in God, constitutes an offense against the honor due to God alone, as required by the first commandment. (CCC, Glossary)

synod: A meeting of bishops of an ecclesiastical province or patriarchate (or even from the whole world, for example, Synod of Bishops) to discuss the doctrinal and pastoral needs of the church. A *diocesan* synod is an assembly of priests and other members of Christ's faithful who assist the bishop by offering advice about the needs of the diocese and by proposing legislation for him to enact. The words "synod" and "council" are sometimes used interchangeably. (CCC, Glossary)

T–W

Tanakh: The Tanakh contains the Scriptures the Jewish people believe to be the inspired Word of God. The word Tanakh is an acronym for **T**orah (or teachings), **N**evi'im (or prophets) and **K**etuvim (or writings). These Scriptures, which are contained in the Old Testament of the Bible, are also sacred to Christians today, as they have been since apostolic times. *See also* **Torah.**

theological virtues: Gifts "infused by God into the souls of the faithful to make them capable of acting as his children and of meriting eternal life" (CCC, no. 1813). The theological virtues are faith, hope and charity (love). *See also* **charity (love); faith; hope.**

Theotokos: A Greek term meaning "God-bearer"; Mary is *Theotokos.* She is the Mother of God. Her Son, Jesus, is the Incarnate Son of God, in whom the divine nature and a human nature are united in the one divine Person, Jesus Christ.

Torah: A Hebrew word meaning "instructions," "teachings" and "laws." The term is used to name the first five books of the Bible, which are also known as the Law or the Pentateuch. *See also* **Tanakh.**

Tradition, Sacred: The living transmission of the message of the Gospel in the Church, flowing from the oral preaching of the Apostles and the written message of salvation under the inspiration of the Holy Spirit (Scripture). Tradition is preserved and handed on as the Deposit of Faith under the guidance of the bishops, successors to the Apostles. (USCCA, Glossary, 530)

traditions of the Church: The diverse ways the people of the Church authentically celebrate and give witness to her Tradition and faith in various times and places throughout the world.

transubstantiation: A term used to describe the unique change of bread and wine into the Body and Blood of Christ. By the consecration, the substance of bread and wine is changed into the substance of Christ's Body and Blood. (USCCA, Glossary, 530)

Trinity: One God in three Persons—Father, Son, Holy Spirit. (USCCA, Glossary, 530)

twelve tribes of Israel: The people of ancient Israel whose origin is the leadership of the twelve sons of Jacob: Asher, Benjamin, Dan, Gad, Issachar, Joseph, Judah, Levi, Naphtali, Reuben, Simeon, and Zebulon.

Vatican/Vatican City: The territorial seat of the papacy that is situated within the city of Rome; the smallest sovereign state in the world. The Vatican is also referred to as the Holy See. It is the location of the central governing body, the Curia, of the Catholic Church. *See also* **Holy See.**

Western Church: *see* **Eastern Churches and Western Churches.**

wisdom: A spiritual gift which enables one to know the purpose and plan of God; one of the seven gifts of the Holy Spirit. Wisdom is also the name of one of the books of the Old Testament. (CCC, Glossary)

worship: Adoration and honor given to God, which is the first act of the virtue of religion. (CCC, Glossary)

Acknowledgments

Scripture quotations taken from or adapted from *New Revised Standard Version Bible: Catholic Edition*, copyright © 1989, 1993, Division of Christian Education of the National Council of Churches of Christ in the USA; all rights reserved.

Excerpts from the English translation of the *Catechism of the Catholic Church* for use in the United States, second edition, copyright © 1997, United States Catholic Conference, Inc., Libreria Editrice Vaticana; all rights reserved.

Excerpts from *Go and Make Disciples* (2002); *National Directory for Catechesis* (2005); *United States Catholic Catechism for Adults* (2006); *Catholic Household Blessings & Prayers*, Revised Edition (2007); "Steps Towards a Reunited Church: A Sketch of an Orthodox–Catholic Vision for the Future" (2010); and from the website of United States Conference of Catholic Bishops (*www.usccb.org*), all copyright United States Conference of Catholic Bishops, Washington DC; all rights reserved.

Excerpts from *Unitatis Redintegratio* (1964); *Joint Catholic–Orthodox Declaration* (1965); *Credo of the People of God* (1968); *Redemptor Hominis* (1979); *Letter to the Bishops of the Catholic Church on Some Aspects of Christian Meditation* (1989); *Redemptoris Missio* (1990); *Letter to the Bishops of the Catholic Church on Some Aspects of the Church Understood as Communion* (1992); *Ut Unum Sint* (1995); *Evangelium Vitae* (1995); *General Directory for Catechesis* (1997); *Fides et Ratio* (1998); *Ecclesia in Asia* (1999); Catholic–Lutheran *Joint Declaration on the Doctrine of Justification* (1999); *Evangelii Gaudium* (2013); homily delivered by Pope Francis on Sunday, August 24, 2014; *Code of Canon Law*; various quotations from St. John Paul II, Benedict XVI and Pope Francis; and excerpts from Vatican Radio and the Vatican website; all copyright © Libreria Editrice Vaticana.

Excerpts from documents of Vatican II from A. Flannery (ed.), *Vatican Council II: Constitutions, Decrees, Declarations* (New York/Dublin: Costello Publishing/Dominican Publications, 1996).

Excerpts from the English translation of *Rite of Baptism for Children* © 1969, International Commission on English in the Liturgy Corporation (ICEL); excerpts from the English translation of *The Roman Missal* © 2010, ICEL. All rights reserved.

Excerpts from *New Catholic Encyclopedia* © 2003 by The Catholic University of America. Published by Gale, an imprint of The Gale Group, Inc., a division of Thomson Learning, Inc.

Excerpt from the Paulist Fathers' mission statement, p. 52, sourced from *www.paulist.org*.

Prayer Reflection, pp. 53–4, adapted from a resource provided by the Pontifical Council for Promoting Christian Unity for the Week of Prayer 2015.

Excerpt, pp. 58–9, from Elliot Eastman, *Life in the USA*, "Discrimination Against Catholics," copyright Elliot Eastman 2014, sourced from *www.lifeintheusa.com*; all rights reserved.

Statement from the World Council of Churches, pp. 61–2, copyright 2015 World Council of Churches, sourced from *www.oikoumene.org*.

Profile of Augustin Cardinal Bea by Oliver P. Rafferty, SJ, p. 71, sourced from *www.jesuit.org.uk*.

Aims of the Tantur Ecumenical Institute, p. 74, sourced from *http://tantur.org*.

Quotations from participants at Taizé, p, 78, sourced from *www.taize.fr*.

Quotations from St. Irenaeus and St. Damasus I, p. 86, sourced from *www.catholicbasictraining.com*.

Description of icons by Fr. Michael Azkoul, p. 91, St. Catherine Mission, St. Louis, MO, copyright 1994 St. Nectarios American Orthodox Church; reproduced with permission from The Orthodox Christian Witness, Vol. XXVII (48), Vol. XXVIII (6) and (8), 1994.

Quotation, p. 99, from *The Dialogue Between the Eastern Orthodox and Oriental Orthodox Churches*, Christine Chaillot, editor, Volos Academy Publications, copyright 2017.

The following resources were used for information relating to the history of the schism between the Orthodox Churches and the Catholic Church: *The Orthodox Church: New Edition* by Timothy Ware (Bishop Kallistos of Diokleia), published by Penquin Books, copyright 1963, 1964, 1993, 1997 by Timothy Ware; and "Schism of 1054" in *Encyclopedia Britannica*, sourced from *www.britannica.com*.

Prayers in the Prayer Reflection, pp. 104–05, adapted from Orthodox prayers sourced at *www.orthodoxprayer.org*.

Statistics under the heading "Many Branches of the Christian Family Tree," p. 108, sourced from *www.pewresearch.org*, from 2014 Religious Landscape Study, conducted June 4–Sept 30, 2014, Pew Research Centre.

Excerpts, pp. 115, 117–18 & 119, from *From Conflict to Communion: Lutheran-Catholic Common Commemoration of the Reformation in 2017*, © 2013 by Evangelische Verlagsanstalt GmbH · Leipzig and Bonifatius GmbH Druck – Buch – Verlag Paderborn.

Excerpt, p. 119, from Preface of *The Hope of Eternal Life: Lutherans and Catholics in Dialogue XI*, copyright © 2011 by Lutheran University Press, the Evangelical Lutheran Church in America, and the United States Conference of Catholic Bishops.

Statement relating to the Episcopal Church's attitude to doctrine, under "Worship and Creed," p. 124, from *Anglicans Online* at *http://anglicansonline.org*.

Figures mentioned under "The Ongoing Reformation of Protestantism," p. 138, from "U.S. Religious Landscape Survey" by the Pew Forum, sourced from *www.pewforum.org*.

The following resources were used for the presentation on Methodism, pp. 140–48: "Methodist Church History" and "Methodist Church Denomination" by Mary Fairchild at *http://christianity.about.com*; "John Wesley Biography" by Jack Zavada at *http://christianity.about.com*; "Methodism" by Rev. Rupert E. Davies in *Encyclopedia Britannica* online at *http://www.britannica.com*; "The Book of Discipline of the United Methodist Church" and "The people of the United Methodist Church" at *http://umc.org*.

Excerpt, p. 143, from *Methodist–Catholic Dialogues: Thirty Years of Mission and Witness*, copyright © 2001, United States Catholic Conference, Inc., Washington, D.C. and General Commission on Christian Unity and Interreligious Concerns of The United Methodist Church, New York, N.Y. All rights reserved.

Excerpts, p. 143, 146 & 147–8, *The Book of Discipline of the United Methodist Church*, copyright 2016, The United Methodist Publishing House, Nashville, Tennessee.

The following resources were used for the presentation on the Baptist tradition, pp. 149–54: the *Catholic Encyclopedia* online; *American Baptist Churches USA* online at *www.abc-usa.org*; Southern Baptist Convention at *www.sbc.net*; *Baptist Origins, Baptist History, Baptist Beliefs* at *www.patheos.com*; and "Christian Baptists.com" at *www.christianbaptists.com*.

The following resources were used for the presentation on the Congregationalist tradition, pp. 155–63: Congregational Library and Archives, "History Matters," at *www.congregationallibrary.org*; Harriet Beecher Stowe Center at *www.harrietbeecherstowecenter.org*.

Quotation, p. 157, from 'Principles of the Christian Church,' United Church of Christ, sourced from www.ucc.org.

Quotations and information about the Evangelical community, pp. 164-5, sourced from *www.nae.net*, the website of the National Association of Evangelicals.

Information for the profile on Rosa Parks, p. 166, sourced from the Hollowverse website at *http://hollowverse.com* and from the bio. website at *www.biography.com*.

Excerpt from John Wesley's letter to William Wilberforce, p. 166, sourced from "Global Ministries: The United Methodist Church" website at *www.umcmission.org*.

Quotations, pp. 173 & 181, from *Jewish Encyclopedia*, sourced from *jewishencyclopedia.com*, copyright © 2002-2011, JewishEncyclopedia.com. All rights reserved.

Quotation, p. 174, from *New Advent* Catholic Encyclopedia, sourced from *www.newadvent.org*, copyright © 2017 by Kevin Knight.

Explanation of the rituals of the Haggadah, pp. 181–2, from *The Passover Haggadah: A Guide to the Seder*, The Jewish Federation of North America, pages 4–5; sourced from *http://jewishfederation.org*.

Excerpt, p. 182, from Rabbi Evan Moffic, *What Every Christian Needs to Know About Passover* (Abingdon Press, Nashville), copyright 2014 by Evan Moffic; all rights reserved.

Excerpt, p. 187, from Pope Francis' Letter to the Founder of *La Repubblica*, September 11, 2013, translated by Zenit (Zenit.org News Agency), sourced from *www.ewtn.com* .

Quotations from Abraham Heschel, pp. 194–5, from *No Religion Is An Island: Abraham Joshua Heschel and Interreligious Dialogue*, edited by Harold Kasimow and Byron L. Sherwin (Maryknoll: Orbis Books, 1991), sourced from www.cs.auckland.ac.nz.

Quotation from Muhammad Yunus, p. 201, from Muhammad Yunus' Nobel Lecture, Oslo, December 10, 2006, sourced from *www.nobelprize.org*.

Quotation from Muhammad Yunus, p. 202, from *Banker to the Poor, The Story of the Grameen Bank*, Muhammad Junus with Alan Jolis (Penguin Books); copyright Muhammad Yunus and Alan Jolis, 1998, 1999.

Quotations, pp. 214 & 215, from Islamic Supreme Council of America, sourced from *www.islamicsupremecouncil.org*.

Excerpt, p. 217, from A Common Word Between Us and You © 2009 The Royal Aal al-Bayt Institute for Islamic Thought, Jordan.

Information under the heading "Non-Christian Religions in North America," p. 224, sourced from Pew Research Center website at *www.pewforum.org*.

The following resources were used for the presentation on Hinduism, pp. 227–34: *Understanding Differently: Christianity and the World Religions* by Jo O'Donovan (Dublin, Ireland: Veritas, 2012); the Kauai's Hindu Monastery webpage at *www.himalayanacademy.com*; "The Heart of Hinduism" at *http://hinduism.iskcon.org*; and Britannica.com at *http://www.britannica.com*.

Verse from the Vedas, p. 228, translated by V.V Raman, University of Rochester; sourced from *www.allabouthinduism.info*.

The nine Hindu beliefs listed on pp. 229–30 sourced from *www.himalayanacademy.com*.

The following resources were used for the presentation on Buddhism, pp. 235–42: *Understanding Differently: Christianity and the World Religions* by Jo O'Donovan (Dublin, Ireland: Veritas, 2012); Buddhist Studies: Basic Buddhism at *www.buddhanet.net*; ReligionFacts, "Buddhism" at *www.religionfacts.com*; Shambhala, "Buddhism" at *http://shambhala.org*.

Summary of and quotations from *New York Times* article of July 25, 2014, "In Scarred Chinese Tibetan City, Devotion to Sanctity of Life" written by Andrew Jacobs, p. 235, sourced from *www.nytimes.com*.

The following resources were used for the presentation on Confucianism, pp. 243–47: *Encyclopedia Britannica* at *www.britannica.com*; Patheos Library: Confucianism at *www.patheos.com*.

The following resources were used for the presentation on Sikhism, pp. 258–62: *Sikhism, An Introduction* by Nikky-Guninder Kaur Singh (I.B. Tauris & Co Ltd, London, copyright 2011 by Nikky-Guninder Kaur Singh); "Jesus Through Sikh Eyes" by Nikki Singh, at *www.bbc.co.uk*; Sikhs.org at *http//ww.siks.org*; Sikh Religious Philosophy at *http://sikhs.org*; "Five Things to Know about the Sikh Religion" by Jahnabi Barooah, at HuffPost Religion, *www.huffingtonpost.com*.

Quotations under heading "Sikh Woman Finds Enlightenment in Jesus," p. 258, from "Jesus Through Sikh Eyes" by Nikki Singh, at *www.bbc.co.uk*.

The following resources were used for the presentation on the Bahá'í faith, pp. 263–7: the website of the worldwide Bahá'í community at *www.bahai.org*; Frances Worthington, *Bahá'í Basics: A Guide to the Beliefs, Practices, and History of the Bahá'í Faith* (Illinois: Bahá'í Publishing, 2012); "Jesus Christ in the Bahá'í Writings" by Robert Stockman, published in *Bahá'í Studies Review*, 2:1 (London: Association for Baha'i Studies English-Speaking Europe, 1992), available on the Bahá'í Library Online website at *http://bahai-library.com*; "Resurrection: A Bahá'í Perspective" by Mark A. Foster, available on the Bahá'í Library Online website at *http://bahai-library.com*; "Welcome to the Bahá'í Faith," available at *http://www.us.bahai.org* and maintained by The Bahá'ís of the United States; *Course on Teaching Christians about the* Bahá'í *Faith* by Dianne Bradford, available on the Bahá'í Library Online website at *http://bahai-library.com*.

"A Bahá'í's view of Pope Francis and his critics," p. 263, written by Christy Besozzi, sourced from *http://toledofavs.com*.

Excerpt, p. 263, from Kenneth E. Bowers, Testimony to the United States House of Representatives, May 22, 2014, sourced from *http://docs.house.gov* .

Quotation, p. 266, from Bahá'u'lláh, *Gleanings*, sourced at *http://reference.bahai.org*.

Quotation, p. 266, from Shoghi Effendi, *High Endeavors: Messages to Alaska* (69–70), sourced at *http://bahai-library.com*.

The following resources were used for the presentation on Mormonism, pp. 268–74: *Mormonism 101: Examining the Religion of the Latter Day Saints: Revised and Expanded*, Bill McKeever and Eric Johnson (Grand Rapids, Michigan: Baker Books © 2000, 2015); *Doctrine and Covenants and Church History: Study Guide for Home-Study Seminary Students* (Kindle Edition); Frequently Asked Questions at *www.mormon.org*.

Quotations from *Joseph Smith—History* sourced from *www.lds.org*.

Quotation, p. 269, from Bruce R. McConkie, *Mormon Doctrine*, 2nd edition (Salt Lake City: Bookcraft, 1966).

Quotation, p. 271, from *Ensign*, February 2013, sourced from *www.lds.org*.

Quotation, pp. 271–2, from *True to the Faith: A Gospel Reference* (Salt Lake City: Church of Jesus Christ of Latter-day Saints, copyright 2004).

Excerpt from "Somewhere Over the Rainbow," p. 285, lyrics by E.Y. Harburg (1896–1981).

Image credits:

COVER: *Main image:* Detail from *Maundy Supper at Emmaus* (2001) by He Qi. © 2001 He Qi.

p. 9: Photo: Nheyob.

p. 13: Photo: Paweł Cieśla

p. 15: Andrey Mironov

p. 19: Walters Art Museum, Baltimore, Maryland

p. 20: Photo: Marsyas

p. 22: Photo: Andreas Praefcke

p. 24: Photo: Andrew R. Abbott

p. 25: Photo: Andy Katz/Thinkstock

p. 27: Photo: Matthias Kabel

p. 28: Photo: Mossot

p. 29: Photograph of Thomas Merton by John Lyons, used with permission of the Merton Legacy Trust and the Thomas Merton Center, Bellarmine University.

p. 35: The J. Paul Getty Museum

p. 37: Photo: Wolfgang Sauber

p. 38: The J. Paul Getty Museum

p. 39: Photo: Alexey Borodin/Thinkstock

p. 40: Photo: MIQU77/Thinkstock

p. 43: Photo: Mario Tama/Thinkstock

p. 44: Photo: Karmakolle

p. 45: Photo: Philippe Alès

p. 46: Photo: Shakko

p. 48: Photo: Panek

p. 49: © TASS/ITAR-TASS Photo/Corbis

p. 50: Bogdan Khmelnytskyi/Thinkstock

p. 53: Photo: Tin2little

p. 55: Photo: UOAE11

p. 59: New York Public Library

p. 60: © Sid Hastings/Corbis

p. 61: © TOLGA BOZOGLU/epa/Corbis

p. 65: New York Public Library

p. 66: Photo: ITPOW/Thinkstock

p. 69: Photo: Jochen Jahnke

p. 71: Photo: Ambrosius007

p. 85: Map by Lir Mac Cárthaigh

p. 87: Photo: Buda Mendes/Thinkstock

p. 92: Wellcome Collection

p. 94: Photo: Paterm

p. 96: Photo: Alexey Anashkin/Thinkstock

p. 102: Photo: Ori~

p. 116: Photo: Karmen Media

p. 120: Photo: Artur Widak/Corbis

p. 121: Photo: Sailko

p. 123: Library of Congress

p. 127: Fotos International/Getty Images

p. 131: Wellcome Library, London

p. 132: U.S. National Archives and Records Administration

p. 139: Walters Art Museum, Baltimore, Maryland

p. 142: Print Collection; Miriam and Ira D. Wallach Division of Art, Prints and Photographs; The New York Public Library; Astor, Lenox and Tilden Foundations

p. 149: Wellesenterprises/iStockPhoto

p. 150: Print Collection; Miriam and Ira D. Wallach Division of Art, Prints and Photographs; The New York Public Library; Astor, Lenox and Tilden Foundations

p. 154: Wellcome Library, London

p. 155: U.S. National Archives

p. 159: Photo by Gordon Chibroski/Portland Press Herald via Getty Images

p. 164: Middelveld/iStockPhoto

p. 165: John Moore/Thinkstock

p. 166: © Bettmann/CORBIS

p. 169: Wellcome Collection

p. 174: Gerald R. Ford Presidential Museum

p. 176: Photo: Marsyas

p. 178: Photo: Jastrow

p. 179: Phillip Medhurst Collection

p. 180: Andrey Mironov

p. 185: Photo: Thesupermat

p. 187: Photo: Wjarek/Thinkstock

p. 190: Photo: Gianni Giansanti/Corbis

p. 192: Photo: Chris McGrath/Thinkstock

p. 193: Sedmak/iStockPhoto

p. 194: Photo: Bettmann/Corbis

p. 202: Photo: Softdelusion/Thinkstock

p. 205: numbeos/iStockPhoto

p. 209: Elifranssens/iStockPhoto

p. 210: Photo: Wolfgang Sauber

p. 217: Photo: Miqu77/Thinkstock

p. 218: Photo: Andrew Burton/Thinkstock

p. 235: Photo: Jules2013/Thinkstock

p. 236: Photo: Dominique Dalbiez

p. 246: Photo: Tom@hk

p. 250: FangXiaNuo/iStockPhoto

p. 257: Andrey Mironov

p. 258: Photo: Orhideja/Thinkstock

p. 259: Wellcome Collection

p. 260: Photo: Bike World Travel/Thinkstock

p. 262: Photo: Isaji/Thinkstock

p. 263: Photo: Andy Katz/Thinkstock

p. 266: Photo: David Haslip

p. 270: Adi Holzer

p. 272: Photo: Chris Light

p. 273: Photo: GFreihalter

p. 276: Walters Art Museum, Baltimore, Maryland

Index